Trance on Trial

The Guilford Clinical and Experimental Hypnosis Series
Michael J. Diamond and Helen M. Pettinati, Editors

Trance on Trial
Alan W. Scheflin and Jerrold Lee Shapiro

Hypnosis: A Jungian Perspective
James A. Hall

Hypnosis, Will, and Memory: A Psycho-Legal History
Jean-Roch Laurence and Campbell Perry

Hypnosis and Memory
Helen M. Pettinati, Editor

Clinical Practice of Hypnotherapy
M. Erik Wright with Beatrice A. Wright

Trance on Trial

Alan W. Scheflin, LL.M.
Santa Clara University School of Law

Jerrold Lee Shapiro, Ph.D., ABMP
Santa Clara University Division of Counseling Psychology
OHANA Family Therapy Institute, Los Gatos, California

Foreword by David Spiegel, M.D.

The Guilford Press
New York *London*

To the loving memory of Anthony C. Amantea

For my precious daughter, Hallie Scheflin

For the Bernadett-Shapiros:
   Susan Trese
   Natasha Leilani
   Gabriel Faustino

© 1989 The Guilford Press
A Division of Guilford Publications, Inc.
72 Spring Street, New York, NY 10012

Printed in the United States of America

This book is printed on acid-free paper.

Last digit is print number: 9 8 7 6 5 4 3 2 1

Library of Congress Cataloging-in-Publication Data
Scheflin, Alan W.
   Trance on trial.
   Bibliography: p.
   Includes index.
   1. Witnesses—United States.   2. Forensic hypnotism.
3. Hypnotism—Law and legislation—United States.
I. Shapiro, Jerrold Lee.   II. Title.
KF9672.S34   1989   347.73'066   347.30766   88-1674
ISBN 0-89862-749-4
ISBN 0-89862-340-5 (paperback)

Foreword

Just as it is said that truth and falsehood are two sides of the same coin, it is not surprising that hypnosis, a technique that has been associated with the ability to retrieve otherwise unavailable memories, should likewise stand accused of creating false memories. What has this odd phenomenon to do with eyewitness testimony? Does it help or hinder? The authors, law school professor Alan Scheflin and psychologist Jerrold Shapiro, do indeed put trance on trial and admirably fill the roles of both prosecution and defense, skillfully cross-examining the literature for evidence regarding uses and misuses of hypnosis.

By the standards of our modern disposable culture, hypnosis has ancient roots. It began as a formal discipline some two centuries ago and represents the first Western conception of a psychotherapy, a talking interaction between a doctor and a patient that could lead to improvement in symptoms. Over the ensuing two centuries, it has been repeatedly discredited and then rehabilitated. The French commission that investigated the work of the famous Dr. Mesmer, founder of the field, was composed, interestingly enough, of the chemist Lavoisier, our own Benjamin Franklin, and a doctor known for his work in pain control by the name of Guillotin. They reached the then devastating conclusion that hypnosis was nothing but "heated imagination." The report itself, however, took pains to underscore the power of suggestion in maintaining the social fabric as well as in therapeutic interactions. The members of the commission specifically took aim at Mesmer's theories of magnetic influence and some of his methods and claims of success, rather than the principle of suggestive influence.

Sigmund Freud likewise started his psychoanalytic investigations with the use of hypnosis, using it to develop his original idea that unconscious conflicts led to conscious symptoms. He gave it up when he came to believe that hypnosis represented just one form of a more general phenom-

v

enon, the irrational thoughts and feelings patients have about therapists, drawn from their early experiences with parents and other caretakers, which he called "transference."

What relevance does this have for the courtroom? One need but see one patient who develops a traumatic amnesia, a rape victim who has no memory at all that the crime occurred even though she was fully conscious at the time and gave a report to the police afterwards. She has lost time, is mystified by her inability to recall any details of the event. Hypnotized, she goes back in time to the period just before the rape and suddenly, with vivid and painful detail, relives the assault as though it were occurring again. The whole walled-off, or dissociated, body of memories suddenly becomes available, along with intense dissociated emotions. This warded-off material is accessed through the formal use of hypnosis, a state of intense, focused concentration with a relative suspension of peripheral awareness. Now the victim can identify her assailant, can give a vivid description of the circumstances of the alleged crime, whereas numerous attempts by herself and with the police were unavailing. Can a phenomenon that can be so powerful in such a setting be easily dismissed?

Cases such as this led to widespread training of professionals of various types, psychiatrists, psychologists, and law enforcement officials, in the use of hypnosis to enhance the recall of witnesses, victims, and occasionally defendants. This led to no small amount of concern that hypnosis was being used, not to uncover information, but indeed to suggest it. For while hypnotized people may tap into memory stores they seem otherwise unable to access, they are also unusually responsive to instructions because their attention is so focused that they are less likely to critically judge and evaluate instructions they are given. Thus, the very method that supposedly allows people to bypass their defense against emotional pain and uncover memories may also be used to implant or contaminate memories. The dangers of a leading police interrogation are well enough known anyway: "How tall was the black man when he shot you?" is an example of an unduly suggestive question. The dangers of suggesting rather than eliciting an answer are amplified when a subject is hypnotized and therefore relatively uncritical about the information produced in an effort to comply with the hypnotist.

The adversary approach to ferreting out truth complements nicely the two-edged sword quality of hypnotic influence on memory. The same phenomenon that can focus attention toward the recall of detail surrounded by a storm of emotion may be misused to push a subject to believe in fantasies. The hypnotic state gains its intensity at the expense of critical judgment. Thus, since the hypnotized person utilizes less critical judgment, we must use more such judgment in evaluating what happens during an hypnotic encounter. More than that, our knowledge of the hypnotic state, and how easy it is to enter and exit, makes it clear that hypnotic phenomena occur spontaneously: during traumatic episodes and in their aftermath; when one is absorbed in reading a good novel; or is transported by a movie to the point where one loses awareness of being in a theater watching a movie and enters the imagined world. Hypnotic phenomena occur all the time and as such are a concern for anyone interested in evaluating the truth. For example, intensive interrogation in the back room of a police station can have its hypnotic components. Subjects have been led to confess to crimes they did not commit with a line of questioning like, "Well if you did something that terrible, you probably would develop an amnesia for it, so how would you have done it if you did it?" This could be a clever way to get a guilty person to confess, but it could also be a subtle hypnotic instruction that an innocent person should confess to a crime he or she did not commit.

When it comes right down to it, studying hypnosis is a lesson in humility. The law cherishes a standard called the reasonably prudent man. We all like to think that we are one. Yet what we observe with hypnosis teaches us that we are not always reasonably prudent, that we sometimes will firmly believe things that are strange or untrue. We become convinced that one hand is lighter than the other, although this is physically impossible. We do not see something that is right in front of us after hypnotic instruction. We sniff ammonia and think it perfume. The massive neocortex that sits on top of the structures at the base of the brain that process perception allows us to do a great deal of work: modulating perception, accessing memory and planning future actions. This is a unique advantage to humans, but it can also be a disadvantage. Our ability to transform signals allows us to reduce or eliminate pain, yet it sometimes makes it hard for us to discriminate between real and fantasy perceptions. Yet accurate perception and memory is often at the heart of the judicial process. Because hypnosis helps us understand these processes, and demonstrates to us our abilities to store and retrieve memory, it represents both our opportunities for improving this process and the risks inherent to it. Hypnosis is thus both entrancing and threatening.

Thus, hypnosis has come to be seen as a two-edged sword, possibly useful, especially in cases where there is traumatic amnesia, and yet potentially dangerous, contaminating the memory or conviction of a witness who goes through the ceremony and therefore somehow comes to believe with more certainty the "truth" of his or her own productions.

Yet, despite the calls of some for the death penalty for hypnosis, it still stands charged but not convicted. Indeed, there is renewed interest in the phenomenon in this context because of the observed association between dissociative experiences and posttraumatic stress disorder. Many aspects of the trauma that victims of crime undergo, suddenly living an event as though it were in the present, the loss of pleasure in usually enjoyable activities, and the sensitivity to stimuli that remind them of the crime, are reminiscent of hypnotic experiences: hypnotic age regression, dissociation, and suggestibility. Several studies have found that Vietnam veterans with posttraumatic stress disorders are unusually hypnotizable. Thus, even an official sentence of death could not keep hypnosis out of the courtroom, since it may be that individuals vividly reliving a traumatic experience are in a spontaneous hypnotic state. Hypnosis may, in fact, occur when nobody intends its use. An intense interrogation about a traumatic event in the back room of a police station may be enough to induce hypnosis in a highly hypnotizable witness, victim, or defendant. This may account for some of the spurious confessions to crimes exacted from defendants, or well-meaning but erroneous testimony provided by witnesses and victims. If the phenomenon is there, it is a normal part of human nature. Widely distributed in the population and useful for various forms of problem-solving, hypnotic capacity is spontaneously mobilized in many kinds of traumatic responses and will find its way into the courtroom, whether we like it or not. Hypnosis deserves a fair trial. Here it gets one. Remember that defendants are innocent until proven guilty, and enjoy reading this book.

David Spiegel, M.D.
Stanford, California

Preface

For more than half of the 20th century, hypnosis was of little concern to judges, lawyers, and police. In 1897, the California Supreme Court announced that "the law of the United States does not recognize hypnotism" (*People v. Ebanks*, p. 1053). There the matter was to stay until the late 1960s, when a few courts were willing to soften the judicial hard line against the admissibility of hypnotically refreshed testimony. This initial sprinkle of judicial acceptance soon grew into a stream, then a river, and now a flood. Since 1980 more books have been published, more law review articles have been written, and more cases have been decided involving forensic hypnosis than in the entire preceding century. Incredibly, the literature and case law on forensic hypnosis more than doubled in 5 short years!

This renaissance of interest in hypnosis has proceeded at an astonishing pace. Today psychologists, psychiatrists, counselors, therapists, doctors, nurses, and other professionals use hypnosis, meditation, guided imagery, visualization, neurolinguistic programming, and related techniques in thousands of cases and for multiple purposes. Each year the number of professionals who seek training in hypnosis expands enormously. However, despite the vast volume of material now available on the legal aspects of hypnotic interventions and investigations, practicing therapists have been without a handy reference source that details the implications of hypnotherapy on the legal rights of clients. We had to discover this fact the hard way.

In 1981, Dr. Shapiro was requested to provide hypnotherapy for the relief of amnesia blocks suffered by a woman who had been traumatically raped. Because his sole initial interest was in symptom relief, he proceeded in a therapeutically rather than a legally oriented manner. When his client regained her memory, she became aware that she had been molested by a second, previously unidentified perpetrator. Upon her report of this fact to the authorities, the culprit was subsequently arrested. (This case is described in more detail in Chapter Two of this volume.)

Shapiro found it necessary to address many legal issues involving his use of hypnosis. It was important for him not only to satisfy the clinical needs of the client, but to proceed in a manner that satisfied judicial requirements as well. Although the procedures Shapiro followed were deemed acceptable, he discovered that identical therapy in another jurisdiction could have inadvertently deprived the client of the right to be a witness in court actions against her attackers.

In the late 1970s, Professor Scheflin encountered a parallel problem. Several trial attorneys consulted him for assistance in handling legal cases involving hypnosis issues. In his search through the literature, Scheflin found very little practical information that would be helpful to them. Because hypnosis questions had rarely been raised in courtrooms, lawyers were generally unfamiliar with how hypnosis works and with its impact on memory. Though they were quite conversant with the rules of evidence governing the admissibility of testimony, they were unsure of the nuts-and-bolts issues involving direct examination and cross-examination of hypnosis experts. No available materials addressed the everyday concerns of a lawyer working to put together a case involving hypnosis for trial.

The motivation to write a book that could function as a practical reference handbook was further fueled by our experiences as expert witnesses in court. In the witness chair, one soon discovers that the atmosphere of a trial is unlike any other environment an expert tends to inhabit. As with any mission into foreign terrain, careful advance preparation is one's best ally. For us, such preparation had to be the product of endless hours spent accumulating scattered pieces of information from diverse and often unrelated sources.

Therapists are increasingly called to court to testify as practitioners or expert witnesses. How does a hypnotherapist who is not trained in the law prepare for a court appearance? How does he or she handle direct examination and, especially, cross-examination? What guidelines are recommended for routine therapeutic procedures that will ensure protection of the legal rights and interests of clients, while also meeting the legal and ethical standards of professional codes? It is our desire to equip therapists, hypnosis experts, lawyers, and others with enough useful references and suggestions to save dozens of hours of research. It is also our intention to provide specific and detailed information about hypnosis topics that will enable therapists and lawyers going into court to prepare themselves properly and to perform well.

Naturally, no one text can be expected to function as the sole source of consultation, and this book is no exception. Indeed, the nature of the subject matter discussed requires that other material be examined and read. This book will help professionals to locate that material. We have made an exhaustive search to find and list every hypnosis case decided in this country and every pertinent hypnosis statute currently in force. (The cases and statutes pertaining to hypnosis are listed in the Appendix of this book; all other material is listed in the "References and Bibliography" section at the end of the book.)

As professionals, regardless of our chosen callings, our first concern must be with the welfare and protection of those entrusted to our care—itself a demanding task. Often it seems as if the client is trapped in a free-fire zone as lawyers, therapists, and police reciprocally undermine one another's best efforts. In such a battle there can be only losers. And, as in a game of Russian roulette, the question of whom the "liability" bullet will strike is left to the hands of fate.

But, as professionals, we can influence the odds. We can do so by making sure that in our zeal to protect one set of our clients' interests, we do not neglect another set normally protected by others. For example, a therapist or police officer who hypnotizes a crime victim without explaining and following the legal requirements for testimonial admissibility is risking a suit for malpractice or deprivation of civil rights. In such a case, the great irony is that the criminal goes free and the helping professional must pay. For the sake of innocent clients, we hope that this book will equip us all to work better in individual situations, and in closer harmony with one another.

The marriage of skills and styles that led to the completion of this book has been, like most fruitful unions, arduous as well as productive. The fields of law and psychology do not easily mesh, and practitioners from each discipline tend to approach problems from distinctly different orientations. When trance goes on trial, even within each discipline sparks fly as conflicting viewpoints rub uncomfortably against one another.

Forensic hypnosis is a volatile field engendering strong opinions. True believers abound. It would not be possible to write a practical book on this subject that would satisfy everyone. Because professional positions on these topics have become so polarized, our first goal to our readers has been to present each perspective as impartially and as fairly as possible. Every effort has been made by direct interview and correspondence to make sure that the views of each major participant in the forensic hypnosis debate have been stated accurately.

To our colleagues in law and mental health we owe a very great debt of gratitude. Over the years we have benefited from discussions and correspondence with many people. We acknowledge them here: Martin T. Orne, David Spiegel, Campbell Perry, Jeffrey Zeig, Ernest Rossi, Martin Reiser, Helmut Relinger, Thomas Worthington, and Howard Varinsky.

We also wish sincerely to thank the Erickson Foundation for allowing us the opportunity to present this material on two different occasions. The warm reception we received convinced us that hypnotherapists were looking for a safe path to provide effective healing without courting legal calamity.

In the course of the preparation of this book, many other people have provided support, help, and assistance. Professor Scheflin would like to express appreciation and affection to his parents, his brother Larry, sister-in-law Toni, and nephew Scott. Dr. Rhona Fisher and Denise Amantea, Esq., provided warmth, encouragement, and strength, especially in the crucial closing months.

Dr. Shapiro gratefully acknowledges the calming, effective advice of his wife, Susan Bernadett-Shapiro. In addition to her inestimable love and support, she also managed to provide an addition to their family in 1988. He also extends his appreciation to many teachers in hypnosis from the American Society of Clinical Hypnosis, Dr. Milton H. Erickson, the Erickson family, The Rape Crisis Center of Honolulu, Hawaii, Mr. Darwin Chang and the Office of the Attorney General of the State of Hawaii, and the staff of the King Kalakaua Center for Humanistic Psychotherapy in Aina Haina, Hawaii.

Mary Hood and the law librarians at Santa Clara University deserve special thanks for the hours and hours of aid they provided to us over the years. Barbara Norelli, in particular, tracked down obscure journals and articles dating back over a century. Her search for the long-forgotten literature on the legal aspects of hypnosis was conducted with the zest and skill of a Sherlock Holmes.

We wish to thank our research assistants: Barbara Edmonston, who helped us with the psychological issues, and Wini Gross, Elizabeth Harris, Jamie Caploe, Richard J. Davis, and Laura B. Choper, who helped with legal citations.

The production staff at Guilford Publications deserves special commendation. The copyediting by Marie Sprayberry was thorough and uniformly excellent. Pearl Weisinger, the Production Editor, shepherded the manuscript, and then the proofs, with consummate skill. In their capable hands, the hundreds of pages of text became a book.

The assistance provided by the editorial staff at Guilford Publications made our task an easier one. Dr. Michael Diamond, coeditor of The Guilford Clinical and Experimental Hypnosis Series, encouraged our project from its inception and provided emotional support, valuable knowledge, and friendship. Dr. Helen Pettinati, the other coeditor, shared her special expertise for the chapter on memory and provided thoughtful commentary and guidance throughout. Seymour Weingarten, the Editor-in-Chief, courageously kept us on track.

Alan W. Scheflin
Jerrold Lee Shapiro

Contents

Part I

Introduction

CHAPTER 1

The Legal Status of Hypnosis: An Overview

INTRODUCTION

In 1987, Andrea H. was sexually assaulted.[1] This experience was so traumatic that in its aftermath she was unable to remember what had happened or who had violated her. Suffering from posttraumatic stress, Andrea sought the assistance of Dr. Mitchell O'Connor, who used hypnosis to help restore her memory and promote healing. Following successful treatment, Andrea regained her memory of the assault. After she presented the police with this information, Mark White was arrested and charged with the crime.

At trial, White's attorney argued that the hypnosis performed by Dr. O'Connor had so tainted Andrea H.'s memory that she would have to be disqualified as a witness. The attorney cited dozens of cases holding that the police use of investigative hypnosis constituted an impermissible tampering with the memory of a witness. The prosecutor acknowledged these cases, but raised a critical distinction between them and the present case. Police hypnosis was not involved, and hypnosis was not used for investigative purposes. The rule disqualifying a witness from testifying, the prosecutor urged, should not be extended to situations where qualified and licensed mental health professionals had used hypnosis for therapeutic purposes unrelated to legal proceedings.

The judge was moved but not swayed by this argument. He was willing to recognize that hypnotic suggestion might be less of a problem in

---

[1] All the names in this case have been changed.

the therapeutic setting, but he was nevertheless persuaded that even in this benign setting the mind of the witness had been altered. Andrea H. was not permitted to testify; White went free.

Andrea H.'s day in court had been denied her. Only one other potential *legal* remedy was available to her: She might have wanted to sue Dr. O'Connor for failing to protect her legal rights. Her argument would be simple: He had a duty to tell her before he used hypnosis that the treatment might place her legal rights in jeopardy. Although she had no quarrel with the hypnosis as therapy, nor with Dr. O'Connor's competence as a hypnotherapist, if he failed to provide her with complete information, he might have innocently violated her right to informed consent. (We do not know what information Dr. O'Connor provided Andrea H., and we state Andrea H.'s legal remedy as a hypothetical possibility only.) Every hypnotherapist may face the same potential threat.

The therapeutic use of hypnosis can lead to unanticipated legal consequences. This book is about those consequences.

Healing techniques have often been the subject of fierce legal debate. Drugs, psychosurgery, electroshock treatment, behavior modification, and aversion therapy continue to face court and constitutional challenges. Recently, lawyers, legislators, and litigators have turned their attention toward hypnosis and its practitioners. It is quite possible that many mental health professionals who read this book will learn that they have been unnecessarily risking legal liability or unknowingly violating the law.

Today, therapeutic or investigative work with hypnosis will be judged not only by the ethical and performance standards of one's own profession, but also by the legal requirements currently in force in the locality of one's practice. Hypnotherapists are required to exercise extraordinary sensitivity to meet dual, and occasionally conflicting, responsibilities. Furthermore, these obligations do not remain fixed in time. A court ruling on any particular day can dramatically alter the way in which hypnosis may be delivered to the public. Therapists who use hypnosis with their clients cannot afford to be unaware of the legal consequences of their work. Wisdom dictates that an ounce of prevention is worth a pound of malpractice.

For the benefit of everyone using hypnosis, and of everyone upon whom it is practiced, therapists have a right to be completely informed about the legal status of hypnosis and the legal responsibilities of those who utilize it.

Legal Influences on Psychotherapy

It is a contemporary reality for all therapists that work performed in the office may no longer remain strictly limited to that private setting. Evolving trends in law have altered the manner in which therapy may be conducted. For example, the scope and extent of confidentiality and privileged communication have been progressively reduced in the last decade. For the therapist, this means that revealing what occurs in the sanctity of the treatment room no longer seems an impossibility. Indeed, in certain circumstances, it is becoming more of an inevitability. In addition to this retrenchment in the latitude of privilege, recent court decisions have shown a willingness to expand the longitude of obligation owed by therapists to clients and even to nonclients.

A natural result of these developments is the fact that the volume of litigation brought against therapists has been steadily on the rise. Insurance companies, recognizing that more professionals will be sued on an expanding variety of legal theories in the current litigious climate, have dramatically increased malpractice premiums. In fact, the major insurer for clinical psychologists (in conjunction with the American Psychological Association Insurance Trust) instituted a sixfold increase in premiums between 1984 and 1988.

Legal Influences on Hypnotherapy

The professional work of hypnotherapists and the legal implications of hypnotherapeutic interventions are currently being scrutinized more closely by the courts than at any other time in legal history. When hypnotherapy work is evaluated not only by the standards of the mental health professions, but by legal mandates as well, the therapist must walk a very fine line to satisfy professional ethical guidelines and simultaneously protect the client's rights to legal redress.

An avalanche of hypnosis-related cases has cascaded through the courts in the last half decade. Judges have been asked to evaluate the use of hypnosis in a variety of settings, ranging from the therapist's office to the police station interrogation room. Who may legally practice hypnosis? Who may qualify in court as an expert in hypnosis? May a person who has been hypnotized testify in court? These questions have only begun to be answered with clarity within the last 10 years. The answers differ across jurisdictions.

The most potentially significant question for hypnotherapists has yet to be answered. Can a therapist be sued successfully for failing to fully inform a client or patient of the potential legal consequences involved in undergoing hypnosis? To put it another way, is there a duty to warn clients that they may lose legal rights in order to gain mental health?

The Current Popularity of Hypnosis

The growing attention that law now pays to hypnosis is paralleled in the healing professions. For the last two decades, hypnosis has made enormous strides in proving itself as a valuable therapeutic technique. Consider these recent developments.

First, more people within each health profession are using hypnosis. Conferences on hypnosis are enjoying the largest attendance in history, and the subject of hypnosis is appearing ever more frequently in workshop and panel discussions of professional organizations and associations. There is a corresponding explosion in the hypnosis literature. No fewer than 27 new texts on hypnosis were on display at the 1985 American Psychological Association meetings, compared to 9 in 1983.

Second, the number of professions using hypnosis continues to increase. It is no longer the sole province of psychiatry, psychology, anesthesiology, obstetrics, and dentistry. Marriage and family counselors, pediatricians, oncologists, nurses, habit control specialists, educators, and a host of workshop leaders offer hypnosis as part of their trade.

Third, innovative hypnotic techniques, such as the naturalistic indirect inductions pioneered by Dr. Milton H. Erickson (see Erickson, 1980), are spawning a host of methods as the latest generation of hypnotherapists makes its own contributions to the field. Authors such as Haley (1963) and, more recently, Ritterman (1983) have brought hypnosis into the field of family therapy.

Finally, a variety of theories related to hypnosis incorporate fresh insights from other disciplines with established observations about altered states of consciousness, trance behavior, and learning. Visualization, imagery, meditation, progressive relaxation, and neurolinguistic programming are perhaps the best-known hypnosis-related counseling systems.

Even beyond these professional arenas, today almost anyone can buy popular books and cassette tapes on hypnosis in local bookstores. Training courses on hypnosis are being advertised and offered to anyone able to meet the tuition price. No prior qualifications to enroll are necessary. Guarantees of graduation and new careers are given freely.

One example of the extent to which hypnosis has gone public, and the excessive claims that are made in reference to it, was evident in a full-page advertisement that appeared in the Sunday, August 25, 1985 edition of the *Los Angeles Times*. Dr. Dante, a convicted felon with no formal mental health training or license, offered a course in hypnotherapy as part of a pleasure cruise. Dante, who legally changed his first name to "Dr.," promised students that they would be legally licensable by the state of California as hypnotherapists. Dante also claimed that his graduates would be able, within 2 weeks, to charge $65.00 per hour for hypnotherapy services.

It is clear that hypnotic procedures are being employed by larger groups of persons, in a wider variety of occupations, with an increasing number of clients, and for an expanding number of purposes. It is not surprising that established professional organizations and the law have become concerned about these developments. Professional associations, fearful that excessive claims by untrained or unethical practitioners could resurrect the image of hypnosis as part of the occultist's art, have already begun to put pressure on both legislators and the popular media to encourage a perception of hypnosis as a serious therapeutic tool best utilized only by qualified practitioners.

Section 2 of the *Code of Ethics* of the American Society of Clinical Hypnosis (ASCH) specifically prohibits its members from supporting the work of nonprofessional hypnotists: "Members of ASCH shall not support the practice of hypnosis by lay persons. In particular, a member of ASCH shall not teach hypnotic techniques to lay persons" (ASCH, 1983). In an attempt to exercise greater control over the regulated price of hypnotherapy, ASCH members were asked to adopt an amendment to the bylaws that would allow licensed master's-level practitioners to become affiliate members. In 1988, the proposed amendment was rejected by a 56–44% vote.

In addition, Division 30 (Hypnosis) of the American Psychological Association has pressured *Psychology Today* magazine to eliminate personal classified hypnosis advertisements with unprofessional claims.

The battle between health professionals who use hypnosis in their work and lay hypnosis practitioners is once again beginning to heat up. Future legal rulings will play an important role in determining who may utilize hypnosis, for what purposes, and with what consequences.

HYPNOSIS AND THE LAW

For the law, there are two basic questions regarding the regulation of hypnosis. First, who shall practice hypnosis? Second, what are the consequences of its use?

Who May Practice Hypnosis?

Three groups of professionals regularly engage in the practice of hypnosis: (1) medical, dental, and mental health professionals; (2) lay hypnotists (not including stage performers); and (3) law enforcement personnel. Each group claims a right to practice within its own sphere of expertise.

Health professionals cite their specialized academic and clinical training, knowledge of pathology, and ability to therapeutically manage the elicited contents of hypnotic procedures. They also point out that misuse of hypnosis can be hazardous to the mental health of the subject. The inner recesses of the mind should not be probed by those not trained to protect it.

Lay hypnotists, by contrast, claim to have received more complete training in the specific techniques of hypnosis than the health professionals. They argue that most legal cases concerning the inappropriate use of hypnosis have involved licensed professionals and police. They further claim that many of the health professionals have received their training from the lay hypnotists. Their position is basically that hypnosis is a nonhazardous tool that can be safely taught and learned by the general public for self-help and motivation.

The police claim primacy in using hypnosis to solve crimes. As support for their view that law enforcement personnel should be the hypnotists of choice in situations where court cases may ensue, they cite their (1) particularized training and competence in investigative and interrogative questioning; (2) knowledge of the criminal codes and the rules of evidence; (3) experience with crime victims, witnesses, and suspects; and (4) generalized understanding of court proceedings.

To the criticism often leveled at police hypnotists—that their training in hypnosis is frequently quite limited in duration and scope—the police reply by pointing out that many professionals have equally limited hypnosis training. Indeed, as the most thorough of the police training books on hypnosis (Hibbard & Worring, 1981) observes: "[A]n historical survey would probably show that a sizeable percentage, if not the majority, of practicing hypnotists, whether lay or professional, were self taught" (p. 6). This argument is losing some of its validity as hypnosis courses proliferate in academic curricula, however.

The legal issue of who may practice hypnosis will necessarily depend on the purpose of the hypnotic intervention. Mental health professionals claim that hypnosis is a medical, therapeutic procedure of which they are the only qualified users. Lay hypnotists do not challenge the supremacy of licensed health practitioners to handle matters of medicine, but claim that psychologists and psychiatrists cannot stake out a monopoly on a procedure that is also effective in stimulating motivation and maximizing self-help opportunities for success. Finally, law enforcement officers argue that training in techniques of forensic hypnosis must be augmented by an understanding of the intricacies of criminal law and investigative procedures, which they alone possess.

Despite the obvious disagreements among these three groups of hypnosis practitioners, they all share one common circumstance: They must await ultimate clarification of their rights and responsibilities regarding hypnosis from the courts and legislatures.

What Are the Consequences of Practicing Hypnosis?

For most of the 20th century, health professionals, lay practitioners, and the police were able to practice hypnosis without close legal scrutiny. Each group held to its own particular sphere of influence. In this relatively unregulated condition, only the police suffered adverse consequences. They were the ones who invited the current judicial attention.

The Police Officer's Dilemma

Mental health professionals could practice hypnosis during this entire century with virtually no legal restriction. The police, however, were blocked from using hypnosis as anything beyond an investigative tool to develop leads and clues to solve crimes. Before 1968, no American court would allow into evidence the testimony of a witness whose memory had earlier been refreshed by hypnosis. The universal rule was stated by the very first case to address the issue: "The law of the United States does not recognize hypnotism" (*People v. Ebanks*, Cal., 1897, p. 1053).[2]

This placed the police on the horns of a very unpleasant dilemma. On the one hand, they could forego using hypnosis on a witness in order to qualify that witness to testify. However, the evidence that might have been discovered if the witness had been hypnotized prior to trial would remain unobtainable. On the other hand, the police could guess that the evidence that *might* be produced under hypnosis was sufficiently significant or independently confirmable to sacrifice the witness's testimony at trial. There was no guarantee. Before actually putting the witness in a trance, how could they know what his or her subconscious might reveal?

Rather than continue to make this painful choice, law enforcement groups wisely sought to eliminate the dilemma. In 1968, they succeeded for the very first time. The Maryland Court of Special Appeals, in *Harding v. State* (1968), permitted a witness who had been previously hypnotized by the police to testify in court. The modern field of forensic hypnosis was born.

The rights gained by the police to liberalize the rules for evidence obtained by hypnosis initially opened the door for more liberal rulings with regard to work done by therapists as well. However, several events within the last 10 years have had quite the opposite effect. Indeed, it is now the therapists who find themselves faced with virtually the same dilemma that the police had encountered earlier.

The Hypnotherapist's Dilemma

In most jurisdictions, a therapist may well be faced with a quandary. On the one hand, he or she can forego the use of hypnosis in order to protect the legal interests of the client, at the expense of not being able to provide therapeutic relief. On the other hand, the therapist may have to determine, prior to utilizing hypnosis, whether the therapeutic gain from the hypnosis will outweigh the client's potential loss of legal redress. How did this predicament emerge?

---

[2]Complete citations for all state, federal, and foreign cases and state statutes specifically pertaining to hypnosis appear in the Appendix of this book. Full information on relevant but non-hypnosis-related cases (e.g., *Tarasoff;* see "Expanding Duties Owed to Clients," below) and all other material is given in the "References and Bibliography" section at the end of the book.

The therapist's dilemma is the unwelcome consequence of three related, but distinct, influences. These are described below.

Therapy versus law enforcement. For a variety of reasons, therapists and police officers now espouse opposite positions in the controversy regarding who may lawfully utilize hypnosis. Professional hypnosis associations have been active in seeking clarification of the proper role of investigative hypnosis performed by the police. Should police officers, who may be minimally trained in suggestion and untrained in psychology, be permitted to employ hypnotic procedures with witnesses and victims? Or should this work be done only by neutral, impartial mental health professionals who specialize in hypnosis?

Professional therapists argue that the police are inadequately trained to be aware of such problems as confabulation, excessive suggestion, accuracy of recall, and deception in a trance state. Police organizations, on the other hand, insist that they are better trained for *investigative* hypnosis work than mental health practitioners, who have no training in criminal investigation and interrogation.

The territorial battle lines between law enforcement organizations and mental health professional associations have now been drawn. The American Society for Clinical Hypnosis (ASCH), the Society for Clinical and Experimental Hypnosis, and other mental health associations have gone on record opposing police use of hypnosis unless the hypnotist has professional therapy credentials. To justify their conclusions that the police are ill equipped to recognize and handle the complicated issues concerning memory, suggestion, confabulation, and simulation, mental health specialists have amassed an overwhelming volume of studies, experiments, and data detailing the pitfalls of hypnotically refreshed testimony (cf. Orne, 1985; Orne, Soskis, Dinges, & Orne, 1984).

Ironically, this very proof that police should not be permitted to use hypnosis to refresh the recollection of victims and witnesses has convinced courts to view such testimony with great skepticism, regardless of the qualifications of the hypnotist. By trying to shut out the police, mental health *researchers* have helped create the dilemma faced by mental health *practitioners*. This, of course, represents yet another battleground for the traditional experimental-versus-clinical conflict that has historically divided psychology.

The return to inadmissibility. Since the mid-1970s, the courts have reversed the liberalizing trend toward increased openness to hypnosis work. Jurisdiction after jurisdiction has limited or eliminated the rights of a witness to testify after undergoing hypnosis procedures. Two separate lines of cases have narrowed or closed the door on such testimony.

One line of cases is exemplified by the decision of the New Jersey Supreme Court in the 1981 *State v. Hurd* case. According to the court, hypnotically refreshed testimony is admissible only if the hypnosis has been performed according to strict guidelines, such as those recommended by Dr. Martin Orne. Under these guidelines, only a licensed psychologist or psychiatrist should perform the hypnosis, and then only under certain limitations. For example, the professionally licensed hypnotist must be independent of the police, prosecutor, or defense, and must not receive any information from the police unless it is in writing and therefore later available to be produced in court. In addition, the hypnotist must take a prehypnotic statement of the facts from the subject; must audiotape or videotape all transactions between them; and must not permit anyone else in the room at any time during the prehypnotic, hypnotic, and posthypnotic procedures.[3]

A second line of cases makes a more critical assessment of the ability of hypnosis to accurately refresh a person's recollection. These courses cite evidence and testimony by experts suggesting that hypnosis may taint memory and nullify the effectiveness of cross-examination. On the basis of these data, many courts have refused to allow hypnotically refreshed testimony in court, even when stringent safeguards have been met. This line of cases has been steadily gaining ground and is becoming dominant across the country. Although it was not the first case to so hold, the California Supreme Court opinion in *People v. Shirley* (1982) is perhaps the best known and the most vehemently debated.

In the *Shirley* case, the court fully closed the door on the trend begun in 1968, which permitted the admissibility of hypnotically refreshed testimony. In a long and heavily footnoted opinion, the court declared that hypnosis is unduly suggestive as an investigative tool, and therefore any witness who has been hypnotized prior to trial should not be permitted to testify about matters discussed during the hypnosis session. A later amendment to the decision allows for a single exception: The defendant in a criminal case has a constitutional right to testify on his or her own behalf, even if he or she has been hypnotized.

The *Hurd* and *Shirley* lines of cases address the issue of whether hypnotically refreshed recollection is admissible at trial. The impact of these rulings on hypnotherapists whose patients may subsequently testify in court requires a brief look at one further legal development.

Expanding duties owed to clients. Therapists are well aware that in the last two decades judges have expanded the scope of duties owed to patients. Indeed, many courts have expanded the duties owed by therapists to nonclients.

---

[3] This final requirement may be revised under certain circumstances (i.e., with minor children).

In the *Tarasoff v. Regents of the University of California* case (1976), the California Supreme Court created a duty for mental health professionals to warn nonclients of threats against them revealed to the therapist in confidence by clients. Many other states have chosen to follow the lead of *Tarasoff* by continuing to expand the therapist's legal responsibilities beyond the confines of the therapy room.

The *Tarasoff* case requires therapists to consider the future implications to nonclients of the present practice of therapy with a client. The *Hurd* and *Shirley* cases may suggest a parallel development in requiring therapists to consider the future implications to clients of the present practice of hypnotherapy with those same clients. If the courts have been willing to create duties to nonclients, it is reasonable to expect that they will feel little hesitancy in expanding the duties owed to clients. It is now quite clear that therapists must look beyond the traditional scope of the therapy session in meeting their obligations to the law.

Implications. What is the significance of these three influences for the psychologist, psychiatrist, physician, or therapist who utilizes hypnosis?

In states following the *Shirley* approach, the hypnotherapist must now evaluate far-reaching potential *legal* events prior to engaging in therapeutic interventions with a client who might be in substantial mental distress. Hypnosis may have to be rejected as a treatment of choice in order to protect the client's potential legal rights. Therapists find themselves in the position of having to provide full disclosure of potential legal consequences to clients prior to beginning therapy with those clients. Therapists must also decide at that time whether or not they would be willing to be called to court to testify regarding the therapy.

In states following the *Hurd* safeguards approach, therapists have to be exceptionally careful in documenting hypnosis therapy sessions. Although full attention to these details may partially distract both a therapist and a patient from complete absorption in the healing process, inattentiveness to these details can cause the entire procedure to be inadmissible in court proceedings.

TRANCE ON TRIAL

How does a therapist carefully and effectively respond to the psychological needs of a client without violating the client's legal rights? How does a therapist, operating in good faith and performing high-quality therapeutic work, avoid facing the ordeal of a malpractice suit based on conditions dictated by a separate professional field?

Hypnosis is a treatment of choice only in certain limited situations in a therapeutic practice. In addition to the purely clinical questions regarding the advisability of uncovering certain types of information, the timing of doing so within the patient's ego framework, and the type of hypnotic procedures to employ, there are also special questions that arise when a legal process may ensue.

A special consideration may arise when hypnosis is used on a victim of rape or another form of intrusive violence. Hypnosis specialists Martin T. Orne and Campbell Perry have independently expressed their concern that hypnosis in such cases might be perceived as a form of "psychological rape" in which the rape victim submits to the dominance and power of the hypnotist (personal communications, 1989). The victim, having once been forced to comply physically, may again feel pressure to comply psychologically. This factor should be carefully weighed by the therapist before deciding to use hypnosis as treatment or for refreshing the victim's memory.

Memory refreshing is the most common situation in which the performance of hypnosis is scrutinized by the law. This area poses particular problems for both the clinician and the court. At issue are these considerations: (1) the ability to cross-examine a previously hypnotized witness, (2) simulation, (3) confabulation, (4) suggestibility, and (5) demand characteristics. In addition, difficulties are created by the fact that the evidence for the efficacy of hypnosis in amnesia recall and memory enhancement in both experimental and clinical settings is equivocal (see Smith, 1983).

To demonstrate the range of decisions that the therapist must encounter and resolve, we will examine the hypothetical (though common) scenario of Dr. Smith and his patient, Ms. B. Two potential professional problems involving hypnotically refreshed memories are explored in this example. The first is the dilemma of a therapist who, in a jurisdiction that refuses to admit hypnotically refreshed memory, fails to warn a client properly. The second consists of the greater intricacies involved in jurisdictions that admit such testimony subject to certain restrictions. Following this discussion, a brief overview is presented of what Dr. Smith would have been asked, had he testified in court.

A Case Example: The Hypnotherapist in Practice

On January 5, 1985, Ms. B. was referred to Dr. Smith by her family physician. Intake interview information indicated that she had been suffering from nightmares, anxiety attacks, and some amnesia following her report of an unspecified traumatic event that had occurred a month earlier. Dr. Smith felt that hypnosis could help Ms. B. regain her memory. He believed that through reliving the event and re-experiencing the emotions of that trauma, she could achieve a therapeutic emotional catharsis. Once this occurred, he anticipated helping her to obtain symptomatic relief, to rebuild her damaged ego structures, and to regain her self-esteem. Dr. Smith explained this procedure to Ms. B., and she consented to undergo treatment.

Approximately 6 weeks into the hypnotherapy, while in a hypnotic trance induced by Dr. Smith, Ms. B. relived the trauma of a brutal rape. With her memory refreshed, she was now able to identify the man who assaulted her. This information was given to the police, and Mr. R., a neighbor of Ms. B. who had a prior record of assaults on women, was arrested. He was subsequently charged with the rape, and brought to trial approximately 10 months later. Ms. B. continued her therapy, and was able to attain significant relief from her symptoms.

In December 1985, Ms. B. was called to testify in the case of *State v. R.* for the crime of rape. Because she had undergone hypnosis, she was disqualified from testifying in court. Lacking the testimony of the victim, the case was dismissed, and Mr. R. was set free. This event rekindled many of her psychological difficulties, and she returned for additional therapy, but with another therapist.

Dr. Smith operated at all times in good faith, used appropriate therapeutic interventions, and was successful in helping his client. However, the nature of the treatment, while psychologically sound, deprived Ms. B. of her legal right to testify in subsequent court actions.

When Ms. B. consulted a lawyer, she was told that Dr. Smith should have informed her that the hypnosis would disqualify her as a witness. Furthermore, the lawyer worried that Ms. B. might also be disqualified in her civil suit against Mr. R. for damages caused by his tortious conduct against her. Deprived of her right to compensation from her attacker and of her right to provide the testimony central to his criminal prosecution, Ms. B. authorized the attorney to file suit against Dr. Smith.

What happened? By any therapeutic standard, Dr. Smith acted in a correct and competent manner. He was successful in helping his patient recover from her symptoms. Yet now his patient was suing him for his failure to warn her of potential *legal* consequences. Though Dr. Smith might win this lawsuit, his time and effort in defending himself would be substantial. Furthermore, the suit would be likely to taint his reputation.

There must be other options. What could Dr. Smith have done to protect both Ms. B. and himself?

States Prohibiting Hypnotically Refreshed Testimony

In a sense, the rules in a *"Shirley"* jurisdiction are quite clear. The only real mistakes that a therapist can make are (1) failing to warn the client and obtain written informed consent, and (2) failing to record the prehypnotic memories adequately.

In any state in which hypnotically refreshed testimony is held to be inadmissible, Dr. Smith should also have considered the possibility of using the hypnosis sparingly. Most courts do not restrict all testimony because the witness has been hypnotized, but exclude the testimony that is the product of hypnosis. Ms. B. might have been permitted to testify about matters not covered in the hypnosis sessions.

If Dr. Smith maintained precise records, along the lines suggested in the following section, and was careful in limiting the scope of the hypnosis, he might have been able to provide hypnotherapy without subverting Ms. B.'s legal rights. Naturally, Dr. Smith would have had to perform a very careful balancing act here.

Some therapists have attempted to avoid the problem of legal disqualification by using techniques akin to hypnosis. They believe that if they do not use the word "hypnosis," courts will not impose the strict admissibility test. This approach has been suggested to therapists at hypnosis conferences. Any therapist following this method, however, should be advised that the courts may not be so easily fooled. For those judges who are critical of the inadmissibility rule, but are nevertheless bound by it, this approach may provide a convenient loophole. However, this tactic is risky: It still may put the legal rights of the patient in some jeopardy. At minimum, the patient should be so informed.

States Permitting Hypnotic Testimony Subject to Guidelines

In states that admit hypnotically refreshed testimony, but only when certain specific guidelines are met, a therapist has more freedom to engage in the best therapeutic practice, but far greater potential for malpractice liability. In these states, certain additional requirements must be met:

1. In any case in which legal action may ensue, and certainly in any case where there is amnesia for a traumatic event, the therapist should maintain especially complete records, beginning with the recording or reconstructing of all the information presented in the initial telephone contact.

2. The therapist must be careful to maintain the integrity of the therapist–patient relationship. He or she should not accept payment for therapeutic services from law enforcement agencies. Any interaction with these agencies, or with attorneys, should be fully documented.

3. Prior to the first session, the therapist should explain the need for hypnosis and its legal ramifications to the patient. The patient should be asked to sign a written informed consent form certifying that he or she has received full information about the potential legal consequences of hypnotherapy and still desires that it be undertaken. Consent should also be obtained for permission to tape the therapy sessions.

4. Prior to beginning any hypnosis, the therapist must take a complete history of the events as remembered by the patient. This history should be, at a minimum, audiotaped, and preferably videotaped, for subsequent referral to determine whether a casual comment or remark acted as a suggestion.

Patients should be encouraged to tell what they remember in a free narrative style. Research indicates that this style is the least likely to be influenced by inadvertent suggestion (Hilgard & Loftus, 1979). Specific questions to a patient should be avoided until after the patient has completed the narrative, and should at that point be carefully phrased so as not to hint at or suggest specific answers.

The therapist should be especially careful to avoid making comments, promises, or assurances about the power of hypnosis to aid recall. Although it may be therapeutically beneficial to suggest that hypnosis will allow the patient to remember what has been forgotten, or to supply missing details, these remarks are unduly suggestive and act as an invitation to fantasize or confabulate. Statements that "all memories are recorded in the brain" should also be avoided.

5. Alternative memory-refreshing techniques, including the mnemonic interview procedure described by Geiselman and colleagues (Geiselman, Fisher, Cohen, Holland, & Surtes, 1986; Geiselman, Fisher, MacKinnon, & Holland, 1985), may be employed before hypnotic procedures are utilized.

6. As noted earlier, all hypnosis sessions should be videotaped. Strong arguments can be made for the fact that audiotaping alone is insufficient; only a clear *visual* record of the interaction between therapist and patient provides an opportunity to properly evaluate the hypnosis session. Courts have not yet insisted upon videotaped records. However, Laurence and Perry (1988) sensibly recommend that the videotape show both the therapist and the patient, and that an on-screen timer device be incorporated into the recording.

7. The therapist must be able to demonstrate the hypnotic capacity of the patient and the fact that a hypnotic state was or was not achieved. Some measure of the depth of the hypnotic state should also be demonstrated.

8. In conducting the hypnosis sessions, the therapist must be especially careful not to lead the patient or assist him or her in filling in (confabulating) any of the lost memory by providing "logical" or more socially acceptable alternatives.

9. When the hypnosis session ends, any posthypnotic interactions between the therapist and patient should also be videotaped. The therapist should avoid statements or suggestions that might have the effect of "concretizing" the information revealed during the hypnosis or that might encourage the patient to believe that hypnotically refreshed recollection is likely to be more accurate.

10. The tapes should be securely stored in a safe place.

The clinical hypnotherapist at this junction may well ask, "Is it truly necessary for me to rigorously adhere to these guidelines when all I intend to do is therapy with a patient?" Laurence and Perry (1988) have argued that the answer is "yes":

> If [hypnotically refreshed] recollections are to form the basis of subsequent testimony, it is essential to follow the guidelines. . . . Without a complete and adequate electronic record of all interactions between a therapist and patient, it would be totally inappropriate to permit an individual to testify on the basis of recollections that occurred during a therapeutic hypnosis session. (p. 383)

Let us assume for what follows that our hypothetical Dr. Smith had done all that could be required of him to meet his legal obligations, and that Ms. B. was allowed to testify in the trial of *State v. R.*

A Case Example: The Hypnotherapist in Court

It is certain that if Ms. B. were allowed to testify on the basis of her refreshed memory, Dr. Smith would be called to the stand to explain and support the hypnotic procedures that were used. Once on the stand, he would be questioned both by the prosecuting attorney attempting to support the criminal charges against Mr. R., and by the defense attorney trying to discredit both Dr. Smith and his treatment.

First, Dr. Smith would have to be qualified as an expert. This process would involve inquiries into his background, training, and experience. Once qualified as an expert, Dr. Smith would be expected to answer questions about hypnosis in general, the use of hypnosis in this particular case, basic psychology, memory, the divergent literature and expert opinions on these issues, guidelines for the use of hypnosis in forensic situations, and a host of other related subjects. The court would be especially interested in Dr. Smith's assurances as to the accuracy of the patient's recall. There would also be questions about the capacity of Ms. B. to lie or confabulate under hypnosis, and about Dr. Smith's ability to detect such deception or inaccuracy.

Dr. Smith might bring personal feelings about the case to the trial. He certainly would have some emotional connection to Ms. B. and her interests, and might believe that a conviction would be beneficial to her healing process. A further complication might arise if Dr. Smith were to harbor personal doubts as to the accuracy of Ms. B.'s refreshed memory. These doubts might not be of central significance to the therapy, but they would create a conflict between his professional obligation to provide effective therapy and his legal obligation to testify truthfully.

CONCLUSION

The differing goals and dissimilar methods of lawyers and therapists are often difficult to reconcile.

What the law requires of hypnotherapists forms the subject matter of this book. The ensuing chapters will familiarize clinicians with the following:

- An actual clinical case that subsequently involved courtroom testimony by the therapist.
- A historical overview of the development of forensic hypnosis issues in courts and legislatures.
- A description of the law's evolving view of hypnosis.
- A guide to the techniques lawyers use to handle expert witnesses in hypnosis cases.
- A presentation of data on crucial psychological issues of memory and hypnosis.
- A guide for therapists through the pretrial, trial, and posttrial legal proceedings.
- A thorough listing of the relevant cases, statutes, and legal and psychological literature.

Forensic hypnosis need not be a mystery or a pitfall to the informed practitioner.

Part II

A Clinical Case

CHAPTER 2

Jennifer: A Case Portrait

In January 1981, Dr. Shapiro received an apparently standard referral call from Sandra P., a case worker at the local rape crisis center.[1] Sandra indicated that she was working with Jennifer L., a young woman who had been raped the previous October and who was currently suffering from a variety of posttrauma symptoms, including amnesia. Sandra wanted to know whether hypnotherapy might be helpful in allowing Jennifer to recall the events of the assault. It was hoped that by reliving the trauma in a trance state, the patient could be freed from the nightmares, insomnia, and feelings of dread that often accompany posttraumatic amnesia.

Hypnosis is a common therapeutic technique for amnesia. It is hypothesized that in a trance state, information from the unconscious mind becomes more available. Frequently, in cases of trauma-induced memory loss, repressed or inaccessible recollections and the attached emotions recur with hypnotic procedures. It is believed that by reliving these experiences in the "safe" therapeutic environment, the patient will gain some emotional relief and cognitive mastery over the events.

In recent years, however, the use of hypnosis has not been restricted to clinicians in mental health fields. Hypnosis has become a common tool of investigation in law enforcement as well. Because of this use and a general confusion concerning the parameters and limitations of hypnotically influenced testimony, a major legal controversy has ensued.

This chapter details the four hypnotherapy sessions that resulted in a full remission of Jennifer's amnesia and subsequent posttraumatic symptoms.

---

[1] With the exception of the therapist, pseudonyms are employed to maintain confidentiality.

THE SETTING

Jennifer arrived early for the first session, accompanied by Sandra. She completed the intake forms and arranged with the receptionist at the office for payments for the hypnotherapy sessions. Jennifer paid personally for each appointment.

Jennifer appeared to be in her early to mid-20s and was dressed in a T-shirt and jeans. Of mixed racial heritage, she spoke in "pidgin English," seemed alert and intelligent, and had a normal amount of anxiety for the session.

Sandra was an experienced case worker at the rape crisis center. She was a tall, slender woman, approximately 30 years of age, and was professionally dressed.

The four appointments took place on January 27, February 5, February 17, and February 19, 1981. Each session took place in the same large room, which contained no furniture except a soft rug, pillows on the floor, and a video camera and tape recorder in the furthest corner of the room.

EVENTS OF THE RAPE

On October 18, 1980, Jennifer L. was beaten and forcibly raped by M. B. after she had accepted a ride home from a party with him and two of his friends. Following the attack, Jennifer began having nightmares and other symptoms commonly associated with post-rape trauma. She also suffered from amnesia for certain parts of that evening and morning. Four periods surrounding the rape incident were lost from her conscious memory; all of these occurred between the time immediately prior to the actual rape and her admission to the emergency ward at a local hospital. When the memory deficits became a major factor in loss of sleep and in her general psychological and emotional discomfort, she was referred for hypnotherapy.

The four hypnotherapy sessions were designed solely for memory retrieval. Each session was conducted by Shapiro with only Jennifer and Sandra present. With the aid of hypnosis, Jennifer was able to regain a full memory of the events of October 18. This refreshed memory was subsequently available both in trance and waking states.

One particularly significant component of the refreshed memory was that Jennifer remembered that she had also been assaulted by one of M. B.'s companions (A. M.). At the recommendation of Sandra, Jennifer was voluntarily reinterviewed by the police at her home on February 20, 1981, and picked A. M.'s picture out of a photographic lineup. She stated for the record that she now remembered that A. M. had also molested her. As a result, A. M. was arrested, and both he and M. B. were brought to trial in December 1982.

Jennifer's hypnotically refreshed memory was deemed legally admissible, and she was allowed to testify as a witness for the state. At the conclusion of the trial, both men were found guilty and sentenced to multiyear terms in the Hawaii State Prison.

At the time the hypnosis sessions were conducted, there were no legal rulings in Hawaii governing the admissibility of hypnotically refreshed recollection. However, judicial decisions in other states were beginning to suggest that before such testimony would be allowed in court, several procedural requirements for the conduct of the hypnosis sessions had to be met. With these precedents as a guide, the following precautions were taken in Jennifer's case:

1. All four sessions were videotaped in their entirety.
2. All four sessions were conducted by a licensed clinical psychologist.
3. A complete statement of Jennifer's conscious memory was taken prior to the beginning of any hypnosis.
4. The hypnotherapist had no prior knowledge of the events that had occurred.
5. The hypnotherapist was not at any time hired by the police or prosecutor.
6. Jennifer's regular case worker, Sandra, was present for all sessions.
7. The hypnotherapy was expressly geared for Jennifer's functioning and comfort. Neither the hypnotherapist nor the client had any intention of using the contents of any retrieved memory to pursue legal action.

A SESSION-BY-SESSION ANALYSIS OF THE HYPNOTHERAPY

Each session of the hypnotherapy consisted almost entirely of an induction, deepening, and extension of hypnotic trance. There was a pretrance segment to help set the stage, create a comfortable rapport, and discern whether there were any counterindications for the hypnosis. This was followed by a relaxation induction, deepening procedures, and a "watch the movie" technique of memory *recall* from the unconscious. Finally, the subject was brought out of the trance and debriefed.

After each hypnosis session, recommendations were made to Sandra, the case worker, for follow-up work in her regular therapy sessions with Jennifer.

Session 1: January 27, 1981

The first session was designed to assess Jennifer's ability to be a hypnosis subject, and also to determine the advisability of pursuing hypnotic work for memory recall.

The beginning of the session was devoted to familiarizing Jennifer with the setting and procedures. The presence of the video camera was pointed out; written releases of information and confidentiality were discussed and signed; and Jennifer's control over the disposition of the tape was described.

Prior to any induction, Jennifer's knowledge of hypnosis was elicited. Her prior exposure was minimal:

JENNIFER: . . . like on TV you just fall asleep and start doing whatever they [the hypnotist] say . . . like other people control your mind.

The hypnotic procedures for the current setting were then carefully explained. Hypnosis was described as a "learned skill," under which Jennifer, rather than the hypnotherapist, would maintain control. The unconscious mind was then described for her, using the analogy of a twilight state between waking and sleep.

SHAPIRO: *So what hypnosis is doing is a kind of asking your conscious mind to just stand aside for a while and watch. . . . What we will do today is just try and see how quickly you can learn the skill.*

In this initial meeting, Jennifer was fully informed that only her current hypnotizability was being assessed at this time. There would be no delving into the trauma at any point during this session.

The trance induction consisted of a series of progressive relaxation suggestions, moving from Jennifer's forehead out over her entire body and culminating in a state of deep bodily relaxation. After all major organs and muscle groups had been relaxed, a resistance suggestion was made that if any area of her body remained tense, it represented doubts or questions. She was told that it was important for her to pay attention to those doubts.

SHAPIRO: *And now try and explore your body and see if there's a place or two that's much less relaxed than all the other places. It's important if there is, because very often in our unconscious mind there's a part of our mind that really wants to be hypnotized, and another part that's kind of scared, and it's saying, "Hey, I'm skeptical, I'm not so sure about this." And that skeptical part, the part that is not so sure, is the part that keeps tension in those one or two areas of the body. It's really important to pay attention to that and to listen to the skepticism. It's really important to know that there's doubt . . . but once your conscious mind becomes aware that there is doubt, the tense parts have done their job. Now there's no longer a reason for those body parts to remain tense any longer. So if there is a body part or two that is more tense, we now know that they represent a message of skepticism, and now that the message is clear, these parts can also begin to get a well-deserved rest. Let's see if they can also relax now.*

Following this suggestion, a hypnotic induction by reverse counting from 10 to 1 was given:

SHAPIRO: *And now I am going to count from 10 all the way down to 1, and by the time I reach 1 allow yourself to be in a trance, a special state of mind for your unconscious mind, the part of your mind that is active in dreams and daydreams, and that special time between waking and sleep just before you fall asleep. Allow that part of your mind to be more active, and your conscious mind to be an observer, to watch, and listen but to not take over . . . and with each number allow yourself to drift deeper and deeper into this trance state, until you're feeling totally comfortable. Your body totally relaxed, and your mind alert, aware, and focusing on its own inner work and the sound of my voice. Ready now: 10, 9, . . .*

During the reverse counting, Jennifer showed several signs of relaxation. Her muscle tone eased, her breathing became slower and more regular, and she showed the beginning of some rapid eye movements (REMs). All were positive indicators of an altered state of consciousness. After she was allowed to experience this state, a deepening technique (peripheral heat transfer) was employed to help reify the trance for her, and also to allow her to access her unconscious mind more clearly.

SHAPIRO: *And you know, in this state, it is possible to do things and experience things that we normally cannot do. Maybe we could try one of these and see. You know, Jennifer, the unconscious mind works automatically. It controls our blood flow, our breathing, our temperature without our ever having to think about any of these. One of the things that the unconscious can do that the conscious mind cannot do very well is to change the temperature of various parts of our body, simply by slightly increasing the blood flow to that part of the body.*
Let's see what happens if the blood flow were to increase in one of your two hands, and see if that hand gets warmer than the other hand. Try that now, increasing the blood flow to one hand ever so slightly and seeing if there is a sense of warmth. It might get comfortably warmer, but it will never get too hot, just enough so it's noticeable. . . . And if that starts to happen, allow yourself to take one deep breath when you notice it.

Jennifer took a deep breath at that point, and was informed that if she wanted to, she could take another one and go even deeper into the trance. She did.

This particular deepening technique was used because it tends to be nonthreatening, and because the room in which the work was taking place was very cool. The suggestion of warmth could have the additional effect of helping Jennifer be a bit more physically comfortable.

The next phase of the hypnosis was to establish whether Jennifer could develop a fantasy in trance and could experience several sensory aspects of the fantasy. She was asked to form a picture of a place that was pleasant for her, and then was asked to go to the place:

SHAPIRO: . . . *a place of comfort and freedom, and just allow yourself to be there now, . . . to see the sights of the place, hear the sounds of the place, feel the feelings, smell the aromas, and even perhaps taste the tastes of the place.*

When Jennifer was able to experience this place, she gave a finger-lifting response, and then was given instructions to linger and enjoy being there. These pleasurable images were then identified as a "haven" to which she could return at any time, to feel safe and comfortable.

SHAPIRO: *If at any time, you feel like you're becoming too uncomfortable, you can return in your mind to this place and re-experience it.*

At one point, a tear rolled down her face. Shapiro made a note to query her about that.

Once Jennifer was able to experience the fantasy place, the next test appraised her ability to use age regression for the memory enhancement produces to be used in subsequent sessions. Suggestions were made for her to experience the feelings of first being in school. A form of Erickson's "learning the letters" induction was utilized here (M. H. Erickson, personal communication, 1979). She asked to be the young Jennifer going to school, experiencing her teacher and her classmates. Following being in school, she was instructed to leave the school and go home:

SHAPIRO: . . . *taking the same route, and looking at the home, seeing the place and the people, and maybe even hearing a conversation, seeing the people there, experiencing the place and finding the part of the home that you like the best, some special area.*

Again she was asked to experience all of her senses in that setting. After a few minutes of internal exploration, she was informed that she could enjoy the home for just a few moments and then she would have to return to the room. A suggestion for permissive amnesia was then given:

SHAPIRO: *One of the things that happens, while being in a trance like this, is that sometimes memories come up that are real important to remember. If any memories do come up that you want to remember, it's good to go ahead and remember them once you are awake. By the same token, if there is anything that is best left in your unconscious, that you don't want to remember, or don't need to remember, that's perfectly OK too. That's the nice part of it. You can remember what you want to remember and leave behind whatever is best left behind.*

She was then brought out of the trance state on Shapiro's counting from 1 to 10. On awakening, she seemed a bit dazed and asked, "Can I have a cigarette now?"

Debriefing occurred immediately, and Jennifer recounted her subjective experiences. She described being very tense at the beginning and being surprised at how quickly she relaxed and seemed to begin "to float." She was also surprised by the peripheral heat transfer. As her right hand got warmer, she began to "really have more hopes that this would work." The special place was a quiet graveyard near her home where she spent many meditative hours. The graveyard image also brought up for her the recent death of her mother (14 months previously). Jennifer described feeling very sad. She began to sob when she talked about her mother's death. When asked whether she was aware of crying during the trance, Jennifer replied that she had not felt it then, but her face felt now as if she had cried a little.

The school images were fairly vivid, and she appeared to have a particular ability to experience visual and kinesthetic images. She was able to re-experience raking the leaves after school, something she did every day while she was "thinking about things."

At several points, Jennifer was given positive reinforcement for her abilities at hypnosis. She was an atypically good subject, and this fact was communicated to her.

In concluding the session, therapist and client discussed future plans.

SHAPIRO: *What we would want to do, if you would like to continue, is in future sessions to go ahead and try to relive—to try and remember from your unconscious mind those events that you had that are blocked out.*

It was recommended that she and Sandra "take some time and talk it over" before deciding whether she wished to continue with additional hypnosis sessions.

Jennifer then mentioned that the experience of her mother 15 years ago was very vivid and nice, but it brought up the pain of her mother's recent death. She began crying again, and the discussion shifted to whether remembering the events of October 18 might also be very painful. Jennifer felt that though she was indeed afraid that they would be, she also had to know what happened.

As a final issue, the videotape was again discussed, and she was told that she had control over what happened to it. She was also told that if she chose, she would be able to see it at any time. An agreement was made that Jennifer would call to set up the next appointment if she chose to continue, which she did. Jennifer then left the room so that Sandra and Shapiro could have a short conversation regarding the therapeutic importance of her tears about her mother.

Session 2: February 5, 1981

The second session was designed to serve three purposes:

1. To confirm that Jennifer did wish to continue the hypnosis and attempt to recover her lost memories.
2. To take a complete history of events as she remembered them prior to the hypnosis.
3. To begin the task of retrieving the memories by reliving the traumatic experiences while in trance.

The first goal was accomplished easily. Jennifer was "eager but anxious" about the continuation. With reassurance that she could terminate the process at any time, she decided to try to re-experience the events.

So that recovered memories could be distinguished from continuing recollection, a complete history of the events of the trauma as recollected was taken prior to any regressive hypnosis. This history is presented below in summary form, preceding the description of the hypnotic phase of the hour.

The session began with a few rapport-creating comments and reassurance of termination on Jennifer's terms. History taking then began:

SHAPIRO: *Well, let's begin by telling me everything you do remember about the events of that time.*

The Prehypnosis History

Jennifer described drinking beer with her friend V. They were joined by V.'s cousins and friends, who had been sleeping in another room. Then they began smoking marijuana and tobacco.

JENNIFER: [I was] a little uncomfortable there. . . . One of the girls had a baby. . . . I never saw anything like that . . . people, like, just pushed and slapped the kid and punch 'em, see how strong she is and stuff like that.

Jennifer retreated to a corner with a beer and the baby. She played with the baby by herself. Her friend V. "thought I was a little weird because I wasn't talking. So I just told her, well, I'm just going to leave pretty soon. . . . I'm tired."

The drinking continued until the beer ran out and V. asked everyone for money for more beer. Jennifer was the only person to offer. She and two others from the party went to the store to buy a "few more six-packs." When Jennifer subsequently prepared to leave, V. said that everyone was going. The group headed for V.'s cousin's car.

JENNIFER: . . . and I felt weird. As soon as we were down, V. waved goodbye and I thought she was going [to] come. So I began telling them where I lived.

SHAPIRO: *Who do you mean now? Who was in the car?*

JENNIFER: A. M. [the driver], me, and M. B. and R.

She described a long period of time during which the driver kept getting lost, but refused to take directions. When the car finally approached her house, the others asked her to buy them some beer, claiming that it was a long way home and they "didn't want to fall asleep at the wheel." After she purchased beer, chips, and cigarettes for them, they suggested a trip to a local swimming hole to see whether any of their friends were there. When they arrived, nobody else was present.

JENNIFER: . . . So they say that they usually come up here. . . . So I told them, "Well, that's funny, I never seen you guys before, I come up here quite often."

One of the guys brought the cooler with beer so they could continue drinking. A. M. and R. began swimming. Jennifer reported that she became frightened that they might push her into the water from the cliff, so she started to walk down the path to a lower level closer to the water level. M. B. noticed her leaving, and asked her, "Where are you going?"

JENNIFER: [I said,] "I'm going to sit down there." So he said, "I'll take you." As soon as we were walking, he said, "Let's go this way, the other path is slippery." So as we were going down, I slipped and asked him, "Are you sure you know where you are going? I think I went down this path before and it's a dead end." He said, "No, this is the back way." So we went, and then I remember walking all the way down, and then that's what I don't remember. The next thing I remember, you know, he was on top of me, then again, I just blacked out.

Then I remember again. I could hear him laughing, and he was calling the guy A. M. and saying, "come, come." So I heard both of them laughing. Then I felt like a bottle going up [into her vagina]. So then I don't know, I just blacked out again. Then the next thing I know . . . I woke up, and, you know, my clothes and stuff, nothing was around. So I got up and started running to the parking lot where they had the car, and as soon as I came around the bend I just saw them shut the trunk. So I asked M. B., "Go get my clothes." He was yelling at me "shut up, shut up," and the driver was yelling at me, and the guy R. looked real scared, like he was looking at me.

M. B., the man who assaulted her, offered to go with her to find the clothes, but she refused and continued her demands that he go alone to get them. She was standing at the open front passenger door and screaming until M. B. got into the car, and A. M. threw her his pair of pants and told her to put them on.

JENNIFER: Then he pulled me into the car, and told me, "shut up," so I just told him, "hey, just drop me off anywhere."

She talked at length about the ride with them and asked to be let off at any one of many places that were familiar to her.

JENNIFER: So they just kept going. Then the next thing I remember was when I was in the hospital.

After the narrative concluded, there was a discussion about three gaps in her recollection of the events, and Jennifer was asked about her feelings.

JENNIFER: Well, now I can talk about it. I'm curious about what really happened. I wonder, like I was telling Sandra, a lot of times, when the incident first happened I used to have nightmares, dreams like people killing each other . . . beatings . . . visions coming in my head like they were beating me. I don't believe it, but I don't doubt it either. Just not so sure.
SHAPIRO: *Do you have any ideas, any other ideas about what might have happened any of those times?*

She responded by shaking her head from side to side.
At the conclusion of this history taking, Jennifer was given hypnotic suggestions to re-enter trance.

Hypnosis

SHAPIRO: *Again, Jennifer, you know, it will be totally under your control, just like the last time. This time I will kind of give you an opportunity to see what your unconscious wants to tell you about that day, but there will be no forcing, no pushing. Whatever comes up will come up when your unconscious is ready to do it. OK?*

Trance inductions were identical to those described in the first session. A connection to the first session was made to deepen the trance and to allow Jennifer to re-experience the home in which she grew up. Once she signaled that she was able to be in that place, a suggestion was made to relocate her consciousness in her current home. Then the focus shifted to the night in question.

SHAPIRO: *And now we're going to go to the day when the incident happened, and while you relax, and become more and more comfortable, think back to when you were at V.'s house, and the baby was there, and that was really confusing why people would treat a baby so roughly . . . and you were treating the baby differently . . . there's a contact between the two of you.*

And then just like a movie that you are watching, where you are part of the movie, and where you can also be outside of it and watch what's happening, start watching the events that happened that day, and while you are doing that, allow your voice box to open up and just talk about . . . just say the things that you are experiencing. Maybe you could start by describing V. Just allow yourself to talk and tell what she looks like on the day.

JENNIFER: Tall, skinny, long black hair.

SHAPIRO: *What is she wearing?*

JENNIFER: Dark pants.

SHAPIRO: *And now let's move. You're coming down the stairs, and V. isn't with you. Notice your feelings, and now you're approaching the car. What kind is it?*

JENNIFER: Kind of a Mustang like a copper color . . . an old one.

In order to make the experience safer, Jennifer was asked to experience Sandra, the trusted case worker, as if she were with her and as if they were watching the movie together. At this suggestion, Sandra did shift her position to get closer to Jennifer.

SHAPIRO: *And Sandra is getting settled in to watch with you. I am going to count down from 3 to 1, and as I count allow yourself to go deeper and deeper, so there will be more details, so that the two of you can watch them more clearly.*

Jennifer then recounted the sequence of events, with greater detail than before. As she did so, she moved from a past-tense recollection to a present-tense, experiencing mode. Nonverbal signs such as respiration, muscle tone, and REMs coincided with this alteration, and provided some indication that she was in a trance state.

When she came to the first occurrence of memory loss, the following exchange occurred:

JENNIFER: . . . So I just started—they were asking me if I lived there all my life. . . . They just asked me if I wanted to go up there and just see who was up there [by the pond], so I said, "sure, why not."

SHAPIRO: *What are you feeling now?*

JENNIFER: Scared.

SHAPIRO: *Scared?*

JENNIFER: I guess just thinking about it. I guess that if I didn't really, you know, trust people as easy as I do, maybe they wouldn't have attacked me.

SHAPIRO: *What's happening now?*

JENNIFER: Then we went and left. They parked [the car] in the parking lot, so M. B. told R. to carry the cooler and stuff. So we started walking. So as we were walking, we went up and went straight to the first cliff. Then R. opened a beer, gave me a beer, then they all started to swim. So then I just told myself, you know, that if I was to slip or something . . . I could get hurt.

SHAPIRO: *It was scary to be on the top of the cliff?*

JENNIFER: So I just decided to go down to the road, and then M. B., he saw me walking, so he asked me where I was going to go. So I told him that I was going to go by the road and sit down.

So he told me to avoid my getting hurt and stuff, you know, he would help me to go down. So I started walking, then told me, he grabbed my hand and told me to go down the other path. And I said, "So how come we going to go on this one?" and I tell him that one has a lot of plants and stuff, so I just start walking that way. I don't want to slip. Then he tells me, "the other path is too wet, too muddy." I think I went down this path before and it's a dead end.

As we were walking, he was in front of me and he was holding my hand, so I slipped and then he pulled me up and is telling me, "We're almost there."

SHAPIRO: *How does he pull you up?*

JENNIFER: He just grabs me and pulls me up by the waist and shoulder.

SHAPIRO: *As he is pulling you up, how does his face look?*

JENNIFER: Kinda creepy to me.

SHAPIRO: *What is going through your mind now as you see the creepy look on his face?*

JENNIFER: Just reminds me of some other crazy people I know. My cousin and brother-in-law. They get same kind of looks when they do inconsiderate stuff.

SHAPIRO: *He picks you up. . . . OK, Jennifer. Now you and Sandra can watch the movie as it unfolds, you can be right there now for a few minutes. What is happening?*

JENNIFER: Just walking. I feel very scared now.

SHAPIRO: *Scared?*

During this time, Jennifer began to shake, and her face indicated a great deal of fear.

SHAPIRO: *What are you feeling afraid of?*

JENNIFER: Finding something out.
SHAPIRO: *What are you afraid of finding?*
JENNIFER: *(Tearfully)* Beating me or making fun of me?
SHAPIRO: *If you'd like, you could ask your unconscious mind about that. Is that happening as you experience it?* (Silence) *What's happening now?*
JENNIFER: Fighting.
SHAPIRO: *Who's fighting?*
JENNIFER: Him and me.
SHAPIRO: *Describe the fight as it is happening.*
JENNIFER: He keeps pushing me down.
SHAPIRO: *You keep getting up.*

During this time, Jennifer was crying noticeably, her chest was heaving, and REMs were marked.

JENNIFER: [I] keep getting up and punching him. He slapping my face.
SHAPIRO: *What happens now?*
JENNIFER: I . . .
SHAPIRO: *Hard to talk about?*

Jennifer's crying was continuing, but the REMs were slowing. She seemed very agitated.

SHAPIRO: *OK, Jennifer. What I would like to ask you now is to focus back on Sandra, who is your therapist and friend and who really cares, and just focus on the fact that you have this friend with you. In just a moment we'll come out of this special place, and come back to the room, and she'll be sitting here just like she's been the whole time, and also aware of whatever parts of the "movie" that are best remembered.*

I'll count from 1 to 10 and when I reach 10, you can come back to the room, being alert and refreshed, feeling like you have had a really good nap, and being able to remember anything that's new that you want to remember, and leaving behind in your unconscious mind anything that's better left behind. 1, 2, 3, 4, 5— halfway back now—6, 7, 8, 9—your eyes can open at any time now—and 10. How are you feeling?
JENNIFER: OK . . . Can I smoke a cigarette now?
SHAPIRO: *You can do whatever you'd like. Do you have any new memories?*
JENNIFER: So I remember fighting.
SHAPIRO: *You hadn't remembered that before?*
JENNIFER: I'm so nervous.
SHAPIRO: *Yeah. Say what you feel nervous about.*
JENNIFER: Fighting. I hate to fight. I fought a lot, but I hate to fight.
SHAPIRO: *I think it's going to be real important for you to talk to Sandra about*

some of the things that are coming up right now, OK? Could you sense her being
with you this time?

JENNIFER: I . . . yeah . . . I feel a little bit of faith, you know.

SHAPIRO: *OK, Jennifer, we have to quit now. There are a few things that I need*
to tell you. First, you're very good at this, and I want you not to force it until the
next time we can get together. I don't want you to go any further with it. OK?

JENNIFER: Oh, so I don't have to think about it?

SHAPIRO: *You don't have to do a thing, except that if something bothers you,*
get in touch with Sandra, and talk to her about it, or if you want to talk to me,
you can call at any time before our session.

Session 3: February 17, 1981

At the beginning of the third session, Sandra encouraged Jennifer to discuss a poem that she had written the week before. The poem had suicidal
references. The refreshed memories of fighting and the recurrent pictures
of the assault had bothered Jennifer substantially. In particular, she reported discomfort with what she referred to as "half-memories" where a
man or men were yelling at her, but she couldn't understand what they
were saying. Exploration into Jennifer's past indicated several suicidal gestures and active suicidal ideation. She also indicated a great deal of fear
concerning what she "might remember here. In a way I didn't want to
come here, and in a way I did."

Shapiro explained to her that the memories being refreshed also meant
that feelings were being re-experienced. She was told that things could get
worse before they got better. Jennifer and Sandra talked at some length
about Jennifer's strengths and weaknesses, her fears about men, and how
the difficulty of the previous week was experienced as a setback in her
recovery from the assault.

After about 20 minutes, the hypnosis began. Once the trance was induced, the scene was reset on the path where the rape occurred. Jennifer
continued describing her experiences, beginning with the fight: "He pushed
me down. . . . He starts to get on top of me." At that point she reported
that the screen went black. A reverse-counting deepening technique was
used, and specific questions were posed about the surroundings on the
path.

Jennifer continued, slowly and emotionally, with several long pauses between sentences:

JENNIFER: He keeps pulling my head down . . . like he's trying to pull
my head off. . . . My head hurts . . . it's bad, somehow I can't move.
. . . He's trying to take my pants off. . . . [I'm having a] hard time breathing 'cause he's so heavy. . . . [I'm] so scared. . . . Now he's laughing.

SHAPIRO: *Still right on top of you?*

JENNIFER: Still right on top. Now he's calling his friend.
SHAPIRO: *Which friend? . . . What's happening now?*
JENNIFER: His friend A. M. is right [on] top of my head. . . . Then they both start taking off their shorts.

Jennifer was in obvious emotional pain. Tears rolled down her cheeks. She appeared very frightened.

SHAPIRO: *What's happening now?*
JENNIFER: [I] start yelling my head off, then A. M. holds my head and my mouth. . . . He's laughing at me.
SHAPIRO: *What are you feeling now?*
JENNIFER: Sore. Stiff.

At this juncture, an attempt was made to halt the trance and bring Jennifer back to a state of relaxation. However, as she tried to return, she still continued the description of the events. It seemed therapeutically most proper not to interfere with this natural process.

SHAPIRO: *The projector wants to stay on. Just let that happen and let's see what comes next.*
JENNIFER: Now he starts playing with me . . . starts forcing it way inside of me . . . painful. He keeps laughing at me.

Her crying intensified.

SHAPIRO: *What's happening now?*
JENNIFER: He's telling his friend that it's his turn now. He [A. M.] lets go of my head and starts to come on top of me now. . . . He keeps laughing at me. He force . . . he forces hisself.
SHAPIRO: *What's happening?*
JENNIFER: Can I go home? A. M. getting off me now and his friend . . .

After this sequence, Jennifer seemed exhausted. She was brought out of the trance state after being given a suggestion for permissive amnesia.

She initially awoke with a severe headache. Trance was reinstated to supply a suggestion of analgesia, with a reminder that her head had been banged around and needed time to heal. When she came back out of the trance, Jennifer reported that he head pains were markedly reduced.

The therapeutic impact of this session was significant. The amnesia had previously blotted out many of the details of the assault, including the entire participation of the second rapist. It was this revelation, and Jennifer's subsequent decision to report it to the police, that created the potential for conflicts between Jennifer's emotional and legal interests.

Session 4: February 19, 1981

Jennifer had two immediate reactions to the preceding session. First, she got drunk. However, she also wisely sought emotional support by taking a few close friends and an employer into her confidence. This disclosure received positive reinforcement from Sandra. Jennifer also reported that for the first time in months, she had slept well both nights between the sessions.

She appeared to be in a much better mood for this final session. She seemed more calm and confident, a far cry from her initial anxiety and depression. Early in the session, she expressed amazement that she had forgotten about the second assailant.

The hypnosis began approximately 10 minutes into the session, using the same induction that had been previously employed. Jennifer resumed her account with the assault by the second rapist.

JENNIFER: I remember A. M. getting off me, and him and M. B. kept laughing. And I'm not sure which one of them tried to force a beer bottle up me. I can't tell which one, but I can hear him laughing.

SHAPIRO: *Do you want to know which one?*

An affirmative answer led to a trance deepening (reverse counting), and she affirmed that it was A. M.

SHAPIRO: *What's happening now?*

JENNIFER: They're taking my clothes—my pants and my shoes. . . . They start to run away. For some reason I can't get up.

SHAPIRO: *What's holding you there?*

JENNIFER: Probably 'cause I'm so scared.

SHAPIRO: *Makes a lot of sense. Are you scared? Maybe some shame too?*

She was sobbing now, and continued hesitantly.

JENNIFER: I guess being there without my clothes. They just keep laughing at me. . . . I get up and start running . . . hurt . . . angry . . . scared . . . clothes are nowhere around me. Start running up path. As I come around corner I can see M. B. and A. M. closing the trunk. I think my clothes are in there.

She then described the argument by the open car and being dragged into the car in fuller detail:

JENNIFER: I sat in the car, and I told them to give me my clothes and shoes. "If it's money you want, you can have it, just give me my clothes."

So A. M. told me he would take me home. As we were going down the freeway, I told him to take the cutoff and he could drop me right there. I think I can go to my friend's house right around the corner. But they went straight on the freeway. I keep yelling and screaming at them . . . tell them to let me out. A. M. kept slapping my head and telling me to shut up.

She requested to be let off at several exits, but at each one they kept going. Then the screen went blank again. A deepening technique allowed continuation.

SHAPIRO: *So you are yelling and A. M. is hitting you and telling you to shut up, and you just want to get to some friend's house.*
JENNIFER: Where are they going to take me?
SHAPIRO: *What are you thinking?*
JENNIFER: That they are going to kill me or throw me out of the car someplace.

That inference on her part was based in reality. During the previous several months a number of women had been raped and murdered, and their bodies had been found in the fields by the road they were traveling.

JENNIFER: Somehow I was more angry than afraid. I would like to kill them, but I knew I wouldn't. . . . I was just so hurt because they are all local people, and I guess where I was brought up I got more guy friends than girl friends, and they're like brothers to me . . . they don't hurt me. They take care of me.
SHAPIRO: *Local people are supposed to be safe.*
JENNIFER: And it just hurts. If you see someone local in trouble, you just go there and help.

Jennifer had come out of the trance state at this time, and it was reinduced. She described seeing the sign for an exit where she wanted to disembark, but they passed it.

JENNIFER: All I see is the back of the sign. Turn back and look at it. I'm yelling at 'em . . . crying.

She then reported an out-of-body experience that felt "spooky." She saw her face all red, and heard "a wicked weird laugh, and tears are shooting out of my eyes." She finally got out of the car in a distant town.

JENNIFER: I don't know how, but I am getting out of the car, and I can see my friend's apartment, about two doors away. I keep telling myself to

look at the license plate, but as soon as I get out I am running . . . upstairs
. . . there's beer bottles in each hand. I start pounding on my friend's
door, and as soon as she opens it she looks at me and stares and says,
"What's wrong, Jennifer?" I just throw the bottles in her house and start
beating up my friend. . . . She calls her friend and they get me down on
the floor. I can hear her telling a friend to call the ambulance. I can't remember what kind of ambulance it is. I am going to the hospital.

After some additional information was collected about the time of the
rape and the incident at her friend's home, Jennifer was asked whether
there were anything else she wanted to remember. She said, "No, other
things I don't want to know."

Jennifer was brought out of the trance. She reported feeling greatly relieved. She even managed to smile and joke about how she thought the
three guys were more frightened than she was, and how she took it all out
on her friend. Later, she spoke about how frightening it was to have the
sensation of losing her mind as she relived the experience in the car. A
connection was made between this fear and the suicide attempts, which
she and Sandra agreed to discuss further in their regular sessions.

PSYCHOLOGICAL AND LEGAL AFTERMATH

As a result of her refreshed memory, Jennifer was able to gain substantial
relief from her insomnia, headaches, and other symptoms associated with
her trauma-induced amnesia. She also decided to bring the new information to the police. Based on the hypnotically refreshed testimony, a warrant was issued for the arrest of A. M. Prior to the hypnosis, he had not
been indicted for any part of the crime of rape; M. B. had previously been
the only person charged.

The presiding judge ruled that Jennifer could testify, despite the hypnosis sessions. The judge also ruled that Shapiro could testify at the trial
within the guidelines established by the 1981 *Hurd* case. Had this experience occurred in many other jurisdictions, neither could have testified, and
the second assailant would not have been brought to justice.

In December 1982, both men were tried and found guilty of rape. After
an appeal, a retrial was ordered in 1984. On the eve of that trial, the second assailant plea-bargained for a lesser sentence.

It is important to note that this case serves as an example of the therapist's dilemma of attempting to meet both therapeutic and forensic goals.
The hypnosis described above was both therapeutically successful and acceptable to the court.

However, practitioners who would utilize similar approaches are advised that recent court rulings could call into question three components

of the procedure. In some jurisdictions any hypnosis, even an induction unrelated to memory enhancement for the case in question, prior to a free narrative recall, could invalidate subsequent testimony. Secondly, the "watch the movie" technique has similarities to the generally discredited "TV" technique, although it does not promote particularly contaminating qualities such as the "zoom in" capacity of the latter. Third, Shapiro's encouragement and praise, and comment that "the projector wants to stay on," could be seen as leading or suggestive.

The reasons for this level of scrutiny become evident from an understanding of the uneasy relationship between hypnotherapy and the law.

Part III

Investigative Hypnosis

CHAPTER 3

The Road to Admissibility

Now that mesmerism, under its new name of Hypnotism, has been divested of the charlatanry which for so long obscured the subject, and its principles are being scientifically investigated and discussed, jurisprudence may afford to pay some attention to it. —Brodie-Innes (1891, p. 51)

Though hypnosis is as old as speech, legal issues concerning its use are of remarkably recent vintage. For a subject as mysterious and controversial as hypnosis, history does not record many judicial skirmishes before the late 1800s. However, in our own century—particularly in the last two decades—hypnosis issues have made frequent court appearances.

Throughout the entire United States, appellate courts considered hypnosis questions in only 44 cases from the 1800s through 1968. By contrast, from 1969 to March 1, 1989, 464 cases filled the pages of law reports. Almost every appellate court in America has had to study and rule on this distinctive form of human interaction.

A century ago, the law was quite unfamiliar with hypnosis and hypnotic phenomena, as was the medical profession. An address delivered by the president of the Medico-Legal Society of New York in 1889 laments the lack of interest in hypnosis by physicians (Bell, 1889):

> The medical profession in America do not give this subject the attention its importance deserves.
> We know of no medical man of prominence in America who has publicly identified himself with the investigation of this science as some of the most eminent men in foreign countries have recently done. (p. 363)

Though hypnosis had begun to break free from its association with magnetism and spiritual healing, it had not yet been embraced by medical practitioners. Most physicians equated hypnosis with quackery.

The law's first glance at hypnosis also did not reveal a flattering portrait. Its unscrupulous use was what first attracted the jurists' attention. In the formative period from the late 1800s through the 1920s, courts and legislatures were asked to resolve three major issues: (1) Did the defendant use hypnosis to commit crimes or offenses upon unwilling victims? (2) May the defendant in a criminal case plead hypnotism as a defense? and (3) May the use of hypnosis be banned from the stage and restricted to licensed practitioners?

Courts in the last century were especially concerned about the *dangers* of hypnosis. But its *benefits* also have been the subject of judicial apprehension. Even in the hands of competent and ethical practitioners, hypnosis has posed difficult legal questions. Judicial skepticism about the use of hypnosis in the *commission* of crimes was matched by skepticism about the use of hypnosis in the *solution* of crimes. Few issues have posed more complications and controversy for the law than the proper scope to be given to investigative hypnosis. After hundreds of cases and thousands of pages of legal commentary, hypnosis as a tool to solve crimes still sparks debate.

HYPNOTIC INTERROGATION OF CRIMINAL SUSPECTS

Involuntary Hypnotic Interrogation

In 1893, the Dutch government captured a vicious killer named De Jong. He was accused of murdering several women whose whereabouts were unknown. To assist their investigation, the police proposed to hypnotize De Jong to extract from him some clue about the fate of the missing women. Legislation in the Netherlands forbade the introduction into evidence of hypnotically obtained testimony, but no law prevented the police from using hypnosis as an investigative technique to gather evidence. Under the law, the police could use hypnosis to develop leads, but nothing the suspect would say in trance could be used against him in court.

When news of the police proposal was made public, an international outcry ensued that forced the police to abandon their plans. An editorial in the October 14, 1893 edition of the *Law Times*, a British legal journal, stated flatly that "such a thing as the hypnotisation of a prisoner against or with his will is utterly alien to English juridical ideas" (p. 500). Under Anglo-Saxon concepts of adversarial justice, such a procedure would trample on the rights of the defendant. Under the Dutch inquisitorial system, however, such a procedure would be legal, though unwise, because "the most competent hypnotists declare that hypnotic subjects can and do tell lies as readily as if they were awake" (*Law Times*, October 14, 1893, p. 500).

The use of hypnosis to extract information or a confession from a criminal suspect without his or her consent is clearly impermissible under the governing principles of our constitutional democracy, which protects the privilege against self-incrimination by nullifying any statements that are not voluntary and reliable. On rare occasions, the police push this restriction to the limit. Such a case arose in the early 1950s and was litigated in the New York courts, the federal courts, and ultimately the U.S. Supreme Court.

In *People v. Leyra* (N.Y., 1951), the police used a procedure long held to be improper. In marathon shifts they questioned Leyra, the defendant, a 50-year-old man accused of murdering his parents. They denied him sleep, food, and water for extended periods of time during the interrogation. This interrogation alone would have voided the confession, but the police had an unusual trick up their sleeves. They called in a physician who specialized in psychoanalysis to question the defendant. The physician explained that he was there to help Leyra. "I'm your doctor," he said as he began asking the defendant about his sinus condition.

Gradually the questions turned toward the criminal offense. Using a combination of relaxation, regression, and sympathy, the doctor's inquiries produced a second confession. Leyra was convicted at trial on the basis of these confessions. On appeal, he urged reversal on the grounds that he had been hypnotized involuntarily into giving a confession that was untrue (Levy, 1955).

New York's highest court was outraged by the police conduct. According to the court, "torture of the mind is just as contrary to inherent fairness and basic justice as torture of the body" (*Leyra*, 1951, p. 559). The combination of fraud and chicanery practiced by the police required that the conviction be reversed. The U.S. Supreme Court agreed by the narrowest of margins. In a 5–4 opinion, the Justices reversed Leyra's conviction on retrial because all of his confessions were mentally coerced and therefore involuntary (*Leyra v. Denno*, 1954).

Some police departments, however, were not prepared to follow the law of the land. During the 1950s, police interest in hypnosis was kindled by a number of pioneers, including lay hypnotist Harry Arons. In his book *Hypnosis in Criminal Investigation* (1967), Arons claimed he first began holding courses for police detectives in September 1959 in Ridgefield, New Jersey. Some idea of what he taught may be gleaned by examining the case he chose to begin his book.

The defendant was aged 17, "a gangling kid with overlong arms and a baby face" (p. 3). Hours of police questioning were unsuccessful in linking him to several muggings and a murder. On the verge of giving up, one detective suddenly had an idea: "Why don't we get 'Doc' Arons down here?" (p. 3). As Arons explained, "the 'Doc' business has been prearranged for suitable situations" (p. 4). In other words, unlike the *Leyra* case, in which a real physician was involved, here the police were using a non-licensed hypnosis practitioner.

Arons falsely presented himself as a doctor and soon had the boy in trance. A confession was obtained, and Arons's work had ended. Closing his commentary on this case, Arons wrote:

> Had I placed this boy in a hypnotic trance? If I had, he certainly was not aware of it. Whether it was hypnosis or not is not the point. I had cajoled him into a "subjective" mental state. It helped "break" his mental set. (p. 5)

With the elimination of "third-degree" tactics used by police in the 1920s and 1930s, interrogations turned away from the physical toward the psychological. Psychologists and psychiatrists assisted law enforcement officials in developing sophisticated questioning techniques to aid police interrogators. A number of police manuals were written in the 1960s explaining these procedures, many of them of questionable legality.

The manuals were quite inclusive. Even the revelations about Communist "brainwashing," which filled the headlines in the 1950s, provided grist for the police interrogators' mill. In *Criminal Investigation and Interrogation* (1962), Gerber and Schroeder begin their discussion of "brainwashing" by observing that "this is a very handy device . . ." (p. 361). They also included a chapter entitled "The Possible Role of Hypnosis in Criminal Investigations." Written by an Ohio psychiatrist named Levendula, this short chapter made the modest assertion that hypnosis could be effective as an investigative technique. The author cautioned, however, that the "use of hypnosis shall not be substituted for proper interrogative techniques" (Levendula, 1962, p. 345).

The trend toward psychologically sophisticated forms of influence and interrogation reached its pinnacle in the U.S. Supreme Court's landmark case of *Miranda v. Arizona*, decided in 1966. Although the case today is generally cited for the proposition that police must read a suspect his or her rights before questioning, and must not question the suspect if he or she objects, the lengthy judicial opinions contain an extraordinary compendium of quotes from police interrogation manuals. The majority of the Supreme Court viewed many of these tactics as inquisition rather than interrogation.

By the late 1960s, police departments across the country were aware that hypnosis could play a role in detecting crime. The impulse to use the technique on suspects during questioning would occasionally prove irresistible. Claims of involuntary hypnotic interrogations by police appeared from time to time in the cases. One such case is *State v. Walker* (Mo., 1967). The defendant was questioned by a psychologist trained in interrogation techniques and a law professor/criminologist. During questioning, the law professor began asking the defendant to think back to the day of the crime. As they talked, the professor took out a key chain with a multicolored disk on it. As he continued inquiring about the day of the crime, he swung the key chain back and forth, again and again, intermittently suggesting that the defendant should close his eyes, that he was getting sleepy, and that he should relax.

The Missouri Supreme Court upheld the conviction, making two brief points about the hypnotic interrogation. First, the law professor denied any knowledge of hypnosis and denied any attempt to place the defendant in trance. The court appeared to accept this testimony, despite the fact that the professor had been one of the attorneys involved in the *Miranda* case and therefore could have been expected to be more familiar than most with sophisticated methods of interrogation.

Second, and more significantly, the court noted that when on the witness stand, the defendant bragged about how he was "wise to" the police tricks. The defendant, a 39-year-old man with 2 years of high school education, testified, "I knew exactly what it was when I seen the chain, what he was trying to do, because I have seen the same thing performed once or twice in Chicago; it kinda amused me . . ." (p. 142). The court held that because the defendant knew his legal rights and nevertheless "voluntarily matched wits with his interrogators," his legal rights were not infringed.

One year later, the U.S. Supreme Court reviewed another case involving a claim of involuntary hypnotism. *Darwin v. Connecticut* (1968) raised the question of whether a defendant's rights were violated when the police brought into the interrogation room a revolving disk that was permitted to turn continuously for 30 minutes while the defendant was told to stare at it and relax. Unlike the situation in *Walker*, where the interrogator claimed no knowledge of hypnosis, here the trial judge held that the police knew exactly what they were doing. The defendant, however, testified that he did not look at the disk, and so the Court did not address the hypnosis issue.

One of the most recent cases on involuntary hypnosis raised a special problem. *State v. Cochran* (Or., 1985) involved a murder witness initially contacted for information about events before the crime. When the police brought Cochran in for questioning, they had no reason to believe that he was a suspect. Police Lieutenant O'Rourke and Sergeant Button questioned Cochran for 7 hours, from 7:45 P.M. until 2:40 A.M. As the questioning progressed, the officers began to surmise that Cochran might have committed the crime. Although their superior officer instructed them to inform Cochran of his *Miranda* rights, the officers did not want to do so.

As one of them testified, "I thought maybe if I advised him of his rights and he had information pertaining to the murder, he wouldn't give it" (p. 1117).

Finally, Cochran was read the *Miranda* warning, and he signed a card stipulating that he was aware of his legal rights. When he asked Button whether he was a suspect, Button threw the card into a wastebasket and said, "No." At this point, the questioning ventured into the surreal. O'Rourke brought in a black light that caused Cochran's hand to glow orange. O'Rourke told him that the orange color meant he had blood on his hands. O'Rourke played the tough guy in the famous "Mutt and Jeff" or "good guy and bad guy" interrogation technique. Cochran said he wanted to talk with Button.

Button encouraged him to sit back, relax, close his eyes, and imagine he was watching a motion picture screen while concentrating on the questions. As the interrogation continued, Cochran was told he had a special "gift" that he could use "to tell Button about things that [Cochran] did not claim to have personally observed" (p. 1118). On several occasions Button told Cochran to "freeze" the frame "just like a movie projector" (p. 1118). When the questioning turned to another murder, "Button elicited from [Cochran] a description [of the murder]" (p. 1120), despite the fact that Cochran could not possibly have been the culprit because he was in another state at the time. The appellate court had little difficulty in reversing Cochran's conviction, based on the coercive and deceptive practices utilized by the police.

Most state and federal police departments specifically prohibit the use of hypnosis on criminal suspects (Ault, 1980). As a consequence, cases involving the administration of hypnotic techniques on involuntary criminal suspects have been rare and easy to decide. Of more difficulty and frequency have been cases where the defendant *voluntarily* requests hypnosis to assist in the preparation of his or her defense.

Voluntary Hypnotic Interrogation

We now examine cases that involve a defendant's voluntary choice to undergo hypnosis to aid in the preparation of a defense. Here the defendant makes no claim to have committed a crime while in trance, excusing him or her from culpability. Rather, the defendant desires to use hypnosis either (1) as a memory refresher or (2) as proof that exculpating statements made during trance prove his or her innocence.

The law on this subject begins in 1897 with *People v. Ebanks* (Cal., 1897), involving an appeal of a murder conviction. The defendant claimed that the trial judge had erred by refusing to admit the testimony of an expert hypnotist. The expert had hypnotized Ebanks and was prepared to testify that (1) he had denied his guilt in trance, and (2) the expert believed the trance statements proved Ebanks's innocence. The trial judge's refusal to permit the expert to testify was briefly stated: "The law of the United States does not recognize hypnotism. It would be an illegal defense, and I cannot admit it" (p. 1053).

The California Supreme Court upheld this ruling with the terse comment, "[W]e shall not stop to argue the point, and only add the court was right" (p. 1053). Three members of the Supreme Court wrote a separate opinion to keep open the possibility of admitting testimony showing that a defendant committed a crime while in "a hypnotic condition." As to the testimony the defendant sought to introduce in the present case, they agreed with the majority that it was clearly inadmissible. *Ebanks* slammed the door shut on the admission of testimony resulting from hypnotically refreshed recollection. Fifty-three years passed before another appellate court in the United States addressed similar questions.

In *State v. Pusch* (N.D., 1950), a defendant was convicted of poisoning his wife. On appeal, he argued that the trial judge should have allowed him to place on the witness stand a psychologist specializing in hypnosis who was prepared to testify that, on the basis of his questioning of the defendant in trance about the crime, he believed the defendant was innocent. To buttress this testimony, the defendant offered to introduce into evidence the wire recordings of the hypnosis sessions. The Supreme Court of North Dakota dismissed the defendant's request in two unenlightening sentences:

> No case has been cited by either party relating to the admissibility of the evidence proffered and no case has been found. We think that the evidence was clearly inadmissible and that no error was committed in sustaining the objection. (p. 522)

Three separate points were involved in the *Pusch* case:

1. May an expert who has interrogated a criminal defendant using hypnosis testify as to what defendant said in trance?
2. May an expert who has interrogated a criminal defendant using hypnosis testify that he or she believes the defendant was telling the truth in trance?
3. May the recordings of the hypnosis sessions be introduced into evidence?

Since *Pusch* in 1950, each of these questions has generated substantial legal commentary. Although these issues were initially raised by defendants, by the 1970s prosecutors were also making similar arguments on behalf of previously hypnotized witnesses and victims. Many courts have been asked to address these issues. Their conclusions are briefly summarized below.

Statements Made in Trance

The rules of evidence determine what testimony is admissible in court. Although some legal theorists have argued that any relevant evidence be admitted for the jury's consideration, most courts place restrictions on testimony. One such restriction is the "hearsay rule," which actually is a complex set of principles and exceptions.

The hearsay rule precludes the admission of testimony by a witness about what someone else said if the testimony is introduced to prove the truth of those statements. For example, suppose William, a witness, testifies that John told him that the boiler broke down. This testimony is inadmissible to prove that the boiler actually did break down. The reason behind the hearsay rule is easy to grasp: If John is lying or is wrong, there is no way to cross-examine him to show his deception or error.

Let us now turn to a hypnosis-related issue. Suppose a psychologist specializing in hypnosis is prepared to testify that the defendant made certain statements in trance. One such statement might have been that the defendant was not present at the scene of the crime. The defendant may not want to take the stand and be cross-examined on that point. If the psychologist were permitted to relate what the defendant had said, the jury would hear the defendant's alibi, and he or she would escape cross-examination. The law is well settled that an expert cannot testify about what a subject said in trance if that testimony is introduced to prove the truth of those statements (*People v. Smith*, N.Y., 1983; *Strong v. State*, Ind., 1982).

An Expert's Belief in the Truth of Trance Statements

Some courts have permitted experts to express an opinion concerning the veracity of statements made by a subject in trance (*State v. Turner*, N.M., 1970). The usual case involves a previously hypnotized defendant who wants the hypnotist to testify that the hypnotist believes the defendant was telling the truth in trance. An expert may express an opinion about the hypnotized subject's veracity; however, the jury will be instructed to accept the expert opinion not as proof that the subject was telling the truth, but rather as part of the basis upon which the expert has reached a conclusion. The fact that the expert believes the defendant is not proof that the defendant was telling the truth. It is evidence, however, of the factors used by the expert to formulate a professional opinion.

Some judges exercise their discretion to exclude the hypnotist's opinion, reasoning that it is the jury's province to determine truth, not the expert's. The expert's opinion on this ultimate question could unduly influence the jurors.

Recordings of the Hypnosis Sessions

As a general proposition, recordings of hypnosis sessions are not admissible, for reasons similar to those discussed in connection with the hearsay rule. The tape cannot be cross-examined. Upon occasion, however, lawyers have succeeded in having recordings admitted into evidence, provided that the jury is specifically cautioned not to accept what is said on the tape as proof of the truthfulness of the remarks.

People v. Thomas (Cal., 1969) is an apt illustration. The defendant, Antonia Thomas, was on trial for the murder of her 6-day-old son. Her lawyer, Dudley Gray, asked the trial judge, Robert Gardner, to allow the jury to see a 47-minute film of Thomas in trance. Gray knew the tape could not be introduced to prove the truth of his client's statements. He suggested another line of reasoning. A defense psychiatrist was prepared to testify that in his opinion Thomas could not have killed her child. He wanted the jury to observe the film so they could better evaluate the basis for the psychiatrist's expert opinion.

The film graphically showed Thomas's distress and confusion concerning the circumstances leading to her baby's death. Gardner was concerned. Could the jury watch the film for one purpose and discount it for another? Could they view it with an eye toward evaluating the psychiatrist's opinion and yet not accept Thomas's statements as testimony? Gardner instructed the jury to watch the film only as to whether it supported the psychiatrist's conclusion, not as proof that Thomas's denials were factually accurate. He also instructed them that statements made while under hypnosis could be fallible.

The jury deliberated for 2 days before returning a verdict finding Thomas guilty of murder. Judge Gardner told reporters that "my gamble paid off. The verdict has confirmed my faith in the jury system. They viewed that film . . . and considered it only as bearing on the psychiatrist's testimony" (*Time*, April 12, 1968, p. 57). The California Court of Appeal affirmed Gardner's ruling (and Thomas's conviction) in an unpublished opinion. Gardner's bold experiment was widely reported in the media. Ten years later he would return to the hypnosis limelight once again, this time as a judge on the Court of Appeal. It was his unpublished opinion in the *Shirley* case that the California Supreme Court vehemently reversed, as we shall see in Chapter Five.

Although judges have the discretion to admit recordings of hypnosis sessions, they also have the discretion to exclude them if the tapes would confuse, mislead, or unduly prejudice the jury. In *People v. Milner* (Cal., 1988), a psychiatrist had videotaped 11 hours of hypnosis sessions with the defendant. The defense wanted to introduce these tapes, or a 1-hour edited version of their highlights, into evidence to show the basis for the psychiatrist's diagnosis of the defendant as mentally ill.

The judge refused to admit the edited version on the grounds that it "took things out of context" (p. 721, fn. 10), and refused to admit the full version on the grounds that it would be too time-consuming and misleading to the jury. However, the psychiatrist was permitted to testify fully about those portions of the sessions that "were important to the formation of his opinion" (p. 722), so the defendant was not deprived of presenting the essence of those sessions to the jury.

Trance in the Courtroom

May a defendant be hypnotized in court and be questioned while in trance? This question arose, apparently for the first time, in an Ohio courtroom in 1962. Arthur Nebb, a 38-year-old man separated from his wife pending their divorce, was indicted for attempted murder of her and the murder of her lover (*State v. Nebb*, 1962). After the trial had commenced and testimony had been taken, Nebb's lawyer moved that the jury be excused so that an expert on hypnosis could be permitted to hypnotize Nebb in the courtroom. The prosecutor had no objection.

Dr. T. R. Huxtable, Jr., took the witness stand and testified that statements made under hypnosis are "with reasonable medical certainty [likely to be] truthful, correct statements" (Teitelbaum, 1963, p. 208). Upon completion of his preliminary testimony, Huxtable placed Nebb in trance before the watchful eyes of the judge. After satisfying the prosecutor, defense attorney, and judge that Nebb was sufficiently hypnotized, Huxtable questioned Nebb about the crime. Nebb claimed that he did not see his wife's lover and therefore did not mean to kill him when he shot at his wife. Spectators in the courtroom were visibly impressed by the trance testimony (Herman, 1964). So too was the prosecutor, who immediately dropped the murder charge to manslaughter and allowed Nebb to plead guilty to that lesser offense.

The case was first reported by Teitelbaum (1963), who was critical of the hypnotist's performance:

> Certainly Dr. Huxtable did not lay a sufficient foundation in this case to establish that the subject was telling a factual account. Dr. Huxtable did not instruct the subject to tell only the truth. He did not motivate the subject to want to tell the truth. He did not set up any conditioned reflexes which would automatically signal the telling of an untruth. He did not interrogate the subject to determine if the subject had been pre-suggested to give certain answers. (p. 209)

In fact, as Teitelbaum (1963) and Herman (1964) have both observed, Nebb did lie in trance and was given highly leading and suggestive questions.

Nebb is the first reported instance in American law where a witness was permitted to be hypnotized in court. Unfortunately, the case is of marginal value as a precedent, because the trial judge never had to rule on the admissibility of Nebb's testimony once the prosecutor dropped the initial charges.

Five years later, a Canadian court faced a similar issue in *Regina v. Pitt* (1967). The defendant's husband had pressured her to have sexual relations with his male friend. The defendant had reluctantly consented, but did not enjoy the experience. One afternoon the friend came over for lunch, and the defendant feared her husband would once again renew his sexual demand. She went to talk with her husband, and the next thing she recalled was standing over him as he bled from a head wound. She was charged with the attempted murder of her husband. Trial began in October 1967.

At trial, the defendant's amnesia was established. Her counsel requested the court to permit her to be hypnotized to aid her memory. The trial judge granted the request with one stipulation: She was not to be questioned while in trance. The hypnosis was permitted solely to give her a posthypnotic suggestion that she would remember the details of her husband's injury. As the jury watched, the defendant was hypnotized. A posthypnotic suggestion was given, and the defendant was brought out of the trance. The defendant then claimed to remember the entire incident. She told the court that her husband had once again propositioned her on behalf of his friend. She had grabbed a hammer and hit him.

The defendant's testimony tended to demonstrate that although she had assaulted her husband, she had not done so with premeditation. The prosecutor sought to shake this story on cross-examination, but after 15 minutes the defendant became very upset and claimed that her amnesia had returned. The jury found the defendant guilty of assault, not attempted murder. She was sentenced to 1 year in prison (Block, 1976, p. 68).

The trial judge was impressed by the hypnosis. He wrote that hypnosis was a valid medical procedure to revive recollection and lift amnesias. "It would be unfair to deny to the accused the right to have the assistance of [hypnosis]" (*Pitt*, p. 516). The medical hypnotist, Dr. F. W. Hanley, advocated a position beyond the one accepted by the trial judge (Hanley, 1969). In his view, because "hypnosis has the great advantage of providing more reliable and accurate testimony" (p. 352), witnesses should be hypnotized in court and questioned while in trance. Cross-examination should provide an adequate safeguard.

Only one additional reported case raising the question of in-court hypnosis has been found. In *State v. Pitts* (Fla., 1970), one of the participants in a criminal act was hypnotized in court at a pretrial hearing. The court had appointed two psychiatrists to examine her before and after she was put into trance. They observed the entire process and later testified about it.

The trial judge ruled that only the hypnotist, and no one else, could ask

questions. All questions had to have prior judicial approval. This procedure was followed, and the witness "was put in an hypnotic trance and
again related or, in a manner of speaking, relived the events of the crime"
(*Pitts*, p. 414). The appellate court provides no discussion of this issue,
other than to say that because the defendants had failed to submit questions to be asked, they could not complain that their right to cross-examine
had been infringed.

None of the three cases just discussed serves as a solid precedent to
permit in-court hypnosis. *Nebb* was an experiment that did not require a
judicial ruling on the admissibility of such testimony; *Pitt* did not involve
testimony while in trance; and *Pitts* dealt with a pretrial hearing on a defense motion. No other appellate cases raising the issue have been found.
Scott (1977), however, has reported a trial decision in Oregon that raises
an interesting additional question.

One morning the estranged husband of the defendant, B. G, was found
dead on her front lawn. Shortly after the shooting, B. G.'s 12-year-old
daughter told ambulance personnel that her mother had acted in self-defense. B. G. confessed to the shooting, but the police did not believe her.
Two facts were especially troubling: Why had the revolver been wiped
clean, and why had the defendant's boyfriend fired a pistol outside B. G.'s
husband's camper the night before? Another fact also troubled the police.
On the morning of the shooting, B. G.'s boyfriend "just happened" to
drive by her house when, according to his testimony, he observed the
husband breaking in. He entered the house; a struggle ensued; and, according to the boyfriend, B. G. got the pistol and fired it at her husband.

A psychiatrist who examined B. G. suggested she be examined by Scott,
a psychologist. The hypnosis was performed, and while B. G. was in trance
she claimed that her boyfriend had done the killing but she had confessed
out of fear. Immediately after the shooting, the boyfriend said to her, "Why
did you shoot your husband?" and he threatened to kill her if she did not
confess. Scott's hypothesis was that B. G. had "paramnesia": This false
memory of her shooting her husband was implanted in her, and fear kept
it in place.

B. G.'s lawyers, who were present during the hypnosis, immediately
moved to have Scott hypnotize B. G. in court. The judge agreed, but the
jury was not to witness the induction or questioning. The jurors did know
she had been hypnotized in court. The jury acquitted B. G., but the basis
for their acquittal is unknown. Scott noted that in this particular case

> the defendant was *already* in the state of hypnosis—the suggestion "given"
> (demanded) by [her boyfriend]. My task was to de-hypnotize her. . . .
> De-hypnosis, or the deleting of a paramnesia can be as dramatic as hyp-
> nosis itself. (1977, p. 165)

Although in-court hypnosis has not engendered much legal commentary, out-of-court hypnosis has received extensive judicial attention. In fact, no hypnosis issue has raised more questions or aroused greater judicial debate than the out-of-court hypnosis of witnesses or victims.

HYPNOTISM COMES OF AGE

From 1900 to the 1960s

By the turn of the century, hypnosis had firmly established medical and scientific roots, first in Europe and then in the United States. Harvard University researchers William James, Boris Sidis, and Morton Prince conducted extensive investigations of hypnosis and altered states of consciousness. Legal scholars and medical practitioners at academic institutions, clinics, hospitals, and private offices also participated in exploring hypnotic phenomena. Unfortunately, only a small percentage of the medical community was seriously involved in studying and practicing hypnosis. Professional associations were unwilling to make a formal endorsement. However, medical interest in hypnosis got a boost during World War I as doctors reported beneficial results using hypnotherapy treatments for war neuroses.

After World War I, hypnosis research progressed surprisingly slowly. Few medical or academic institutions considered it worthy of study. That negative viewpoint changed when behaviorist Clark Hull published *Hypnosis and Suggestibility* (1933), which was based on 10 years of laboratory experiments of hypnotic behavior initiated at the University of Wisconsin and concluded at Yale University. In Hull, hypnosis finally found the laboratory objectivist it needed to rescue it from the obscurity of side shows and seances. Hull's use of quantitative data and rigorous scientific methods demonstrated that hypnosis could be studied legitimately in academic settings. Though drawn to the subject of hypnosis, Hull initially had misgivings. It took, as he wrote, "courage to brave the semi-superstitious fears of the general public and the uneasy suspicions of their orthodox scientific brethren" (Hull, 1933, p. 403).

Hull was hopeful about the significance of his work. As he wrote in his notebook, "I believe it is an important contribution, and it may mark a new epoch in that form of experimentation." Hull thought it would be read "for a long time, possibly a hundred years" (Hull, 1962, p. 852). His extensive laboratory research proved more influential than his conclusions. The publication of the book brought academic respectability to the study of hypnosis. Gradually, medical professionals began to examine the therapeutic possibilities of hypnosis; in 1939, for example, the Menninger Clinic received funding to inaugurate hypnotic experiments (LeCron & Bordeaux,

1947). During the 1930s and 1940s, however, most professionals who learned hypnosis did so from books or from lay hypnotists. Medical schools did not include hypnosis as part of their curricula. Few hypnosis researchers could be found at academic institutions (Pattie, 1943).

World War II brought a resurgence of medical interest in the therapeutic potential of hypnosis. When hundreds of soldiers returned home with combat-related mental disorders, hypnosis and narcoanalysis were the treatments of choice. An extraordinary glimpse of these treatments may be found in filmmaker John Huston's documentary *Let There Be Light* (Huston, 1948). Commissioned by the Army, the 59-minute film traced a group of returning soldiers as they spent 2 months in an Army mental hospital receiving medical and psychiatric attention. Dramatic scenes of hypnotherapy and narcoanalysis were filmed as they happened. Huston was moved by what he observed. As he later reported:

> I felt what some people feel in church. These men came in from the boats in batches of 75 and 100, mute, shaking, with amnesia, blind, with paralysis, as a result of warfare. Many were healed. (Dorn, 1981)

Immediately after its completion in 1948, the Pentagon suppressed the film. Although the documentary had been designed to encourage potential employers to hire men who had received mental treatment, the Pentagon felt that the film was in contradiction to the "warrior myth" of the soldiering experience and could be viewed as "anti-war." Huston angrily retorted, "Gentlemen, if I ever make anything other than an anti-war film, I hope you take me out and shoot me, because I'll very well deserve it." For 36 years, Huston's documentary languished in Army vaults until it was finally cleared for public release.

In the early 1950s, in part as a response to the therapeutic use of hypnosis in World War II, medical professionals began traveling across the country holding weekend seminars for medical practitioners. William J. Kroger, Milton H. Erickson, Seymour Hershman, and Irving Secter presented one course of instruction, "Seminars on Hypnosis" (Erickson, Hershman, & Secter, 1961). David Cheek and Leslie LeCron presented another, "Hypnosis Symposiums" (Cheek & LeCron, 1968).

Regrettably, the history of hypnosis at this crucial juncture has not yet been thoroughly chronicled. It is known that a rather acrimonious debate occurred concerning (1) who might properly receive hypnosis instruction and (2) who might be qualified to teach it. Some medical and psychological professionals objected to lay hypnotists' conducting hypnosis training courses.

A bitter rivalry developed between the two camps. The doctors felt that hypnosis was too important and delicate a therapeutic technique to be practiced by people untrained in the workings of the mind. Severe physical and mental damage could be done by entertainers and amateurs; the public was entitled to protection from such threats. Only qualified medical professionals with training in therapeutic hypnosis should utilize this power and intimate procedure.

The lay hypnotists, on the other hand, felt doubly betrayed by the doctors. After rejecting hypnosis for centuries, then learning it from the lay hypnotists, the doctors now wanted to endorse hypnosis and declare their teachers incompetent. The lay hypnotists saw this turnabout by the medical profession as an attempt to extend its monopoly. They challenged the doctors to substantiate the claims of harm from lay hypnosis beyond the anecdotal stories told in the media.

Some aspects of this debate, coupled with a fascinating look at the world of the lay hypnotists, are available in back issues of *Hypnosis*, a magazine that first appeared in the mid-1950s. *Hypnosis* (later named *Hypnosis Quarterly*) was produced under the editorial supervision of lay hypnotist Harry Arons, a tireless crusader for the virtues of hypnosis. The magazine was filled with pictures, and it lived up to its motto as an "Illustrated Journal of Hypnotism in All Its Phases." *Hypnosis* was widely circulated, offering hypnotists from across the country and abroad a forum to exchange their views on legal issues and other matters.

Increasing numbers of professionals were learning hypnotic techniques, and increasing numbers of lay practitioners were teaching, performing, and healing with hypnosis. By the mid-1950s, it was clear that hypnosis was again becoming popular. An article in *Time* (March 30, 1953) heralded this movement:

> Hypnosis has been a hard-luck kid among medical techniques. A century ago, it was just beginning to win acceptance as a painkiller when ether anesthesia was discovered, and hypnosis was discarded. It was making a comeback 60 years ago when Freud hit upon the idea of psychoanalysis, and the experts again lost interest in hypnosis. Now, the third time around, it is once more winning the support of reputable men in both the physical and psychic areas of medicine. (p. 34)

The time was ripe for official medical recognition of the therapeutic value of hypnosis. That recognition came rapidly. In 1955 the British Medical Association endorsed hypnosis for certain purposes. It was recommended that all physicians and medical students receive training in hypnosis (*British Medical Journal*, April 23, 1955). Three years later, an editorial in the *Canadian Medical Association Journal* (1958) recognized the therapeutic benefits of hypnosis and urged acceptance of the British Medical Association's report.

In the same year as the Canadian Medical Association's action, the Council on Mental Health of the American Medical Association (AMA) was moved by two imposing pressures to endorse hypnosis (Council on Mental Health,

AMA, 1958). After the positive experience with hypnosis during the war years, physicians and dentists in increasing numbers were requesting information on legitimate training programs. At the same time, the rise in stage hypnosis and lay treatment with hypnosis caused alarm at the threat to public knowledge and health. The council's report endorsed the therapeutic use of hypnosis by medical and dental professionals. Although the report noted that many fundamental questions about hypnosis had not been answered, medical schools and postgraduate training centers were encouraged to teach hypnosis. The council went on to specifically condemn the expanding use of hypnosis by stage performers and unlicensed amateurs.

According to an editorial in the *British Journal of Medical Hypnotism* (Ray, 1962),

> Legally and ethically medical hypnosis (in the U.S.A.) was born in the year 1958 at San Francisco, California, following an exhaustive two-year "labour" within the committee-rooms of the American Medical Association Council on Mental Health. Immediate reactions to the "birth-announcement" were quite varied. A small percentage of physicians were exuberant and overjoyed; a slightly greater number were appalled and dismayed; and the vast majority acknowledged the event with sceptical tolerance or amused indifference. (p. 15)

In 1960, 2 years after the AMA's approval, the American Psychological Association endorsed hypnosis as a branch of psychology (Hilgard, 1965, p. 4). Subsequently, the Council on Mental Health of the AMA (1962) recommended 144 hours of hypnosis training over a 9- to 12-month period at undergraduate and postgraduate levels of medical training. Hypnosis had been given a professional stamp of approval.

The law took notice of these developments. During the 1950s, two law journals published articles encouraging courts and legislators to address hypnosis issues more directly and favorably. Both articles—the first by an anonymous student (*Nebraska Law Review*, 1952) and a later one by a New York county assistant district attorney (Levy, 1955)—favored the use of investigative hypnosis, except to obtain confessions. Levy was blunt: "Hypnosis has outgrown its infancy. It now demands its legal emancipation. A court that will not heed this plea bespeaks rigidity and unenlightenment" (1955, p. 333).

At the close of the decade, there was some indication that the courts might be willing to take a more lenient approach to claims involving hypnosis. In 1959, the California Supreme Court granted a defense lawyer's request to have his client examined by a lay hypnotist (*Cornell v. Sup. Ct.* 1959). By 1963, the same court permitted a qualified expert to testify in court about her use of hypnosis to examine the defendant's mental condition (*People v. Modesto*, 1963).

Hypnosis was making courtroom appearances, and judges were willing to take a close look. Two books published in the 1960s encouraged lawyers and law enforcers to press for a greater role for hypnosis in the law.

Dr. Bryan and Mr. Arons

The first modern book on the law's relation to hypnosis was published in 1962 by Dr. William J. Bryan, Jr. *The Legal Aspects of Hypnosis* surveyed the situations in which the use of hypnosis might raise legal questions. Some of these topics were familiar, such as whether hypnosis can induce criminal conduct and whether hypnosis should be used to obtain investigative information. Other topics covered by Bryan were less familiar—for example, a chapter titled "Winning Cases through Hypnosis," and sections on "brainwashing" and "powerization."

Bryan had one very good reason to publish this book. A year earlier, the California Supreme Court had declared him unqualified to serve as an expert witness in the case of *People v. Busch* (1961), involving a defendant's mental state. At the trial, the defendant attempted to use Bryan as an expert to testify about the defendant's mental state at the time the crime was committed. Bryan based his opinion in part on his hypnotic examinations of the defendant. The prosecutor successfully objected, claiming that hypnosis was not a sufficiently scientific means to examine mental states and that, even if it were, Bryan lacked the credentials to qualify as an expert in this kind of investigation.

The trial judge's opinion that Bryan was not qualified was affirmed by the California Supreme Court. Even though Bryan claimed that he had been licensed to practice medicine in California in 1953 and in two other states shortly thereafter, he admitted that he was not a psychiatrist, had only begun to specialize in hypnosis less than a year before the trial, and had never appeared in court as an expert on a defendant's state of mind at the time of the crime.

Presenting a novel technique (hypnosis) by using a neophyte "expert" was further than the court was willing to go. At the very least, the court noted, an expert seeking to validate an exploratory or investigative technique should have some experience with that technique in circumstances similar to those in the case. Even though in *Cornell* (1959) the court had permitted a defendant to be examined by a lay hypnotist, it had not ruled on the admissibility of evidence arising from that examination. *Busch* was not a setback for hypnosis, only for Dr. Bryan. But not for long.

Bryan's unbridled support for the potentials of hypnosis came to the attention of the legal community. Melvin Belli, an attorney noted for pioneering "demonstrative evidence" such as films, charts, and other visualizations to assist jurors, invited Bryan to make two appearances at the 1961 Belli Seminars. His presentations were well received. Within a few years, Bryan would become involved with many court cases. Bryan next teamed up with famed attorney F. Lee Bailey to use hypnosis for the defense in some of the most dramatic cases in the 1960s, including the trial of the Boston Strangler (convicted of several strangulation murders) and the trial of Carl Coppolino (accused of murdering his wife in a sordid love triangle mess). Years later, Bryan wrote about some of these experiences in *The Chosen Ones* (1971). Bailey wrote favorably about Bryan's hypnotic assistance in *The Defense Never Rests* (1971).

While he was enjoying success with lawyers, Bryan's work fared less favorably with his fellow hypnotists. In January 1963, the *American Journal of Clinical Hypnosis* published a special book review of *The Legal Aspects of Hypnosis* (Weitzenhoffer, 1963). This review was a devastating rejection of the book. Critical of the scholarship, style, and ego of Bryan, Weitzenhoffer pulled no punches. Calling Bryan "doubtfully competent to write such a work" and suggesting that his qualifications as a medical hypnotist and a teacher "should be seriously re-examined" (p. 222), he wrote that "the present work has harmful potentialities and it would have been much better if it had never been published, and even better [if it] never had been written" (p. 214).

This negative appraisal was not noticed by legal writers, who cited Bryan's book favorably throughout the 1960s and 1970s. Bryan himself ran a successful hypnosis institute in Los Angeles. He trained hundreds, perhaps thousands, of professionals and others in hypnosis before sexual improprieties with his female clients led Nevada and Los Angeles authorities to restrict his hypnosis activities. The negative side of Bryan's skills and conduct did not affect his impact on forensic hypnosis. Bryan's open endorsement of investigative hypnosis found favorable response with dozens of legal commentators and provoked discussions throughout the legal community. Many judges and lawyers first became attracted to hypnosis as a result of his 1962 book.

Unlike Dr. Bryan, Harry Arons was not a medical doctor, nor was he a psychologist. His credential was experience, but he was, as Dr. William Kroger wrote in a foreword to Arons's 1967 book, "one of the few non-medical hypnotists to initially teach the technics [sic] of hypnosis to physicians and dentists. His first course for professionals was conducted in 1932 . . ." (Arons, 1967, p. vii). Arons began teaching police investigative hypnosis in New Jersey in the late 1950s. By the time his *Hypnosis in Criminal Investigation* appeared in 1967, Arons had been very successful in convincing skeptical police departments to add hypnosis to their investigative armamentarium.

Hypnosis in Criminal Investigation was dedicated to "the law enforcement officers and attorneys who had the courage and resourcefulness to try a new approach in the interest of justice—thus becoming the pioneers in the field of hypnosis in criminal investigation" (1967). To these pioneers and those who would follow them, Arons's book was a training manual. From it, one presumably could learn enough to go out and practice hypnosis. Chapters on memory, age regression, induction techniques, detection of faking, and so on provided sufficient information to whet the appetite for actual experience.

During the 10 years Arons taught hypnosis to law enforcement officials, the momentum for police use of hypnosis slowly increased. *Hypnosis in Criminal Investigation*, which was widely circulated in law enforcement departments throughout the country, added to this momentum. As the 1960s drew to a close, lawyers predicted that some court would open the door the California Supreme Court had shut in *Ebanks* in 1897. Perhaps it was no accident that the case to do so was the very first case to reach any appellate court where the *government*—not the *defendant*—asked the court to recognize the value of investigative hypnosis.

THE ERA OF ADMISSIBILITY

Prior to 1968, courts had consistently excluded posthypnotic testimony on the grounds that it was unreliable and apt to influence the jury unduly. Prosecutors opposed such evidence; in every case it was the defense that wanted hypnotic testimony to be admissible. The very first appellate case in the United States involving a *government* request for the admission of hypnotically refreshed recollection, *Harding v. State* (Md., 1968), started an avalanche of cases that continues to cascade through the courts.

Harding involved gruesome facts. The defendant had picked up a young woman, Mildred, and invited her to join his friends. Mildred agreed. Later in the evening, when they were alone, Mildred rebuffed the defendant's sexual advances. The defendant pulled out a pistol and shot her in the chest. Believing she was dead, he dumped her body by the side of the road. When she was found by the sheriff, several miles from where she had been abandoned, Mildred was barely alive. There was evidence she had been raped.

The police brought Mildred to a psychologist for hypnosis to refresh her memory of the postshooting events. On the stand at trial, Mildred claimed the hypnosis had brought back her memory. She recalled the defendant's return after dumping her, when he raped her and once again abandoned her body by the roadside. Defense counsel questioned the sufficiency of the expert's qualifications, focusing on the expert's having only a master of arts degree in psychology. The court found him to be qualified on the basis of his 4 years of experience and his previous qualification as an expert in other cases.

At trial, the expert testified that Mildred was in trance for 45 minutes. During that time, two police officials were in the room recording the hypnosis session. At the close of the trance, the expert gave Mildred the suggestion that when she awakened she would tell the same story she told in trance. The expert was asked whether the information he obtained from Mildred while she was in trance was reliable. He responded:

> [It is reliable] because there was certain information that was provided by the police to me later and there were also self-corroborative statements she made. Also, her recall afterwards was essentially the same. (p. 310)

When Mildred was called to testify, the defense objection was overruled. The defendant was convicted on the basis of Mildred's hypnotically refreshed testimony.

The Maryland Court of Special Appeals had little difficulty with the issue. Mildred could tell what she remembered. According to the court, "the fact that she had told different stories or had achieved her present knowledge after being hypnotized concerns the question of the weight of the evidence which the trier of facts . . . must decide" (p. 306).

The opinion in *Harding* lacked sophistication. As commentators frequently noted later, the judges uncritically accepted the self-serving testimony of the psychologist that there were no improper suggestions made to Mildred, and that there was no reason to doubt the accuracy of her recall. More recent cases tend to exercise greater scrutiny over expert testimony.

The *Harding* Approach: Credibility, Not Admissibility

The *Harding* approach was economical and simple. Hypnotically refreshed recollection was admissible, with the jury making the decision on whether to believe it or not. In justifying this approach, courts repeatedly emphasized two important factors.

First, judges chose to look at hypnosis as just another, though perhaps more unusual, way to refresh memory. The law usually has been generous in permitting a variety of methods to refresh recollection. In the words of *Jewett v. United States* (9th Cir., 1926):

> It is quite immaterial by what means the memory is quickened; it may be a song, or a face, or a newspaper item, or a writing of some character. It is sufficient that by some mental operation, however mysterious, the memory is stimulated to recall the event, for when so set in motion it functions quite independently of the actuating cause. (p. 956)

Hypnosis was viewed after *Harding* as one more way to move mental gears. The important fact was that the witness was testifying from *present* recollection. The other fact, that such recollection had been stimulated by hypnosis, was deemed less significant. If there was a problem with the method by which the memory was revived, it could be handled by attacking the reliability of the hypnotic process, not by refusing to allow the witness to testify at all.

Second, the previously hypnotized witness and the hypnotist could be thoroughly and fully cross-examined. Furthermore, the challenging party could bring forth its own experts to demonstrate the unreliability of hypnotically refreshed memory. Full cross-examination satisfied constitutional mandates of due process, as well as evidentiary requirements permitting the credibility of witnesses to be questioned. Courts felt that a complete cross-examination could handle inherent deficiencies in hypnotic techniques.

A Decade of *Harding:* 1968–1978

The flood of cases that *Harding* would eventually produce took a long time gathering momentum. Only 54 cases reached appellate courts during this 10-year span; they reflected some unusual patterns. For one thing, compared to the 41 appellate cases decided before *Harding,* the case law had doubled in one decade.

Of the 54 total cases decided in this decade, 19 involved circumstances where the *defendant* argued a *pro*hypnosis position. These arguments included the following claims:

1. The defendant was in trance during the commission of the crime (*People v. Baldi,* N.Y., 1974; *Barfield v. State,* Ala., 1975; *State v. Smith,* Ohio, 1976).
2. The defendant is entitled to the services of a hypnotist (*South v. Slayton,* W.D. Va., 1972) (claim denied).
3. The defendant is entitled to have a hypnotist testify on the defendant's behalf (*Jones v. State,* Okla., 1975).
4. The defendant is entitled to have audio or video recordings made of the hypnosis sessions admitted into evidence (*People v. Hiser,* Cal., 1968).

It is not surprising that so many cases, more than one-third, involved *defendants'* making favorable hypnosis arguments. Defendants made prohypnosis arguments consistently before *Harding.* What is surprising is how few cases there were where the *prosecution* was prohypnosis. Only 11 such cases were decided; most of them followed the admissibility approach. *Harding's* open-admissibility policy found favor in Oregon (*State v. Jorgensen,* 1971), North Carolina (*State v. McQueen,* 1978), and New York (*People v. Hughes,* 1979), and with several federal courts (*United States v. Narcisco,* E.D. Mich., 1977; *Connolly v. Farmer,* 5th Cir., 1973; *Wyller v. Fairchild Hiller,* 9th Cir., 1974).

The *Harding* approach did not require minimum standards or guidelines. Under this open-admissibility policy, how far would the courts be willing to go in tolerating unqualified hypnotists or sloppy hypnotic procedures? The Wyoming Supreme Court has provided one answer in a series of five cases, three of which are discussed here.

In *Chapman v. State* (1982), the victim was hypnotized twice by a city police officer. The videotape of the sessions was inaudible. The court held the victim's testimony to be admissible. Two justices disagreed. They began their dissent dramatically: "Stripped of its veneer, this case holds that a police officer who occasionally plays around with hypnotism can manipulate the recall of a witness and receive the blessing of this court" (pp. 1286–1287). The justices had further concerns about the qualifications of the police hypnotist, who had never had a psychology course. His hypnosis training was acquired from a fire marshal and an attorney, one of whom, the hypnotist testified, had certified him. There was no evidence in the record demonstrating by what recognized authority this certification was bestowed.

The dissent closed its argument on a devastating, but less legal, note:

> The writer of this dissent knows the hypnotist personally. He is a well-qualified law enforcement officer and his honesty and integrity are not in question, but his skills as a hypnotist, and the reliability of the procedures used here, are totally deficient. (p. 1287)

One year later, the issue of qualifications was back before the Wyoming Supreme Court. In *Gee v. State* (1983), the dissent again pushed for some minimum qualifications for the police hypnotist. In this case, the person hypnotized could not remember the name of the hypnotist, and the prosecutor had trouble listing the hypnotist's qualifications. The dissent began simply: "I undertake the disconsolate task of differing from the majority, with a feeling that I am probably right" (p. 105). The problem was that *Chapman* did not require that the hypnotist possess any qualifications or experience, nor did it require any verification procedures so that the hypnosis session could be later evaluated: "It follows, therefore, that a hobo passing through town or a derelict in the county jail could hypnotize a potential witness, and the witness' testimony would be admissible at trial" (pp. 105–106). The absence of minimal criteria lends itself to parody or ridicule:

> There is a man in Oakland, California, who is the dean and lone "professor" at "Croaker College." For the sum of $150 each, this man trains frogs to jump. (Many graduates, after receiving their degrees, go on to compete in the famous jumping contest of Calaveras County.) As part of his rigid training curriculum, the "professor" claims that he hypnotizes the frogs; while they are in their hypnotic trance, he plays an attitude-improvement

tape to them. Under our present standards the dean of "Croaker College" would be over-qualified as a hypnotist. (p. 106, note 3)

The dissent proved prophetic. *Haselhuhn v. State* (1986) involved hypnotic interviews conducted by, in the words of the majority, "a non-professional with meager training in hypnotic techniques" (p. 283). In fact, as the dissent specifically notes, the "non-professional" hypnotist was a maintenance person at the Pacific Power and Light Company. His "meager training" consisted of a "32-hour home course." Despite the hypnotist's obvious lack of qualifications, and the threat to justice his meager technique created, the three-member majority of the Wyoming Supreme Court was not moved to set minimum standards.

The Police Respond

During the late 1950s, police interest in hypnotic interrogations began to develop. Army Major Charles Derrick, writing in the March 1959 issue of *The Police Chief*, encouraged law enforcement agencies to examine the unique potential benefits of hypnotic questioning:

> Do you want the subject to know that you have obtained the information from him? Then have the hypnotist tell him that he will remember giving the information. Do you want the subject kept in ignorance? Then have the hypnotist tell him that. Do you want the subject to repeat something to someone else on signal? That too is possible. The potentialities of hypnosis are vast. (p. 28)

Because of these possibilities, Derrick encouraged caution: "Hypnosis is not a parlor game. Permanent, serious, far-reaching damage to the mind, personality and physical health of a subject can result from improper use of this art" (p. 28). Derrick recommended that all hypnosis sessions be tape-recorded and that the hypnosis be performed only by a "skilled operator."

The general public had been introduced to the possibilities of investigative hypnosis several months earlier. *This Week Magazine*, in its January 25, 1959 issue, published an article by Dr. Samuel R. Gerber entitled "Hypnotism—New Weapon against Crime?" A group of police officers were attending a routine lecture at Western Reserve University when suddenly a violent quarrel broke out between two stenographers who were present to record the talk. One of the women took an object out of her purse, stabbed the other woman, and fled the room. The officers were stunned. But, as Dr. Gerber described, the fight was staged for the purpose of testing whether hypnosis could effectively enhance memory.

The hypnosis was conducted by a medical specialist who told the officers while in trance that when they were awakened they would remember additional details of the incident. Gerber reported that the posthypnotic reports contained more information than did the prehypnosis reports. Gerber believed that hypnosis would prove useful in criminal investigations. Only "properly trained medical personnel" should be permitted to utilize hypnotic techniques. With their assistance, Gerber felt that "it will not be long before hypnosis takes its valuable place in our growing arsenal against crime" (p. 8).

By the late 1960s, police interest in hypnosis had spread nationwide, but the hypnosis techniques were rendered useless unless the witnesses who had been hypnotized could later testify in court. The police could still use hypnosis to generate leads, which could then be corroborated, but the people who provided those leads under hypnosis were prevented from testifying. Once *Harding* cleared this testimonial barrier, police departments across the country were alerted to the potential of hypnotic interrogations.

It is difficult to trace precisely when police departments began to use hypnosis. Harry Arons had encouraged its use and taught hypnotic techniques to police officials in New Jersey as early as the mid-1950s. Federal authorities may have begun even earlier. Milton Erickson reported a visit from FBI personnel prior to 1962 and perhaps as early as the 1940s (Estabrooks, 1962, p. 270). Udolf (1983) reports that "FBI policy on investigative hypnosis is based on guidelines set out by the U.S. Department of Justice in 1968 and revised in 1979, to include the use of specially trained Hypnosis Coordinators" (p. 48). FBI agent Richard Doucé (1979), on the other hand, has written that the FBI "became genuinely interested in hypnosis during 1976 with the approval of a pilot program designed to test its value in highly selective criminal matters" (p. 61).

Regardless of the beginning dates, hypnosis as a tool for the investigation of crime did not achieve national prominence until a group of Los Angeles police experimenters began practicing it in an extensive and highly visible manner. At the forefront of those developments was police psychologist Martin Reiser, Ed.D. In 1970 (Reiser, 1976) or 1972 (Reiser & Nielson, 1980), Reiser began receiving frequent calls from police officers requesting hypnosis assistance in murder, rape, and kidnapping cases. By 1978, he claimed a 60% success rate in obtaining new and valuable information based on the hypnotic questioning (Reiser, 1978).

As word of Reiser's work spread, Los Angeles police officials approved a 1-year pilot program to commence in 1975. Police and outside consultants prepared a 48-hour hypnosis training course that included lectures and practice sessions. Participation was to be limited to specially selected officers. The program was deemed a success. It received professional recognition by winning the 1977 American Express/International Association of Chiefs of Police Award as the most "outstanding advancement in police science and technology" (Reiser & Nielson, 1980, p. 76).

Articles and stories in the popular media heralded the new forensic breakthrough. An article in *TV Guide* (Stump, 1975) was unstinting in its praise:

> Charlie Chan had his inscrutable stare, Sherlock Holmes his deductive power and Lord Peter Wimsey his jolly good luck, but 48-year-old "Marty" Reiser is one of a number of specialists with something more to offer—a means by which victims and witnesses can re-experience a crime on the mental screen of a hypnotically induced television box, and do so with clear perception. (pp. 33–34)

Media stories often centered around some remarkable successes apparently achieved by hypnosis. Most frequently cited was the bizarre kidnapping in Chowchilla, California (*Time,* September 13, 1976, p. 56). Thugs stopped a school bus, kidnapped the children and the driver, and buried them alive in the school bus under a mound of earth. The driver and some of the older children heroically dug their way out, allowing everyone to be freed. Police investigators hypnotized the bus driver to assist his memory in recalling the license plate numbers of the vans driven by the thugs. Under hypnosis, the driver remembered enough letters and numbers to aid the police in identifying the vans, thereby leading to the solution of the crime (Kroger & Doucé, 1979).

The wave of publicity was backed up with a flow of statistics. Reiser and Nielson (1980) reported impressive figures:

> Follow-up data to April 1979 revealed that in approximately 374 sessions, 92.5% achieved a light to deep state of hypnosis, 85.2% had improved memory from slight to a significant degree, 80.2% elicited additional information under hypnosis, 67.5% being considered valuable. Of the information obtained with hypnosis where corroboration was possible, 90.7% was found to be accurate (161 sessions), 49.7% of the sessions' accuracy could be determined, and in 6.8% was determined to be inaccurate. At the time of follow-up, 31.3% of the cases were solved, with hypnosis considered valuable in 65% of these cases. (pp. 76–77)

To satisfy the growing interest in and demand for forensic hypnosis, Reiser founded the Society for Investigative and Forensic Hypnosis in 1977. Its goals included the formulation of ethical standards and educational guidelines for this growing specialty. Reiser also established the Law Enforcement Hypnosis Institute, Inc. (LEHI) to run 32-hour training courses for police officers and others to become what he called "hypno-technicians."

The law enforcement response to this program was positive. From 1976 to 1984, over 1,000 police officers received training at LEHI (Serrill, 1984). To help meet the demand, in 1980 Reiser published his third book, *Handbook of Investigative Hypnosis.* By this time, he was making frequent appearances in courtrooms across the country as an articulate and persuasive spokesman for the admissibility of testimony that had been hypnotically refreshed by police officers. In 1985 Reiser reported:

> Our data in over 600 major crime cases at the Los Angeles Police Department show that hypnosis interviews with cooperative, traumatized witnesses enhances investigatively useful recall in approximately three-fourths of the cases, using original police reports as the criterion measure. Adequate follow-up has been possible in only 50% of these cases, where accuracy levels of the hypnotically-elicited information were around 90%. (1985a, p. 515)

Federal, state, and municipal law enforcement agencies also were forming hypnosis units (Diamond, 1980; Millwee, 1979; Stratton, 1977; Udolf, 1983). The FBI described in a series of articles its "team approach" to hypnotic questioning (Ault, 1980; Doucé, 1979; Kroger & Doucé, 1979).

The New York Police Department established its own hypnosis unit on November 1, 1976, as a pilot project. Detective Sergeant Charles Diggett was the unit's chief hypnotist. As he noted in *Hypnocop* (Diggett & Mulligan, 1982), within a few years he had been involved with "more than four hundred criminal investigations . . . as a forensic hypnotist" (p. 2). Consistent with Reiser's early statistics, Diggett also reported a 60% success rate.

On February 25, 1979, Sergeant Diggett made a guest appearance on a local Boston television talk show hosted by Joe Oteri. In explaining hypnosis, Diggett told his audience that "there are actually hundreds of ways of hypnotizing a person, you know; the important thing is to con him into thinking he wants to be hypnotized. Once you've done that, the rest is easy. It really doesn't matter what method you use." Oteri was startled by this answer. "Is hypnosis a con job?" he asked. Diggett responded affirmatively: "If you don't convince him that he wants it to happen, it's not going to happen." If hypnosis was at least in part "a con job," Oteri wanted to know, was it possible to "plant stuff in someone's mind"? Diggett responded by noting that the police "wouldn't know what to put there. Police are looking for leads, not trying to implant information."

The Television Technique

The issue of whether the police suggest or induce the answers they receive from subjects in trance is intimately tied up with the hypnotic technique they use for memory retrieval. The most widely practiced and discussed method used in investigative hypnosis is the highly controversial "television technique," described as follows by Reiser (1980):

> After an optimal state of hypnosis is achieved, the hypno-investigator indicates that the subject, in imagination, will be watching a special docu-

mentary film on television from a safe, secure and comfortable place. This special documentary can be speeded up, slowed down, stopped, reversed, with close-ups possible on any person, object or thing in the film. The sound can be turned up high so that anything that is said, even a whisper, can be heard very clearly. This will be a documentary film of the incident in question and will depict accurately and vividly everything of significance and importance the subject perceived and experienced in relationship to that crime event. And even though what occurred was very traumatic, the subject watching the TV documentary will be able to remain calm and relaxed, feeling detached from what is happening on the television set. The subject will be observing it as a reporter, covering an event to be written up accurately for a news story. (p. 158)

Kroger and Doucé (1980) describe a somewhat similar technique designed to dissociate the subject from the recollections:

It was suggested that [the subject's] own "hidden observer" was looking through a magic lens which was projecting action sequences on a large television or motion picture screen. The actions on the screen could go forward or backward, they could be played back in slow motion or the image on the screen could be stopped or "frozen." Also, when indicated the subject could "zero" in on any part of the projected image. (p. 88)

The television technique has become a focus of debate by experts in courtrooms across the country. Proponents argue that it spares witnesses and victims additional trauma from re-experiencing the criminal events without sacrificing the accuracy of the recall. Opponents strongly argue against its use.

Martin Orne, a psychiatrist and psychologist, has conducted numerous hypnosis experiments on memory, age regression, and related investigative questions. He is a staunch adversary of the television technique, on the grounds that by its very nature it encourages the hypnotized subject to imagine and fantasize. As he explained from the witness stand in a Boston murder trial (his testimony was shown on an episode of *Walter Cronkite's Universe;* Minor, 1981), "you can create the *illusion* of it but you don't really zoom. . . . This can lead to profound distortion."

Even worse, as Orne testified, not only can the technique lead to false memories, but these memories will "harden":

[If the hypnotized subject] was uncertain about something before hypnosis but thought it might be so and you hypnotize him and have him watch his own videotape with that material on it, he now becomes convinced as if he had seen a documentary where it happened and he now instead of being an uncertain witness becomes a convinced, assured witness. (Minor, 1981)

The sincerity with which the witness believes this inaccurate recollection will provide additional reason for the jury to accept the memory as genuine. The television technique, rather than providing a means to extract accurate memories, may in fact contaminate those memories and increase the likelihood that a witness will believe in the truth of something false.

As the 1970s came to a close, police interest in hypnosis was at a record level. Courts were admitting hypnotically refreshed recollection, and police hypnotists were permitted to conduct hypnosis sessions and testify about them in court. Judges accepted the police argument that forensic hypnosis was not a medical specialty, did not involve therapy, and could be effectively practiced by police officials specially trained in investigative techniques. Forensic hypnosis, in short, was at the height of fashion.

CHAPTER 4

The Search for Safeguards

THE LAW TURNS CAUTIOUS

Clouds of darkness began to dim the bright light of investigative hypnosis by the mid-1970s. Though investigative *uses* of hypnosis were now judicially endorsed, some courts began to fear investigative *abuses*. The possibility that police or prosecutors might use hypnosis to tamper with the mind became real in two dramatic instances brought before federal district judges.

Shaw v. Garrison (E.D. La., 1971) was only one mysterious wrinkle in the controversy surrounding the tragic assassination of President John F. Kennedy on November 22, 1963. For reasons that still remain unclear, Jim Garrison, a district attorney in Louisiana, decided to conduct his own investigation of the crime. After several years of work, he prosecuted Clay Shaw, a Louisiana businessman, for involvement in the assassination (*Shaw v. Garrison*, E.D. La., 1971). The jury acquitted Shaw in less than an hour. After the verdict, Garrison indicted Shaw for perjury. Shaw, in turn, sued Garrison and others for violating his civil rights by bad-faith prosecution and harrassment.

Shaw demonstrated that virtually the only evidence against him was the testimony of Perry Raymond Russo, which was procured by the use of "hallucinatory drugs and hypnosis" administered by doctors under orders from Garrison. Shaw claimed that Russo's testimony was programmed into him. The district court agreed: "A fair inference to be drawn is that these *ex parte* procedures were used to implant into Russo's mind a story implicating the plaintiff in an alleged conspiracy plot. This could have been accomplished by post-hypnotic suggestion" (p. 395). At a later point, the court also observed that Garrison "resorted to the use of drugs and hypnosis on Russo, purportedly to 'corroborate,' but more likely to concoct his story" (*Shaw*, 1971, p. 396). The plan failed. At trial, Russo's testimony contradicted his earlier statements, and he did not identify Shaw as a co-conspirator. The court granted Shaw relief from further prosecution.

Shaw v. Garrison was the first time an appellate court had reason to comment on unacceptable prosecutorial motivation involving the use of hypnosis. Unfortunately, it would not be the last. A double murder of husband-and-wife pathologists in Georgia set the scene for judicial concern about prosecutorial motives. Two Georgia Supreme Court opinions would deliberately ignore the problem before a federal court stepped in to do justice. The *Emmett v. State* (1974) and *Creamer v. State* (1974) cases put hypnosis in a bad light, and both are a monument to judicial insensitivity.

The state's chief witness against defendants Emmett and Creamer was Debra Ann Kidd. The government gave her immunity from prosecution for her testimony against the defendants. Kidd told her story to the police, who then decided to send her to a hypnotist to refresh her memory. Dr. Edwin P. Hall saw Kidd 12 times for a total of approximately 35 hours. Fewer than half of these sessions were taped. For his services, Hall received over $3,500. The state was shortchanged.

At trial, Kidd testified that the purpose of the hypnosis sessions was to use "age digression" [sic] to help her remember. The defendants requested that the tapes of the sessions be given to them. The judge claimed that the tapes were protected by physician–patient privilege, despite the strenuous (and legally correct) objections by defendants that no treatment was involved and all confidentiality, if any, had been waived.

In *Emmett*, the Georgia Supreme Court held that hypnotically refreshed recollection was unreliable and therefore inadmissible. The judges let Kidd's testimony stand, however, because she told basically the same story before and after the hypnosis. How the judges knew this to be true is somewhat mysterious, because the court specifically noted that "it does not appear which details she may have remembered after her hypnotic sessions" (p. 235).

In the companion case, *Creamer*, the Georgia Supreme Court upheld the trial judge's ruling that the defense was not entitled to the tapes of the sessions, using as its main argument the fact that the defendants had an extensive and thorough opportunity to cross-examine. How a cross-examination could be "extensive" and "thorough" when the most significant and relevant evidence upon which to base it was not made available is not explained in the court's opinion.

Hall's skills as a hypnotist were in constant demand. *Newsweek* (August 5, 1974) reported that he had "conducted about three dozen hypnotic examinations of witnesses, victims and suspects for police officials, district attorneys and defense attorneys in Georgia and Alabama" (p. 57).

One year later, Emmett and Creamer's case found its way to the federal district court, which viewed it in an entirely different manner than did the

Georgia Supreme Court. *Emmett v. Ricketts* (N.D. Ga., 1975) was a scathing rebuke of the prosecutorial conduct of the case. It now emerged that Debra Ann Kidd was an admitted drug addict, a prostitute, and a shoplifter. At the time she was being investigated and hypnotized, she began living with one of the detectives assigned to solve the case. It was also revealed that she told police she was so full of pills she could not remember many details of the crime. As the district court described it, her prehypnosis testimony, "riddled as it was with inconsistencies, implausibilities and gaps, was in dire need of shoring up if the prosecution were to obtain convictions" (p. 1036).

Dr. Hall was brought in for the cure. He claimed to use age regression techniques, but no tape was ever produced demonstrating the use of such techniques with Kidd. Indeed, tapes had a strange way of disappearing in this case, leading the district court to state, "[T]he unavoidable conclusion is that either there has been a deliberate destruction of vital and highly material evidence, or that no age regression or hypnosis ever took place. The former involves the unlawful obstruction of justice and the latter evidences perjury by an agent of the State [Dr. Hall]" (p. 1038).

The court castigated Hall and called his actions "a thinly veiled effort to prop up the prosecution's case" (p. 1041). What little evidence still remained of the hypnosis sessions with Kidd and with others showed that Hall used such flagrantly suggestive techniques as "extending to Johnson [another prosecution witness] the stick of continued imprisonment and the carrot of immunity and release from jail in an attempt to induce her to change her story to conform to Kidd's" (p. 1040).

Emmett was a reprehensible case, although not recognized as such by the Georgia courts. The prospect of using hypnosis to shore up a sagging or inconsistent memory of a witness rears up again several times in later cases, especially in the important *Shirley* decision in California.

In essence, the decade after *Harding* showed judicial acceptance of hypnotically refreshed recollection. Little attention was paid to the scientific literature on hypnosis and memory; legal discussions were brief. Except for the scattered concerns of a few courts, the judicial attitude was clearly prohypnosis for investigatory purposes.

United States v. Adams (9th Cir., 1978) was the first case to suggest that the rule of open admissibility might be too naive. A postal robbery and murder had occurred. Postal authorities found an eyewitness and hypnotized him. At trial, the defense called the eyewitness and tried to limit his testimony to his prehypnosis statements. The judge, however, permitted the prosecutor to use the posthypnotic statements to impeach the eyewitness. The court followed the rule it had applied earlier in two civil cases (*Wyller v. Fairchild Hiller*, 9th Cir., 1974; *Kline v. Ford Motor Co.*, 9th Cir., 1975), permitting hypnotically refreshed recollection to be admitted.

The Ninth Circuit was not happy with the prosecution's use of an uncertified hypnotist who kept no records: "We are concerned . . . that the investigatory use of hypnosis on persons who may later be called to testify in court carries a dangerous potential for abuse" (p. 198). In a footnote, the court suggested that police follow minimal guidelines, such as record keeping that would identify who was present, what was asked, and how questions were answered. Audiotaping or videotaping "would be helpful" (p. 199, fn. 12).

There is a clear indication from the court that if the defense had objected to the adequacy of the foundation laid for the receipt of the testimony—in other words, the qualifications of the hypnotist and the inadequacy of the records of the session—the evidence would have been excluded. Instead, the defense argued a different point: that *all* hypnotically refreshed recollection should be excluded. The court declined to adopt a rule of total exclusion.

Beginning with *Adams,* courts began a more cautious look at hypnosis. Thus the search for safeguards commenced. The age of innocence gave way to a more critical assessment, as questionable practices came to light and voices other than that of law enforcement began to be heard.

Courts

After *Adams,* additional cases of incompetent or improper police hypnotic procedures started to surface. Producers of British and American television documentaries on forensic hypnosis focused attention on one such instance (Barnes, 1982; Minor, 1981).

People v. Kempinski (Ill., 1980; see Laurence & Perry, 1988) involved a police hypnotist trained at Dr. Reiser's LEHI. This officer conducted an unduly suggestive interrogation, which led the hypnotized witness to make an identification of the defendant. The officer took no notice of the witness's self-contradiction during the trance, and he did not realize that his suggestive promptings induced the witness's identification of the defendant. The case ended when an expert on vision conclusively demonstrated that the witness could not possibly have seen the criminal.

Whereas *Kempinski* involved an honest but incompetent police hypnotist, other cases raised questions about police motives in using hypnosis. In *State v. Long* (Wash., 1982), the defendant was charged with assault. A witness who had observed the incident told police that the victim might have had a knife and had lunged at the defendant. On the eve of trial, the witness was hypnotized by a police officer who had learned the technique at a 3-day course held at a local community college. During the hypnosis session, the witness "remembered" that the victim did not have a knife and did not lunge at the defendant. The defendant's claim of self-defense was severely impaired by this change in the witness's story. At trial, the witness was asked:

Q: Are you sure today that [the victim] had nothing in his hand?
A: Yes, I am.
Q: Why are you sure?
A: I was hypnotized. (p. 847)

The Washington Court of Appeals questioned why the hypnosis was conducted on the eve of trial and not during the long months of police investigation conducted earlier. The court answered its question by noting that "the purpose could only have been to change the story of the key witness . . . from what she had said in a statement written shortly after the event" (p. 847) The case was dismissed, rather than sent back for retrial, because "the improper hypnotic episode arranged by the prosecuting attorney and conducted by a police officer deprived the defendant of a material witness who cannot be rehabilitated" (p. 847). Other courts would also have occasion to question the legitimacy of police use of hypnosis.

Legislatures

Legislators also became aware of the growing use of hypnosis by the police and the controversies surrounding such use. In 1977, Oregon enacted the first legislation in the country concerning investigative hypnosis. The Oregon Court of Appeals had earlier accepted the *Harding* admissibility rule (*State v. Jorgensen*, 1971), and the legislators had no quarrel with this result. To protect the interests of all parties concerned, however, the new legislation imposed minimal conditions on obtaining hypnotically refreshed recollection.

Section 136.675 of the legislation required any party seeking to admit such testimony to furnish to the adversarial party "an unabridged videotape or mechanical recording [of] the entire session." Section 136.685 added an additional requirement for police officers. Before conducting any hypnosis, they were mandated to explain the following to the intended hypnotic subject:

(a) He is free to refuse to be subject to the [hypnosis];
(b) There is a risk of psychological side effects resulting from the process;
(c) If he agrees to be subject to [hypnosis], it is possible that the process will reveal emotions or information of which he is not consciously aware and which he may wish to keep private; and
(d) He may request that the [hypnosis] be conducted by a licensed medical doctor or a licensed psychologist, at no cost to himself.

The Oregon legislation was an additional indication that the open-admissibility rule of *Harding* had failed to provide adequate safeguards.

Attorneys

Some defense lawyers pushed harder to get courts to declare hypnotically refreshed testimony scientifically unreliable. Among these lawyers were members of the California Attorneys for Criminal Justice (CACJ). In the 1970s, they began a crusade to curtail police use of hypnosis on victims and witnesses. Ephraim Margolin, Thomas Worthington, and Stephen Hiser led the fight. Though most of their advocacy was conducted in California, they also filed briefs in significant cases in other states. Their efforts began to change judges' views across the country.

Court opinions on investigative hypnosis had been remarkably devoid of analysis of the scientific findings about hypnosis and its ability to refresh memory. With the help of expert testimony on hypnosis and memory, the CACJ lawyers hoped to alert courts to the defects of hypnotically refreshed recollection. In order to accomplish this goal, the attorneys turned to the scientific researchers for evidence that hypnosis could not guarantee the accuracy of refreshed recollection and, worse, that it could contaminate the existing memories by subtle but undue suggestion. Furthermore, because the serious problem of confabulation had yet to be confronted or addressed by the courts, expert testimony on this crucial topic was also vital.

Dr. Orne's Safeguards

Police use of hypnosis was growing rapidly by the late 1970s. Encouraged by the open-admissibility rule being followed in most states and by the overblown claims in the media concerning remarkable successes, law enforcement officials rushed to embrace investigative hypnosis.

Prominent hypnosis researchers noticed this trend and began to address it directly. Dr. Martin Orne surveyed the developments in "The Use and Misuse of Hypnosis in Court" (Orne, 1979). He explained why he made the transition from the clinic to the courtroom:

> Because of our laboratory's work on the nature of hypnosis, I have become involved in a number of cases where our work was directly relevant to the proposed forensic use of hypnosis. Of particular relevance were our empirical studies dealing with: the nature of hypnotic age regression . . . ; the potential use of hypnosis in interrogation . . . ; the question of whether antisocial behavior can be elicited by the use of hypnosis . . . ; the nature of posthypnotic behavior . . . ; the simulation of hypnosis . . . ; and posthypnotically disrupted recall . . . [citations omitted]. (p. 312)

In cases ranging from California to New York and from Wisconsin to New Jersey, Orne filed affidavits and made court appearances urging courts to apply caution in their consideration of hypnotically refreshed testimony. Whether he appeared by invitation of the prosecution, the defense, or the court, Orne's message remained consistent: Hypnosis had serious draw-backs in the search for truth. In his opinion,

> There are instances when hypnosis can be used appropriately provided that the nature of the phenomenon is understood by all parties concerned. It must be recognized, however, that the use of hypnosis by either the prosecution or the defense can profoundly affect the individual's subse-quent testimony. Since these changes are not reversible, if individuals are to be allowed to testify after having undergone hypnosis to aid their mem-ory, a minimum number of safeguards are absolutely essential. (Orne, 1979, p. 335)

Orne first proposed his safeguards in an affidavit filed in the case of *People v. Quaglino* (Call., 1977). At that time he stipulated four basic re-quirements. A Wisconsin judge (*State v. White*, 1979) expanded the list to nine, as did a New York court (*People v. Hughes*, 1979). The Orne safe-guards received their definitive formulation, however, in the 1980 *State v. Hurd* case from New Jersey.

Hurd involved a woman, Jane Sell, who had been attacked during the predawn hours in her home while her husband slept on the couch in an-other room. According to the court, Sell was "unable or unwilling" to identify her attacker, but she told police to "check out" her ex-husband, Paul Hurd. To assist Sell's memory, the police brought in Dr. Herbert Spiegel to hyp-notize her. Spiegel, one of the early pioneers of medical hypnosis, per-formed the hypnosis in the presence of several detectives and a physician studying Spiegel's technique. During the session, when Sell began to be-come emotional, one of the detectives asked her whether she knew her attacker. Sell said, "Yes." The detective then asked whether it was her husband. Sell answered, "No." The detective next asked whether it was Paul Hurd. Sell, who by this time was crying hysterically, replied, "Yes."

After being brought out of the trance, Sell expressed misgivings about what she had said. She was encouraged by Spiegel and the detective to make a positive identification of Hurd. They told her "that unless she iden-tified her attacker he would remain free to attempt to attack again, and that should a subsequent attack prove successful her children would be without a mother" (*Hurd*, 1980, p. 294). Furthermore, they urged that if she did not make an identification, her current husband "could not be eliminated as a suspect" (p. 294). Sell made the identification. As a conse-quence of the hypnotic abreaction, Sell's "previous posttraumatic stress disorder, which included insomnia, nightmares, irritability, and reduced ability to function, was reversed" (Spiegel & Spiegel, 1987, p. 494).

The police sought no additional corroborative evidence before placing Paul Hurd on trial. Four experts testified. Spiegel told the court that it was possible for a hypnotist to implant completely false ideas in the minds of certain subjects and to cause them to recall events contrary to fact at the suggestion of the hypnotist. He insisted, however, that the procedure he followed was "completely free from seduction, suggestion, coercion or taint of any kind" (*Hurd*, 1980, p. 296).

Unfortunately, none of the other experts agreed with Spiegel that his procedures were free from taint. All of them testified that it appeared to them that Spiegel believed Paul Hurd was guilty and had pushed Jane Sell to reach this conclusion as well. One expert, Dr. Edward Lowell, went so far as to describe Spiegel's hypnosis work in this case as "coercive persuasion," another name for "brainwashing" (Schein, 1961).

The appellate court also had problems with Spiegel's work. The New Jersey Superior Court felt that Spiegel had a tendency to change his testimony to suit his needs:

> Initially, Dr. Spiegel characterized his efforts with [Sell] as an interrogation process. Thereafter the defense, through the testimony of Dr. Orne, challenged the neutrality of that interrogation, particularly in the post-hypnotic session. It was then that Dr. Spiegel's contact with [Sell] was characterized as therapeutic, designed to cure a traumatic neurosis, as opposed to investigative. (p. 308)

Other expert testimony in the case claimed that when Spiegel, before trial, had spoken and written about his work with Sell (Spiegel, 1980), he had described the case far differently than he did in court.

Dr. Spiegel found himself in an unanticipated and conflicted role. His dilemma serves to highlight a latent danger for therapists and mental health professionals involved in investigative hypnosis. Once the police had failed to seek out corroborating evidence of Sell's identification, Spiegel's testimony on the validity of the identification assumed an importance he had never intended it to have.

Spiegel was originally contacted by the police to help them develop a lead. A crime had been committed and the police needed assistance in their investigation. If Spiegel could use hypnosis on Sell to uncover enough initial information to get a search for evidence underway, the police could then develop a solid case.

Unfortunately, when Spiegel got to court, he discovered the police had not done their homework. Unexpectedly, he was the case for them. Confronted on the witness stand with this absence of additional corroboration, he was asked to provide what evidence he could that her identification was genuine. Spiegel expressed the opinion that it was unlikely that the symptoms of posttraumatic stress disorder would have resolved had her identification been confabulation. He therefore concluded that her identification was accurate. Because of his concern about Sell's psychological state, and as a consequence of this new role he had been forced to play, it appeared as if he had switched from being an investigator to being a therapist. This role confusion hurt his credibility on the stand.

The battle of the experts left the Superior Court with a clear preference for the safeguards suggested by Orne. On appeal, the New Jersey Supreme Court upheld the necessity for safeguards and made only minor changes in them (*State v. Hurd*, 1981). The following list accommodates both versions:

1. The hypnotic session should be conducted by a licensed psychiatrist or psychologist trained in the use of hypnosis.

2. The qualified professional conducting the hypnotic session should be independent of, not regularly employed by, and not responsible to the prosecutor, the investigator, or the defense.

3. Any information given to the hypnotist by law enforcement personnel or the defense prior to the hypnotic session must be in written form or recorded, so that subsequently the extent of the information the subject received from the hypnotist may be determined.

4. Before induction of hypnosis, the hypnotist should obtain from the subject a detailed description of the facts as the subject remembers them, carefully avoiding adding any new elements to the witness's description of the events.

5. All contacts between the hypnotist and the subject should be recorded, so that a permanent record is available for comparison and study to establish that the witness has not received information or suggestion that might later be reported as having been first described by the subject during hypnosis. The use of videotape is strongly encouraged but is not mandatory.

6. Only the hypnotist and the subject should be present during any phase of the hypnotic session, including the prehypnotic testing and posthypnotic interview.

An additional point insisted upon by Orne, and also by Spiegel, was recognized in the *Hurd* case. That point is "the importance of independent verification of hypnotically-induced recollection. . . . [T]he most we should legitimately expect from hypnotic interrogations is further data which may serve as leads for more conventional evidence gathering" (*Hurd*, 1980, p. 299). The charges against Paul Hurd were ultimately dropped.

Courts began accepting the Orne guidelines as a precondition to the admissibility of hypnotically refreshed recollection. Without them, there was no way to test the reliability of such memories.

Professional Associations Take A Stand

Alarmed by the increasing use of hypnosis by poorly trained police officials, two major hypnosis associations passed a resolution addressing the issue. In October 1978, the Society for Clinical and Experimental Hypnosis condemned police hypnosis. The same resolution was passed by the International Society of Hypnosis in August 1979, and was reprinted in the

International Journal of Clinical and Experimental Hypnosis in that year (Society for Clinical and Experimental Hypnosis, 1979).

The resolution emphasized that the health of the hypnotized subject is jeopardized when police officers with minimal skills in hypnosis and without adequate understanding of human psychology and psychopathology practice hypnosis on vulnerable witnesses and victims. It was not argued that hypnosis should play no role in forensic matters; instead, a safeguards approach was advocated. Police, the resolution stated, should not be given training in hypnosis. Only "trained psychiatrists or psychologists with experience in the forensic use of hypnosis should be employed" (Society for Clinical and Experimental Hypnosis, 1979, p. 452). In addition, it was stressed that all interactions between a hypnotist and a subject *"must"* be videotaped. The resolution concluded by noting that it is "unethical to train lay individuals in the use of hypnosis, to collaborate with laymen in the use of hypnosis, or to serve as a consultant for laymen who are utilizing hypnosis" (Society for Clinical and Experimental Hypnosis, 1979, p. 453).

As might be expected, the police response to this resolution was negative. The defenders of law enforcement's position stressed two basic points. First, police are better trained in interrogation and criminal investigation than are licensed healers. Although it would clearly be improper for lay police officers to attempt to heal or cure with hypnosis, it is equally wrong to place psychologists and psychiatrists in the role of crime solvers, a position for which they are insufficiently trained. Second, evidence of psychological damage to hypnotized subjects is more fiction than fact. Although claims of such damage are often made, no hard data demonstrate that police use of hypnosis has caused physical or emotional harm.

In general, the police hypnotists, like stage hypnotists and other lay practioners before them, view such regulations as an attempt by the medical profession to maintain an economic monopoly. Reiser has been most outspoken on this point. In language directed primarily at Orne and Dr. Bernard Diamond, Reiser (1985a) complains:

> A few hypnosis "authorities" with impressive credentials have been on an avowed crusade to "shoot down" the police use of investigative hypnosis. In the process, they have misinformed the courts, colleagues and the public on many key hypnosis and cognition issues. Using assertion and fiat, without the required relevant data, these individuals, claiming to represent the "scientific community," have engaged in scientism in the guise of science and injected proprietary guild interests under the cover of ethical concerns.
>
> An underlying territorial motive can be seen in the identical resolution passed by two separate clinical hypnosis societies declaring it unethical for members to teach, supervise or consult with police who use investigative hypnosis in criminal cases [citations omitted]. Attempts are also being made to extend the power play, still in the guise of an ethics problem, to other psychological and hypnosis associations. (p. 513)

In numerous courtroom battles, Reiser has found himself testifying in opposition to Orne and Diamond. To support his position, Reiser (1985a) disputes Orne's research data concerning vital questions of hypnosis and memory, and reaches the following conclusions:

1. "The assertion that hypnosis always involves hyper-suggestibility and that hypnotic recall is essentially unreliable . . . is linked to the old Svengali myth of mind control" (1985a, p. 514). Reiser argues that "suggestibility per se plays a relatively small part in hypnosis processes" (1985a, p. 514).

2. Confabulation and fantasy in hypnotic recall are exaggerated in the literature. Although an "occasional instance of abuse or misuse" (1985a, p. 515) of investigative hypnosis has been noted, confabulation and fantasy are no greater in hypnosis than they are without hypnosis, when proper procedures are followed. "The legal–psychological literature on eyewitness problems and the misidentifications of suspects by non-hypnotized witnesses clearly indicate that this is a generic problem involving individual cognitive processes, sensory perceptual mechanisms, apperceptive mass, attitudes, values and belief systems" (1985a, pp. 515–516).

3. Memory is not distorted or tainted by hypnosis, and hypnotized persons are able "to discriminate among events before, during and after hypnosis if indeed they had that capacity to start with" (1985a, p. 517).

Reiser's points raise two basic questions about the potential fragility of the mind in trance: (1) *Can* hypnosis distort memory? (2) If so, *must* hypnosis *necessarily* distort memory?

The Malleability of Memory

When I was a young man I could remember everything,
whether it happened or not.   —Mark Twain

Documentation of the potential for memory distortion. For well over a century, hypnosis investigators have documented the potential for memory distortion in hypnotic suggestion. The ability of hypnotists to create or implant false memories or inaccurate recollections has been consistently observed and reported, especially with reference to the legal arena. Albert Moll (1889/1958) put the point succinctly: "Retroactive hallucinations are of great importance in law. They can be used to falsify testimony. People can be made to believe that they have witnessed certain scenes, or even crimes" (pp. 345–346).

Moll's observations mirror those of Bernheim (1891/1980): "I have shown how a false memory can cause *false testimony given in good faith,* and how examining magistrates can unwittingly cause false testimony by suggestion" (p. 92). To demonstrate his point, Bernheim told a patient in trance that the patient had been awakened from sleep the night before by a neighbor who coughed, sang, and made a racket opening windows. The patient also was told that other neighbors had been aroused from slumber by the noise. When the patient was brought out of trance and asked about the previous night, he reported being awakened by a loud neighbor, just as Bernheim falsely suggested in trance. Bernheim then pressed the patient for further details, which the patient readily supplied. During the waking state, the patient fantasized and confabulated details not suggested by Bernheim.

Orne duplicated this experiment before cameras filming a documentary for the BBC (Barnes, 1982). A hypnotized subject, who had reported an excellent night's sleep, was told in trance that she had been awakened by loud noises that sounded like gunshots. She was also given a suggestion as to the time at which this incident had occurred. Upon awakening from trance, she reported these noises and the time she had heard them. When Orne played a tape for her of her prehypnosis statement that she had slept peacefully through the night, she was puzzled, but insistent that she had been awakened by loud noises. In other words, she was more confident of her hypnotically induced *false* memories than she was of her tape-recorded prehypnotic *true* memories.

The possibility of creating pseudomemories with hypnosis has also been demonstrated by a team of Canadian researchers who have provided the fullest documentation of the literature (Laurence, Nadon, Nogrady, & Perry, 1986).

The fact that hypnosis can be used to distort memory or to create false recollections has not escaped the attention of legal commentators (Allen, 1934, pp. 19–20; *Criminal Law Magazine*, 1891; Levy, 1955, p. 340).

Dr. Herbert Spiegel's "Honest Liar" syndrome. At the annual meeting of the American Psychiatric Association in May 1968, Dr. Herbert Spiegel conducted a demonstration designed to show that false memories are easily implanted by hypnotic suggestion (*Time*, May 24, 1968). As NBC-TV cameras filmed the experiment, Spiegel placed a subject in trance and told the man that Communists intended to take over radio and television stations. Details were not provided, but Spiegel told his subject that he would remember specific information. When the trance ended, the subject began talking about the plot. The subject told an intricate and elaborate story, replete with minor details such as the furnishings and posters in the room where he first heard about the Communist plan. The subject also incorporated waking suggestions given to him by the people he talked with about the plot. Spiegel then removed the false story, and the subject was shocked when he saw the film. Although objections were raised about the scientific nature of the experiment, it did indicate a need for caution in evaluating hypnotically refreshed recollection.

A dozen years later, Spiegel (1980) referred to this ability of a subject to fervently believe hypnotically implanted memories as the "honest liar" syndrome. Referring to his earlier experiment, Spiegel wrote that the subject, a successful businessman in his 40s, leaned politically to the left, yet he was induced to act and sound like an ultraconservative:

> During the experiment, in response to the hypnotic signal, the subject created a totally false story to rationalize his compliance. He sincerely believed it to be true. Since he was locked into the hypnotic bind, he suspended his own critical judgment. He lied but did not actually know he was lying. At the time, he was in effect an honest liar. (p. 78)

"Honest liars" would, of course, make perfect witnesses, because they would be impervious to cross-examination and would be sincere in their belief that what they were saying was true. The danger such witnesses pose for the legal system would seem to mandate, at the very least, minimal safeguards.

The Late 1970s Approach: Admissibility If Safeguards Are Satisfied

As the 1970s drew to a close, evidence was accumulating that hypnosis could affect memory in ways detrimental to the discovery of truth. From the police perspective, the fact that hypnotically refreshed recollection might not be entirely accurate was not viewed as a serious handicap, because any new information developing from trance might provide investigative leads that could be further corroborated or proven.

Thus, if a license number were to be remembered in trance, the police could shift their investigation to verify this information. Should the memory prove incorrect, nothing but time would be lost. On the other hand, if the information should prove accurate, hypnosis would be the source of vital clues that otherwise could not have been obtained.

When hypnotically refreshed recollection is introduced in court, however, additional considerations become significant. Juries are apt to attribute great power to hypnosis. Thanks to Hollywood and media images, it is a common belief among the public that people tell the truth under hypnosis. Law enforcement officials upon occasion benefit from that belief. In the *White* case (Wis., 1979), one such senior official testified under oath that hypnosis lends "credibility and strength to your investigation" (Orne, 1979, p. 333).

Based on the overwhelming data demonstrating the impact of suggestion on hypnotically refreshed recollection, courts responded by imposing safeguards before such testimony would be admissible. Although the Orne guidelines listed earlier in this chapter became the standard, other courts added to or rewrote them to suit individual preferences (*People v. Lewis,* N.Y., 1980).

What would happen if the Orne safeguards were to be substantially, but not entirely, complied with by the police? A weaker version of the safeguards approach was applied by some courts in this situation. These courts favored a pretrial hearing during which the trial judge would evaluate the *"totality of the circumstances"* before ruling on the admissibility of hypnotically refreshed recollection (*Hughes,* N.Y., 1979, p. 649, italics added for emphasis). Under this test, no safeguard would be absolutely mandatory. A judge would have discretion in each particular case to evaluate the entire set of circumstances surrounding the hypnosis sessions. Although this approach would be more costly, failure to meet each safeguard would not be fatal.

Are Safeguards Necessary or Sufficient?

*Imagination and suggestion are twin artists ever ready to retouch
the fading daguerrotype of memory.* —Gardner (1933, p. 401)

No sooner had the safeguards approach been developed than it was attacked from opposite directions. The police, as we have seen, objected on the grounds that the safeguards were unnecessary and unduly restrictive. To buttress their argument, they pointed to the expanding literature, both scientific and legal, demonstrating the general fallibility of eyewitness testimony and memory. In addition, they argued that suggestion is just as powerful in causing memory distortions in everyday life without any hypnosis.

The police argument was accepted in part in the *Hurd* case. According to the New Jersey Supreme Court, "hypnosis can be considered reasonably reliable if it is able to yield recollections as accurate as those of an ordinary witness, which likewise are often historically inaccurate" (*Hurd,* 1981, p. 92).

To the police, the general inaccuracies in memory and eyewitness testimony, coupled with the power of suggestion outside of trance, indicated that hypnosis should be treated no differently from any other type of witness testimony. In their view, special procedures, restrictions, and limitations were not warranted, because they were designed to address problems that occur in nonhypnosis settings as well.

The safeguards approach also was attacked from the opposite perspective. Hypnosis researchers and defense lawyers argued that the safeguards were insufficient to protect against memory tampering, and therefore were too weak. Instead of safeguards, they clamored for a flat rule barring hypnotically refreshed recollection from the courtroom as the only legitimate protection. If it is true that ordinary memory can be inaccurate or altered by suggestion, the possibility of even greater unreliability would be present with the use of hypnosis, especially in the hands of inadequately trained police officials who have a vested interest in solving crimes.

Just as the safeguards approach began to find some favor in the courts, a devastating attack on the reliability of hypnotically refreshed recollection appeared from the pen of Dr. Bernard Diamond. No other article has engendered such controversy or had a greater impact on the law of investigative hypnosis. The fact that hypnosis *may* distort memory encouraged courts to adopt a safeguards approach. Diamond went further; he argued that memory contamination is an *inevitable* by-product of hypnotic questioning.

DR. DIAMOND'S 14 POINTS

Hopes that the newly detailed safeguards would persuade courts to permit the use of hypnosis soon were dashed. In 1980, a broadside against admissibility was fired by Bernard Diamond. In a major article published in the *California Law Review*, Diamond marshaled scientific data and legal arguments to urge courts to disqualify any witness from testifying if that witness had been previously hypnotized. Diamond is a professor of law at the University of California at Berkeley, and a clinical professor of psychiatry at the University of California at San Francisco. His prior law review articles had helped shape the California Supreme Court's thinking on many issues where law and psychiatry cross paths.

The timing of Diamond's hypnosis article could not have been better. Courts were just beginning to have second thoughts about hypnosis and had not yet explored in any depth the scientific literature concerning hypnosis and memory. The newly developed safeguards might prove a real temptation to judges who would not want to deprive the police of an important new aid in criminal investigation. If there were problems with the hypnosis, these judges could now say, "Let the experts fight about it in court." As long as the police followed the simple rules spelled out by Orne, the hypnotically refreshed recollection could be admitted.

The persuasiveness of this approach troubled Diamond. It rested upon a foundation that was unsteady. The scientific literature, according to his reading, clearly demonstrated that hypnotically refreshed recollection had four major flaws. First, it was apt to be filled with fantasy, confabulation, and perhaps deliberate deception. Though memory might be enhanced, and new information obtained, there would also be an increase in erroneous information. Memories would be stimulated, but many would not factually be accurate. Second, no expert could consistently and correctly tell whether the subject was simulating hypnosis; whether statements made in trance were truthful; and whether the refreshed recollection was fact or fiction. Third, even the witness would be unable to tell whether a memory had been inspired by the hypnosis or recollected independently.

Fourth, and most importantly, the witness would have more confidence in the accuracy of the memories as a result of the hypnosis. This confidence, even in memories that were impermissibly suggested or incorrectly recalled, would be impervious to effective cross-examination, because the witness would believe fully that his or her memories were true. This last point was especially crucial, because it answered the argument that rigorous cross-examination would weed out fact from fiction. The judiciary's trust in cross-examination as the deterrent to error was often cited as a reason to admit hypnotically refreshed recollection. If cross-examination could not do this job, the essential foundation of the admissibility approach, and even the safeguards approach, would crumble.

In short, Diamond's thesis was that all hypnosis involves interfering with memory and therefore tampering with evidence. If a witness were to be hypnotized, no aspect of the testimony would be trustworthy. The witness would be confident, but possibly mistaken as to both the *source* and the *content* of the memories. Because cross-examination would not be effective, the defendant's constitutional right of confrontation would have been compromised.

The centerpiece of Diamond's article was his articulation of 14 questions "which might be asked in court of an expert in the field of hypnosis" (1980, p. 332). Diamond believed that negative responses to these questions demonstrated that hypnotically refreshed memory should be inadmissible.[1]

1. Can a hypnotized person be free from heightened suggestibility?
2. Can a hypnotist, through the exercise of skill and attention, avoid implanting suggestions in the mind of the hypnotized subject?
3. After awakening, can the hypnotic subject consistently recognize which of his thoughts, feelings, and memories were his own and which were implanted by the hypnotic experience?
4. Is it rare for a subject to believe that he was not hypnotized when in fact he was?
5. Can previously hypnotized persons restrict their memory to actual facts, free from fantasies and confabulation?
6. After the hypnotic subject is awakened, do the distorting effects of the hypnosis disappear?
7. Can an experienced hypnotist or other expert detect the simulation of hypnosis?
8. During or after hypnosis, can the hypnotist or the subject himself sort out fact from fantasy in the recall?
9. Is the specificity and richness of the recalled memories an assurance that the hypnotic or posthypnotic subject is recalling fact?
10. Does the independent corroboration of some of the hypnotically enhanced memories assure that all or most of the witness' memories are reliable?

11. Is it possible or practical to make an adequate record of the hypnotic experience?
12. Does a witness' posthypnotic demeanor, attitude of self-confidence, and appearance of integrity and honesty remain unaffected by pretrial hypnosis?
13. Can an experienced hypnotist or other expert have a reliable and valid opinion that the recall of a particular witness whose memory has been enhanced by hypnotism is reliable and valid?
14. Are the uncertainties of ordinary eyewitness testimony and those of hypnotically enhanced recall sufficiently similar that the legal rules of procedures designed for coping with the one are sufficient for the other?

"No" was the emphatic answer Diamond gave to each question. Constructed as a blueprint for cross-examination of the hypnosis expert, these questions were designed to lead the court to reject hypnosis as untrustworthy in the *accurate* recall of memory.

Diamond's article created a firestorm of controversy. Its advocacy of a rule of total exclusion obviously did not find favor with prosecutors, police, law-and-order judges, and many clinical hypnotherapists. Despite this resistance, Diamond's position had an immediate persuasive impact. Barely had the article appeared when courts began to accept his conclusions. A formidable array of state court decisions conducted the most thorough and detailed investigation into the literature of hypnosis and memory yet undertaken by the judiciary. When the judges emerged from their reading, hypnosis was called into serious question, and a new era of inadmissibility was inaugurated.

[1]© 1980 by California Law Review, Inc. Reprinted from *California Law Review*, Vol. 68, No. 2, March 1980, pp. 313–349, by permission.

CHAPTER 5

The Rise and Fall of Inadmissibility

THE RETURN TO INADMISSIBILITY

By 1980, the volume of cases raising legal issues related to investigative hypnosis had swelled mightily. The rising tide of trials involving questions about forensic hypnosis was a natural by-product of the two approaches articulated by the courts—open admissibility and admissibility if safeguards were met. Both rules encouraged police to continue expanding the number of witnesses and victims hypnotized for memory recall. As this volume of litigation increased, courts became aware of the pitfalls of hypnotically refreshed testimony. Expert opinion on hypnosis questions was now frequently sought. As a consequence, the judiciary became more familiar with the hypnosis studies contained in the literature.

Court opinions began to reflect this increased sophistication. Prior to 1978, judicial opinions on hypnosis generally failed to analyze or even to mention the extensive experimental literature on hypnosis and memory produced in the preceding 40 years. Judges drew their understanding of hypnosis primarily from the police and from clinical practitioners, who had little need to be familiar with the technical laboratory experiments that did not have a clinical or therapeutic orientation. After 1978, by contrast, the laboratory experts took over. Their research presented a picture of hypnosis far different from the vision previously presented to the courts. Diamond's 1980 article, described in Chapter Four, crystallized this perspective.

Although rumblings of a hard-line approach to hypnotically refreshed recollection were discernible earlier, in 1980 the first major cases reversing the two admissibility rules were decided. From 1980 through 1982, a rule of per se (i.e., total) exclusion of hypnotically refreshed memory was articulated in Minnesota (*State v. Mack*, 1980), Arizona (*State v. Mena*, 1981), Nebraska (*State v. Palmer*, 1981), Pennsylvania (*Commonwealth v. Nazarovitch*, 1981), and Maryland (*Collins v. State*, 1982). These courts gave hypnosis a sustained and extensive examination, but concluded that, for a variety of reasons, the best approach was to return the law to where it began— that is, to the position that testimony refreshed by hypnosis is inadmissible. The judges found support for their position in *Frye v. United States* (D.C. Cir., 1923), an old but important case that spelled out the test for admitting expert testimony in a trial when that testimony is based on scientific techniques.

The *Frye* Rule

Courts sensibly believe that the value of an expert opinion in part depends upon the trustworthiness of the information that is the foundation for that opinion. If a psychiatrist were to testify that his or her opinion was based upon a throwing of the tarot cards, courts might be inclined to give such a view little if any credence. The advancement of science poses a special problem for the judiciary. When a new technique or procedure is developed, and an expert testifies based upon it, how is the reliability of that experimental procedure to be evaluated? The 1923 *Frye* case provides an answer.

Frye concerned a primitive version of a lie detector. Was this machine sufficiently *reliable* to justify believing in its accuracy? If not, the results of the lie detector test ought not to be admissible. In an oft-quoted passage, the District of Columbia Court of Appeals articulated the test followed by a majority of courts today:

> Just when a scientific principle or discovery crosses the line between the experimental and demonstrable stages is difficult to define. Somewhere in this twilight zone the evidential force of the principle must be recognized, and while the courts will go a long way in admitting expert testimony deduced from a well-recognized scientific principle or discovery, *the thing from which the deduction is made must be sufficiently established to have gained general acceptance in the particular field in which it belongs.* (p. 1014; emphasis added)

The purpose of the *Frye* rule's requirement of "general acceptance" is in part to prevent juries from being swayed by the "aura of infallibility" surrounding scientific techniques and procedures. Jurors tend not to be very skeptical of scientific methods and to imbue them with a high degree of accuracy and certainty. The requirement that a procedure be generally accepted by the scientific community helps ensure that juries will not be unduly swayed by techniques of dubious validity.

Courts did not immediately apply the *Frye* test to hypnosis, because the test had been almost exclusively used for evaluating physical or mechanical devices, or chemical or electrical procedures. Blood typing, voiceprint analysis, neutron activation analysis, electron microscope scanning devices, paraffin tests, polygraphs, and gunshot residue tests were the types of procedures that usually triggered the *Frye* rule (Giannelli, 1980). Hypnosis does not comfortably equate with the physical procedures listed above. Furthermore, *Frye* affects the admissibility of expert opinion deduced from a scientific technique, not the admissibility of eyewitness or victim testimony. For these reasons, courts did not generally ask whether hypnosis was a scientific procedure that had gained "general acceptance" in the scientific community.

Although a few early opinions on hypnosis raised the issue of *Frye* (*People v. Harper*, Ill., 1969; *Greenfield v. Commonwealth*, Va., 1974; *People v. Hangsleben*, Mich., 1978), it was not until the *Mack* case in Minnesota in 1980 that the courts first began to exclude hypnotically refreshed recollection on the grounds that hypnosis did not have scientific support as an accurate memory refresher. Since 1980, a substantial number of courts have excluded hypnotically refreshed testimony on the basis of *Frye*. Although the trend toward total exclusion had already been building, no case has achieved more notoriety, or has been the subject of more controversy, than the California Supreme Court's 1982 *People v. Shirley* decision.

The *Shirley* Case

California courts had decided hypnosis questions in dozens of cases before the Supreme Court was asked to make a definitive ruling on the police use of hypnosis for investigative purposes. In 1977, the court had declined to rule on the issue in *People v. Quaglino*, and had left standing a lower court's decision to admit hypnotically refreshed testimony. The police had interpreted this refusal to overturn the admission of the testimony as an indication that the court was not opposed to police hypnosis of witnesses and victims. That interpretation might well have been correct, but by 1982 the judicial climate across the country had cooled considerably toward hypnosis. Prosecutors and police were nervous that the prohypnosis attitude presently prevailing would be altered or even reversed.

For the very first time in its history, the California Supreme Court permitted the oral argument in the *Shirley* case to be filmed for television audiences. KQED, a San Francisco PBS affiliate, took its cameras into the court's hearing room to record the arguments of the prosecution and the defense (Ornstein, 1981). A great deal was at stake in the case. According to the prosecutor, Deputy Attorney General John Carney, 59 cases involving the use of hypnosis by the police would be affected by the court's ultimate ruling (Carrizosa, 1982). Some of those cases included brutal and sensational crimes such as those of Angelo Buono, Jr., who was accused of involvement in the Hillside Strangler serial killer cases. Even more at stake were the hundreds of cases not yet brought to trial, and, indeed, the very future of hypnosis as an investigative tool.

Given the seriousness and importance of the Supreme Court's ruling in *Shirley*, the factual elements of the case could not have been worse for the police. It was, as Justice Mosk pointed out in his majority opinion, "a classic case of conflicting stories" (p. 244). Catherine C. brought charges against Donald Lee Shirley, the defendant, claiming he had raped her and forced her to commit other sexual acts against her will and without her consent. The defendant admitted the sex, but denied that she had been forced. No other witnesses were present at the crucial times. The entire case against Shirley rested on the testimony of Catherine.

Catherine was not the best of witnesses. She had been drinking heavily all night and had varied her alcohol diet with Mellaril, a major tranquilizer. As Justice Kaus noted in his separate opinion, because of her intoxication, "there is a good possibility that she has no clear memory to be refreshed by hypnosis" (p. 278). Shirley, on the other hand, was not the typical criminal defendant. At the time of the alleged crime, he was in the military. During the trial, several Marine officers, including his superiors, testified that he had a good reputation, had no history of violent or aggressive behavior, and was regarded as being honest and truthful.

Catherine told several different stories to police officers before she was hypnotized. Her story during hypnosis, and afterwards, also varied. As the majority opinion noted:

> Catherine's performance as a witness was far from exemplary: the record is replete with instances in which her testimony was vague, changeable, self-contradictory, or prone to unexplained lapses of memory. Indeed, on occasion she professed to be unable to remember assertions that she had herself made on the witness stand only the previous day. (p. 245)

Catherine admitted that before hypnosis the events of the night in question were "vague" in her mind. She said that the hypnosis helped her fill in the gap in her memory.

The prosecutor called no experts in hypnosis. The defense called Dr. Donald Schafer, a board-certified psychiatrist with impressive credentials in hypnosis. Schafer's testimony was consistent with Diamond's position that hypnosis does not guarantee the accuracy of recall and may, in fact, make it easier for a subject to lie. As Schafer testified on cross-examination (Hosford, 1980):

Q: If I understand you correctly, Doctor, what you are telling us is that hypnosis is not a truth serum, is that correct?
A: Correct.

Q: Person can stand here in this room and lie while not under hypnosis just as easily as they can while under hypnosis?

A: They might even do it easier under hypnosis because the hypnosis would put the responsibility on the shoulders of the hypnotist, as the patient would see it, or as the subject would see it.

Q: What do you base that opinion on?

A: Experience. (pp. 9–10)

Schafer also testified that no one is able to tell whether a person under hypnosis is telling the truth. The effect of hypnosis, he continued, is to make a person more convinced of the truth of what he or she said in hypnosis, especially when that person is asked *after* hypnosis to remember the same events he or she was asked to recall in trance.

The hypnosis of Catherine C. raised serious concerns, apart from Schafer's criticisms of hypnosis as a memory refresher. The session was conducted *at the courthouse by a deputy district attorney, the day before trial was scheduled to begin*. Despite these problems, and the fact that Schafer's testimony was basically unchallenged, the jury convicted Shirley. His lawyer immediately appealed. In a very brief unpublished opinion (four typed pages), the court of appeal affirmed the conviction. Hypnosis was not discussed as an issue.

Shirley's petition for hearing before the California Supreme Court provided details not addressed in any published court opinion (Hosford, 1980). Catherine had reported that her father had raped her, but she had not filed a complaint against him. She had also revealed that she had spent time in a mental institution in Indiana 2 years before the incident in question. Defense lawyers were not permitted to question her about these facts.

At the Supreme Court, the crucial issue became the hypnosis conducted by the prosecutor's office. The entire court agreed that the conviction had to be reversed. Neither the hypnotist nor the setting was impartial. The court stopped short of agreeing with the defense that the prosecutor had basically "manufactured evidence" by its last-minute hypnosis designed to get Catherine to tell one consistent story; there was no doubt, however, that this possibility was present.

The court could have reversed the conviction and dealt with the case as an unusual and seriously flawed aberration. It chose instead, however, to use the case as a vehicle to pronounce a rule of total exclusion. Following in the footsteps of the emerging trend of cases using *Frye* to prevent the admission of hypnotically refreshed recollection, the court slammed the door shut on investigative hypnosis.

The majority rejected the safeguards approach for several reasons. First, the safeguards enunciated in *Hurd* failed to prevent the dangers they were designed to alleviate. Second, the safeguards did not even address certain other, and more serious, dangers that the subject (1) would lose his or her critical judgment and begin to credit "memories" that were formerly viewed as unreliable; (2) would confuse actual recall with confabulation and would be unable to distinguish between the two; and (3) would exhibit an unwarranted confidence in the validity of his or her ensuing recollection. The majority was also persuaded that the safeguards approach was costly, time-consuming, and likely to produce extensive litigation as each aspect of each guideline was challenged in court. The best rule, and the simplest to administer, was total exclusion.

The majority backed up its decision with a lengthy and detailed examination of the hypnosis literature and with an examination of contemporary studies on memory. The court flatly rejected the police belief that memory acts like a "tape recorder," and the opinion singled out Reiser's work as an illustration of this false view. Instead, the court accepted the theory that memory is "productive, not reproductive." Memory augments; it does not simply "play back." Two members of the court, though not disagreeing with the court's reading of the literature, preferred the *Hurd* safeguards to the total-exclusion rule announced by the majority.

The *Shirley* case was decided on March 11, 1982. On June 4, 1982, the court issued a revised opinion that permitted a defendant who had been previously hypnotized to testify on his or her own behalf, as is the defendant's constitutional right. The court expressly limited this exemption from the rule of total exclusion of hypnotically refreshed testimony to defendants, and did not extend it to defense witnesses. This last point, exempting defendants, bothered Schafer. In the *Division on Psychological Hypnosis Newsletter* of the American Psychological Association, Schafer (1984) wrote:

> I wish therefore at this time to state that the use of hypnosis with a defendant in the pre-testimony phase of a trial approaches unethical actions— on the part not only of the "hypnotist," but also on the part of the defending attorneys—for it usually obfuscates the testimony by making it concrete, convincing to the defendant and also the court, and not subject to cross examination. (p. 2)

The *Shirley* case was not the first to advocate a total-exclusion rule, but it was one of the most influential. As the early 1980s unfolded, it appeared to represent the trend. The revolution that had begun in 1968 with the *Harding* case appeared to be ending.

The Early 1980s Approach: Inadmissibility

After the initial explosion of cases in the early 1980s that held hypnotically refreshed testimony to be inadmissible, two other developments strengthened this approach.

First, courts that had earlier adopted *Harding's* open-admissibility policy reversed themselves and embraced total exclusion (*State v. Peoples*, N.C., 1984). In no state was the reversal more dramatic than in Maryland, where courts overruled *Harding,* the case that had spawned the admissibility movement (*Polk v. State,* 1981; *Collins v. State,* 1982; *State v. Collins,* 1983).

Second, Orne's later work appeared to reject the guidelines that bear his name. In his important 1979 paper "The Use and Misuse of Hypnosis in Court," Orne had written that "if individuals are to be allowed to testify after having undergone hypnosis to aid their memory, a minimum number of safeguards are absolutely essential" (p. 335). Courts naturally interpreted Orne to mean that adherence to his guidelines should be the test for the admissibility of the hypnotically refreshed testimony. Other courts may have believed that adherence to the guidelines was a guarantee that the hypnotically refreshed testimony was reliable. Orne tried to discourage both interpretations.

As the North Carolina Supreme Court noted in the *Peoples* case, "Dr. Orne, who designed the safeguards generally followed by courts which have adopted them, has admitted that they are ineffective in eliminating the dangers associated with hypnosis" (p. 188). Despite the fact that each guideline is scrupulously followed, a subject still may fantasize, confabulate, or lie while in trance. An expert will be unable to tell the false from the true memory, and even the subject may be unable to tell fact from fantasy, unless independent corroboration can be found.

On the more significant second misinterpretation, Orne presented a clear statement of his view in a talk before a convention of law professors held in Miami Beach in January 1988 (Orne, 1988). In his presentation, he stated that he had never intended the safeguards to be *criteria* for the admissibility of testimony. They were intended to provide the minimum requirements necessary for an expert to make an informed judgment concerning the hypnosis session. Without the safeguards, an expert's opinion would be less informed and less reliable.

The unfolding story of investigative hypnosis has been one of twists and turns. Just as it looked as if the total-exclusion rule would settle the issue, more convolutions appeared to complicate matters and throw the law back into turmoil.

THE RETREAT FROM INADMISSIBILITY

The first indication that the law would not settle down came when courts that had decided on total exclusion opened a loophole for prehypnotic testimony. Courts in Arizona, Colorado, Michigan, Minnesota, Nebraska, New York, and Pennsylvania from 1981 to 1983 adopted the total-exclusion rule, but permitted a person who had been hypnotized to testify about matters that had been adequately recorded before hypnosis was used.

The reasoning of the judges accepting this view was that the hypnosis did not contaminate information given before it was used. Matters remembered before hypnosis could be the subject of testimony. The courts did not especially concern themselves with the fact that the initial story, if erroneous, would be told with more conviction and confidence after the hypnosis. The prehypnosis exception satisfied the judicial concern that the total-exclusion rule might be unduly harsh. Despite the pitfalls of hypnotically refreshed recollection, courts were still sympathetic to witnesses and victims, and to the police who sought to curb the rising tide of crime.

Dr. David Spiegel's Rebuttal

Judges and police were not alone in their desire to protect witnesses who had been hypnotized from testimonial disqualification. Clinical therapists who treated victims of brutal crimes also wanted to preserve a place for the therapeutic use of hypnosis without risking a loss of their patients' legal rights. David Spiegel of the Stanford University Medical School is among those who have raised serious questions about the legitimacy of the *Shirley* ruling. His rebuttal of its basic premises attempts to find a middle path that does not deny to victims the therapeutic relief hypnosis may offer.

Spiegel (1987) begins by noting that the *Shirley* case was a factual nightmare that should never have been brought to trial. The victim was not credible, and her intoxication prevented retrieval of accurate memories. Furthermore, the *prosecutor* performed the hypnosis *on the eve of trial* and got her to change her story in significant detail. The California Supreme Court had valid reasons to be alarmed about the conduct of this growing army of "hypnotechnicians" who were "programming" witnesses. Instead of issuing a narrow ruling to prevent such misconduct, however, the court issued a broad ruling that unnecessarily invaded the province of therapists. According to Spiegel,

> What about the rape victim whose therapist used hypnosis to help her deal with the posttraumatic stress disorder and reviewed the events of the rape as part of a process of helping her overcome them? Prosecutors and police began discouraging victims and witnesses from obtaining such help, even strictly for treatment purposes. (1987, p. 102)

Spiegel cites an unreported California case concerning a rape victim who had received therapy involving "relaxation techniques." Her therapist testified that on one occasion she had probably been in trance. On the basis of the *Shirley* ruling, the trial judge dismissed the case, despite the fact that several witnesses were available and the fact that the alleged rapist was arrested at the scene of the crime. "As a psychiatrist who helps victims of violent crimes, it seems to be astounding and unconscionable that the Court [in *Shirley*] is attempting to tie the hands of therapists in helping these people," Spiegel concludes (1987, p. 103).

The *Shirley* case went wrong in overreacting to the fact that false memories can be elicited by hypnosis. That such contamination is *possible* is not proof that it is *probable*. After all, "even in the best of cases it is possible for a subject to come up with material that is responsive to internal needs or external factors rather than the truth" (Spiegel & Spiegel, 1987, p. 492).

The laboratory studies relied on by the court in *Shirley* are not necessarily indicative of how memory or hypnosis works in the clinical setting. The laboratory cannot duplicate the real emotional anguish of victims, nor can it duplicate the motivational factors leading a person to recall vital facts. Furthermore, laboratory experiments report immediate results, whereas hypnotically refreshed recollection must wait months or longer before court testimony is given. Finally, the global amnesia following traumatic events, and the clinical treatment of this amnesia with hypnosis, cannot be replicated in experimental settings in university laboratories.

Even beyond his critique of these experimental (as opposed to clinical) data, Spiegel (1987) believes that the court focused on the wrong point in *Shirley*. The crucial variable is not *hypnosis,* but rather *hypnotizability.* Spiegel begins his argument by noting that everyone is not hypnotizable even when hypnosis is attempted. Of those people who are hypnotizable, not all of them are put into trance during a hypnotic session. Of those who do enter trance, the possibility that their memories may be contaminated by undue suggestion is minor. Courts should therefore focus less on the fact of hypnosis and more on the subject's amenability, or vulnerability, to suggestion.

To illustrate this point, Spiegel observes that individuals who are highly hypnotizable, or exceptionally suggestible, can be unduly influenced *without* a formal induction of trance. Astute police interrogators and attorneys proficient in the use of leading questions have known for a long time that the answers one receives are influenced by the questions one poses. More recently, social psychologists (Goodman & Loftus, 1984; Hilgard & Loftus, 1979; Loftus, 1979b) have studied how language outside of trance can be unduly suggestive. Psychologists and lawyers have also studied the influence process with reference to eyewitness testimony (Moore, 1949; Wells & Loftus, 1984; Yarmey, 1979). They have concluded that contamination of memory occurs without the induction of trance.

Spiegel (1987) concludes that it is unfair and unwise to penalize individuals who have been hypnotized when mounting evidence demonstrates that memory taint is equally as likely in nonhypnotic encounters. Highly hypnotizable individuals, who are extremely vulnerable to suggestion, may in fact enter a spontaneous trance while being questioned

and find themselves compulsively complying to signals implanted by a forceful examiner. This scenario is even worse than the one envisioned by [Dr. Bernard] Diamond and the [*Shirley*] Court, because it is entirely possible that neither the examiner nor the subject is aware that hypnosis has taken place. (Spiegel, 1987, p. 108)

Instead of singling out hypnosis, the *Shirley* court should have asked more relevant questions:

> Is information elicited from hypnosis substantially less reliable than that elicited by other techniques? Or, to put the question another way: Is it so unreliable that the experience of a formal hypnotic induction should disqualify a witness, when, for example, a witness who has been convicted of perjury is not prohibited from testifying? (Spiegel, 1987, p. 111)

By not asking these questions, courts that follow a per se exclusion rule wind up reaching legal conclusions that are both ridiculous and unjust. One such instance occurred in Arizona, when prosecutors could not bring to trial a hypnotist who was accused of using hypnosis to seduce and rape several of his clients. "Why? You guess it—since the clients were hypnotized about—in fact, during—the crime, they could not testify. How far must this absurdity go before we can regain a more reasonable perspective?" (Spiegel, 1987, p. 117).

In states following a total-exclusion rule, judges have labored mightily to find ways to obey the rule and yet not reverse convictions. Loopholes have been devised to soften the harsh impact of a rule absolutely forbidding hypnotically refreshed recollection. California courts have pioneered in this pursuit. Because this state has seen just about every variation on the theme, we now take a closer look at what happened after the highest court in the state announced its rule of total exclusion in *Shirley*.

The California Experience

No state can boast a more convoluted encounter with forensic hypnosis than California. It was the first state to rule on investigative hypnosis (*People v. Ebanks*, 1897), and it has been in the vanguard ever since. When the door slammed shut in *Shirley* in 1982, it appeared that the matter was finally closed. But that was not to be the case. At first, all went smoothly; the first two appellate courts to consider the issue of hypnotically refreshed recollection after *Shirley* followed its rationale (*People v. Aquino*, 1982; *Guadalupe v. Sup. Ct.*, 1982). Then came the counterattack.

People v. Williams (1982) involved a police hypnotist who had refreshed the memory of a rape victim. After the hypnosis session, the victim identified the defendant as the assailant; the defendant claimed that this identification was tainted by the hypnosis. The court correctly noted that the rule announced in *Shirley* was not necessarily meant to apply in this case, but only in future cases. Whether or not to give the per se inadmissibility rule retroactive effect had been left to the discretion of the judges. Noting that the victim's testimony was crucial to the conviction, the court summed up its refusal to apply the *Shirley* rule by saying that "if we apply *Shirley* retroactively, this defendant escapes responsibility" (p. 925).

Judge Robert Gardner wrote the court's opinion. In a most unusual move, he also wrote a separate concurring opinion to vent his annoyance at the *Shirley* decision. He had reason to be angry: He had authored the unpublished court of appeal decision in *Shirley* that was so devastatingly overruled by the California Supreme Court. Gardner's concurring opinion in *Williams* made little attempt at legal analysis, but was forceful and emotional in its articulation of what a substantial number of judges believed.

The opinion began with a point of persuasion:

> *Shirley* is really more of a polemic than an opinion. As a polemic it makes interesting reading. The protagonists are so clearly defined.
>
> The prohypnosis expert is a lowly police psychologist, wretchedly educated ("Ed.E"), who is, of all things, a director of a "proprietary school" in Los Angeles. . . . This police psychologist is so dumb that he accepts at "face value" and "without question" the "somewhat extravagant conclusions" of a neurosurgeon who is apparently pretty much of a dummkopf himself.
>
> On the other hand, the antihypnosis experts are "highly experienced," "nationally known," "pioneers" and "respected authorities" who present the "generally accepted view" which is set forth in "scholarly articles" and "leading scientific studies." Thus, the guys in the white hats and those in the black hats are clearly defined and appropriately labeled. (p. 926)

The plain fact, Gardner continued, was that a majority of the states did permit hypnotically refreshed recollection to be admitted. Such testimony should be treated no differently from testimony refreshed by any other means. Cross-examination and expert testimony would demonstrate any infirmities in the hypnotically remembered testimony. Gardner trusted that the jury could see through "flaky testimony and pseudoscientific claptrap":

> I quite agree that we should not waste our valuable court time watching witch doctors, voodoo practitioners or *brujas* [sorcerers] go through the entrails of dead chickens in a fruitless search for the truth. However this is only because the practice is too time consuming and its probative value is zilch. (p. 928)

Granting that some evidence must be ruled out because it is too untrustworthy, Gardner summed up his point:

> [T]he idea that an eyeball witness to a transaction [can] be denied the opportunity to tell a jury his recollections of what he saw is disturbing to me whether that recollection has been refreshed by hypnosis, truth serum,

drugs, intimidation, coercion, coaching, brainwashing or impaired by the plain old passage of time. (p. 928)

Gardner was further dismayed by the fact that *Shirley* did not apply to defendants: "The idea that the predator may testify and yet his victim may not offends my sense of justice. It appears to me that the scales of justice are tilted—dangerously" (p. 928).

Gardner's eloquent rhetoric made no effort to evaluate the extensive hypnosis literature or to carefully examine the growing legal literature on hypnotically refreshed recollection. In short, it was almost completely devoid of any reasoned legal analysis. Nevertheless, his views found emotional favor throughout the courts of appeal. The next two cases followed his conclusion that *Shirley* should not be retroactive (*People v. Adams*, 1982; *People v. Parrison*, 1982). In 1984, however, the California Supreme Court decided the case of *People v. Guerra*, which eliminated this retroactivity argument, expressly rejecting Gardner's position. *Shirley* now was held to apply to every case in California.

With one loophole closed, the courts of appeal found others. In fact, from the 1982 *Williams* case through 1987, every decision of these courts managed to avoid the direct mandate of *Shirley*.

The Loopholes

Once the retroactivity loophole closed, others developed. The typical case facing the courts of appeal involved a defendant who claimed that his or her conviction should be reversed because the trial judge had permitted a previously hypnotized prosecution witness (or victim) to testify. The courts did not want to reverse these convictions on that ground, because (1) they did not distrust hypnosis, and (2) they favored admitting the testimony along with a warning to the jury to be cautious in fully accepting it. In order not to reverse *Shirley*, the courts needed arguments that would bypass Shirley's emphatic holding.

The courts found many loopholes to satisfy this goal. Though the loopholes are discussed in conjunction with California law, all of them have been applied by other courts in other states.

The hypnosis didn't work. Quite sensibly, the courts reasoned that if hypnosis was tried but was not successful, the testimony would be admissible because it was not hypnotically refreshed (*People v. Lopez*, 1980). This loophole has been especially appealing to courts across the country during the last few years. Many cases now permit a witness to testify even though hypnosis had been used or attempted, provided an expert is prepared to testify that the hypnosis was unsuccessful (*People v. Romero*, Colo., 1987) or that the subject was not hypnotizable (Spiegel, 1987).

There was no prejudicial error. Shirley permitted the appellate courts to uphold convictions, despite the admission of hypnotically refreshed memory, unless it was reasonably probable that a result more favorable to the defendant would be reached on retrial with the hypnotic testimony eliminated. If the defendant could demonstrate that the admission of the testimony was highly prejudicial, the conviction would have to be reversed.

The basic idea is simple. Even if a judge made a mistake in admitting hypnotically refreshed testimony, that mistake did not hurt the defendant's case, because sufficient other evidence was present to warrant conviction. Though an error, the law considers it "harmless." Several California courts have used this "harmless error" idea to uphold convictions (*People v. Glaude*, 1983; *People v. Brown*, 1985).

The California Supreme Court addressed such a case in its 1987 *People v. Johnson* decision. Here the government conceded that *Shirley* had been violated, but claimed that the error was not prejudicial to the defendant. The court disagreed. The victim's testimony was the only direct evidence linking the defendant to the crime. If this evidence were excluded at a retrial, the defendant would be substantially better off. As a consequence, the trial judge's ruling permitting the testimony harmed the defendant. The conviction had to be reversed.

Wholly unrelated matters. Suppose a witness is hypnotized, but the hypnosis session only explores one small piece of the criminal event. May the witness testify about other aspects of the crime not discussed during hypnosis? The answer is "yes," according to *People v. Huber* (1986). Nothing precludes the victim's testimony on matters not covered in trance.

Prehypnotic recollection. The possibility of an additional "escape hatch" from *Shirley* was suggested in some of the opinions of the California Supreme Court's 1984 *Guerra* decision. The invitation proved irresistible. In *People v. Zamarripa* (1985), the court of appeal applied the prehypnotic testimony exception. Many factors in the case made the court comfortable with that result. The victim's recollections *before trance* were tape-recorded and played to the jury. The evidence showed (1) that her prehypnosis and posthypnosis statements were consistent, and (2) that independent evidence supported her story. The hypnosis itself was conducted only for a limited purpose; all testimony related to that purpose was excluded at trial. Based on this strong record, the prehypnosis recollection exception seemed just.

The Guerra Case

Two years after its landmark opinion in *Shirley*, the California Supreme Court returned to investigative hypnosis issues in *People v. Guerra* (1984).

The facts of *Guerra* were not favorable to the police. Two men were charged with rape. The victim, Judy, and both men denied that there had been penetration, an essential element of the crime. A police officer who had taken one 4-day course and one 3-day course at Reiser's LEHI hypnotized Judy for the purpose of determining whether she could "remember" whether there might have been penetration. Judy was aware that this was the purpose of the hypnosis. To make matters worse, Judy and the police hypnotist were not strangers. They lived in the same apartment building, and the victim was grateful to the officer for fixing her automobile on a previous occasion.

Another police officer was assigned to tape-record the session, but he did not record the whole proceeding because he "kept going into hypnosis himself." The prehypnosis and posthypnosis discussions with the hypnotist were not recorded. During trance, Judy did not report penetration, but made equivocal remarks on the subject. She was given suggestions that she would recall other events more vividly after trance. It was during this unrecorded posttrance discussion that Judy first affirmatively claimed that she had been violated.

Both defendants moved to have Judy's posthypnosis testimony disqualified. The prosecutor claimed that "the penetration was something that she accidentally recalled after she was hypnotized" (p. 168). By contrast, a defense psychiatrist testified that the hypnotic session was an example of "psychological brainwashing" designed to induce her to "remember" that she had been penetrated. Another defense witness, a clinical psychologist, testified that she was responding in a "programmed" manner to the obvious demand characteristics of the situation. She knew what was desired from her and she delivered.

Despite strong pressure from police and prosecutors, the court held fast to its inadmissibility rule. Other state courts had by this time followed the reasoning of *Shirley*, and the California Supreme Court cited these cases with enthusiasm to justify its point that the prevailing trend was decidedly against investigative hypnosis. Cases holding to the "admissibility with safeguards" approach were discounted in light of Orne's "repudiation" (p. 188) of his own guidelines.

Failing to persuade the justices with case law, the prosecutor turned to the scientific community for assistance. Articles by psychiatrist David Spiegel (1987) and psychologist Helmut Relinger (1984) were presented as evidence that hypnosis can and should play a role in memory retrieval. Spiegel's article, unpublished at the time the court considered it, challenged *Shirley's* conclusions on several points:

> . . . how significant is the risk of intentional or unintentional cueing by the hypnotist, how often the hypnotized subject produces confabulations or other pseudomemories, how difficult it is to distinguish true from false

memories, how resistant the subject will be to cross-examination at trial, and how effective are procedural precautions in minimizing the dangers of using hypnosis to restore a witness's memory. (Spiegel, as cited in *Guerra*, 1984, p. 183)

The court objected to the tone of the article by stating that it was not "a dispassionate, objective report of a new clinical or experimental study of the reliability of posthypnotic testimony that might show some change in the consensus of the scientific community"; rather, it was "a frontal assault on the *Shirley* decision itself—and through it, on Dr. Bernard Diamond, one of the principal participants in that consensus" (p. 183).

Relinger's article claimed that hypnosis does enhance recall, provided that the material is meaningful and the recall is the product of free narrative rather than specific questioning. The court discounted his conclusion because (1) he summarized other studies, all of which were conducted before *Shirley* and all of which reached results with which the *Shirley* court was familiar; and (2) his article did not address the vital question of whether the enhanced recall was *accurate*. On that last point, the court cited several studies demonstrating that hypnotic hypermnesia "is purchased at the price of increased errors and probably also an increase in the subject's misplaced confidence in those errors" (p. 184). One portion of Relinger's paper did satisfy the court: his rejection of the television technique as unduly suggestive.

More important than the court's disagreement with the conclusions reached by Spiegel and Relinger was the manner in which the court treated that disagreement. The court freely acknowledged that a minority position within the scientific community supported the view that hypnosis does not necessarily, or excessively, taint the reliability of memory when compared to other memory retrieval techniques. The very fact that the scientific community was sharply divided was proof for the court that hypnosis as a reliable technique to refresh memory had not yet gained "general acceptance" to meet the requirements of the *Frye* rule:

It is not our function, however, to resolve any such disputes within the scientific community, any more than it is our task to determine whether posthypnotic testimony is reliable as a matter of scientific fact. . . . [T]he courts view the professional literature on hypnosis "as 'evidence,' not of the actual reliability of [hypnosis], but of its acceptance *vel non* in the scientific community." (p. 183)

Thus, the court planned to adhere to its rule of total exclusion for as long as the experimentalists and the clinicians introduced conflicting data or disagreed. The more heated the debate became, the more adamant the court planned to remain.

By the middle of 1987, it was clear that the California Supreme Court and the state courts of appeal were headed in opposite directions. Every Supreme Court case on hypnosis in the 1980s (*Shirley*, 1982; *Guerra*, 1984; *Johnson*, 1987) had been a *reversal* of convictions based on improperly admitted hypnotically refreshed memory. Every court of appeal decision after the middle of 1982, on the other hand, *upheld* convictions on the basis of the loophole arguments just discussed. This divergence might have continued, but fate had other plans. It was time for the people and their representatives to step into the controversy.

The Voters and the Legislators

Proposition 8 and the Supreme Court shakeup. The mood of the country in the early 1980s was conservative. Victims' rights organizations pressed public campaigns to stop judges from "coddling criminals." From the perspective of the public, and an increasing number of judges, it looked as though the law protected only the vicious and the deadly. Cries for the death penalty, fewer restrictions on police, and fewer inhibitions on courtroom testimony coalesced into an extensive and well-financed public campaign to loosen the rules of criminal procedure and to vote "liberal" judges off the California Supreme Court. Both campaigns succeeded.

In the June 1982 election, California voters passed Proposition 8, the so-called "truth in evidence" law. Under its terms, the per se exclusionary rule of *Shirley* appeared to be overthrown. Hypnotically refreshed recollection was now arguably admissible without restriction. The California Supreme Court upheld the constitutionality of Proposition 8 in *Brosnahan v. Brown* (1982). Four years later, the voters who had changed the law now acted to change the justices. In the November 1986 election, several judges were voted off the court, thereby giving the conservative California governor, George Deukmejian, the opportunity to appoint more conservative justices.

Meanwhile, as the voters were busily rewriting the law and redesigning the philosophical makeup of the Supreme Court, the legislators were also busy. Something had to be done to harmonize the polar opposites of exclusion under *Shirley* and admission under Proposition 8. At that point in time, no one was quite sure what the law in California was regarding investigative hypnosis.

California evidence code section 795. In 1984, the legislators sought a middle ground. They added a new provision to the California Evidence Code: Section 795, which permitted the admissibility of hypnotically refreshed testimony, provided the testimony was limited to those matters recalled and related prior to hypnosis. Furthermore, certain safeguards were necessary, especially the taping or recording of prehypnotic, hypnotic, and posthypnotic sessions.

The crucial question of who might perform the hypnosis was answered, to the detriment of the police. Though the police argued strenuously that investigative hypnosis is a specialty not requiring medical training, the legislature specified that only licensed physicians or psychologists experienced in the use of hypnosis were qualified. Section 795 further required that the hypnosis be performed independently of both the prosecution and the defense. In each case, a pretrial hearing would have to be held to determine whether the requirements of Section 795 had been met.

Now that police hypnotists are not qualified under the law, the volume of hypnosis cases in California is likely to shrink. If the police do use hypnosis by means of a licensed professional, adequate note taking and taping will be required.

Ironically, the prehypnosis solution reached by the legislators was in agreement with the thinking of some of the California Supreme Court's justices in the 1984 *Guerra* case, which had not yet been published at that time. For the first time since these investigative hypnosis issues had been raised, the judges, the legislators, and the voters had found a common meeting ground.

In its debut in the courts, Section 795 has been favorably received. *People v. Burroughs* (1987) held the section to be applicable to all cases tried after January 1, 1985, the day the section went into effect, even if the hypnosis had been performed before the section became law.

Section 795 was amended in 1987 to expand the list of professionals qualified to perform investigative hypnosis. In addition to the licensed physicians and psychologists originally designated, the amendment added (1) licensed clinical social workers experienced in the use of hypnosis; and (2) marriage, family, and child counselors certified in hypnosis by the Board of Behavioral Science Examiners.

The full text of Section 795, as amended through 1988, reads as follows:

> (a) The testimony of a witness is not inadmissible in a criminal proceeding by reason of the fact that the witness has previously undergone hypnosis for the purpose of recalling events which are the subject of the witness' testimony, if all of the following conditions are met:
> (1) The testimony is limited to those matters which the witness recalled and related prior to the hypnosis.
> (2) The substance of the prehypnotic memory was preserved in written, audiotape, or videotape form prior to the hypnosis.
> (3) The hypnosis was conducted in accordance with all of the following procedures:
> (A) A written record was made prior to hypnosis documenting the subject's description of the event, and information which was provided to the hypnotist concerning the subject matter of the hypnosis.
> (B) The subject gave informed consent to the hypnosis.
> (C) The hypnosis session, including the pre-and post-hypnosis interviews, was videotape recorded for subsequent review.

(D) The hypnosis was performed by a licensed medical doctor, psychologist, or licensed clinical social worker experienced in the use of hypnosis or a licensed marriage, family and child counselor certified in hypnosis by the Board of Behavioral Science Examiners and independent of and not in the presence of law enforcement, the prosecution, or the defense.

(4) Prior to admission of the testimony, the court holds a hearing pursuant to Section 402 of the Evidence Code at which the proponent of the evidence proves by clear and convincing evidence that the hypnosis did not so affect the witness as to render the witness' prehypnosis recollection unreliable or to substantially impair the ability to cross-examine the witness concerning the witness' prehypnosis recollection. At the hearing, each side shall have the right to present expert testimony and to cross-examine witnesses.

(b) Nothing in this section shall be construed to limit the ability of a party to attack the credibility of a witness who has undergone hypnosis, or to limit other legal grounds to admit or exclude the testimony of that witness.

A qualified professional called by the police or the defense in California for hypnotic memory refreshing should be familiar with the specific requirements of Evidence Code Section 795. Violation of its terms could create liability for professional malpractice.

Four cases concerning investigative hypnosis were decided by a conservative California Supreme Court in 1988. None of the four cases altered already existing California law, thus providing some reason to believe that the law finally may have stabilized.

While the law may have stabilized, the practice of investigative hypnosis continues to pose new questions. In particular, a case presently pending in the California Supreme Court raises some disturbing accusations of police use of covert hypnotic techniques in routine interrogations. *People v. Alcala* (1988) involved a highly vulnerable and suggestible witness who dramatically altered her story after being questioned by two police hypnosis specialists. They denied intending or attempting to hypnotize the witness and the trial judge accepted their word. Should the judge have permitted a psychologist to express his professional opinion that covert hypnotic techniques were employed?

After examining the transcripts, tapes and investigative reports documenting the questioning of the witness, the defense expert was prepared to testify that the following techniques were used to induce hypnosis without the witness's consent:

1. Repeatedly encouraging [the witness] to relax, disassociate, and watch her dreams and memories like a movie.
2. Influencing [the witness] to believe that she could easily hypnotize herself and that she did it all the time.
3. Repeated use of a technique known as "shingling suggestions"

whereby the hypnotist adds several unrelated suggestions to help the subject see what the hypnotist wants . . . [and] mixing actual memories or dreams with impressions or feelings, mixing actual memories or dreams with suggestions made by the hypnotist.

4. The use of a confabulation metaphor to get [the witness] to fill in gaps [in] her memory.
5. Erickson's "My Friend John" technique.
6. A game of "guess and think."
7. Causing [the witness] to mix dream with reality and influencing her to accept the truth of her dreams.
8. The use of role reversal to manipulate certainty of information.
9. Influencing [the witness] to believe that only others were responsible for evaluations of the truth of her memories so as to create dissociation.
10. Suggesting the need to become an eyewitness to protect herself from [the defendant].
11. Suggesting that the man she saw had been in a fight, had blood on his shirt, and had menacing eyes.
12. Repetition of a variety of techniques to break down her resistance to being certain.

Alcala points to a potentially difficult legal problem: Will the police be able to bypass the barriers erected by *Shirley* and the legislature by utilizing hypnotic techniques but not calling what they are doing "hypnosis?" The California Supreme Court may choose to answer that question in 1989.

Two other important questions await resolution by the California Supreme Court. Section 795 of the California Evidence Code specifically applies only to *criminal* proceedings, thus leaving open the possibility that less stringent admission rules may be applied in *civil* cases. Litigators throughout the country have indicated that they intend to utilize hypnosis more frequently in civil trials. The civil arena may be the next frontier for forensic hypnosis.

A second issue yet to be resolved was raised but not answered in two recent California Supreme Court cases. Suppose a hypnotherapist or an expert uses one or more hypnosis tests to determine the depth of trance or the hypnotizability of the subject. Must these tests pass the *Frye* rule standard of general acceptance in the scientific community?

In *Caro* (1988) and in *Johnson* (1989), Dr. David Spiegel had testified that after examining the recordings of the hypnosis sessions, and testing the hypnotizability of each subject, it was clear that the prosecution witnesses had not been hypnotized. Spiegel based his opinion in part on his use of the Hypnotic Induction Profile (Spiegel & Spiegel, 1978). The defense claimed that the Profile failed to satisfy the *Frye* test. In each case, the California

Supreme Court sidestepped the issue by noting that Spiegel did not exclusively rely on the Profile in forming his opinion and that other evidence supported his conclusion.

These cases may signal a new defense strategy to challenge hypnotherapists: If no standardized procedures or tests were used to determine hypnotizability and depth of trance, the hypnotic procedure may arguably be flawed. If such tests were used, however, they may be challenged under the *Frye* rule as lacking general acceptance in the hypnosis community. Guidance from courts on this crucial issue hopefully will soon be forthcoming.

THE AMERICAN MEDICAL ASSOCIATION SPEAKS

The 1985 Report

In 1958, the AMA first recognized hypnosis as a valid medical and therapeutic procedure. The proper use of hypnosis in investigative settings was not discussed at that time, but by the mid-1980s the controversy surrounding this issue had grown so strident that the AMA appointed a panel of its Council on Scientific Affairs to prepare a study and state a position. In 1985 the council released its report, entitled "Scientific Status of Refreshing Recollection by the Use of Hypnosis."

The panel consisted of eight members, including Martin Orne, Bernard Diamond, Herbert Spiegel, and David Spiegel. Several specialists in memory and hypnosis were consulted to assist the panel members in their deliberations. As might be expected whenever such a varied cross-section of professional opinions is represented, the panel members engaged in intensive and occasionally heated debates.

The panel noted two basic methods of refreshing memory with hypnosis: age regression and direct or indirect suggestion. With each method, however, the panel found problems.

Age Regression

Are memories recollected by age regression accurate? Freud intitially believed that they are, but later recognized that such memories contain a strong emotional mixture of fears, facts, and fancies. Controlled laboratory studies have generally not attempted to establish the accuracy of re-experienced events, but in those instances where such attempts were made, the evidence does not support accuracy. By consensus, the panel concluded that age regression is "the subjective reliving of earlier experiences as though they were real—which does not necessarily replicate earlier events" (Council on Scientific Affairs, 1985, p. 1919).

Direct or Indirect Suggestion

The second, and more frequently utilized, method of memory retrieval in investigative hypnosis is the use of direct or indirect suggestion. The panel had in mind the "television technique" which it described as follows:

> Prior to hypnosis, it is explained to the subject that everything a person sees, hears, or experiences is recorded in the subconscious and can be accurately accessed in hypnosis. Once hypnotized, the subject is told to imagine a television screen in his mind and that he will soon begin to see a documentary of the to-be-remembered event. As in a sporting event on television, he will be able to stop motion, go fast forward or backward, and "zoom in" in order to see any detail that might otherwise not be clear. Finally, it is explained that, while he may see himself in this documentary and accurately observe what happens, he need not experience any of the troublesome feelings or pain that may have occurred at the time, but rather will see in an objective manner the events that transpired. (p. 1919)

In this technique, the television metaphor is presented to the subject as fact. But is it true that the mind stores memories in the same way in which a videocassette recorder stores images? If not, the television technique is a suggestion for confabulation that may have the effect of irrevocably tainting the subject's recollection.

In order to answer the question of whether memories are accurately stored in the mind, the panel explored the literature on memory, clinical case studies, field reports, and other evidence. When it had fully digested this material, the panel reached the following conclusions:

1. There is no scientific evidence that hypnosis increases the recall of meaningless or nonsense material (which it would do if the mind acts like a tape recorder).
2. Hypnosis does not increase "recognition" memory.
3. Hypnosis can enhance "recall" memory, but at a price: The subject will produce *more* memories, both accurate and inaccurate. Hypnosis stimulates productivity, not accuracy.
4. Hypnosis may make the subject more vulnerable or susceptible to subtle cues given wittingly or unwittingly by the hypnotist.

The panel was forthright in acknowledging the fundamental problem in exploring questions of hypnotically refreshed recollection: Laboratory studies cannot duplicate the trauma experienced by real-life victims, nor can they duplicate the motivation such victims have in memory recall. On the other hand, real-life experiences do not meet scientific standards of rigor and replication. For this reason, clinicians have dismissed laboratory studies as irrelevant, and experimentalists have dismissed clinical reports as anecdotal.

In essence, the panel concluded that at best hypnosis may aid in the production of memories, but these memories will not necessarily be accurate. An unfortunate by-product of this increase in accurate and inaccurate memory, however, is an increase in the subject's confidence about the accuracy of *all* such memories: "[H]ypnosis may increase the appearance of certitude without a concurrent increase of veracity" (Council on Scientific Affairs, 1985, p. 1921). Neither the subject nor the hypnotist can correctly differentiate between accurate recall and pseudomemory or confabulation.

What, then, is the proper role for hypnosis in investigative settings? The panel recognized that that the production of new information by hypnosis may be of value to police agencies as potential leads. It is for this purpose, and this purpose only, that hypnosis may be beneficial. But even in this restricted setting, the panel suggested two limitations:

1. Any information produced as investigative leads should be subjected to corroboration. Furthermore, the fact that some information is physically corroborated will not guarantee the accuracy of other recollected information, nor will it guarantee that the recollection of any information was free of impermissible suggestion.

2. Even in the limited investigative setting, certain procedural safeguards must be followed. These safeguards are similar to the Orne guidelines adopted in the *Hurd* case and to the guidelines set forth in California Evidence Code Section 795.

Reaction to the Report

As might be expected, the AMA panel's report drew mixed reviews. Stories about internal dissent and dissatisfaction on the part of panel members began to surface. Overt attacks on the panel's reasoning and conclusions also began to appear.

Reiser's Response

The report did not please police psychologist Martin Reiser (1986), because it provided a very limited role for forensic hypnosis and because it urged as a safeguard that only licensed psychologists or psychiatrists, not police officers, perform the hypnosis. Reiser objected to the report on both scientific and political grounds.

On the technical side, according to Reiser, the panel made misstatements of fact in its evaluation of the existing literature and ignored significant studies supporting the view that hypermnesia does occur when hypnosis is used to assist in the recall of meaningful material. In addition, the panel discounted police studies clearly demonstrating that the use of hypnosis produced information of value in over 75% of the cases; when this information was independently checked, it was found to be accurate approximately 80% of the time.

Reiser's main objections were political. He suggested that some panel members might have an antipolice bias. Why, for example, had the panel not sought input from police officials with the most experience in these matters? Would it not make sense to request input from officers who had handled hundreds of these investigative cases?

Reiser further argued that the report was unsatisfactory even to its members. Citing the internal grumbling that surfaced after the report was completed, Reiser claimed that the document was not a neutral scientific study, but rather a political compromise that left no one pleased.

Why had the AMA even addressed the issue of investigative hypnosis? According to Reiser,

> [I]nvestigative hypnosis is not a medical procedure, it is an investigative interview. It seems odd that the AMA is now attempting to dictate the parameters of practice in an essentially criminal justice area involving witnesses to crimes and not patients in treatment. (1986, p.1)

In conclusion, Reiser argued that the AMA report should not be supported "because of the political motivations, the lack of scientific accuracy, and the unwarranted conclusions" (p. 3).

Clinicians' Response

Police officials were not alone in finding some aspects of the AMA report unsatisfactory. Clinicians providing hypnotherapy to victims of trauma and crime also found the document too restrictive.

Whereas Reiser concentrated his disagreements on what the report said, Beahrs (1988) chose a point of attack based on what the report did not say. Beahrs argued that the rule of exclusion advocated by the report was grounded on three assumptions that were barely addressed by the panel. Each assumption, he claimed, was factually weak.

First, the report was based on the idea that the hypnotic state can be differentiated from nonhypnotic situations. Although this notion may be plausible in structured laboratory experimentation, it is not plausible in everyday situations, where shock, trauma, or other events may create hypnotic-like conditions. The second assumption follows from the first: The hypnotic condition is preceded by a formalized procedure known as an "induction." This ritual may help to define laboratory work, but the literature is filled with illustrations of people entering spontaneous trances without any formal, or informal, inductions.

The final assumption concerns the alleged ability of hypnosis to create false or inaccurate memories and an increase in confidence about all recollections. To justify a rule of exclusion on this ground, "problematic distortion and false certitude must occur to a profound degree in hypnosis and only to a relatively trivial degree outside it" (Beahrs, 1988, p. 21). The evidence does not support this assumption. In fact, similar distortions occur in eyewitness testimony and the use of clever or sophisticated leading questions in interrogations. Furthermore, posthypnotic recollections are not always, and not necessarily, tainted. Quite often, they are accurate and independently verifiable.

Beahrs, extending arguments initially made by David Spiegel, concluded that the panel's rule of exclusion, by failing to give appropriate weight to these considerations, was seriously flawed. It is only legally and logically sensible to exclude recollections refreshed by hypnosis if (1) hypnosis is a distinct and separate state, readily distinguishable from nonhypnosis; (2) hypnosis can be shown to be *the* cause of memory contamination or distortion; and (3) the contamination caused by hypnosis is greater than the contamination ordinarily present in eyewitness and interrogation situations. Because these assumptions are not correct, the rule of exclusion, which singles out hypnosis for censure, is wrong.

Not only is the rule of exclusion wrong, according to Beahrs; it is also unjust because it adversely affects those who are the most vulnerable and the most in need of therapeutic and legal assistance—crime victims and the highly suggestible. Beahrs would allow the legal system's use of cross-examination and the hypnotist's adherence to procedural guidelines to be the criteria for evaluating hypnotically refreshed recollection. Exclusion, he insisted, is too harsh a remedy for too minor a disease.

As the 1980s began to draw to a close, experimentalists, clinicians, prosecutors, police, defense lawyers, and almost every state and federal court had been heard from on the issue of hypnotically refreshed recollection. Only one voice had been silent: the U.S. Supreme Court.

THE U.S. SUPREME COURT SPEAKS

Rock v. Arkansas

After hundreds of cases on investigative hypnosis had appeared in appellate courts throughout the country, the U.S. Supreme Court finally issued its first significant ruling in the summer of 1987.

Rock v. Arkansas involved a wife accused and convicted of killing her husband. Though Rock could not remember some details of the quarrel that left her husband shot to death, she claimed it was an accident; she had no intent to harm him. At the suggestion of her attorney, Rock consulted a neuropsychologist with experience in hypnosis. The psychologist took notes on her story and then hypnotized her twice. Both hypnosis sessions were taped, but the initial prehypnosis interview was not.

At trial, the *prosecutor* made the argument that hundreds of *defense* lawyers had made in other cases: Posthypnosis testimony is inadmissible because it is unreliable. The trial judge followed the per se inadmissibility approach, but ruled that Rock could testify about matters that were contained in the psychologist's notes of the prehypnosis interview, augmented by whatever else the psychologist could remember was said at that time.

Defense counsel argued for an exception for defendants, as opposed to witnesses, based on the constitutional right to testify on one's own behalf. The Arkansas Supreme Court decided against this claim. The court cited two cases to support its decision that a defendant who uses hypnosis to refresh recollection can constitutionally be held incompetent to testify about posthypnosis information. Both cases involved defendants in worse circumstances than Rock, because they remembered virtually nothing before hypnosis.

But the Arkansas court failed to read those cases with sufficient care. In both cases, the courts took pains to observe that the testimony of the defendants was "completely uncorroborated." Rock, however, did have other proof, which the Arkansas Supreme Court chose not to mention in its opinion. She appealed to the U.S. Supreme Court.

The Justices had no easy time; they split 5–4 on the hypnosis issue. Justice Blackmun, writing for the majority, revealed the information excluded by the Arkansas courts. Rock had no new memories under hypnosis, but after the sessions she remembered two vital facts: (1) that her finger was not on the trigger, and (2) that the gun had discharged when her husband forcibly grabbed her arm. After this revelation, defense counsel had the gun sent to an expert for analysis. The expert reported that the gun was defective. It was prone to fire when jostled, *even if the trigger was not pulled.*

Blackmun noted that the Arkansas per se rule "operates to the detriment of any defendant who undergoes hypnosis, without regard to the reasons for it, the circumstances under which it took place, or any independent verification of the information it produced" (p. 2712). The severity of this rule, which excludes "all posthypnosis testimony," violated Rock's right to testify on her own behalf. According to the majority, "the Arkansas Supreme Court failed to perform the constitutional analysis that is necessary" in this case (p. 2712). Rock's conviction was overturned and the case was sent back to the trial judge, who now had to reconsider admitting her posthypnotic testimony. Rock could show that the psychologist made no improper suggestions, that the sessions were taped, and that there was corroborating evidence. The trial judge was instructed to consider these factors.

Before reaching its conclusion, the U.S. Supreme Court majority recognized that although hypnosis has been officially endorsed for therapeutic purposes by physicians or psychologists, its use "in criminal investigations . . . is controversial, and the current medical and legal view of its appropriate role is unsettled" (p. 2713). The majority stayed neutral on the larger question of the admissibility of hypnotically refreshed recollections of witnesses, rather than defendants, by stating that "we express no opinion on that issue" (p. 2712, fn. 15). True to its word, the majority opinion was written just carefully enough to make it unclear whether the Justices favored or feared hypnosis in the courtroom.

No such ambiguity existed with the four dissenting Justices. Led by Chief Justice Rehnquist, the conservative wing of the Court took a decidedly antihypnosis stance:

> [A] hypnotized individual becomes subject to suggestion, is likely to confabulate, and experiences artificially increased confidence in both true and false memories following hypnosis. No known set of procedures . . . can insure against the inherently unreliable nature of such testimony. (p. 2715)

The dissent challenged the legal analysis of the majority Justices and faulted them for not permitting the states the right to set their own laws on hypnosis. Despite substantial reservations about the reliability of hypnosis, the dissenting Justices did not wish to tread on what they regarded as discretionary powers reserved to the states. In their view, with so many different approaches adopted by different states, Arkansas was reasonable in adopting the one it did, and its choice should not be overturned.

Now that the U.S. Supreme Court has spoken, what has it said? Unfortunately, very little. *Rock* involved a very limited factual situation. Very few cases focus on a defendant seeking to testify after hypnosis. (Defendants usually have wanted hypnotists to testify as to what the defendants said in hypnosis, or have asked to have the tapes introduced into evidence.) No other factual circumstance is covered by the Court's ruling. Even in the single, limited circumstance that *Rock* covers, the trial judge still may exclude a defendant's posthypnotic testimony. The Supreme Court struck down a per se exclusion; it did not require a per se admission.

The holding in *Rock* is narrow. The potentially more far-reaching issue is yet to be decided: What will the U.S. Supreme Court do when faced with a case of a witness or victim rather than a defendant? Because the majority was noncommittal, it is difficult to predict how the Justices comprising it might vote on this broader issue. One member of that majority, Justice Lewis Powell, Jr., has retired. His replacement, Justice Anthony Kennedy, was confirmed in February 1988; his views are not known.

The dissenters took an antihypnosis position. Does this mean that they will decide against the prosecutors? Not necessarily. In *Rock*, Arkansas courts had taken a hard line against hypnosis. The dissent stood up for the right of each state to make its own choice. The antihypnosis language could be explained as support for the reasonableness of the selection made by Arkansas judges, not as a decision against hypnosis. In other words, the dissent could take a prohypnosis position where witnesses or victims were involved without being bound by its *Rock* language.

Thus, the question remains open; nothing in *Rock* foretells the answer. Because of its limited factual setting and inconclusive opinions, the U.S. Supreme Court's one major case on investigative hypnosis is likely to have little impact on the law—unless, of course, people do not simply *read* the case, but *read into* it.

Lawyers have appeared on television talk shows proclaiming that the Supreme Court has endorsed hypnosis. Even though the Court's decision does not necessarily support this view, these lawyers have expressed their intention to make more frequent use of hypnosis. They predict an increase in the number of cases involving hypnotically refreshed recollection. Will the lower courts reach this same conclusion? The initial evidence suggests that judges are willing to read more into *Rock* than the case actually holds. By so doing, these judges hope to keep alive some role for investigative hypnosis in the courtroom.

Post-*Rock* Cases

There have been more than three dozen cases decided since *Rock*; about one-third of them have been in federal courts and two-thirds in state courts. Half of these cases fail to mention *Rock*. Most of the other half discuss *Rock* briefly or distinguish it on factual grounds. Only half a dozen cases add additional insight (see *State v. Adams*, S.D., 1988; *Bundy v. Dugger*, 11th Cir., 1988; *People v. Romero*, Colo., 1987). They read *Rock* as strongly suggesting or requiring that hypnotically refreshed recollection be admissible if proper safeguards are met. Ironically, just as the movement throughout the country has shifted dramatically toward a per se exclusion rule (except for prehypnosis testimony meeting adequate guidelines), what the U.S. Supreme Court did not say may send the law spinning off in another direction.

The Colorado Supreme Court illustrates this movement. In *Romero* (1987), the police questioned Romero about the murder of two sisters. Arrangements were made for Romero to undergo hypnosis, but he would only do so if given immunity for what he might say. The police arranged what is called "passive-involvement" immunity, and Romero consented to the hypnosis. When Romero was charged with participation in the crime, his counsel sought to bar prosecution on the basis of the immunity. The court of appeals agreed and overturned Romero's conviction. He was freed, but only temporarily. The government appealed to the Colorado Supreme Court.

The court interpreted the immunity narrowly, against Romero's position. Having thus cleared the way for Romero to be tried, the court addressed the further issue of the hypnosis of Romero and of two witnesses. Romero did not testify at trial, so no issue was raised as to the admissibility of his hypnotic recollections. He had, however, made posthypnotic incriminating statements to several people. Romero argued that these witnesses could not repeat his statements because the hypnosis had tainted his remarks. The court easily dismissed Romero's hypnosis by noting that Romero was not in "an altered hypnotic state" during the sessions. No trance, no taint.

The hypnosis performed on other witnesses provided a tougher issue. Earlier Colorado appellate courts had applied a per se exclusion rule, permitting only prehypnotic recollections to be admitted. In *Romero*, the Colorado Supreme Court rejected this approach in favor of a case-by-case determination by trial judges of the reliability of hypnotically refreshed recollection. To assist trial judges in performing this duty, the Court listed "procedures [that] should be followed in future cases." Because these procedures also serve as the basis for an expert to make an informed judgment concerning the use of investigative hypnosis techniques in a particular case, they are quoted at length here:

> [T]he trial court should consider the totality of circumstances bearing on the issue of reliability, including the following factors: the level of training in the clinical uses and forensic applications of hypnosis by the person performing the hypnosis; the hypnotist's independence from law enforcement investigators, prosecution, and defense; the existence of a record of any information given or known by the hypnotist concerning the case prior to the hypnosis session; the existence of a written or recorded account of the facts as the hypnosis subject remembers them prior to undergoing hypnosis; the creation of recordings of all contacts between the hypnotist and the subject; the presence of persons other than the hypnotist and the subject during any phase of the hypnosis session, as well as the location of the session; the appropriateness of the induction and memory retrieval techniques used; the appropriateness of using hypnosis for the kind of memory loss involved; and the existence of any evidence to corroborate the hypnotically-enhanced testimony. (p. 1017)

The Colorado Supreme Court upheld the trial judge's decision to admit the hypnotically refreshed testimony. Colorado thus moved from per se exclusion to admissibility with safeguards.

Justice Lohr, in a specially concurring opinion, revealed the court's underlying motivation when he noted that "in light of the implications of *Rock*, I accept the approach adopted by the majority" (p. 1019). He noted that the trend across the country was to accept the per se rule, but *Rock* "seems to dictate an approach" requiring a more individualized determination in each case. It is clear, however, that *Rock* demands no such interpretation. At a later point in his opinion, Justice Lohr acknowledged that "the actual holding in *Rock* is limited to rejection of a *per se* rule that prevents *a defendant* from testifying" (p. 1021, emphasis added). Nevertheless, he concluded that "the language of the opinion has broader implications" (p. 1021).

Rock certainly does not require the result reached in *Romero*. The Colorado Supreme Court's decision says a great deal about the judges' preference for hypnosis, but not much about their ability to read U.S. Supreme Court cases with precision. In other words, these judges used *Rock* as an excuse to favor hypnosis. The Colorado Supreme Court could just as easily have upheld the lower court's per se rule without violating constitutional principles.

Why are judges willing to read implications into *Rock* beyond the actual language of that case? Justice Lohr has suggested an answer:

> [I]t is difficult to find a principled basis for allowing the defendant to offer post-hypnosis testimony while excluding that of other defense witnesses. Similarly, if the defense witnesses can present hypnotically enhanced testimony, it is unfair to prevent the prosecution from introducing such evidence. (p. 1021)

The "slippery-slope" argument—that it is difficult to find a principled basis to accept a defendant's evidence and yet to reject the evidence of the defendant's witnesses—is not logically persuasive. Slippery-slope problems are the most common in law; every branch of jurisprudence faces them on a daily basis. Sometimes a line must arbitrarily be drawn somewhere, because anywhere it is drawn will in fact be arbitrary. Here, however, the line is not arbitrary. There is a difference between a defendant and his or her witnesses. The witnesses are not on trial and do not have a constitutional right to present a defense on their own behalf.

Once his mistaken premise is gone, Justice Lohr's other argument falls as well. The defense does not have the right to place hypnotized witnesses on the stand, nor does the prosecution. All witnesses are treated equally; whether they would be called by the prosecution or the defense is immaterial.

Lohr's real objection is to the point that a victim cannot testify and a defendant can. This superficially appears to be favoring the predator over the prey, and indeed it does do so. Whether such a preference is unfair depends upon whether, as Aristotle noted so long ago in Book V of his *Nichomachean Ethics,* equals are being treated unequally. In this case, they are not. As an illustration, juries and judges are more likely to accept the testimony of victims who have been hypnotized and offer *incriminating* evidence than they are to accept the testimony of defendants who have been hypnotized and offer *exonerating* evidence.

Our constitutional democracy expressly protects the rights of criminal defendants. This principle is often capsulized in the expression that it is better that nine guilty persons go free than that one innocent person be convicted. Although this might seem an expensive tradeoff, it must be remembered that our constitution was forged in an era of oppressive government that did not balk at reversing the formula. Justice Lohr's concerns strike an emotional chord within us. But it must be remembered, as Aristotle pointed out, that it is also unjust to treat unequals equally. That is what Justice Lohr would have us do.

Because of its emotional resonance, other courts will respond to Lohr's points by doing what the Colorado Supreme Court did: reading *Rock* so broadly as to negate the constitutional feasibility of a per se exclusion rule. The Texas Court of Criminal Appeals has provided a clear illustration. In *Zani v. State* (1988), the court went even further than *Romero* in rejecting a per se rule. The *Zani* court was *persuaded* that the per se approach was correct, yet felt constitutionally blocked from so holding:

> Were we writing on an entirely clean slate we would be inclined to hold that it has not been shown that hypnosis is a generally accepted means of refreshing memory that is either historically accurate or comparable in accuracy to pristine recollection. Thus we would likely follow those jurisdictions which have fashioned a rule of per se exclusion of any evidence not documented or otherwise memorialized as the product of prehypnotic memory. The recent opinion of the Supreme Court of the United States in *Rock v. Arkansas* . . . , however, has rendered such a position untenable. (p. 242)

Justice Lohr's reasoning was used to support the *Zani* conclusion that hypnotically refreshed recollection is admissible if certain safeguards are met. Thus, the *Zani* opinion is a compelling illustration of how poor logic can sway even critical minds.

If courts continue to misread *Rock*, every state that has adopted a per se rule may now expect to have that rule constitutionally challenged. All the questions previously raised and apparently settled may once again be brought before the courts for reconsideration. The law of investigative hypnosis remains in flux.

THE STATE OF THE LAW AND THE LAW OF THE STATES

The explosion of cases in the first half of the 1980s began tapering off during the second half of the decade. By the middle of 1988, judges had evolved four approaches for handling investigative hypnosis claims involving the testimony of prosecution witnesses or victims:

1. *Hypnosis is admissible.* The defendant can question the credibility of the testimony and may receive a cautionary instruction for the jury about the imperfections of hypnotically refreshed recollection.

2. *Hypnosis is admissible if safeguards are met.* The prosecutor has to demonstrate that the hypnosis sessions were conducted with proper safeguards to reduce the possibility of suggestion and confabulation. Some courts require the prosecutor to meet this burden of proof by "clear and convincing evidence," whereas other courts have settled for the less stringent "preponderance of the evidence" ("more likely than not") standard.

3. *Hypnosis is admissible if the trial judge concludes that the hypnotically refreshed recollection is reliable.* Unlike the first approach, here a judge performs an initial screening of the testimony; unlike the second approach, here no prior safeguards have to be met. The judge may look at "the totality of the circumstances" of the case in deciding whether the hypnotically refreshed memory was reliable. This approach has been favored by a majority of the most recent decisions.

4. *Hypnosis is inadmissible per se.* Most courts following this approach permit the witness or victim to testify about prehypnosis memories, provided that those memories are adequately documented or recorded. Other safeguards, as in the second approach, may also be imposed before prehypnosis memories can be admitted.

In states where the police are expressly forbidden to perform the hypnosis, licensed physicians, psychiatrists, psychologists, or other specifically designated professionals may be brought in to conduct the forensic hypnosis. If the *Rock* decision continues to be interpreted as favoring hypnotically refreshed recollection, an increasing number of investigative uses of hypnosis can be expected.

One of four additional events could seriously alter the law of investigative hypnosis:

1. Definitive laboratory studies' producing compelling data for or against the accuracy of hypnotically influenced recall.
2. The U.S. Supreme Court's issuing a conclusive ruling squarely on the issue of hynotized witnesses or victims.
3. Legislators' passing statutes regulating police use of hypnosis.
4. Professional hypnosis associations' lobbying successfully on behalf of clinicians who use hypnosis.

Short of these possibilities, the law governing the investigative use of hypnosis is now temporarily settled in most states, but only until the next round of post-*Rock* questions begins the process anew.

Part IV

Hypnosis and Memory

Hypnosis and Memory

CHAPTER 6

Defining Hypnosis

The expert witness and the lawyer both need to be able to define clearly what hypnosis is and what it is not. Unfortunately, this is no simple task. The plethora of divergent definitions provides us with more of a labyrinth than a clear path to our goal. Not only do visions of hypnosis shift substantially when delineated by psychologists and lawyers; there is almost as much disagreement within disciplines as there is between them.

A dictionary of psychology and psychiatry defines hypnosis as follows:

> A superficial or deep trance state resembling sleep, induced by suggestions of relaxation and concentrated attention to a single object. The subject becomes highly suggestible and responsive to the hypnotist's influence, and can be induced to recall forgotten events, become insensitive to pain, control vasomotor changes and, in the hands of an experienced hypnotherapist, gain relief from tensions, anxieties and other psychological symptoms. (Goldenson, 1984, p. 358)

Psychologists in different camps take varying views of hypnosis:

> An artificially induced state, usually (though not always) resembling sleep, but physiologically distinct from it, which is characterized by heightened suggestibility, and as a result of which certain sensory, motor and memory abnormalities may be induced more readily than in the normal state. (Weitzenhoffer, 1953, p. 3)

> [B]ehavior resulting from positive attitudes, strong motivations, and positive enhanced expectancies toward the situation in which the subject finds himself thus willing to follow suggestions of the hypnotist. (Barber, Spanos, & Chaves, 1974, p. 23)

> [A] state or condition where the subject focuses his mind on the suggestions of the hypnotist so that he is able to experience distortions of mem-

121

ory or perception. For the time being, the subject suspends disbelief and lowers his critical judgment. (Orne, 1983, p. 67)

[T]he induction of a peculiar psychological state which permits the subject to reassociate and reorganize his inner psychological complexities in a way suitable to the unique items of his own inner psychological experiences. (Erickson, 1980, Vol. III, p. 188)

[A] natural state of mind better understood in terms of two familiar functions . . . imagination and self suggestion. (Araoz, 1981, p. 1)

[A]n induced psychological regression, issuing in the setting of a particular regressed relationship between two people, in a relatively stable state which includes a subsystem of the ego with varying degrees of control of the ego apparatuses. (Gill & Brenman, 1959, p. xxiii)

[A]n altered state of the organism originally and usually produced by a repetition of stimuli in which suggestion (no matter how defined) is more powerful than usual. (Marcuse, 1959, p. 21)

More briefly, hypnosis has been defined as follows:

1. Altered states of mind (Hilgard, 1965; Orne, 1959)
2. A trance (Erickson, 1967)
3. A controlled dissociated state (West, 1960)
4. Intensified concentration (Debetz & Sunnen, 1985; Frankel, 1976; Spiegel & Spiegel, 1978)
5. Concentrated awareness (Morgan, 1983)
6. Atavism (Meares, 1960)
7. A non state explainable by experimental and relationship characteristics (Barber, 1969)
8. Role enactment (Sarbin & Coe, 1972)
9. A habit of heightened susceptibility to prestige suggestion (Hull, 1933)
10. Goal-directed behavior (White, 1941)

Many investigators have taken a "mix-and-match" technique, combining definitional elements to fit their particular clinical or experimental utilization of hypnosis. Some researchers argue that there is no such "state" of hypnosis at all (e.g., Barber, 1957, 1962).

Fromm and Shor (1979) address this problem by looking to the philosophical bases of the study of science. They explore hypnosis both as a subjective experience that can be best understood by reference to the internal workings of the subject, and as a group of objective, observable behaviors. This distinction has direct relevance for the practice of hypnotherapy in conjunction with the legal process.

In approaching our own working definition, we examine the multiplicity of phenomena classified as "hypnosis" and the variety of theoretical approaches before turning attention to the host of misconceptions that surround the use of hypnosis.

PHENOMENA OF HYPNOSIS

Distinguishing Hypnotic from Nonhypnotic Behavior

Many phenomena that occur in daily life have been classified as hypnotic. We are regularly exposed to propaganda, advertisements, music, repetitive exercise, mothers rocking or singing their infants to sleep, dramatic performances, and television. The more a person experiences these events as personally meaningful and his or her reactions as self-generated, the more likely an uncritical acceptance is. Whether influence or suggestion of this sort is best defined under the rubric "hypnosis" may be open to question. What is clear is that the subjective experience of hypnosis has a great deal in common with a number of other mental events that require intense concentration, altered states of consciousness, and at least a partial suspension of disbelief.

However, hypnosis is also different from personally induced mental events (e.g., meditation) or engrossing external events in both quantitative and subjectively qualitative ways. Although many authors have argued that all hypnosis is essentially self-hypnosis, hypnosis as we are examining it here occurs in an interpersonal situation. It is generally assumed that the greater the rapport with the therapist, the more likely the client is to go into trance and the deeper the hypnotic trance is likely to be.

Addressing this point, Orne (1972) has distinguished hypnotic from normal behavior:

> Hypnotic phenomena can only be distinguished when suggestions are given which distort his perception or memory. The hypnotized individual can be identified only by his ability to respond to suitable suggestions by appropriately altering any or all modalities of perception and memory. (p. 102)

Characteristics of the Trance State

Hilgard (1977) and others have catalogued a host of different characteristics that have been used to define the hypnotic trance. Determination of whether a subject is in hypnosis can be made when he or she experiences any of them. The deeper the hypnosis (trance), the more characteristics are likely to be present.

1. *Dissociation:* The ability to detach oneself from an environment and also observe one's own self. This requires the ability to split awareness. Hypnotic subjects are subjectively able to step out of their selves and watch.

2. *Detachment:* A splitting process in which distortions of one's body in space and time occur. People often report alterations in their perceptions of their arms or legs. They report being able to observe themselves from a distance, as if out of their bodies.

3. *Suggestibility:* The increased ability to respond positively to ideas offered by the hypnotist or by the self. This is associated with suspension of the critical ego.

4. *Ideosensory activity:* The capacity of an individual to develop sensory images that are different from those objectively present in the physical environment. These images can be positive, such as tastes (chocolate, banana), aromas (fresh baking bread, fish), sights (an old photograph, the happy look in someone's face), sounds (the opening of Beethoven's Fifth Symphony, the sound of one's child calling), or sensations (the feeling of rowing a boat in calm water, or of sinking into a nice warm bed). Conversely, negative images are also possible, These may include denial of a particular sensory presence (e.g., an uncomfortable chair, an aroma of perfume, or potentially distracting sounds outside the room).

More complete experiences of ideosensory activity include *positive and negative hallucinations.* These are stronger and more complete, and involve a perception that a stimulus is actually present or absent. Thus a positive hallucination of one's best childhood friend may be compelling enough to induce one to enter into a conversation with that person. An example of a negative hallucination is the inability to perceive a third person sitting in the room observing the hypnosis.

5. *Catalepsy:* A physical state characterized by involuntary muscle contractions of any part of the body. Eyeballs become fixed and a nonblinking gaze ensues; limbs become immovable or conform to a waxy flexibility sometimes characteristic of catatonic schizophrenics. An arm can be raised in some manner and simply hang in the air in that position without signs of tiredness or strain.

6. *Ideomotor responsiveness:* The involuntary capacity of the muscles to respond instantaneously to external stimuli. Ideomotor responses are often learned in a trance state and then built upon in treatment (e.g., "Notice that you can relax more deeply each time you breathe in and out. As you exhale, the whole body can relax more and more"). Finger-raising "yes–no" answers to questions can also be utilized. This functioning can be used to increase suggestibility.

7. *Age regression:* The ability to experience prior life events while retaining all abilities of the present. Thus a patient may re-experience a traumatic event while remaining calm, relaxed, and capable of using skills obtained subsequent to the trauma in understanding and correcting it.

8. *Revivification:* Actual reliving of earlier events. This is similar to age regression, but in revivification the client relives the experience at the age in which the experience actually occurred (e.g., handwriting changes to

more childlike forms). Events that occurred and skills that were developed subsequent to the relived events are unavailable. Often this is accompanied by a marked change in demeanor and a switch to the use of the present tense in descriptions.

9. *Hypermnesia:* The ability to recall events in greater detail than at non-hypnotic levels of awareness. This is often associated with age regression and revivification. In work with trauma victims and the courts, hypermnesia and the accuracy of such remembrances play a significant role in the admissibility of evidence.

10. *Amnesia:* Loss of memories for a specific time period. The amnesia can be automatic or suggested.

11. *Posthypnotic responses.* Actions carried out after the termination of hypnosis that are suggested during a trance. Usually these posthypnotic suggestions are accompanied by a suggestion of amnesia for the instruction. Thus a subject may be told,

". . . and when you awaken from the hypnosis, you will feel confident that when you take the test, all of the information you studied and need will be available. You will not remember where this confidence comes from; it will simply be there as a part of you on test day."

The strength and efficacy of posthypnotic suggestions are related to the subject's motivation and to the suggestions' consistency with the individual's character structure.

12. *Hypnotic analgesia and anesthesia:* Deadening or altering of the experience of pain. Often patients can undergo operations, difficult dental procedures, or other medical treatments using hypnosis; the pain is present, but there is no normal irritating awareness of it.

13. *Glove anesthesia:* Insensitivity of a part of the body to external stimuli or pain. The classic example of this is when the entire hand becomes insensitive—a phenomenon that is physiologically impossible without an almost total severing of the hand.

14. *Somnambulism:* One of the deepest states of hypnosis, characterized by deep trance-like sleep walking. It is sometimes equated with the *nirvana* state of gurus. In this state, subjects take all suggestions without exercise of critical judgment.

15. *Automatic writing:* The ability to write about a subject that is different from the one being discussed.

16. *Time distortion:* The expansion or condensation of time. Frequently subjects will subjectively experience the passing of only a few minutes while they have been in hypnosis for 30 minutes or longer.

17. *Release of inhibitions:* The suspension of inner sanctions against expressing emotions, attitudes, or thoughts. The very act of having bodily relaxation simultaneously with mental awareness of stressful thoughts is significant in this regard.

18. *Change in capacity for volitional activity:* A lessening of interest in direct response to external environmental demands. Under hypnosis, a subject may be aware that a phone is ringing, that something fell off a shelf, or that people are talking outside the room, but does not evince a desire to do anything about it. The subject's attention is concentrated either on the hypnotherapist or internally.

19. *Trance logic:* The ability to tolerate logical incongruities that are ordinarily disturbing to waking subjects.

20. *Effortless imagination:* The ease with which subjects can access imaginative and fantasy aspects of consciousness. Many spontaneously report the effortlessness of the process.

With such a wide array of experiences qualifying as characteristics of "hypnosis," it is hardly a surprise that definitions of the phenomenon itself are so widely divergent. This is not necessarily a problem for the clinician. Clinicians' definitions of hypnosis will be determined by functionality in particular cases and by their personal theoretical stances. Some clinicians will focus on the operator and behavioral manifestations, others on the subject and subjective manifestations, and still others on the induction or interpersonal process. It is the clinician's theory and expectations that determine what he or she will call "hypnosis," what meaning it will be given in treatment, and what criteria will be set for success. Specific delineations are the property of the theory in which the definition is embedded.

The definition becomes problematic only when the clinical applications become important in nonclinical settings such as legal procedures, wherein specification of the exact definition is crucial.

THEORIES OF HYPNOSIS

Any definition of hypnosis must be firmly rooted in a theoretical position in order to generate and test hypotheses, and even to determine what constitutes examples of the phenomenon itself. One investigator of hypnosis may well perceive the very field of study dissimilarly from another.

Three major groups of theories have dominated psychology since its inception: physiological theories, behavioral theories, and psychodynamic theories. Each position provides adherents with characteristic methods for locating, evaluating, and understanding meaningful data. The phenomena collectively called "hypnosis" are no different in this regard. There are physiological theories of hypnosis dating back at least as far as the 1700s (together with a closely allied view of hypnosis as a form of sleep), and there have been recognizable behavioral and psychodynamic theories since the 19th century. As Sheehan and Perry (1976) so lucidly indicate, each theoretical model is best equipped to identify and solve those problems that are most important within its own operational definition of hypnosis.

Because our own view of hypnosis requires certain precepts to make it viable for forensic concerns, it is important to survey the major positions briefly.

Physiological Theories

Psychophysiological concerns dominated theories of hypnosis in the 18th and 19th centuries. Mesmer's theory of "animal magnetism" was organically based. He believed that magnetic fluids responding to planetary movements were essentially responsible for the "crises" and cures his patients experienced. Although the theory itself has been discredited, its popularity and investigation by scientific commissions of the day were significant developments in the history of the scientific study of hypnosis.

Another early influence in hypnosis was the Salpêtrière school in Paris, led by spokesmen Charcot, Pere, and Binet (see Ellenberger, 1965). Hypnosis was defined by this school as a product of central nervous system disease. Hypnotic trances were believed to occur as the result of a pathological neural phenomenon. Charcot, placing the emphasis on the supposed neural substrate of both conditions, argued that both hysteria and hypnosis arise from a disordered nervous system. In dramatic demonstrations, he showed that hysterical paralyses could be altered and shifted through the use of hypnosis. This position was soon overshadowed by the more psychologically based theory of the rival Nancy school, led by Liebeault and Bernheim.

Opposition to organic theories have not completely eliminated their regular re-emergence. West (1960) employed specific psychophysiological constructs in defining hypnosis. He believed that the hypnotic trance is a controlled dissociative state. In his theory, altered consciousness is maintained through parassociative mechanisms mediated by the ascending reticular system. These mechanisms serve to restrict input by excluding from awareness considerable amounts of incoming information that would ordinarily be consciously perceived in the process of reality testing. Under such restriction of critical judgment, the information inserted into the restricted area of the subject's awareness by the hypnotist through his or her suggestions is accepted as reality to a greater or lesser magnitude, depending on the extent to which the subject's range of input is restricted. Hypnosis thus serves as enhanced selectivity of incoming data via a physiological mechanism.

Crasilneck and Hall (1975) support the belief that some physiological substrate will be found to account for the amazing cross-cultural similarities in somnambulistic trance states. Graham (1978) localizes hypnosis in the nondominant hemisphere required for imagery and emotions. Olness

(1984) predicts that a much closer connection between psychophysiological and psychodynamic factors will mark the next decade of research.

To date, however, support for a physiological substrate or localized center for hypnosis has not been found. Any number of physiological alterations have been observed under hypnosis, but none have been consistently shown to be necessary for the hypnotic state. Although it is clear that subjects are capable of physiological alterations while hypnotized, there is still no sound evidence that hypnosis works specifically on any organ or physical system. It is, of course, possible that such a mechanism eludes scientists only because the current state of instrumentation is inadequate to measure such changes. Until specific physiological measurements of hypnotic states are possible, little attention will be paid to the pragmatic importance of such theories.

Hypnosis as Sleep

Closely aligned with physiological theories of hypnosis are the theories that hypnosis is a form of sleep. The Marquis de Puysegur (1837), a follower of Mesmer, is credited with the recognition of the somnambulistic quality of mesmerism. By focusing on the sleep-like state in which subjects could talk, walk about, and respond to commands and wishes, instead of emphasizing the convulsive crisis, de Puysegur actually helped bring about a more naturalistic perspective of mesmerism. Although he maintained a physiological theoretical base (he believed that a curative cerebral fluid was transferred through will power from the mesmerist to the subject), the definitional shift from "magnetism" to "a sleep-like state" was significant.

In the early 1800s, the Abbé Faria suggested that "lucid sleep" was produced by heightened expectations of the subject and rapport developed with the operator (Faria, 1819). This was a primary step away from the fundamentally physiological theories.

Braid (1843), who is credited with the naming of the phenomenon "neuro-hypnotism" (after Hypnos, the Greek god of sleep), described this phenomenon as a special nervous sleep resulting from the deliberate fixation on a single monotonous stimulus for a protracted time. The resultant fatigue was thought to create a derangement of the nerve centers and a decrease in central nervous system activity. Braid later suggested that "monoideism"—single-minded engrossment with a single train of thought—would provide the same state, although he retained his faith in the neurological basis by arguing that, once instituted, monoideism was accompanied by physiological changes.

In the early 20th century, Pavlov redefined hypnosis as a selective inhibition of certain brain centers. Pavlov believed that hypnosis is a function of a cortical neural inhibition or partial sleep of the hemispheres. The only differences between hypnosis and sleep were thought to be the difference between localized and general inhibition (which is common in sleep) (Pavlov, 1928).

Several physiological studies have now clearly established that hypnosis resembles certain forms of sleep *only* to the objective observer. As early as 1939, Nygard observed that blood flow to cerebral vessels, which is altered with the onset of sleep, is not altered in hypnotic subjects. Multiple electroencephalographic (EEG) studies have reported no sleep patterns with hypnosis.

Psychodynamic Theories

In a sense, the belief in hypnosis as a psychodynamic phenomenon had its roots in reactions to the physiological theories of Mesmer. One scientific commission headed by Benjamin Franklin was appointed by King Louis XVI of France to investigate mesmerism (Franklin et al., 1785/1970). The commission concluded that the quite verifiable cures were due to imagination, not to the magnetism and the *"baquet"* (Mesmer's bath with magnetic rods and filings). Similarly, even though Charcot's physiological position that hypnosis was due to a disordered nervous system was discredited, his demonstrations of the dissociation component of hypnosis has promoted continuing psychological theoretical advances. From the work of Faria came the seeds of the importance of individual differences, and from Braid the centrality of subjects' expectations.

One core influence in most modern psychodynamic theories was the work of Bernheim and Liebeault at the Nancy school in Paris. These rivals of Charcot in the late 19th century postulated that suggestion, not physiology, is the causative agent in hypnosis. Contrary to Charcot's view of hypnosis as a rare and morbid condition (probably an artifact of the hospital population he studied), their work emphasized the individual differences in normal hypnotic susceptibility.

Early in his career, Freud journeyed to Paris to study with Charcot. Charcot's demonstrations were of great interest to Freud, as was the theory that hypnosis and hysteria are examples of an identical condition. The scientific demonstration of a hypothesized physiological substrate was quite appealing to Freud as a physician and neurologist, as were the dramatic alterations of hysterical symptoms. He subsequently visited the rival school at Nancy and was persuaded by Liebeault and Bernheim of the power of suggestion in inducing hypnosis. At Nancy he also saw demonstrated the power of posthypnotic suggestions. To Freud, the disparities in the positions of the two schools were less important than was the common indication of the power of the unconscious mind. Soon after returning home, Freud's classic *Studies on Hysteria* with Josef Breuer appeared (Breuer & Freud, 1895/1955), in which they began the detailed charting of the unconscious mind that was to influence Western literature, medicine, and science.

As is well known, Freud himself abandoned hypnosis, favoring the method of free association as the "royal road to the unconscious." However, the use of psychoanalytic concepts to define hypnosis continues to this day. Furthermore, for legal purposes, the postulation of an active, significant unconscious is mandatory in hypermnesia work.

For psychoanalytic writers, hypnosis is essentially used for regression within the transference relationship. Gill and Brenman (1959) viewed hypnosis as the subjects' lending of a subsystem of the ego to the temporary control of the hypnotist. This relationship is revocable at any point, with the subject retaining his or her normal waking state. Watkins (1963) described using hypnosis as an "affect bridge," wherein an unpleasant emotion is intensified until it evokes previous traumatic memories.

Milton H. Erickson, who was quite influenced by psychodynamic postulations, consistently eschewed consistent specific definitions of hypnosis. However, it is clear from his writing that he relied on a supposition of an active, significant unconscious. In his collected papers, Erickson characterizes hypnosis as a "dissociation manifested by a quiescence of the 'consciousness' simulating normal sleep and a delegation of the subjective control of the individual functions, ordinarily conscious, to the 'subconscious' " (Erickson, 1980, Vol. I, p. 8).

All of the dissociation theories—in which one part of the mind is watching the other—derive from psychodynamic constructs influenced by the early work of Charcot.

Behavioral Theories

Hypersuggestibility Theories

Clark Hull, a premier behavioral learning theoretician in the first half of the 20th century, saw hypnosis as an example of the conditioned response. Hull (1933) believed that a subject comes to the hypnotic situation with a preset expectancy. Conditioned to respond favorably to legitimate authority, and expecting to perform well, the subject becomes hyper-suggestible, and will respond favorably to this preconditioning.

There was substantial appeal to scientists in this position; it brought hypnosis under the purview of an established literature and empirical procedures. Corollary observations added to this appeal. Crasilneck and Hall (1975), for example, have noted that a strongly accepted posthypnotic suggestion behaves in a manner that is almost identical to a classic conditioned response. There are also clear similarities among typical hypnotic inductions, the Jacobson (1938) relaxation techniques, and Wolpe's (1961) systematic desensitization. Weitzenhoffer (1972) saw the Wolpe technique using reciprocal inhibition as creating a hypnotic-like state to facilitate direct behavior modification and conditioning.

Interpersonal Influence Theories

Closely allied to the hypersuggestibility theories are the interpersonal influence models.

T. X. Barber has been one of the significant figures in hypnosis research for the past 25 years. Because he has been such a prolific writer, and because his position issues a challenge to all those who believe that hypnosis is an independent or altered state of consciousness, he has drawn a host of attacks from other professionals and has been indirectly responsible for more sophisticated research by his detractors. In the rush to refute his suppositions, much excellent research has been done.

Barber (e.g., 1969) believes that "hypnosis" is nothing more than an example of any social influence situation in which one person actively role-plays a response that is created by a host of predictable antecedent factors, such as prior attitudes toward the phenomenon being investigated. He particularly asserts that the notion of a trance is unnecessary, nonparsimonious, and misleading. Refraining from any reference to the unconscious or altered states, Barber stresses the motivation of the subject, the subject's relationship to the examiner, and environmental conditions. Correlative experimental support for the role-playing position is provided by Sarbin and Lim (1963), who show a positive correlation between subjects' ability to take roles and hypnotizability.

Some suggestion theories do not take as polarized a position as that of Barber. Sarbin and Coe (1972) accept the qualitative and quantitative differences in subjects following a hypnotic induction. They also seem less concerned with accepting a state notion of hypnosis. However, they consider hypnosis to be an example of a larger class of psychological processes in which the crucial variable is role behavior. "Role enactment" is defined as directed goal-oriented striving, which involves favorable motivation, a perception of the desired role, and role-taking aptitude. It is seen as involving more of the unconscious than role playing. To Sarbin and Coe (1972), the hypnotized subject has some level of organismic involvement, and hypnosis involves imagination and the self as well as behavior.

Orne (1959, 1962) has also been very concerned with the social environment in which hypnosis occurs. Using constructs derived from social-psychological experiments, Orne has coined the term "demand characteristics" to describe the influence of the totality of environmental factors on a subject's response. The assumption is that the subject will attempt to give responses that will validate a perceived proper experimental hypothesis. Stressing social motivation, Orne has also noted on several occasions that subjects can simulate or fake hypnosis without the knowledge of the hypnotist.

Examples of the impact of social roles or demand characteristics abound in the performances of stage hypnotists, who choose subjects who are highly suggestible and most willing to respond to the social influence. Orne believes that subjectively real alterations of perception and memory take place in accordance with cues that the subject picks up from the hypnotist. The hypnosis occurs while the subject is striving to play the role of good subject.

MULTIPLE THEORIES, MULTIPLE DEFINITIONS

It seems clear that each theoretical position has something special to offer in a comprehensive definition of hypnosis. It seems equally clear that there are substantial differences and direct contradictions between and among theories. These distinctions follow fairly traditional divisions in the field of psychology. One such differentiation, that between clinical and experimental psychology, mirrors the often deep rifts within academic psychology departments.

Clinical and Experimental Definitions

To the clinician involved in normal daily work in hypnotherapy, the precise definition of hypnosis is not a primary concern. Truth must take a back seat to functionality. If a procedure works with a readily diagnosable population, it matters little which aspects of the hypnosis are due to placebo and which to the nature of induction and suggestions themselves. If a patient gets relief from pain or discomfort, the clinician is satisfied.

Such methodological casualness is anathema to the experimental investigator, whose prime goal is to determine precisely which factors are active, under which circumstances, and how they are distinguishable from all other variables under investigation. In hypnosis research, this difference is particularly problematic, because the same word "hypnosis" is used to describe phenomena that are defined and investigated differently. The natural outcome, of course, is that the results of such studies are also quite dissimilar and incomparable.

The wide divergence in construct and method may well have resulted in the study of two related but different phenomena. It is conceivable that variables such as role playing and hypersuggestibility account for much more of the variance found in laboratory experiments with volunteer subjects than they do in clinical patients who are distressed and seeking professional relief. There may even be some significant subjective difference in the trances themselves.

Definitions of Hypnosis and the Court

This problem is magnified in a courtroom setting. The court is far less interested in a clinician's pragmatics than in a clear definition of what it is that the clinician did, and the implications of this for due process. It is often the two different types of definitions that become the object of the court's inquiry during a particular case.

It is not uncommon, for example, for the prosecution in a memory enhancement situation to employ a hypnosis expert who will define hypnosis as an intrapsychic phenomenon. This expert will testify that the victim or witness who was hypnotized was relieved of amnesia through a skillful hypnotic process that accessed the contents of the unconscious mind and reproduced what had been previously recorded subconsciously in a relatively veridical manner that is at least as accurate as normal eyewitness testimony. A psychodynamic, often Ericksonian, definition is utilized.

The defense will counter with an experimentally oriented expert who will warn of contamination, confounds, and the impact of demand characteristics or role enactment. The battle of the experts in a courtroom can become less a battle over justice or the facts of the case than a recapitulation of the split between the positions of behaviorists and analysts, or experimentalists and clinicians, in a new venue. It sometimes looks like Barber for the defense and Erickson for the prosecution.

Because of this, any clinician who will testify in court regarding hypnotically refreshed memories previously obtained in a hypnotherapy session will probably employ a definition of hypnosis that includes the constructs of altered states of consciousness, unconscious functioning, focused or concentrated attention, and the normality of trance states in everyday living. Less attention will be paid to such constructs as hypersuggestibility, social role interactions, and personal motivation.

Our own position is that the most functional definitions for therapists engaged in forensic work who actually do hypnosis with witnesses, victims, or alleged perpetrators of crimes involve primarily the variable of *concentration of attention.*

The Centrality of Focused Attention

Spiegel and Spiegel (1978) present a workable operational definition of hypnosis as "characterized by an ability to sustain in response to a signal, a state of attentive, receptive, intense focal concentration with diminished peripheral awareness" (p. 22). In his classic account of hypnosis, White (1941) instructs the operator "to reduce as far as possible the perceptual supports which might serve to sustain a wider frame of reference" (p. 502). Frankel (1976) is more expansive but similar in orientation. He defines hypnosis as an event developed in the [W]estern world, involving a subject and an operator, and dependent for its occurrence on the trance capabilities of the subject, his or her motivation, the situation, and the relationship between the subject and the operator.

In this state the subject can experience reality differently. The experience included distorted perceptions, unusual achievements of memory (i.e., hypermnesia or amnesia), a tolerance for logical inconsistencies and yet at some level an awareness of objective reality. *The subject is willing to relegate his usually wide perceptual awareness to a position of relative unimportance and replace it with a specific and narrow range of preoccupations, which creates a different experience of reality.* (p. 42, emphasis added)

This is not to suggest that the array of experimental studies is in any way irrelevant. It is our position, along with Shor (1959), that many of the characteristics typically observed in hypnotic subjects are derivative from the internalized, intensified concentration.

Subjective versus Objective Data

Fromm (1972) has suggested that the primary problem with experimental investigations of hypnosis is that these approaches often attempt to measure external, observed behavior as a way of understanding a basically subjective experience. In a sense, no definition is complete without access to subjective data from the person who is hypnotized. The laboratory situation and a crime may well produce qualitatively different hypnotic states. For Fromm, the clinical use of hypnosis is predicated on the notion of an altered state of consciousness. It is most clearly a state of concentrated awareness. Experimental data must remain as cautions that could contaminate, but do not define, the essential core of the hypnotic experience.

This focus on the client's subjective experience is a big potential problem for the court, which strives as much as possible to avoid, or at least to balance, subjectivity in getting to an objective truth.

AN OPERATIONAL DEFINITION

For therapists engaged in forensic hypnosis, we support the following definition as most relevant and least problematic:

Hypnosis is an altered state of consciousness, characterized by intensified concentration of awareness on certain suggested themes, along with a diminished interest in competing perceptions. Subjects who are hypnotized experience perceptual and sensory distortions and enhanced abilities to utilize normally unconscious m ·tal mechanisms.

In order to understand the hypnotic experience, the investigator must elicit the subjective experiences of the patient, and must very carefully and objectively observe the hypnotic subject in the setting. Best efforts must be made to isolate, to eliminate, or at least to catalogue the host of demand characteristics present that potentially influence or contaminate the subject's responses while in the trance state.

These assessments, as well as the requisite clinical skill to facilitate patients' safe exploration of intrapsychic events, dictate the need for well-trained practitioners who are sensitive to patients' needs. The application of memory-refreshing techniques without suitable safeguards and clinical expertise can be harmful to clients' mental health and legal rights.

Within the purview of this definition, it is possible for hypnotherapists to substantiate their clinical work and to debunk the myths that surround hypnotic practice.

POPULAR BELIEFS ABOUT HYPNOSIS

Many misconceptions color the way in which hypnosis is viewed by juries, attorneys, the court, and the public. Most people have formed their impressions of hypnosis from stage performances; operators of quick-weight-loss and stop-smoking centers; situation comedies on television; and old black-and-white B movies, commonly starring Lon Chaney or Bela Lugosi. The expert witness needs to be able to educate the court on the scientific and medical realities of hypnosis and to expose conventional fallacies, the most common of which are discussed here.

Hypnosis as Something Done to the Subject

One of the most common misconceptions is that hypnosis is induced in the subject by the hypnotist. Most professional practitioners of hypnosis would dispute this. The common belief is that however hypnosis is defined, its primary quality is a subjective experience of the subject. In that sense, hypnosis is normally self-induced. As a phenomenon that is primarily in the mind of the subject, the "trance" state is induced and developed by the concentration and imagination of the client.

The hypnotist is essentially a teacher or guide. Frankel (1976) states, "Hypnosis is not so much a way of manipulating behavior as of creating distortions of perception and memory" (p. 43). The hypnotist operates like an orchestra conductor instructing the individual musician to play. The music comes from the musician; in that sense, it is not something the maestro "puts into" the artist. On the other hand, the conductor does shape and structure the performance.

As a way of underscoring the fact that control is centered in the subject, Udolf (1981) and others have suggested the use of the term "trance capacity" in place of the commonly used "hypnotic susceptibility."

The Svengali Myth

A related misconception is that hypnosis involves a battle of wills, with the stronger party (the Svengali-like hypnotist) winning out over the weaker one. By contrast, Erickson and others have repeatedly demonstrated that hypnosis is a normal state that people enter and leave on a regular basis, whether or not a formal trance is induced. Altered states of consciousness—daydreaming while driving or sitting in a class, absorption in a book or film, or other forms of heightened concentration that limit receptivity to external cues—are viewed as naturalistic states similar to hypnosis that are not unusual, abnormal, or artificial conditions.

The hypnotic subject does not give in to the will of the hypnotist as much as he or she selectively gives attention to his or her own inner experience. It is true, however, that a malevolent hypnotist can take advantage of a trusting subject in much the same way that any influential or charismatic individual can deceive and fool a person into believing that his or her interests are being served.

The Hypnotist as a Charismatic Individual

It has commonly been believed that a hypnotist must be a dynamic, forceful, or charismatic person. This is the image portrayed in many films and novels. Thus Svengali can induce the helpless Trilby to do what he wishes by the sheer force of his will, even from across town.

It is true that certain aspects of authority do enhance one's effectiveness in all forms of treatment. Frank (1974) describes well the importance of the accoutrements of the healer in maximizing the patient's expectancy that any healing procedure will be successful. Authority is helpful in creating trust, which does tend to augment the process.

However, it is also generally agreed that a hypnotist can be anyone and that charismatic, forceful, and dynamic personalities do not always make the best hypnotist. Milton Erickson, fabled for being able to entrance so many resistant clients, told long, rambling, boring stories that would offer clients the opportunity to drift, daydream, and become open to developing trances just to stimulate themselves.

Hypnotic Subjects as Foolish or Weak

Many people believe that only fools and weak individuals can be hypnotized. This false conception is another outgrowth of the belief that something is done by the hypnotist to the subject. In fact, the opposite seems more true. J. R. Hilgard (1974) concludes that subjects with the richest imaginations, those who are more easily absorbed, and those who are most creative often make the best hypnotic subjects.

The Hypnotist's Unlimited Power over the Subject

Another common belief is that the subject is completely under the hypnotist's power, and that anything that the hypnotist says or wishes to be done will be done. Experts agree that subjects generally will not violate their ethical codes or do something that they would not do in a waking state. Hilgard (Wilkes, 1986) describes a report by Janet in which medical students attempted to get a hypnotized nurse to remove her clothing. As expected, she awoke, got up, and left. However, at least one attempt to replicate the experiment at UCLA in the mid-20th century found the subject (a nightclub stripper) very willing to remove her blouse.

It would seem simple to conclude that hypnotists have no power to get people to do things that violate their morals. However, hypnosis may not be that benign. It is theoretically possible to distort subjects' perceptions in a trance to the extent that they believe that a particular situation prevails. Their behavior may be very appropriate under that imagined situation and very inappropriate in the actual current situation. Thus it may be possible to convince a person that he or she is in the shower instead of the supermarket, or vice versa. The person may then do things appropriate to one setting that would be quite inappropriate in the other.

To expect that a person with typical ethical standards would become a killer simply because a hypnotist ordered it is absurd. However, if the same person was absolutely convinced that his or her child were endangered by a stranger, the person's desire to protect the child could have serious consequences. Such ability to completely alter the totality of perceptions under hypnosis would require extensive periods of time and total environmental control. Trance logic would have to be replaced by an altered conviction.

To the extent that hypnosis can be used to create a form of total control of the *internal* environment, it is paralleled by techniques of conditioning and brainwashing that manipulate *external* environmental control.

Corollary: Death by Suggestion

Many classic experimenters also believed it possible for hypnotists to convince subjects to hurt themselves or take their own lives. Certainly the media believe so. The film *The Manchurian Candidate* is a classic example of this belief. More recent versions, including episodes of the television shows *Columbo* and *The Greatest American Hero,* show people jumping off a roof or high balcony under the command of an evil hypnotist.

Such scenes are probably purely fictional (although substantial experimentation by the CIA and other intelligence agencies provides support for a belief in the possibility of hypnotically created assassins and victims). Scientific experimentation is, of course, morally impossible.

Corollary: Commission of Crimes by the Hypnotized

Estabrooks (1951) says that almost anyone can be persuaded to do almost anything under hypnosis. Could a hypnotist actually get someone to rob or kill by force of a hypnotic trance?

Few issues have been more heatedly debated throughout the last century. Most extant literature is of course anecdotal, because controlled laboratory experiments inducing criminal behavior in hypnotized subjects are both immoral and illegal. Nevertheless, there are reports in the experimental literature supporting mutually contradictory conclusions: that hypnosis can be used to induce antisocial behavior, and that it cannot.

Most clinicians believe the evidence from studies of influence and persuasion, which suggest that accessing the individual's true beliefs or nature is far more powerful than any trance state. Certainly, interpersonal influence, excessive dependency, and peer pressure have major effects on the production of social or antisocial behavior.

Corollary: Commission of Crimes on the Hypnotized

Will the hypnotized become so malleable that they are easy *victims* of crimes? Many sales promoters obviously believe so. The rash of sales training programs reportedly relying on neurolinguistic programming purport to provide students with the hypnotic inductions and sensitivity to individuals' accessing systems that will make their clients eager to turn over the contents of their wallets. No research exists yet to support claims of the relative effectiveness of hypnosis versus pure salesmanship. Indeed, nonhypnotized students of such courses do seem willing to pay a great deal for the privilege of learning these hypnotic techniques.

There are also reports of hypnotists taking sexual advantage of clients in medicine, dentistry, the ministry, and therapy. Modern authorities do not dispute the *fact* of victimization; they disagree on its *explanation*. Some (e.g., Venn, 1988) attribute it to a violation of the therapeutic or special authority relationship rather than to the hypnotic state.

Hypnosis as Sleep or Loss of Consciousness

It is true that the term "hypnosis," as first applied by Braid, derived from the name of the Greek god of sleep. Early investigators such as the Marquis de Puysegur, the Abbé Faria, and Braid all wrote of the hypnosis as being similar to sleep. Attempts to confirm this have found no such similarity. EEG readings of people in hypnosis are much more akin to waking states than any previously measured sleep stages.

A related belief is that hypnosis involves a loss of consciousness. It is commonly thought that hypnotized persons lose awareness of what is going on, almost as if they are in a state of suspended animation or a coma. Actually, the opposite is true. Hypnotic subjects are most often more alert and aware of a narrower range of stimuli than they are in their normal state. They report being aware of, but uninterested in, events that are peripheral to those in which they are engrossed. The general subjective experience is an increase in signal strength with a coincident narrowing of band width.

Hypnosis as Dangerous and Destructive of the Will

People often fear that hypnosis may be harmful to them—that they will not awaken from the trance, will become unduly dependent or influenced, will develop serious mental or physical illnesses, or will lose control over their volition.

No evidence exists to support inferences that the method itself is potentially harmful. As noted earlier, Erickson and others since Bernheim have noted that people normally go into and out of altered states spontaneously on a regular basis during their daily lives. There is simply no evidence that hypnosis itself is harmful to subjects. We do not turn into automaton "Trilbys," subject to the will, mood, and health of our master "Svengalis." Hypnosis will not weaken a person's will; it wil not produce mental or physical illness or a permanent trance state.

Hypnosis as a Cure-All

Hypnosis has often been promoted as a form of treatment by itself. Just the opposite is true: Going into a trance or hypnotic state is *not* curative in and of itself. The hypnotic state enhances receptivity and concentration. What is then received or focused on becomes the primary source of interest. However, the subjective experience of relaxation that is common in hypnosis can have a somewhat quieting effect on a patient's stress.

Hypnosis as Conferring Special Powers on Subjects

It is often assumed that hypnotized subjects develop special powers, enabling them to perform whatever they wish in a qualitatively and quantitatively superior manner while in a trance state. Subjects in hypnosis cannot do anything that they could not do while awake. People who have never understood Spanish will not acquire any more understanding of that language under hypnosis. However, if at one time they studied or spoke Spanish, they may be more capable of understanding or conversing in that language while in a trance state because of the power of focused attention. There are many clinical examples wherein patients who were regressed to earlier stages of life used the language they had used during those stages.

There is also some evidence that subjects with an aptitude for certain behaviors will learn them more efficiently with the focused concentration common to hypnosis. Thus, if a subject has a talent for the violin, basketball, or Spanish, he or she may be able to use it more effectively without conscious doubts and interference.

Despite examples like Bernstein's (1956) Bridey Murphy, there is no hard evidence of special extrasensory perception or other special powers accompanying hypnosis.

Hypnotic Trance as Irreversible

One common fear about hypnosis is that the hypnotist will not be skilled enough to end the trance, or perhaps may die while the subject is in a trance, dooming the subject to life as a zombie. Trances that are not broken by direct injunction of the hypnotherapist will wear off in a short time. The subject usually will slip from a trance state into a normal sleep and awaken as if from a nap.

Hypnosis as Fakery or Sham Behavior

Many authors, using primarily stage hypnotists' performances as models, have suggested that hypnosis is essentially a faked show perpetrated on a gullible public. No serious investigator or hypnosis has made such arguments. Indeed, even such critics as Barber repeatedly point out how very easy it is to get people to go along and become engrossed in their role of hypnosis. There is no need for fakery. Furthermore, it is hard to believe that patients undergoing root canal procedures, childbirth, or abdominal surgery would be able to fake the apparent relaxation and absence of pain they report.

Hypnosis as a "Truth Serum"

It is commonly believed that hypnotized individuals lose the normal censorship of the ego and will tell embarrassing or inappropriate things to the hypnotist. Reports from hypnotized individuals do not suggest a loss of such control. In fact, they are aware of everything that is going on and are likely to disclose only those secrets that will be ultimately self-serving in some way.

A skillful interrogator using hypnosis can alter a subject's perceptual reality in a way that encourages revelations of private information. However, there is no guarantee that such information will be truthful or accurate. Hypnosis is not a "truth serum."

People Who Cannot Be Hypnotized

Many people maintain the belief that they are so strong-minded or skeptical that they cannot be "put under" by anyone. This myth is partially true. Some people have a far better natural ability to enter into altered states of consciousness than others. Although this is so, it is possible for almost anyone to enter into at least a light trance. Diamond (1984) considers hypnosis a "dual phenomenon," indicating that some natural capacity for it resides in most individuals. Learning how to be a better hypnotic subject requires a facilitating environment, practice, and proper motivation.

The skillful hypnotist will create a setting in which the subject desires the trance state. Erickson devised a host of techniques for "resistant" clients, which essentially allowed them to access their imagination and memories in an environment conducive to trust.

WHY IS THE DEFINITION OF HYPNOSIS IMPORTANT?

To the therapist in a clinical field, a formal definition of hypnosis is little more than a natural component of theory. With the exception of the value of replications with future patients, it is of secondary importance to most clinicians whether the patients get better because of expectations, role playing, or unconscious alteration. If an element of the procedure (certain words, tones, or motions, or the use of the construct of trance) facilitates the patient's creation of anasthesia or recreation of memories, then success is judged primarily by this element's pragmatic usefulness to the patient and the healing process.

It matters little in a normal clinical setting whether the client is defined as being in a state of heightened susceptibility and thus more willing to take suggestions, or whether the client is thought of as being in touch with his or her own subconscious, which is generating information and skills that are typically available. Clinical cases that involve the courts, however, are not normal clinical situations. The court is far more likely to value what it believes are objective indices than subjective reports. The court will be more favorable toward data that it sees as natural emanations from a subject's true experience than toward prompted responses that result from demand characteristics.

In the case of eyewitness memory and hypermnesia, the definition of hypnosis is likely to influence whether or not testimony is acceptable or admissible in legal proceedings. If the operator can so influence the subject as to subtly encourage the subject to alter memories to fit a particular story or theme favorable to one side of a case, the court has to be skeptical and rule that such information may well be unacceptable. By contrast, if hypnosis is a benign method of getting at the real but buried truth, it is unconscionable for a court to declare it inadmissible. The question of the veracity of hypnotically refreshed or aided memory is still open to debate.

We believe that hypnosis is essentially a subject-oriented vehicle to reach normally unconscious mental processes. The hypnotherapist serves as a guide to this exploration. Hypnotherapy expertise can be used to enhance trust and other components of the therapeutic relationship, in order to encourage the patient to focus attention keenly on certain percepts or issues and to exclude all extraneous input. Although the therapist is the guide, the client is the major factor in both the depth of any trance state and the production of memories or other hypnosis-related abilities (pain control, analgesia, trance logic, etc.). Because hypnosis takes place within the context of a therapeutic relationship, any definition of hypnosis must thus examine both the subjective experience of the client and the interactional impact of the relationship with the therapist.

In order to be able to testify in court competently and professionally, the hypnotherapist must able to induce a trance that utilizes what the patient experiences and reports, and to avoid leading the patient to some mutually satisfactory fiction. Thus the hypnotherapist must be aware of his or her own stimulus pull and personal influence on the subject, as well as of environmental press variables present during the hypnosis. This is particularly important in cases involving memory enhancement and hypermnesia.

CHAPTER 7

The Nature of Memory and of Hypnotically Refreshed Recall

For the hypnotherapist faced with justifying clinical work to the legal system, memory and hypermnesia are most likely to constitute the "Pandora's box." The issues are quite complex, with adamant opposing positions commonplace. There are heated debates about such basic matters as definitions of memory and interpretations of the complex scientific literature. Although a comprehensive examination of memory is beyond the scope of this book, the following background material is presented as a basic guide for the expert witness.

Cross-examiners will exploit each area of scientific disagreement in order to discredit the hypnotherapist, his or her clinical work, or the field of hypnotherapy in general. To handle cross-questioning successfully, the clinician must be familiar with the range of major perspectives, issues, and controversies.

Often the initial questioning appears quite straightforward:

ATTORNEY: Now, Dr. Gabriel, you have indicated that Ms. Smith had experienced a "trauma-induced amnesia" as a result of the alleged attack by an assailant. Could you tell the court exactly what you mean by the word "amnesia"?

WITNESS: "Amnesia" is a loss of memory for a certain period of time.

ATTORNEY: So you claim that Ms. Smith lost her memory because of some incident. How would you define "memory"?

We all have an idea of what memory is and how it works. However, those capacities that are in constant use—abilities that we take for granted as "second nature"—are particularly difficult to clarify. Defining memory on a witness stand may be somewhat akin to paying attention to the movements of our legs while descending a flight of stairs and at the same time avoiding a misstep or fall.

This chapter is organized around seven pertinent questions:

1. What is memory? Does it act like a videotape replay reproducing accurately the total of all objective perceptual events, or is it more selective? If it is selective, what kinds of events are remembered and which forgotten?
2. Does hypnosis aid memory?
3. Does the nature of the to-be-remembered material affect hypnotic hypermnesia?
4. Does hypnosis encourage confabulation and creativity at the time of retrieval?
5. Does normal doubt vanish as an artifact of hypnotic retrieval?
6. Is hypnotically refreshed recall dissimilar to other eyewitness recall?
7. What options are left for the clinician?

It is our contention that a therapist's theory of memory will determine the procedures utilized in memory retrieval. Thus, controversies regarding the use of hypnosis in refreshing memory are ultimately based on assumptions regarding the nature of memory itself.

WHAT IS MEMORY?

Since the question of what constitutes memory is so vital, it is unfortunate that the answer is not very clear. Scores of theories have been postulated to account for learning, retention, and forgetting.

A Definition of Memory

"Memory" is normally considered to be *the capacity and faculty to retain information, thoughts, feelings, and other experiences in the mind and to recall what is past.* Common definitions of memory involve three mental processes: learning, retaining, and recalling. Memory involves the abilities to store a variety of inputs from the physical senses, internal thoughts, and emotions, and to reproduce them at some future time.

A Brief History of Memory Research

Serious psychological study of the phenomena of memory began in the latter part of the 19th century, in the earliest psychology laboratories of Ebbinghaus and James and in the evolving clinical work of Breuer, Freud, and Janet. As in most endeavors, the clinical and experimental paths diverged almost immediately.

One-Component Theories

Ebbinghaus (1885), using himself as the only subject, employed nonsense syllables to ascertain the magnitude of learning and retention. Memory was employed as the dependent variable in studying learning. His verbal learning approach and his "curve of forgetting" became the prototypes for behaviorist studies on the nature of learning and performance. The theoreticians and researchers who carried out this research (Guthrie, Thorndike, Hull, Skinner, Underwood, etc.), dominated the field of experimental psychology for decades. Because their theories were primarily based on associationistic theories of learning, they were quite reluctant to postulate any mental mechanisms intervening between stimulus and response. Nilsson (1979) has critically suggested that such studies of learning and performance assessed only a small component of memory, and that because of the influence of these studies, "it is not surprising that memory research as understood today was dormant during this period" (p. 3).

By contrast, Freud (e.g., 1915/1949) focused more on retrieval than on learning per se. His primary interest was in the motivational aspects of memory. Basing his theories on clinical work with his patients, he postulated that some memories, although recorded accurately and unaltered, become unavailable to conscious recall. Such memories, he believed, contain material that is unacceptable to current functioning of the ego. They are "repressed" or maintained solely in the unconscious mind. They can be released from the unconscious directly by hypnosis or symbolically in dreams, slips of the tongue, and psychoanalysis. When released from the unconscious, their remembrance allows for alteration not in their content, but in their early emotional significance. Both the behavioral and early Freudian investigators believed that the content of memory is essentially accurate.

Ego psychologists such as Hartmann, Kris, and Lowenstein (1946) and Rapaport (1942), continuing Freud's concentration on retrieval, underlined the importance of the individual's maturational level in determining what is retained. They postulated that unconscious material can be altered by subsequent events. Thus what is remembered is a constellation of events rather than a completely intact memory trace. Rapaport suggested that when the past is reconstructed and recognized, it becomes possible for an event to be recalled.

Two-Component Theories

Not all early memory investigators postulated memory as a unitary phenomenon. With the development of two-component theories, memory came to be viewed as a creative as well as a reproductive process. The accuracy of specific memories was called into question.

William James (1890) distinguished between "primary" and "secondary" memory in consciousness. James believed that personal remembering of some event from the past requires a consciousness of the continuity between past and present. Later termed "remembrance" by Reiff and Scheerer (1959), this type of memory is considered different from impersonal recall of facts, and subject to different laws.

Bergson (1896/1911) also postulated two types of memory: "bodily" memory and "mental" memory. Imaging or bodily memory *represents* rather than *replicates* the past. Thus memory was thought to be of two varieties, one reproductive and one productive. Clarapede (1911/1951), Katona (1940), Koffka (1935), Lewin (1936), and Stern (1939) all studied this productive quality of memory, In 1932, Bartlett introduced the important concept of "schema." He concluded a series of studies with a definition of memory as

> an imaginative reconstruction or construction built out of the relation of our attitude toward the whole active mass of organized past reactions or experience, and to a little outstanding detail which commonly appears in image or language form. *It is thus hardly ever really exact . . . and it is not at all important that it should be.* (p. 213, in italics in original)

Schachtel (1949) took Bartlett's definition a step further, arguing that recollection of the past often follows the direction of "conventionalization." In this view, memory—a combination of the events that occurred and of the current ego state of the rememberer—operates naturally to serve the present needs of individuals. This is an obvious concern with regard to eyewitness testimony.

A two-component concept of memory was further developed in the late 1950s in the work of Miller, Galanter, and Pribram (1960) and Broadbent (1958), who reconceptualized memory in terms of information processing. Computer language was employed to reach a better understanding of human memory. This perspective helped open the door to an amalgamation of the clinical and experimental approaches to learning (i.e. Brown, 1958; Peterson & Peterson, 1959) and a structural theory of memory (Atkinson & Schiffrin, 1968, 1971).

A Structural View of Memory

Most modern investigators agree that at least three components of mental processes are involved in memory:

1. *Sensory registers* are representations of stimulus events on visual, auditory, kinesthetic, gustatory, or olfactory sensors.

2. *Short-term memory,* such as remembering a person's name, telephone numbers, or where one has parked the car, involves a level of processing far beyond these sensory registers.
3. *Long-term memory* occurs when materials are stored for much longer periods, perhaps for life.

Although there are great differences between theorists, most now accept some form of duplex model for memory structure.

The Duplex Model of Short- and Long-Term Storage

When an event occurs in the presence of an individual, its image registers as a visual icon, auditory echo, or passing aroma, taste, or feeling. Such unprocessed stimuli may be assembled into culturally relevant recognizable patterns or images and fade with time.

Certain of these perceptions do not fade. They are unconsciously chosen, out of the inestimable number of possible images, to be placed in short-term storage. Atkinson and Schifrin (1968) claim that information passes from the environment to the sensory registers and then to short-term memory (also known as "primary memory," "memory of the moment," "conscious memory," or "temporary working memory"). Once in short-term storage, information can be transformed into long-term memory (permanent memory storage).

Computer memory is often described in similar terms. Input is entered onto a keyboard and placed in random access memory (RAM), where it is manipulated and transformed, and then sometimes saved in long-term storage on a diskette, hard drive, or tape in the form of magnetic impulses that can then be recalled and used from storage by means of commands.

Once information is in short-term memory, a variety of control processes (such as rehearsal, coding, and retrieval strategies) determine the strength of subsequent response output. Rehearsal is considered most powerful in directly affecting the strength and quantity of recall. Short-term memories are transformed into long-term memory by coding; to remember a list of words, for example, we may create a meaningful story, an auditory mnemonic of the first letters, or a visual image. Since short-term storage houses primarily conscious material, retrieval is automatic and instantaneous. By contrast, reclaiming information from long-term storage (the repository of unconscious material) requires the selection of an appropriate retrieval strategy and successful search of long-term memory contents.

Losses from short-term memory occur regularly through decay or displacement. Once information is established in long-term memory, however, it is assumed that failure of recall is primarily due to ineffective retrieval strategies. Hypnosis is deemed effective in refreshing memories by providing an alternative effective retrieval strategy.

The postulated differences between short- and long-term storage are supported by physiological theories of memory, to be discussed shortly.

Levels-of-Processing Theory

One paradigm first proposed by Craik and Lockhart (1972), and subsequently studied by Craik and Jacoby (1979) and Craik and Tulving (1975), is designed to account for some of the differences in retention and relearning. In this model, strength of memory is a function of the depth of processing.

Instead of viewing items encoded by perceptual systems as units, which are shuttled between short- and long-term stores, these authors suggest that the level at which events are processed depends on the total current processing load at the time of learning and the amount of time involved. The more attention that can be given and the more meaningful the material, the deeper the level of processing. Limitations are not by structure, but by what Craik and Jacoby (1975) call a "limited-capacity central processor." This central processor works primarily with conscious memory.

This theory, like the duplex and consolidation theories, holds that losses from primary (conscious) memory result from the diverting of attention or interference by contiguous perceptions. Losses from secondary (unconscious) memory are due to alterations in encoding—the transformation of memory components to make them acceptable. Memory strength is directly related to the depth to which an item was taken; the deeper the processing, analysis, or meaning, the stronger the memory.

Craik's group describes two types of memory rehearsal: Type I ("maintenance"), whose sole purpose is to maintain items' availability in memory (common in verbal learning experiments), and Type II ("elaborative"), which involves deeper levels of analysis (more typical in complex clinical and forensic situations). Only rehearsal of this second type can lead to memory enhancement. Thus, the quality rather than the quantity of rehearsal is critical. This concept is particularly important in the controversy between experimental and clinical investigators regarding the relevance of laboratory studies for clinical applications.

If laboratory experiments primarily involve Type I rehearsal and crime situations involve Type II, it is likely that results of laboratory studies demonstrating confabulation, increases in percentages of errors for intentional learning, and even complete failure of hypnotic hypermnesia may have limited generalizability to the forensic setting. This is a core issue that is addressed more completely later in this chapter. For present purposes, these hypotheses stand as an illustration that one's theory of memory can determine both the method of investigation and the interpretation of data.

Toward a Unified Theory of Memory?

There is no single comprehensive and universally accepted theory of memory. Not surprisingly, researchers are divided along traditional lines in psychological thinking. Major positions include the biological, the behavioral, and the psychodynamic. Studies and results have very much been consistent with the values and orientations of the researchers.

Biological Theories

The physiological theories of Hebb, Penfield, and others emerge from two sources: (1) experimentation with surgical procedures and stimulation of brain centers, and (2) behavioral observations of the selective memory ability that commonly occurs in Alzheimer disease or following electroconvulsive shock treatments. Within this approach, the primary search is for individual loci for specific memories, or for chemical alterations that accompany learning and remembering.

Proponents of the consolidation theory of memory, which emanates from this work, posit that a trace is set down at the synapse and creates a biochemical change. It needs time and repetition to become firmly fixed as a memory. Interference with the time needed to acquire and accommodate to the new information will reduce the possibility of effective biological change. Cases of retrograde amnesia are commonly employed to support this position. Traces interrupted by a trauma are never consolidated. They are not available for recall because they were never put into long-term memory storage. In cases of alcohol or drug blackouts, it is assumed that the traces are not sufficiently incorporated to form a lasting memory.

Behavioral Theories

Like the biological investigators, behavioral theorists value measurement accuracy and study errors in recall. They also consider the strength of memory to be affected by the new stimuli interfering with the consolidation of previous traces.

There are differences between biological and behavioral theories, however. Behavioral (associationistic) theories derive primarily from the work of Guthrie and Hull. Guthrie posited that learning and retention were essentially a function of contiguity of events. The memory trace is made by simple association. In his view, memory was enhanced by the number of related associations. Hull's stimulus–response (S-R) position is that memory strength, like all habit strength, is the result of the number of practices with a particular piece of information. Proactive inhibition and retroactive inhibition of learning are produced by related associations.

Literally thousands of studies have tested for this type of learning and retention, using animal subjects and undergraduates who learned nonsense syllables, which varied in perceived meaningfulness. These studies represented a core of experimental psychology research for almost 30 years. There is a wealth of data supporting the intricate constructs of these theories. However, generalizability to more complex human learning and to the clinical setting remains limited.

Psychodynamic Theories

Psychodynamic theories follow an opposite viewpoint. Little attention is given to conscious or short-term memory; it is focused entirely on long-term storage and retrieval methods. Analytic theorists, following Freud, have focused more on forgetting than on learning.

Generally speaking, learning is believed to occur in a single trial in which significant material is fixed in the mind. Differential recall is entirely a function of what is retrieved. Events and memories that are psychologically painful to the conscious ego are repressed and withheld in the unconscious mind until such time as the ego changes sufficiently to allow for their integration, or the memories emerge in an acceptable symbolic form.

Contrary to the early formulations of Freud, modern psychodynamic theorists, influenced by the work of Rapaport (1951) and Jaensch (1923), perceive memories less as a direct, accurate representation of events and more as an interactive experience with the current ego state. Studies of this viewpoint essentially derive from complex clinical cases and reasoning.

Another approach that emerged from psychology laboratories as well as clinical observation is the position advocated by Gestalt writers. The primary Gestalt notion of memory, as studied by Koffka, Katona, Kohler, Lewin, and others, is that each individual memory trace occurs within both an internal ("memory column") and an external context. Items that are unlike any others will have a lesser chance of being remembered, because the symbolic representation (the memory column) is smaller. These isolated individual traces will be more clearly recalled only if they are transformed to fit better within some greater whole.

Gestalt authors, Piaget (e.g., 1953), and the post-Freudians Jaensch and Rapaport all stress the importance of the state of the organism at the occurrence of the event to be learned and remembered. Reproduction of the original learning is dependent both on a reactivation of the trace and on replication of the column in which the ego functions. Stimuli that initially occurred when the ego was functioning at a different operational level are less likely to be recalled.

This is a particularly important point for hypnotic age regression studies. Retrieval utilizing age regression to life periods that preceded causal thinking will be impeded by the current adult ego state of the individual, because the memory was laid down when the phenomenologically functioning child did not automatically make causal assumptions.

Using this perspective, Relinger (1984) makes an important distinction between studies of age regression and of hypermnesia (increasingly vivid recall over time). In the former, there are likely to be both "excessive demand characteristics created by the elaborate regression suggestions," and "inevitable confabulation" caused by the long lapse of time between learning and recall (pp. 212–213). By contrast, hypnotic hypermnesia, in which subjects are asked to recall previously learned material in a free narrative format, can be freer of such sources of inaccuracy.

The Interaction of Hypnosis and Memory

The nature of the hypnosis performed is inextricably tied to the theory of memory espoused. Naturally, S-R experimenters employ different types of hypnosis to refresh memory than do Freudian and Gestaltist practitioners. Those who follow contiguity theory approach hypnosis by carefully attempting to walk through the specifics already recalled, in order to retrieve the parts for which the subject is amnesic. The S-R (Hullian) approach advocates increasing rehearsal and practice with the material. Many experimental laboratory studies of hypermnesia have employed such methods.

Gestaltists, by contrast, attempt to reproduce the entire context in which the original learning occurred. This includes the level of thinking, mood state, and type of cognitive operations that were present. This approach would come closest to fostering revivification as a method to retrieve memories. The Freudian/psychodynamic approach to hypnosis normally involves attempts to recreate the emotion of the moment when the learning first occurred. Abreaction and emotional release are stressed as a way of allowing the memory to come forth.

Because each approach investigates the material from a different perspective and is limited to particular approaches in refreshing recall hypnotically, it stands to reason that the data obtained are often discrepant. Much of the controversy emanating from results of experiments conceived and performed from dissimilar perspectives can be traced to initially disparate beliefs about the nature of memory per se.

Our own perspective is that of the clinical practitioner. Although we draw from the laboratory work of our more experimental colleagues, we do not attempt to explore the intricacies of all variables that are significant for experimental researchers. For the clinician about to testify in court, the following discussion will provide a set of working guidelines. Further research may be necessary for specific cases.

A Working Theory of Memory

1. As an event unfolds, it is perceived and laid down in the senses as a trace that is acceptable to the current ego state of an individual.

2. There is a period (measurable in microseconds) during which these sensory traces are evaluated for meaningfulness to the individual. If there is some internalized reason or motivation to retain the information, it is then processed into short-term storage.

3. Once in short-term storage (conscious levels of processing), the trace can be recalled for some period of time and can be transformed by analysis, coding, or personal relevance and consolidated into long-term storage—the repository of personally relevant material.

Imagine, for example, that a man on a tropical island has a pleasant walk along the ocean; during this walk, he wades in the ocean, sees a sunset, feels the wind, smells the aromas of fragrant flowers and sea life, and so on. Included in the myriad of percepts is the vision of some forms of sea life attached to rocks by the ocean. In the course of his day, he man may experience a plethora of physical sensations and internal reactions. The sunset may conjure up other sunsets, a longing for a dear friend, or a feeling of being close to nature. It is unlikely that the organisms attached to the rocks by the ocean will play a very significant part in these reactions, unless the man happens to be a Hawaiian. In that case, he may pay closest attention to the delicacy *opihi* and store the location for later harvest. Without the personal, cultural knowledge of *opihi*, the man is likely to make little use of long-term storage. With such added personal and cultural significance, the entire experience may well be centered around the discovery and the anticipated feast with friends.

4. The personal meaningfulness of stimuli increases with the number of perceptual systems involved. Thus the visual notice of the *opihi* may well be combined with aromas, a grumbling stomach, and an anticipatory taste. Even the mood present at the time of a percept will have an impact on later recall (see Bower, 1981). The closer the replication of the emotional internal states and the external stimuli, the greater the subsequent recall.

5. The likelihood of remembering an event is increased to the extent that the event fits comfortably into an already known body of knowledge.

6. By contrast, events that are in sharp contrast to expectations may place an indomitable trace in memory because of the high level of surprise or emotion, or because the memory is consciously incidental. Many people, for example, have very clear memories of what they were doing on November 22, 1963, when they heard the news of President Kennedy's assassination.

7. Once a stimulus enters into long-term storage, memory is primarily a function of retrieval strategy and ego state.

8. Remembrance—long-term memory that assumes the continuity of the individual—is different from recall of unrelated facts (see Reiff & Scheerer, 1959). These memories are more likely to be affected by the interactive and productive nature of memory. This may in part explain how so many people can remember hitting a winning home run. An individual who identifies with an event of importance after it occurs may well in personal remembrance *become* part of the event. For a person who came of age in the late 1960s, for instance, this might involve a memory of being at Woodstock, the 1968 Chicago Democratic Convention, or Newport the night "Dylan went electric."

9. Loss of memory preceding and following a trauma is different from amnesia due to drug or alcohol blackout. In the trauma situation, it is presumed that the conscious memory traces are lost; however, because of the number of perceptual systems and internal states involved, some representation of the events has entered long-term storage and can subsequently be retrieved. In such cases of retrograde amnesia, long-term memory may initially suffer from retrieval problems because the short-term trace has been obliterated.

By contrast, during a blackout, only sensory registers and short-term memory are involved. Because of interference from the drugged state and lack of consolidation, no transformation into long-term memories occurs. The events only last during the current state of consciousness—a state characterized by a shutdown of higher centers. It is possible that such a blackout operates like anterograde amnesia, where new learning is affected. In short, no learning remains to be remembered. Retrieval strategies, including hypnosis, can only be expected to work on trauma-induced amnesia.

10. Memory, at least for significant or meaningful personal matters, is interactive rather than static. Available evidence does not support the "tape recorder" notion that memory reproduces events as they objectively occur and replays them exactly. Stimuli in the world are altered in memory first as they are encoded; again as they are stored; and finally in the decoding, retrieval, and expression process.

11. The veracity of any particular unit of remembrance is less important in clinical work than in legal work. In the clinical setting, the goal is to use the recovered memories to aid the patient's insight, current functioning, and/or comfort. In the legal setting, it is to find the facts and take appropriate social action. Normally, these goals are in harmony; however, recent litigation regarding the admissibility of evidence can produce a situation in which correct clinical practice can have the effect of limiting the patient's subsequent legal rights. This is especially likely when hypnosis is used to enhance retrieval and refresh memory.

DOES HYPNOSIS AID MEMORY?

ATTORNEY: Doctor, you used the term "amnesia" earlier. Can you tell the court just what "amnesia" is?

WITNESS: "Amnesia" is a medical term describing a loss of memory that is usually caused by some physical or psychological event. It usually is partial with regard to certain abilities or skills (an individual may forget who he or she is, but not how to speak or drive a car) or time (there may be loss of memory for a period that is in close proximity to some trauma).

ATTORNEY: Now, what is "retrograde amnesia"?

WITNESS: "Retrograde amnesia" is loss of memories that just preceded a traumatic event. For example, a person who has a serious automobile accident may lose not only the memory of the event, but also memory for any events that immediately preceded the crash. It is commonly believed that memory traces need time to consolidate inside the mind before they can be properly stored. If something interferes with that consolidation, it interferes with the storage process and the memory is lost, at least to the conscious mind.

ATTORNEY: Well, then, if the memory is not consolidated or is lost, how can hypnosis possibly help retrieve it?

WITNESS: That's a question of "hypermnesia," the opposite of amnesia. Hypermnesia is the particularly vivid recall of events, usually with substantial detail. In hypnotic hypermnesia, events that are stored in the unconscious mind are brought forth with exceptional clarity even if they were previously unavailable to the person. Now, obviously, hypnotic aid to recall can only happen with memories that are in the mind and are blocked. It cannot work with material that was never laid down in the first place. Hypnosis works on the retrieval strategies, not on the original learning. What hypnotic hypermnesia is designed to do is provide a more effective search procedure.

Hypnotic Hypermnesia: Memory versus Pseudomemory

Clinical writers and practitioners in hypnosis are more likely to believe in the value of hypnotic hypermnesia; experimental researchers are more likely to be skeptical.

Hypnotic Retrieval of Memory

The two cases most commonly cited as evidence favoring the use of hypnosis in forensic settings are the Chowchilla, California, kidnapping case (*People v. Woods*, 1977) and a San Francisco Bay area kidnapping and rape case (*People v. Barbosa*, 1977) (see Kroger & Doucé, 1979).

In the first case, a school bus was hijacked. Twenty-six children and the bus driver were abducted at gunpoint and imprisoned in vans in an underground tomb in a remote rock quarry. After everyone had escaped, the bus driver was questioned in his normal waking state. His memory was sketchy. However, with hypnosis, he was able to remember enough of a license plate (all but one digit) to provide the police with the lead they needed to catch the kidnappers.

The second case involved the kidnapping and rape of two girls aged 7 and 12. In the waking state, the victims' memories could not provide any substantial leads. With hypnosis, however, the older girl remembered rust spot patterns on the perpetrator's car; details of articles in the car; and a transaction between the abductor and a repairman at a San Diego gas station, including use of a "red, white, and blue credit card" for repairs. When the FBI apprehended the kidnapper, they confirmed the details of the girl's hypnotically refreshed memory.

These anecdotes are very persuasive, as are claims by Reiser (1985b), Ault (1980), Stratton (1977), and others. Reiser and Nielson (1980), reviewing over 400 consecutive cases at the Los Angeles Police Department, claimed that new information was elicited in 80% of interviews that employed hypnosis. Furthermore, corroboration of this information, when possible, indicated that 91% was at least "somewhat accurate." (Clear definitions of "accuracy" were not provided, however.)

Indeed, any hypnotherapist working with a patient who experiences hypermnesia of recall with appropriate affect (abreaction) for the event, followed by symptom relief, cannot help being impressed with the vividness and apparent accuracy of the memory. Critics, however, abound.

Kihlstrom (1985) reports that Sloane (1981) extended Reiser and Nielson's (1980) data by investigating 44 consecutive cases. He found no advantage of hypnosis over forensic interviews. A similar result was also reported by Geiselman et al. (1986) with a laboratory simulation study, described in detail below. Attempts to replicate such dramatic instances of accurate memory enhancement in laboratory settings have been generally unsuccessful.

Orne (1979) points out that in cases like the Chowchilla kidnapping, there is no objective verification of the findings. He argues that many license plates that could not possibly have been involved have been recalled under hypnosis. In fact, Franklin Ray, the Chowchilla bus driver, called out one irrelevant license plate number as well as the correct one (Kroger & Doucé, 1979). In another case reported by Orne (1979), a purported witness to the famous Brink's holdup identified the license plate of a university president—a nonparticipant in the holdup.

Early Use of Hypnosis for Memory Retrieval: The Discovery of Pseudomemories

In the late 1800s, Breuer and Freud (1895/1955) employed hypnosis as a means of reaching repressed unconscious memories; the resulting catharsis for patients, they believed, would release their psyches from emotional pain. So vivid were his patients' memories of childhood trauma that Freud based his early theories of childhood sexuality in part on these hypnotically elicited revelations. When later inquiry into some of these memories proved them inaccurate, the theories also matured and changed, as did Freud's methods. Concerned about the accuracy issue, and apprehensive about the high level of affect and emotional expression, Freud settled on the technique of free association as a basis for revelation of the unconscious. It is important to note that the catharsis of earlier patients was reportedly helpful to them. Thus, from a clinical standpoint, the fact that the content of patients' recall was part fantasy was of little consequence.

Janet (1889), a contemporary of Freud, also described the tendency of hypnotized patients to confabulate. He actually employed this skill in treatment and took it one step further: He reported the creation and implantation of a therapeutic pseudomemory that was more ego-syntonic for the patient. The patient in question, Marie, was multisymptomatic and diagnosable as a conversion hysteric. Janet investigated the origin of each symptom hypnotically. Subsequently, he suggested repeatedly to Marie in hypnosis that events she had actually experienced had not occurred. Instead, he substituted "normalization" suggestions (e.g., her menarche was without unusual incident; a child with whom she shared a bed was not ill with impetigo; etc.). Each symptom disappeared with the hypnotic suggestions.

Modern Reports of Pseudomemories

Pseudomemories have also been created in modern times. Coons (1988) described a case in which police use of an extremely suggestive hypnotic technique produced a false (or at the very least, an illegally obtained) confession. Researchers and legal experts have expressed concern over the ability to deliberately create such pseudomemories, as well as the possibility of an interrogator's *inadvertently* creating such pseudomemories (Orne, Whitehouse, Dinges, & Orne, 1988; Perry, Laurence, D'Eon, & Tallant, 1988). In such circumstances, injustice could occur. In the *People v. Shirley* (1982) case (discussed more fully in Chapter Five), police interrogators' possible creation of pseudomemories during their hypnosis sessions with the alleged victim was a prime factor in the extreme position opposing hypnotic memory refreshing taken by the California Supreme court (see also *State v. Mack*, Minn., 1980).

The Hypermnesia Dilemma

Most clinicians and laypersons believe that hypnosis will aid production of recall. There exist, however, two crucial questions: (1) Is it the hypnosis itself that promoted the enhanced recall? (2) Are the retrieved memories accurate?

Addressing the first question, Smith (1983) writes, "If an individual is suddenly able, under hypnosis, to remember important details of a crime that were not reported earlier, the assumption is that it was the hypnosis that was responsible for the improved recollection" (p. 390). However, she postulates that it may have been other factors, such as the relaxation, the longer and more detailed questioning, the reinstatement of context through evocation of environmental and emotional cues, or other personality differences in such subjects.

For a court, the second question regarding the difference between real memory and pseudomemory is more central. Sensational reports from nonlaboratory situations suffer from lack of possible control groups and fail to meet the criteria for accuracy that are mandatory in laboratory experiments or forensic settings. Despite the compelling drama of age regression, and believability exceeding that produced by a Stanislavski-trained actor, the relived memories may contain a mixture of fantasies, personal reactions, and the actual events. There is no evidence that the investigator can reliably distinguish among these.

Nonequivalence of Studies and Data

An additional quandary for clinicians and researchers is that, in addition to their differing needs for information, they may well be encountering different phenomena entirely. According to Smith (1983), studies of nonsense syllables in a laboratory probably involve memory states and operations far different from those experienced by a crime victim. She notes that the type of material being learned; the level of arousal of the subject; the fact that one situation measures intentional and the other incidental learning; and the perceived consequences of recall are all quite different in laboratory and real-life situations. Pettinati (1988), summarizing the extant research, agrees by maintaining that "clinical research on hypnotic hypermnesia in the therapeutic setting . . . is completely lacking" (p. 288).

DOES THE NATURE OF THE MATERIAL AFFECT HYPERMNESIA?

Personally meaningful material should respond more favorably to hypnotic retrieval methods than nonmeaningful material should. A considerable body of empirical literature supports this contention.

At least four major categories of relevant studies exist: (1) laboratory studies of nonmeaningful material; (2) laboratory studies of meaningful stimuli; (3) simulation studies of real-life events; and (4) field reports.

Laboratory Studies of Nonmeaningful Material

As early as 1925, Young reported that hypnosis did not improve subjects' recall of unconnected lists of words. Huse (1930), replicating and extending Young's (1925) work, reported no differences for hypnotized and waking subjects in recall of nonsense syllables after a 24-hour delay. Mitchell (1932) reported similar findings. Rosenthal (1944) also demonstrated that unless the words to be learned were organized into a meaningful context, there was no advantage for hypnosis in memory enhancement. However, Rosenthal did report increased recall by hypnotic subjects when they were stressed. This finding has been cited as supporting the psychodynamic position in two ways: (1) Hypnosis affects retrieval rather then encoding strategies; and (2) more long-term memories exist than can be easily recalled.

In a review of laboratory studies that used hypnosis, Weitzenhoffer (1957) noted the remarkable consistency of studies attempting to use hypnosis to aid recall of meaningless stimuli. None showed any enhancement of recall with hypnosis. Similar conclusions have been drawn by Das (1961), Barber and Calverly (1966), and Rosenhan and London (1963). One exception to this observation is work in Poland by Augustynek (1978, 1979). In his studies, memory was enhanced for all types of stimuli under hypnosis conditions.

By contrast, many studies that have used hypnosis to aid recall for meaningful material have shown positive results.

Laboratory Studies of Meaningful Material

Effects of Personal Relevance and Emotional Stress

Stalnaker and Riddle (1932) found that highly susceptible hypnotic subjects demonstrated better recall for personally relevant learned material under hypnosis. Unfortunately, methodological problems (nonequivalent directions for hypnotic and waking subjects, no control over length or type of selections, accuracy of recall with original stimuli, and problems associated with age regression vs. hypermnesia) make these results less conclusive.

White, Fox, and Harris (1940) demonstrated significantly greater hypermnesia for film scenes and poetry by hypnotized subjects compared to control subjects after a 24-hour delay. No such advantage was found in recall of nonsense syllables. Unfortunately, the small number of subjects in this study allowed one outstanding subject's scores to have an extraordinary impact.

Rosenthal's (1944) unanticipated finding that hypnotic subjects showed enhanced recall of lists of common words learned when the subjects were stressed has an important implication. When learning occurs under stressful conditions, more stimuli are internalized than can be readily recalled from conscious memory. More effective retrieval techniques, such as hypnosis, could produce more recall. Because hypnosis is viewed in the forensic context as a retrieval assister (by reducing stress-induced inhibition), this finding is fairly significant.

Additional support for this has been provided by Goldstein and Sipprelle (1970), who point out that when emotional trauma occurs together with an event, a partial amnesia about the event is possible. Hypnosis is seen as a way to facilitate the recall of such events. Also consistent are Pascal's (1949) results suggesting similar advantages with nonhypnotic relaxation. Under relaxation suggestions, subjects evidenced hypermnesia, recalling material on later trials that they did not remember earlier.

Kroger and Fezler (1976) have commented on the common components shared by relaxation instructions and hypnosis, and Schafer and Rubio (1978) have stressed the importance of relaxation in assisting hypnotic memory.

Swiercinsky and Coe (1970) have demonstrated that it is easier to *learn* emotionally meaningful material under hypnosis than material that is not emotionally meaningful. These findings support Cheek and LeCron's (1968) belief that heightened emotional states are altered states like hypnosis and similarly produce extra receptiveness.

Ten years after Rosenthal's (1944) study, Sears (1954) demonstrated a consistent gain in remembering items in a visual display for hypnotized subjects, both immediately after learning trials and 1 week later. Cooper and London (1973), using a 33-item short-answer response set, found no advantage for hypnotized subjects. However, they did report that repeated testing did enhance memory for both waking and hypnotized subjects. The fact that all improvement could be accounted for by practice effects brings into question Sears's (1954) results, since hypnotic memory improvement for items on a table was shown only after a prior nonhypnotic trial. Cooper and London (1973) concluded, "[T]he findings suggest that the memory for material of little emotional impact and of a highly factual nature is not enhanced by hypnosis involving motivating instructions" (p. 320).

One interesting sidelight in this study was that the passage read by subjects concerned a rare chemical. Students who were chemistry majors or enrolled in a chemistry course demonstrated significantly better recall than other subjects. They were not included in the study, in the authors' attempt to control level of meaningfulness. It is interesting to speculate on the relevance of this factor, particularly because Sears (1954) indicated that motivating instructions had no differential effect for hypnotized and waking subjects. Indeed, the chemistry majors were the subjects who were most likely to have taken the information into long-term memory, and most likely to have shown an enhancement with hypnotic retrieval methods.

O'Connell, Shor, and Orne (1970), using an age regression procedure, reported that recall was greater under hypnosis, but so was confabulation. Some childhood classmates remembered with great vividness were actually not even in the class. Orne (1979) further notes that the actual number of factual events recalled was no greater under hypnosis than in the waking state.

Using meaningful prose and nonsense syllables with both high- and low-susceptibility subjects and a week's delay in testing, Dhanens and Lundy (1975) employed six treatment conditions. Two important findings were reported. For nonsense syllables, there were no differences between hypnotized and nonhypnotized subjects. For the meaningful prose, highly hypnotic susceptible subjects with motivation instructions demonstrated better recall. The authors, stressing the importance of extrahypnosis factors such as motivation, suggested that the advantage was due to memory retrieval organization. As evidence for this, they cited a nonsignificant but interesting improvement shown by low-susceptibility subjects in the high-motivation condition.

The Dhanens and Lundy (1975) study is frequently cited by authors on both sides of the argument. Those who believe in the value of hypnosis for hypermnesia refer to the advantage of the highly susceptible hypnotic group's performance. Others, who believe that nonhypnotic factors are responsible for hypermnesia, cite the small number of subjects in each group and favor an explanation regarding the effect of instructions and motivation by the subjects.

Augustynek (1977) also found evidence of a hypnotic hypermnesia effect for meaningful text (Relinger, 1984). DePiano and Salzberg (1981), using an open-ended question–answer completion task and recall of "incidental" learning, reported better recall for motivated hypnotized subjects than for equivalently motivated waking subjects.

Manner of Presentation: Intentional versus Incidental Learning

The question of incidental versus intentional learning is important in making comparisons between laboratory and forensic situations. Presumably, witnesses to a crime were not focusing on the events that occurred. Instead, they were exposed to such actions unexpectedly and taken by surprise. In such situations, personally meaningful material might well be learned and entered into long-term storage. However, the high level of arousal might obliterate short-term memory, making retrieval more difficult.

This issue of level of arousal was addressed in a laboratory simulation format by DePiano and Salzberg (1981). In their study, they created three levels of physiological arousal through viewing films. Galvanic skin response (GSR), heart rate, and self-report indices confirmed differential levels of arousal for films depicting surgery, sexual activity, and horses in a pastoral setting. They reported no differential effect of level of arousal on recall for hypnotic or waking subjects in the incidental learning task.

This study, unfortunately, creates more questions than it answers. The experimenters did not test for recall of the film material itself, only for the subject matter of an experimentally created "audio disturbance" and contents of the testing room. Level of arousal was measurably different for the three films, but the range was limited to a laboratory situation. The extent to which suspension of disbelief for the films could occur, and the arousal level of empathy for the subjects, were both rather different from a crime situation, in which personal involvement may produce a far greater range of affect and arousal.

An interesting *accidental* experiment that provided another look at the matter of incidental learning occurred in our own laboratories (Shapiro, 1979). During a graduate training class in hypnotherapy, class members had undergone a basic relaxation-oriented induction and were being tested on the Harvard Group Hypnotic Susceptibility Scale (HGHSS), Form A (Shor & Orne, 1962). The class was interrupted by a secretary who announced that the burglar alarm at the instructor's home was ringing and that the instructor was to call his neighbor immediately at a given number. The instructor then turned the class and the remainder of the HGHSS scale over to an experienced teaching assistant, who completed the scale and a standard debriefing after the instructor had left. Because of concerns for any lingering effects of uncompleted suggestions, the induction was repeated a week later, and subjects were asked to recall on paper all the events of the prior class session. Both high- and low-susceptibility subjects all had memories of the instructor leaving and the reason why. There were slight differences in the number of details recalled, which correlated positively with susceptibility. What was astonishing about this event was that four of the eight highly susceptible subjects remembered the name of the neighbor that was mentioned by the secretary, and one of the subjects remembered six of the seven digits in the phone number. None of the low-susceptibility subjects included any such information on the free-form recall sheet.

Simulation Studies

Police investigators (e.g., Reiser, 1984b) argue that a different basic underlying memory mechanism may be involved when significance and impact are enhanced. Because of arguments that laboratory studies fail to tap the same learning, recall, or memory strategies, several studies have attempted to control for extraneous factors in the laboratory, and yet to simulate a real-life situation to obtain a more accurate test of the value of hypnotic hypermnesia. One means of making the laboratory more lifelike involves the manipulation of emotional arousal in the laboratory setting, such as was attempted by DePiano and Salzberg (1981).

Putnam (1979) showed a total of 16 subjects a videotape recording of a bicycle–automobile accident. Half of the subjects were questioned in a waking and half in a hypnotic state. No differences in the number of accurate answers were found on recall. However, he reported that the hypnosis group made significantly more errors on recall, particularly for leading questions.

One explanation of this involves the instructions and expectations given to subjects: They were instructed to remember the details for the police. Such rehearsal instructions might have served as suggestions to guess more. In addition, Putnam did not distinguish between the performance of subjects high and low in hypnotic susceptibility, and included 6 leading questions out of a total of 15 multiple-choice items. Prior work by Loftus and Zanni (1975) and Loftus (1979a) with waking eyewitnesses indicates that both rehearsal and leading questions lead to increased numbers of errors.

Zelig and Beidleman (1981), using a stressful film depicting graphic shop accidents and a 20-minute time delay, also reported no difference in accurate recall between hypnotic and waking subjects on a multiple-choice test. Hypnotic subjects, however, did make more errors on leading questions.

The methodology in the Zelig and Beidleman study is of considerable interest. In the first place, all subjects were highly susceptible (and expected hypnosis to be a part of the study). Second, experimental (hypnosis) and control (waking) conditions varied substantially. Following exposure to an 8-minute film in which the subjects viewed an amputation of a finger and an accidental death by impaling, control subjects "were escorted to an area where they *waited idly for 20 minutes in seclusion*" (p. 407, emphasis added). Hypnotized subjects were hypnotized immediately after the film, using the Weitzenhoffer and Hilgard (1959) method.

It is hard to imagine that the control subjects did much besides think about the film during their 20-minute isolation. Given the likelihood of 20 minutes of rehearsal for control subjects, the true comparison made was one between hypnosis and practice—a test of two methods of enhancing recall that is unlikely in forensic situations. Finally, the subjects in the hypnosis group had to answer their questions using a complicated ideomotor signaling system. It is not reported whether the control subjects had the same instructions.

Buckhout, Eugenio, Kramer, Licitra, and Oliver (1982), using 60 witnesses to a mock crime, found no difference between hypnotized and nonhypnotized subjects over a 3-week interval. Performance of all subjects deteriorated over that time. The authors reported a "disturbing tendency on the part of witnesses to try harder if they had been hypnotized" (p. 2). They did not employ professional hypnotists or interviewers.

Smith (1983) reported on a similar close-to-real-life study by McEwan and Yuille (1982). Although there were again no differences between hypnotized and waking subjects, all subjects were quite accurate in suspect descriptions. This was attributed to the professional police interview mode employed, which differs from research psychologists' questioning procedures.

Payne (1987) and Blatt and Lamarche (cited in Laurence, Nadon, Labelle, Button, & Perry, 1987), using the same stimulus materials but not police interviewers, found no advantage in recall using hypnosis over rehearsal, but greater number of errors.

Schafer and Rubio (1978) report on two unpublished studies in which actual staging of an "as-if" crime occurred in front of a group of police students. Both studies are given as examples in which recall under hypnosis was superior to ordinary recall.

Sanders and Simmons (1983), using a videotaped simulated crime on a television monitor (a pickpocket stealing a wallet), found hypnosis subjects less accurate than controls on both a lineup recognition and a structured recall task. However, measurement artifacts, and the fact that the hypnosis subjects also gave fewer responses and were less confident of their recall, make the overall results questionable. There is also some doubt as to whether the hypnotized subjects were in fact in an altered state at the time of questioning.

Although the comparability of simulation studies is at best questionable, the bulk of the evidence favors a qualified finding of hypnotic hypermnesia for meaningful stimuli, at least for highly susceptible subjects. As we will discuss below, such increases in recall are no guarantee of accuracy.

Field Studies

In addition to the famous *Woods* and *Barbosa* cases cited earlier, a number of additional cases and studies exist that seem to promote the use of hypnosis for refreshing recall. Kroger and Doucé (1979) report on the use of hypnosis in a federal prison murder case (*United States v. Awkard*, 9th Cir., 1979), in which hypnosis allowed a witness to "penetrate a retrograde amnesia induced by the threat of being knifed to death" and identify the murderer of a fellow inmate (Kroger & Doucé, 1979, p. 368). The authors also reported on a kidnap-and-murder case in which several witnesses were hypnotized, but no fruitful information was obtained.

Arons (1967) indicated that eyewitnesses who were initially unable to recall important information were able after hypnosis to remember a license plate number, which led to an arrest. Reiser (1974) and Reiser and Neilson (1980) reported the use of hypnosis of witnesses in providing significant investigative leads in both a murder and a rape-and-abduction case. Reiser (1976) also describes the use of hypnosis with a police officer who was the victim of a shooting during a burglary investigation. When the suspect was apprehended, he still had the officer's gun in his possession.

Schafer and Rubio (1978) reported on 14 cases in which they had been involved with the hypnotizing of witnesses. They claim that "one case was refused and of the other 13, 10 were considered to have been substantially helped by information gathered under hypnosis" (p. 84). By contrast, Karlin (1983) reports on two cases in which "there was considerable evidence that both identifications were based on confabulation" (p. 227). Karlin served as an expert witness for the defense in each trial, and points out that the manner in which the hypnosis was undertaken could have led to pseudo-memories.

A Summary of Experimental Evidence

What conclusions can be drawn from the four categories of studies summarized? Does hypnosis aid memory retrieval?

Nonmeaningful Material

The evidence is clear that hypnosis does not affect recall of nonmeaningful or nonsense material. This is precisely what we would expect. There is no reason to anticipate that nonmeaningful stimuli will be transferred to long-term memory. Because hypnosis serves as an aid to retrieval, it would not have an impact on any memory that is not stored.

Meaningful Material

It appears likely that certain material in some circumstances can be recalled more readily under hypnosis than in a waking state. Hypnosis can affect both the quantity and quality of remembrance when the material is personally meaningful.

Because of its effectiveness in aiding recall of meaningful material, hypnosis can be of particular value in generating investigative leads for material that can be subsequently independently corroborated. Few experts dispute its value in this arena, although Geiselman et al. (1985, 1986) recommend a mnemonic interview procedure that presumably works as well as hypnosis in memory retrieval but has fewer legal disadvantages.

There is, however, considerable disagreement regarding the nature of hypnotically aided recall as testimony in a courtroom. Several crucial points of argument exist. The first of these involves the veridicality of hypnotically refreshed memory.

DOES HYPNOSIS ENCOURAGE GREATER CONFABULATION?

At the present time, empirical data do not clarify the issue of whether hypnosis encourages greater confabulation. Although there is no hard evidence supporting the extent of hypersuggestibility that would produce high levels of confabulation and hardening, there also is no clear-cut proof that hypnotically refreshed memories are exactly the same as normal waking (and questionable) eyewitness memory.

One means of approaching this question is represented by attempts to demonstrate the veridicality of hypnotically refreshed memories. Dywan and Bowers (1983), using a forced-choice recall procedure for 60 line drawings after a 1-week delay, found that there was a hypnotic hypermnesia effect for highly hypnotizable subjects. However, as the number of correct responses increased, the errors increased by a greater proportion. This study has commonly been taken to support Orne's contention that hypnotically refreshed recall is likely to produce more errors than nonhypnotic recall. Sheehan and Tilden (1984, 1986) and others have also noted the increase in memory distortions with hypnosis without hypermnesia. However, other authors (Geiselman et al., 1985; Stager & Lundy, 1985) have reported hypermnesia with no such increase in errors.

The Dywan and Bowers study may be different from other studies, both in procedure and in meaningfulness of the stimuli. Dywan and Bowers had all subjects rehearse answers by reporting on the number of line drawings remembered for each of the intervening days. Such rehearsal alone can have an impact on learning and forgetting. Laurence et al. (1987) indicate that it is the primary factor in recall. There is also some question as to the actual meaningfulness of the materials, since the number of incorrect responses far outweighed the correct answers for all subjects. It has been well demonstrated, as noted above, that hypnosis does not aid differential recall for meaningless stimuli.

Viewpoint of the Investigator

One of the problems with studies in this area is that they are conducted from diverse positions. For the clinician, the question as to whether a memory is accurate is less important than the impact of that memory on the individual. Veracity takes second place to the patient's subjective reality.

The police hypnotist attempting to generate leads to solve a crime wants to generate as many leads as possible in order to investigate and apprehend guilty parties. He or she too is less interested in absolute accuracy, although veracity is somewhat more important than for the clinician.

For the experimental psychologist, by contrast, the ratio of correct to incorrect responses *is* the issue. Studies of memory enhancement must examine quantity produced with reference to its precision. Otherwise, the study of memory can become the study of imagination. If hypnosis, by its very nature, leads to memory distortion and fabrication, then the admissi-

bility of such information as evidence in court is questionable. This is precisely Bernard Diamond's (1980) position:

> I believe that once a potential witness has been hypnotized for the purpose
> of enhancing memory, his recollections have been so contaminated that he
> is rendered effectively incompetent to testify. Hypnotized persons, being
> extremely suggestible, graft onto their memories fantasies or suggestions
> deliberately or unwittingly communicated by the hypnotist. After hypno-
> sis the subject cannot differentiate between a true recollection and a fan-
> tasy or a suggested detail. Neither can any expert or trier of fact. (p. 314)

No data are provided to support this contention, and Reiser (1984b), summarizing the related literature, finds that "aside from a few anecdotal accounts, wherein investigative hypnosis was either misused or abused by
improperly trained psychiatrists (Orne, 1979), there are no convincing data
to support this assertion" (p. 121).

Orne, Soskis, et al. (1984), avoiding the extreme position of Diamond
and espousing the view of a majority of experimental investigators, state
their belief that "[because the hypnosis] often involves encouraging the
subject to experience suggested alterations of perception, memory, or mood,
the hypnotized individual may honestly report these distortions or hallucinations as real" (p. 177). They assert that if an individual is asked to look
at a license plate or event with a "hallucinated" zoom lens, he or she will
imagine the event if accurate recall is impossible. In a variety of publications, Orne has demonstrated the impact of demand characteristics on obtained data in a host of experimental situations. Similarly, Rosenthal (1966)
has shown that experimental subjects produce results that conform to the
experimenter's hypotheses inherent beliefs.

If retrieving memories with hypnosis does in fact make subjects more
likely to confabulate or err in the direction of the investigator's beliefs,
direct suggestions by the hypnotist or accidental inferences could alter the
memory retained. This could be a serious problem when it comes to eyewitness identification or accused perpetrators of crime. Serious injustice
could potentially be caused by an unsuspecting hypnotherapist whose sole
interest is a client's welfare.

This is the question at the core of the controversy. At the present time,
the available studies do not give us a clear answer. Obtained data tend to
support the expectations of the experimenter. Studies done by police investigators find little or no excess confabulation with hypnosis. Clinical
accounts have generally not expressed concern with differential veracity of
hypnotic and normal memories. By contrast, experimental studies often
conclude that the hypnosis itself introduces errors into the memory obtained. The contrasting results serve to heat up the political argument regarding territoriality.

Whether hypnosis causes confabulation can depend on the manner in which the question is posed. Suppose we ask, "Is confabulation an inevitable by-product of hypnotic retrieval?" Our answer is "no." By contrast, suppose we ask, "Can hypnosis lead to confabulation?" That answer is "yes." The harder question requires a comparison between hypnotic retrieval methods and a variety of interrogation methods that use leading questions. Is hypnosis more likely to produce confabulation? No definitive answer is yet supported by available data.

Methods of Interrogation

Many writers have suggested that the method of interrogation may be important in controlling the amount of suggestion given to the subject. There is potential danger in asking leading questions to a subject in even a moderately suggestible state.

The "television technique" favored by many police hypnotists appears to have greater likelihood for implicit suggestions. In particular, this method informs a witness that he or she will safely and comfortably view the events on the television screen in the mind's eye as a "documentary." The videotape, it is said, will allow the witness to zoom in on details, slow down, speed up, stop action, and reverse action. Closeups will be possible on any person or object, and sound can be turned up so that anything, even a whisper, can be heard. It is easy to see that such a method may encourage guessing or creativity in the absence of actual memories.

Klatzky and Erdelyi (1985) postulate that what may take place in hypnosis is a change in response criterion rather than an enhancement of retrieval. Subjects abandon their normal judgment as to what constitute signals and noise, and adopt a lesser standard between remembering and guessing. The "television technique" seems particularly susceptible to such a shift.

For this reason, Relinger (1984) strongly recommends the free-recall method, both to enhance accuracy and to reduce the influence of extra bias. He further distinguishes between hypermnesia for increased recall and age regression, which demands a reliving of a past event. Revivification of events that are (typically) long past involves memories that have inevitably changed because of changes in ego state and elapsed time.

Maximizing Memory

Accurate hypermnesia seems most probable when events to be recalled are somewhat recent and as many aspects of an individual's life as possible are included. The greater the number of visual, auditory, and kinesthetic modalities involved, the greater the likelihood of reliable hypermnesia. Since the original learning presumably involved a number of complementary sensory registers and coding processes, allowance for the recreation of relevant moods, emotions, and various types of imagery should enhance re-membrance. The closer the reinstatement of the original setting, the more likely the hypermnesia.

Hypnosis does not exactly reproduce events in the past, but neither does waking memory. Before turning to the potential problems specific to hyp-notic methods of memory retrieval, and the nature of normal eyewitness memory, we examine two core questions in hypnosis: What constitutes hypnosis, and what level of hypnosis (trance) is significant?

The Problem of Definition Revisited

In Chapter Six, we have discussed the lack of agreement on a generic def-inition of hypnosis. The position of Diamond (and experimental psycholo-gists) employs a definition derived from Hull (1933), in which hypnosis is equated with increased suggestibility.

Orne, Soskis, et al. (1984) characterize hypnosis as a subject's increased responsiveness to the experience of alterations in perception, memory, or mood:

> Regardless of whether hypnosis is conceptualized as an altered state of consciousness, believed-in imagining, role enactment, fantasy absorption, or focused attention, hypnosis is a real experience in the sense that the hypnotically responsive individual believes in it and is not merely acting as if he or she did. By allowing the hypnotist to define what is to be experienced, the hypnotized individual forgoes evaluation both of the na-ture of the suggestion and his or her reaction to it. (p. 174)

According to this definition, confabulation and influence are inevitable. Even suggestions by the hypnotist for *accurate* recall may entice individuals to produce (should they be unable to reproduce) "new" memories that are nevertheless believed to be extremely accurate.

However, many writers do not accept this "hypersuggestibility" model. Erickson, Rossi, and Rossi (1976) do not even consider hypersuggestibility to be a necessary characteristic of a trance. Hilgard (1973) argues that "al-though hypnotic-like behaviors are commonly responses to suggestion, the domain of suggestion includes responses that do *not* belong within hyp-nosis, and the phenomena of hypnosis involve more than specific re-sponses to suggestion" (p. 973). Reiser (1986), citing work by Sheehan and Perry (1976), Bowers (1977), Frankel (1976), and Chertok (1981), refers to Hull's equation of suggestibility and hypnosis as "outdated."

Kroger (1977) seems to be of the opinion that hypnotic suggestibility and general suggestibility are loosely correlated and not one and the same. Frank (1974) makes a clear and compelling case for the suggestibility inherent in any doctor–patient relationship. He discusses the impact of placebo treatment in psychotherapy and the significance of expectation on the part of both therapist and patient, without any reference to hypnosis.

Investigators who are predisposed to view hypnosis as a hypersuggestibility situation are prone to seek out or find a host of unavoidable minute cues and demand characteristics, such as those described by Orne (e.g., 1979). However, if one agrees with Edmonston (1981) that hypnosis is essentially relaxation, or with Erickson (1980) that it is an innate natural capacity that is modifiable (see also Diamond, 1977; Shapiro & Diamond, 1972), there is no reason to expect a hypnotized subject to confabulate (fill in gaps in memory) *more than a waking subject,* to please an interviewer.

One's belief regarding the nature of hypnosis leads inexorably to concern for its utilization in memory enhancement. From our own perspective, hypnosis is best characterized as intense, focused concentration. Any hypersuggestibility is secondary to the relationship between the hypnotherapist and the particular patient. Hypnosis is viewed as naturally eliciting neither more nor less confabulation, susceptibility to demand characteristics, or artifacts than waking therapy states.

Depth of Trance

The level of hypnotic trance employed by experimenters is addressed in several studies. Hilgard (1968) has contended that only highly hypnotizable subjects respond to hypnotic inductions and show differential performance.

The implications for trance depth are quite significant. Experimental data (White et al., 1940) and anecdotal reports (Shapiro, 1979) suggest that highly susceptible subjects in a trance state can provide clearly superior recall. Clinicians frequently relate hypnotizability and depth of trance to success in therapy, at least for therapies that are affected by what Kihlstrom (1985) calls

> absorptive and dissociative processes that are central to hypnosis. Along these lines, Frankel (1976) suggested that for patients who happen to be hypnotizable, the difficulties that bring them to the clinic may have their origins in naturally occurring states similar to hypnosis. (p. 403)

Most writers in this area contend that any significant hypermnesia reported for hypnotized subjects is found in highly susceptible individuals who enter a deep state of hypnosis during the remembrance phase of the studies. This is consistent with our personal clinical experience. Amnesic victims of alleged crimes who show low levels of hypnotizability have not demonstrated hypermnesia for the events.

Experimenters who have addressed this issue have normally limited their inquiry to scores obtained on one of the standard scales of hypnotic susceptibility—the HGHSS (Shor & Orne, 1962) or the Stanford Hypnotic Susceptibility Scales (Weitzenhoffer & Hilgard, 1962). Subjects who score at the higher reaches of suggestion on these scales are considered as highly susceptible. Subjects who are able to respond to few of the suggestions are considered low in susceptibility. The reliability and validity of these scales in experimental settings are well established. How they are used is another consideration.

Some experimenters have arbitrarily determined that 6 suggestions is the cutoff point. They rate subjects who score 7 (of 12) as high and those who score 6 as low (e.g., Dywan & Bowers, 1983). There is serious question whether 1 point on such a scale can indicate significant differences in actual trance depth. In a more conservative use, Cooper and London (1973) defined high-susceptibility subjects as those scoring 8–12 and low-susceptibility subjects as those scoring 0–4. Stager and Lundy (1985) found that highly hypnotizable subjects (those with scores of 10 and above) were far superior to waking or low-susceptibility subjects (those with scores of 3 or below) in recalling specifics from a film viewed a week earlier.

Relinger (1984), reviewing the extant literature, contended that although susceptibility may have been established and employed as an independent variable, none of the studies either established that subjects were in a trance during testing for recall, or controlled for the depth of such trances.

To summarize the issue, it is generally believed that depth of trance is an important factor in hypnotic hypermnesia, but the obtained empirical data are somewhat perplexing. Differences in design, measurement, procedures, and concept make the studies difficult to compare. It does seem important to measure and report trance depth, as well as the induction and deepening techniques, as a precursor to firm conclusions.

DOES DOUBT VANISH AS AN ARTIFACT OF HYPNOTIC RETRIEVAL?

Confidence and Accuracy

The question of whether doubt vanishes as an artifact of hypnotic retrieval is predicated on claims that hypnosis may not affect recall as much as it does confidence in the accuracy of the memory. This is particularly important in a courtroom, since witnesses who are more confident tend to be more believable to the jury (see Deffenbacher, 1980). The separation of confidence and accuracy, it is argued, may well render a witness impervious to cross-examination. Such a witness would be unshakable; he or she would truly believe in the accuracy of the memory, without being aware that it was actually an artifact created in the hypnosis.

Diamond (1980) considers this an *inevitable* outcome of hypnotically refreshed memory. He is not alone. Laurence and Perry (1988), summarizing the literature, reach this conclusion:

It [hypnosis] increases confidence in the veracity of both correct *and* incorrect recalled material. This is perhaps the most consistent finding to date; virtually every study that has examined the issue of confidence has found this increase. . . . [This finding] underlines the possibility that with hypnosis an unshakable witness can be created. This in turn, means that a defendant may lose his or her right to confront an accuser who has become immune to cross-examination (Warner, 1979). (pp. 326–327)

A similar conclusion was drawn by the Minnesota Supreme Court in *State v. Mack* (1980): "Because the person hypnotized is subjectively convinced of the veracity of the 'memory,' this recall is not subject to attack by cross-examination" (p. 770).

Corollary material also supports this supposition. Laurence and Perry (1983b) and Laurence et al. (1987) have shown that pseudomemories (being awakened by loud noises) can be created in a hypnotic situation and confidently reported by highly hypnotizable subjects. It has also been shown that undergraduate students believe that hypnosis "could help individuals remember previously forgotten details" (Labelle, Lamarche, & Laurence, in press); this is consistent with results reported by McConkey (1986) and McConkey and Jupp (1985). However, neither Labelle et al. (1987), McConkey (1986), nor McConkey and Jupp (1985) indicated that they specifically asked subjects whether they believed hypnotically refreshed memory would be *more* accurate than other memory.

Is this a convincing enough case to assume the *inevitability* of increased confidence, regardless of accuracy? The answer is "no." The fact that pseudomemories about being awakened during an insignificant evening by loud noises can be confidently reported as true only proves that this *can* happen, not that it inevitably occurs. The argument that a previously hypnotized witness will inevitably demonstrate an increase in confidence, regardless of accuracy, was disallowed by a Canadian judge in *Queen v. Clark* (Alberta, 1984): "There would appear to be nothing to distinguish hypnotically-refreshed testimony from testimony refreshed by other means" (p. 9). He did, however, note the importance of caution in evaluating special dangers that adhere to hypnosis.

Empirical studies have also addressed this issue, with mixed results.

Experimental Investigation of Confidence and Accuracy

Several studies (e.g., Sheehan & Tilden, 1983, 1986) suggest that hypnotized subjects do have more confidence in their answers than do control subjects, regardless of accuracy, with the effect on confidence greatest for highly hypnotizable subjects. Three other studies (Putnam, 1979; Sanders & Simmons, 1983; Zelig & Beidleman, 1981) found no significant differences between waking and hypnotized subjects on confidence. Zelig and Beidleman did report a post hoc significant correlation between hypnotic susceptibility and confidence. Sturm (1982) found neither greater hypermnesia for hypnotized subjects nor an increase in confidence.

However, there are substantive differences between these laboratory studies and testimony on a witness stand. Asking subjects to rate their level of confidence with an answer on a 5-point scale in a laboratory simulation (e.g., Putnam, 1979; Zelig & Beidleman, 1981) is dissimilar to reporting a crime to the police.

Sanders and Simmons (1983), attempting to make their confidence ratings more lifelike, asked subjects who had watched a videotaped pickpocket incident whether they would be willing to testify in court. Fewer hypnosis subjects than control subjects indicated such a willingness (as measured by a nonsignificant chi-square test). They also reported a "negative relationship between depth and susceptibility to leading questions on the recall task. The deeper the trance, the fewer the number of leading questions answered in the affirmative" (p. 75). Since the hypnosis subjects in this study also made more errors (also nonsignificant) on a decoy situation, it seems probable that confidence and accuracy were somewhat related.

Together, these results fail to support the contention that there is a particular dissociation in hypnosis between accuracy of memory and confidence. These findings are consistent with studies of nonhypnotic eyewitness testimony. Deffenbacher (1980) and Sanders and Warnick (1981) also indicate a variable correlation between eyewitness confidence and accuracy. Hypnotically refreshed memories have not been shown to be necessarily different in this way from refreshed waking memories.

To summarize, because there are numerous instances of hypnotically retrieved memories not resulting in increased confidence, it seems clear that the so-called "concretization" is not an inherent aspect of hypnosis. Equally clear in the experimental literature, clinical studies, and court cases is the fact that enhanced confidence unrelated to accuracy can be readily demonstrated. The important question then becomes whether there is a greater threat of misplaced confidence with hypnotic methods of memory retrieval.

The problem impeding a solution is one of ecological validity. Laboratory studies are too far removed from a crime or court setting. Their relevance in these artificial and less emotional situations is subject to question. Real crime situations, on the other hand, allow for no experimental control.

IS MEMORY REFRESHED BY HYPNOSIS DISSIMILAR TO WAKING RECALL?

Despite many studies indicating the dangers inherent in normal eyewitness recall (e.g., Loftus, 1979a; Wells & Loftus, 1984), decisions as to who is tried for a crime and who is found guilty by a jury often hinge on the believability of eyewitnesses. What constitutes accurate memory—and the retrieval method employed to attain certain pertinent facts—can be the basis for finding a defendant guilty or not.

The adversarial legal system, and particularly cross-examination, are believed to counteract the vagaries of eyewitness memory—at least to the extent that a jury will have sufficient facts to render fair decisions. The significant questions for us involve the efficacy and reliability of hypnotic methods of retrieving such memory.

Will a person with hypnotically refreshed memories be more impervious to cross-examination than a witness who is simply briefed prior to testifying in court? Rehearsal and briefing of witnesses prior to their appearance in court, to help them relax and tell their story without too much anxiety, are common and accepted legal practices. The difference between hypnotic rehearsal and relaxation cum briefing is as yet undetermined.

If we are to accept available data on eyewitness testimony, we must do so in the context of the unreliability of human memory per se. Memory does not work as a reproducer of objective facts; instead, it is a combination of the facts as experienced subjectively and the need states of the individual doing the reporting. Several authors have reported on the incompleteness, dishonesty, unreliability, malleability, and confabulated nature of eyewitness memory (Clifford & Hollin, 1983; Loftus, 1975, 1979a; Loftus, Miller, & Burns, 1978; Wells, Ferguson, & Lindsay, 1981; Wells & Loftus, 1984).

Haward and Ashworth (1980), citing Bartlett's (1932) pioneering work, state,

What the man in the street is not usually prepared to accept is the empirical fact that much of what is later recalled with vividness and detail, and with complete conviction as to its authenticity, has in fact undergone a degree of distortion between the perception of the event and its recall, in some cases to such an extent that the testimony is completely false. (p. 474)

The fact of this unreliability is particularly disturbing because of the weight given to eyewitness testimony in criminal investigations and courtroom procedures (Geiselman et al., 1985; Wells & Loftus, 1984).

Borchard, as early as 1932, listed 65 criminal prosecutions and convictions of people whose innocence was ultimately established beyond a doubt (cited in Hilgard & Loftus, 1979). More recent laboratory studies (Loftus & Zanni, 1975; Wells, Lindsay, & Ferguson, 1979) have described specific aspects of interrogation, such as leading questions, that increase errors but do not necessarily diminish confidence. The latter study also indicated that jurors' attributions of witness confidence were unrelated to witness accuracy, even though these attributions accounted for 50% of the variance in jurors' decisions to believe witnesses.

A comprehensive examination of eyewitness testimony is beyond the scope of this book. From our review of the extant literature on normal witness recall, it seems premature to single out hypnosis for special treatment. No reliable empirical evidence indicates that hypnosis creates greater numbers of inaccurate memories, or that the memories achieved under hypnosis are more hardened or fixed and thus more impervious to cross-examination. This lack of empirical evidence does not in any way guarantee that such increases in inaccuracies or hardening fail to occur. The current state of the art is predominantly unknown.

Given this situation, it is expected that investigators' values, beliefs, politics, and biases will continue to have greater influence than the weight of the evidence warrants. Courts will have to decide which position is the more consistent with community standards, rather than which position is true.

WHAT OPTIONS ARE LEFT FOR THE CLINICIAN?

Hilgard and Loftus (1979), Geiselman et al. (1985, 1986), and Timm (1983) have proposed methods that are designed to decrease the inaccuracies in all types of eyewitness reports. These procedures may well obviate some of the controversy, as they seem to enhance memory for events without being as subject as hypnosis is to the most compelling criticisms.

The Nature and Order of Questions

In memory-refreshing situations, the first step for all clinicians is to establish a base rate for the memory via a *free-recall* report. The clinician should be careful to provide little information or prompting to the client except for indications to continue.

Following this free narrative, specific questions can be asked in a careful, nonleading manner. During this second phase, especial care should be taken to avoid details and definite articles. Thus, the question "Did you see the red Chevy pickup?" is far more likely to lead to errors than the question "Was there a vehicle?"

It is of particular importance that interrogation skills may play a large part in both the quantity and quality of remembrances obtained. Studies that have used experienced law enforcement personnel as interviewers (Geiselman et al., 1985; McEwan & Yuille, 1982) have demonstrated a far greater amount of correct recall in both hypnosis and standard interviews.

In addition to the order and nature of questions, Malpass and Devine

(1981) have suggested the use of guided memory techniques involving "recollection of the vandalism, the vandal and the witnesses' reactions to them" to facilitate recognition performance in lineups (p. 343).

An Alternative to Hypnosis?

Geiselman et al. (1985) have expanded the guided memory procedure into what they call a "cognitive retrieval mnemonic interview." Their technique involves four different instructions to the subject:

1. Reinstate the context in which the incident occurred (including the environment, weather, observers present, etc.).
2. Report everything, even components that seem unimportant.
3. Review the events in different orders, not just beginning to end.
4. Change perspectives, including taking on the role of characters observed.

Subjects in both the hypnosis and mnemonic conditions, in Geiselman et al.'s study comparing this interview procedure to hypnosis and a standard interview, outperformed subjects in a standard interview in number of correct items recalled from a police training film. There were no differences in confabulation across groups. The authors credit the memory retrieval procedures and the professional interviewers for the enhanced memory in both the hypnotic and mnemonic conditions.

There are, of course, similarities in the two procedures, and many authors who view hypnosis as role playing (e.g., Barber, 1962) might well claim that there is little difference in the two procedures. The obvious advantage of the Geiselman et al. interview is that evidence obtained in such a procedure that does not include hypnosis is less likely to be ruled inadmissible. However, we caution the clinician utilizing the cognitive retrieval procedure to employ the same safeguards requisite in a hypnotic memory-refreshing procedure, as a hedge against a judge's ruling that this technique is simply disguised hypnosis.

The Clinician's Dilemma

Often a client appears with a complaint of amnesia in which no court action is anticipated. It is only after uncovering the lost memories that such procedures come into play. Normally speaking, if the client is highly susceptible, and retrieval of specific memory is important to resolve distress, hypnosis may well be the logical treatment of choice, especially if a cognitive mnemonic interview is inadvisable or ineffective.

Typically, clinicians do not think about clients' potential loss of legal rights when they begin treating the clients. Moreover, the information that would guide a clinician is available only after the hypnosis has been performed and memory has been refreshed—in other words, when it is too late in many jurisdictions.

The solution to this dilemma involves a host of safeguards. This chapter concludes with a description of the best procedures we can advise for attempting to deal with this problem.

CONCLUSION AND RECOMMENDATIONS

There are clinical situations in which hypnosis is a therapeutic treatment of choice for crime victims. Because of the hypermnesia or reversal of amnesia possible in such cases, patients may subsequently wish to testify in court against people who have harmed them. In order to maximize the likelihood that they will be allowed to testify, certain guidelines attributed to Dr. Martin Orne (1979) and commonly used by the FBI (Ault, 1979) and the armed services (Orne, Dinges, & Orne, 1984) were discussed in Chapter One and Chapter Four. We recommend the following additional clinical guidelines.

Qualifications of the Hypnotist

Hypnosis in the treatment of a client who may seek relief in court should be performed by a qualified mental health professional with expertise in both hypnosis and forensics. This expert should be unaware of the facts of the case and should be hired solely by the patient. No contact should be made with police, prosecutors, or defense attorneys regarding any aspects of the case until the entire treatment is completed. If any contact does occur between legal counsel and the therapist, it should be in writing, and should be available later for use by the court.

Who May Be Present?

It is best if only the therapist and subject are present in the room when hypnosis takes place, so that inadvertent communication by others does not affect the hypnosis. This is especially pertinent for law enforcement officials or defense representatives who have a theory as to what may have transpired. If such observers must be present, a one-way mirror with remote sound or a television monitor is recommended. It is also best if the camera can use a wide-angle fixed lens, which will prevent the need for a technician. Any camera operator who is present should be completely unaware of the exigencies of the case.

One exception to this rule offered by Orne is that children may require the presence of a parent. Another exception is suggested by Shapiro (1981) for victims of rape: In such a case, it seems appropriate for the victim to be accompanied by her rape crisis counselor or other professional therapist. The feeling of being in less than total control in a relaxed position, particularly in the presence of a male hypnotherapist, may well be aversive to such a client. In such cases as that of Jennifer L. (see Chapter Two), where a rape crisis worker (also independent of the legal parties) was the primary therapist, and the hypnotherapist was called in for the purpose of dealing with the amnesia alone, it seems appropriate to have the primary therapist in the room during the hypnosis sessions.

Hibler (1984b) describes the procedures recommended by the federal government, including use of a mental health professional, an expert hypnosis coordinator, and professional investigators available from behind a one-way mirror.

Hypnotic Induction and Memory Retrieval

Hypnosis should be induced by a standard method. Some measure of depth of trance is also of value. Tests such as hand clasp, finger lock, or arm immobilization are commonly accepted as indicators of moderate to deep trance.

Once the fact of a trance is established, free narrative recall is the best initial choice of method. Hypnotherapist interaction should be limited to encouragement to continue. Should specific information later be needed, more specific directive techniques may be offered. The therapist must be careful to minimize information giving, pressuring, or leading, to reduce the possibility of suggestion and confabulation.

In a situation where observers (in another room behind a mirror) need to communicate with the hypnotherapist regarding specific questions or information, Orne, Dingus, and Orne (1984) recommend brief breaks from the hypnosis so that the observers can submit questions in writing.

Provision for Clinical Follow-Up

The therapist should be available for any of the patient's reactions to the material elicited. Sometimes delayed reactions can be quite troublesome, and clinical follow-up by the hypnotherapist or referral therapist is commonly necessary.

Even with such precautions, the veracity of hypnotically refreshed memory may be suspect, and such memory may not be admissible in a court for many of the reasons discussed above (suggestion, hardening, confabulation, etc.).

Orne (1988), who is primarily responsible for the proliferation of most of these safeguards, presently believes that the safeguards provide insufficient protection. He is of the opinion that hypnotically refreshed recall should be disallowed. A clinician relying on the guidelines we have listed should be aware of this development.

For the clinician with a patient who wishes to recall material that is unavailable through waking memory, the most important consideration is that of best clinical practice, without any undue loss of later legal rights by the patient. The patient must be forewarned that the use of hypnosis for hypermnesia may result in diminished legal ability to testify against an alleged perpetrator. The client and the hypnotherapist must be fully aware that the court will determine what aspects, if any, of the refreshed memory may someday be admitted as evidence. This fact may well influence the eventual choice of therapy methods.

SUMMARY: FINDING TRUTH IN THE ABSENCE OF FACTS

It seems clear that hypnotically refreshed recall does not produce veridical and exact reproductions of past events. Like all other memories, material recalled under hypnosis is altered by the state of the individual, the situation in which the retrieval occurs, and personal motivation.

It is less clear whether hypnotically refreshed memories are different from waking eyewitness testimony. No hard evidence exists to prove either that hypnosis inevitably alters memories or that it provides the best available recall. It does seem possible that hypnotized subjects may be more likely to accept explicit and implicit suggestions from the hypnotherapist, and to incorporate these into memories. In light of this, clinicians are best advised to take several precautions in employing hypnosis.

The question of whether memories from witnesses who have been hypnotized harden to the point that they are impervious to cross-examination, or that juries are likely to place undue emphasis on them, will continue to be decided by courts and legislative bodies. The current trend seems to be away from a per se ruling.

In the absence of solid empirical evidence, underlying belief both supersedes and creates partiality. The equivocal findings to date allow partisans of differing positions to view the same evidence and claim support for diametrically opposing positions, to a well-documented and astonishing extent. Thus Stager and Lundy (1985) comment, "In fact, in the experimental literature, in contrast to case reports, few studies can be found which report hypnotic superiority in a task requiring [a subject] to remember something learned sometime earlier" (pp. 27–28). Relinger (1984), reviewing the same literature, states, "[I]t is difficult to ignore the fact that *every* study which has measured memory of meaningful material via free recall methods, has demonstrated the hypnotic hypermnesia effect" (p. 221). In this current state of affairs, it is strongly recommended that clinicians keep up to date on the status of hypnotically refreshed testimony in their state or jurisdiction, and follow the safeguards proposed by most professionals and law enforcement agencies.

Part V

The Hypnotherapist in Court

CHAPTER 8

Direct Examination

ATTORNEY: Your Honor, we would now like to call Dr. Anna Wallabee to the witness stand.

JUDGE: Call Dr. Wallabee.

So begins direct examination.

INTRODUCTION TO DIRECT EXAMINATION

Direct examination is often overshadowed by its flashier twin, cross-examination, because it lacks histrionics or surprises. Experienced trial lawyers will say, however, that it is far more important. It is during direct examination that the solid foundation of the evidence must be built.

In many ways, the outcome of a trial depends on what witnesses say and how they say it. In a successful direct examination, the witness will present himself or herself and the evidence in a manner that will persuade the jury to accept and support the witness's side of the issue. The role of the expert witness in the drama unfolding before the jury is often pivotal.

Although most witnesses fear cross-examination, direct examination turns out to be harder work for them. Under cross-examination, witnesses may well be restricted to "yes" or "no" answers in response to an opposing attorney's tightly worded leading questions. By contrast, direct examination is conducted by the attorney who called the witness. This lawyer will pose open-ended questions. In response, the witness will be expected to give a narrative answer that conveys the nature of his or her involvement with the issues at trial. The direct examiner wants the jury to hear, understand, and become familiar with the witness. For this reason, the lawyer asks short questions and the witness provides full answers.

When witnesses speak personally, they become more credible to the jury. It is *their* story, not the lawyer's, that is being told. This fact allows the jury to respond directly to them. A strong direct examination will move the jury to accept a witness's testimony as true or persuasive.

Lawyers would like to believe that trials are won by devastating cross-examinations that blow apart an opponent's case and demonstrate a lawyer's brilliance. But the truth is that judgments are more frequently won by the successful building of a solid case during direct examinations. Juries are more likely to respond favorably to the *creation* of testimony in direct examination than to the *destruction* of testimony in cross-examination.

THE THERAPIST'S GOALS FOR
DIRECT EXAMINATION

Therapists have two goals during direct examination. They want to be liked and believed by the jury, and they want to preserve their own professional dignity. The spectre of being made to look foolish in the courtroom is a common fear. David L. Shapiro, a frequent expert witness himself, has written about this anxiety:

> One of the most difficult tasks for the psychologist who becomes involved in forensic evaluations is to move from the relative safety of his own office, or hospital, into the rather unfamiliar and threatening territory of the witness stand. Here, his credentials are torn apart, his testimony and opinion subject to ridicule, and if he is not properly prepared, his ego shattered. (1984, p. 74)

Fortunately, these apprehensions are not likely to materialize during the relatively tame but extremely significant direct examination. For it is here that the expert can establish his or her credentials and composure. An impression that the therapist as a *person* is a confident, trustworthy, and helpful individual creates a favorable basis for the jury's evaluation of the therapist's *professional* actions.

One key to this confidence is the ability to recognize competing or conflicting goals swirling as undercurrents in the shaping of the testimony. A therapist with unresolved, divided loyalties or unclear aims will be vulnerable on the witness stand. Conversely, one who gives consideration to the pitfalls of testimony, such as those listed below, will fare much better.

Client-Oriented Testimony

Often the therapist who serves as an expert witness has treated, or is in the process of treating, someone else involved in the trial. This may be the plaintiff, the defendant, or another witness. Ethical dilemmas and divided loyalties may hamper the therapist who is in this position.

Therapists who have a personal interest in demonstrating their skill as professionals are often tempted to say more than is necessary. It makes them feel knowledgeable, helpful, thorough, and dedicated to presentation of the complete truth. However, an expert witness cannot indulge this temptation, no matter how immediately satisfying it may feel, for several reasons. First, the jury is apt to view the expert as trying too hard, being insecure, or showing off. Furthermore, the jury may be forced to listen to far more information than it needs or wants; this can cause boredom and perhaps resentment. Second, the lawyer will desire that direct testimony cover only certain limited areas. "Too much rope" on direct examination can lead to a "hanging" on cross-examination.

The lawyer will require a great deal of information from the expert, but will modulate its flow and depth. The therapist will be asked to discuss how and why he or she arrived at hypnosis as the chosen treatment for a client. Once that point is established, questions will lead the witness to explain in detail the process of using hypnosis, both as a general procedure and in the specific instance at hand. These details will most likely include some discussion of the following:

1. The inductions used.
2. How the subject's suggestibility was assessed.
3. The level of trance depth.
4. The subject's responsiveness.
5. What mental, emotional, physiological, or behavioral changes were observed.
6. What posthypnotic suggestions, if any, were given.

The therapist may well be faced with the quandary of demonstrating personal expertise in the field of hypnosis, and simultaneously protecting the integrity of the work done with the client. Many therapists confronted with such dual loyalties will be tempted, consciously or otherwise, to tailor their courtroom testimony so that the therapeutic process is not sacrificed or jeopardized.

Frequently, the client will be present in the courtroom. This factor can further influence the therapist to distort the nature of the testimony given. In general, a client can be made uncomfortable by a public examination of very private exchanges. Revelations that occur under courtroom requirements of candid disclosure can strain the trust and confidentiality created between therapist and client. It can be counterproductive to lay open certain aspects of the therapeutic record, such as the client's medical and/or psychological history, diagnosis, or prognosis.

On the witness stand, the therapist has the difficult task of striking an appropriate balance among protecting the client's therapeutic interests, serving appropriate professional interests, and providing accurate information for the jury. Beyond the therapeutic interests of client and clinician, the therapist also has a stake in protecting the client's legal interests. It is natural to want one's client to prevail at trial. The therapist on the witness stand must guard against tendencies to generalize, overemphasize, or underemphasize aspects of his or her professional opinion. The client's legal position cannot be buttressed with unduly weighted testimony.

The possibility that the therapist's own legal interests may be involved should also be recognized. It may be to the advantage of the opposing lawyer to attempt to demonstrate that the therapist's actions fell below the minimum standards of competence. If enough doubt is created, the therapist may feel as if he or she personally is "on trial." Even if competent practice, or more, was delivered, clients may nevertheless feel aggrieved by what they see and hear in the courtroom.

Problems of partisanship can cause a collision of interests. Therapists may feel themselves juggling potentially incompatible goals: to make themselves look good, personally and professionally; to make their clients look good; to make hypnosis look good. It can be difficult for therapists to honor each of these allegiances without damaging the others. Each therapist must resolve these conflicts internally, as well as through pretrial discussions with the lawyer who is presenting him or her as an expert.

Non-Client-Oriented Testimony

Not all expert witnesses have a direct therapeutic relationship with an individual involved in the trial. Some experts are brought into cases to testify on the basis of their knowledge of the hypnosis field. Their testimony will focus on technical issues regarding hypnosis and on an evaluation of the personality and treatment of the hypnosis patient involved in the specific case.

Hypnosis remains a mysterious process to most people. It cannot be seen or touched or measured in as objective a manner as temperature or pulse. This fact may hinder the expert in the presentation of testimony. Expert witnesses who deal with other scientific areas of knowledge can instruct a jury by means of visual demonstrations that illustrate how a specialized technology operates. But hypnosis exists mainly in the medium of spoken words. Because our culture is now largely visual, the auditory attention span of jurors will not be lengthy. It is a sound strategy to keep answers short and nontechnical.

In addition, the nature of hypnosis, trance, and suggestibility lend themselves to varying interpretations. Law professor Irving Younger, whose videotapes on advocacy and evidence have been studied by thousands of lawyers, has noted that unlike any other country, we submit many issues to the courts that don't turn on factual determinations at all. . . . And in virtually every case in this country in which experts end up on the witness stand, there are vast possibilities for honest difference of opinion. (quoted in Jenkins, 1983 p. 102)

Vastly diverging professional opinions often come face to face as opposing attorneys present their differing expert witnesses. As Professor Younger has observed, "experts can testify in good faith and still be testifying to opposites" (quoted in Jenkins, 1983, p. 102).

Although experts who are not actually treating individuals involved in a trial may appear more impartial than those whose clients' interests are at stake, the jury may still perceive them as partisan players in the "battle of the experts." The victors in such a battle will have a superior ability either to communicate a particular perspective to the jury or, more often, to appear more likable to the jury than their opponents.

Therapists Who Are Frequent Expert Witnesses

Expert witnesses who testify about hypnosis issues on a regular basis face a unique double bind. On the positive side, they are the most experienced expert witnesses on their subject. Having testified at numerous trials, they have analyzed forensic hypnosis issues thoroughly and kept up to date with recent developments in the field. As familiar courtroom performers, they may be exceptionally adept in communicating persuasively with juries.

The negative side of their situation is that frequent court appearances leave these expert witnesses vulnerable to charges of bias. Precisely because they have testified often and continue to keep on testifying, juries may perceive them as having a theory to sell. When the same sets of experts face off in courtrooms across the country, the image of neutral evaluators may dissolve into that of partisan warriors. It is not persuasive for an expert witness to appear to be selling his or her side.

An expert who testifies frequently, but only for one side, is especially vulnerable. The jury may perceive such testimony to be sculpted to fit the contours of the expert's ideology.

THE LAWYER'S GOALS FOR DIRECT EXAMINATION

The lawyer's goals for direct examination dovetail with those of the therapist testifying on behalf of a client. By using short, open-ended questions to elicit narrative responses, the lawyer wants the jury to see the therapist's strengths: concern for the client, and competence in meeting the client's needs with appropriate therapy.

The lawyer will have additional goals. He or she must obtain from the witness the necessary factual support to demonstrate, in the closing argument, that the client's claim should prevail. For the lawyer, the therapist is just one piece of the jigsaw puzzle from which a clear and compelling composition must emerge. The lawyer will need to get certain information from the therapist, and also to have it specifically stated in a manner fitting the requirements of the case.

It is wise for the lawyer to discuss the strategy of the case with the therapist so that the therapist can see clearly how he or she fits into the lawyer's "big picture." For example, the lawyer may be planning to call an additional expert on some particular facet of hypnosis, such as amnesia. Therefore, it would be preferable that each expert stay within the limited parameters set by the litigation strategy.

In some instances, the lawyer may want the therapist to testify beyond what the therapist feels comfortable saying. As Massachusetts Superior Court Judge Robert J. Hallisey has observed:

> Lawyers go through a seduction process with their experts. They try to get them to go as far as they can in their direction. You have some experts who are trying to play it straight, and others who are prostitutes. (quoted in Jenkins, 1983, p. 106)

Despite the pressure an attorney may desire to apply to shape the expert's story, at bottom the lawyer knows that the expert witness has the right, if not the obligation, to present testimony that reflects his or her honest assessment. Anything less would be neither credible nor persuasive.

To avoid an in-court split between their goals, the lawyer and the witness should work out the boundary lines between these goals before the trial. This will help prevent an unproductive and perhaps even harmful struggle during direct examination, with the therapist defending his or her mouth from words the lawyer is trying to put into it.

Even in cases where there is harmony between the lawyer and the therapist, the lawyer is bound to be particular about how the therapist speaks in court as a witness. The therapist will be instructed in the basic goals of direct examination. Among the most important of these are the following:

1. The jury must, first and foremost, *like* the witness. Belief in what the witness has to say is much more likely to follow when the jury has a positive attitude about the person who is telling the story.

2. The witness's story should be presented in as full and complete a manner as possible. Testimony is most effective when broken down into manageable pieces. The important task is that the witness be the storyteller, with only minor input from the lawyer.

3. Although the witness wants to present a strong and coherent story, it must also be realistic to be believable. Human imperfections will not turn

off a jury; an attempt to appear perfect will. Juries are willing to believe the words of a therapist who has done his or her professional best to help someone in pain.

4. It is important for a witness to speak in language that is simultaneously vivid and neutral. Words should be chosen to make a maximum impact on the jury without intimating any bias or prejudice on the witness's part. Expert witnesses especially must refrain from delving into technical jargon that alienates the jury.

PREPARING FOR DIRECT EXAMINATION

Long before a direct examination takes place in the courtroom, there is much a witness can and should do to prepare for testifying. Because the witness's main goal on direct examination is to appear confident, knowledgeable, and competent, the witness should prepare to speak authoritatively on the various issues that will arise. Comfort with oneself and ease of presentation will favorably influence the jury.

The expert's training for a courtroom appearance includes attentiveness to the following factors:

1. A review of all legal interrogatories, depositions, or other documents involving the expert in the case.
2. A review of the factual circumstances of the case.
3. A review of the hypnosis literature that is relevant to significant issues in the case.
4. A survey of the scientific hypnosis community's views on important hypnosis issues.

Legal Documents

Preparation begins with an extensive review of all previous sworn testimony. This review will include all records of pretrial oral depositions, written depositions, and written interrogatories. Because the expert has testified under oath during pretrial hearings, that testimony is accorded the same authority as courtroom testimony. It is essential that the witness be prepared to testify in court *consistently* with all previous sworn testimony.

The law places great evidentiary value on consistency as a hallmark of truth. An expert who deviates from prior sworn testimony will be asked, none too politely, to do a lot of explaining. This emphasis on consistency, as Ernest Rossi (personal communication, 1987) has pointed out to us, runs counter to the therapist's orientation, which focuses on growth, change, and evolution.

Many months usually pass between the pretrial and trial phases, so review is both necessary and helpful. The expert should acquire copies of all pretrial records from the attorney and study them, both alone and with the attorney.

If the expert has changed an opinion concerning some aspect of the case, the pretrial sworn testimony may thereby be inconsistent with what will be said on the stand. This inconsistency could have major repercussions unless the expert is prepared to provide good reasons for the change of view. The expert who knows that he or she will deviate from prior testimony should, of course, inform the attorney. The reason for the change will be very significant and upon occasion can be the focal point of the trial. Cross-examiners thrive on ambiguity and inconsistency. The expert should be armed with compelling explanations for the shift in viewpoint.

An expert who has testified in other trials should definitely review the testimony given in those cases. A thoroughly prepared cross-examiner will have read those court records, in the hope that the expert can be shown to have expressed one opinion in one trial and an inconsistent opinion in the present trial.

The more evident it is to the cross-examiner that the expert is thoroughly prepared, the more likely it is that the cross-examination will be shortened. A cross-examiner will stop when he or she sees no opportunity to succeed. A seasoned trial attorney may not even begin to question a highly informed and well-prepared expert; no cross-examination is better than one that fails.

The Factual Circumstances

The expert's opinion will be sought not only on the technical questions of hypnosis theory and practice, but also on the ways in which theory and practice apply to the facts of the particular case at trial.

Pretrial review of the facts is necessary, of course. The expert who gets the facts confused will be very embarrassed on the stand. But this review is very useful beyond saving the expert from a red face: It provides a means to bring to life the drier aspects of hypnosis theory, which might otherwise have a tendency to cause the jurors' minds to wander.

It may be useful to draw a chart that lists the factual elements of the situation along the top, and the relevant literature in support or contradiction of those facts immediately underneath. If this is done, the literature will never be very far removed from the facts crucial to the resolution of the case.

The Hypnosis Literature

Familiarity with the hypnosis literature is absolutely essential. There is no substitute for a thorough understanding of the major works in the field.

As we shall see in the discussion of this point in the next chapter, the cross-examiner will ask the expert whether he or she is familiar with certain selected portions of the hypnosis literature. If the expert answers "no," the jury may lose its confidence in the expert's expertise. But if the expert says "yes," the cross-examiner is then free to question the expert with precision and in detail about those works.

It is generally a good idea to read and be informed beyond the specific issues being contested at the trial. Symbolically and realistically, hypnosis itself will be on trial, and the jury will reach its own verdict about what it thinks of this unique form of human interaction. Hypnosis has generally been given a sinister or sensationalistic treatment in the media. Most people will have doubts and misconceptions about it. The expert's testimony is likely to range across a wide expanse of hypnosis topics, rather than being confined to the narrower channels under dispute in the case. The jury will trust the expert who covers this terrain with skill and understanding.

The Hypnosis Community

It is not enough for the expert witness to have his or her own opinions on the complicated aspects of hypnosis. The expert must also be able to show that these opinions find concurrence and support in the scientific hypnosis community. A necessary component of pretrial preparation is research directed toward documenting the views of hypnosis scholars and practitioners. Naturally, a great deal of this information can be gleaned after a thorough reading of the hypnosis literature. But additional material of value is available beyond the printed page.

An expert preparing for trial may want to speak with other hypnosis practitioners concerning their opinions, techniques, and results. These contacts can be made by telephone, in person, by mail, or at meetings or conferences of professional associations. It is always in the best interests of the expert to establish a network for feedback and the exchange of ideas. When called on to support or justify his or her opinions, as during cross-examination, the expert will benefit by having this additional source of data to cite.

PRETRIAL REHEARSAL

The expert should definitely meet with the lawyer before trial to rehearse the expert's testimony. At such a meeting, simulated direct examination and cross-examination provide the opportunity to be asked and to answer questions similar to those that will be asked in court. As an experienced courtroom performer, the lawyer will evaluate the expert's responses in terms of both content and style. Both components are critical to effective testimony.

To help the expert witness understand how he or she looks when testifying, many lawyers are using videotapes in the pretrial stage. Small details of appearance, which the expert normally might not notice, can be spotted and corrected. After intense observation, the expert and the lawyer can develop more carefully the most desirable image to be projected.

Experienced trial attorneys insist on pretrial rehearsals with witness and experts. Indeed, some trial lawyers feel so strongly on this point that they consider a failure to hold such rehearsals as "malpractice." Although the *value* of such pretrial meetings cannot be denied, the *ethics* of how they are conducted has engendered some concern. The fear is that the lawyer, in his or her zeal to present the best picture for the client, will unfairly pressure or unduly suggest testimony from the expert.

The American Bar Association's (1983) *Model Rules of Professional Conduct*, in Disciplinary Rule 7-102(A), prohibit lawyers from participating in the creation of false testimony. Although the rule is easy to state, it is far more difficult to apply in practice. As Professor Monroe H. Freedman has asked in his provocative book *Lawyers' Ethics in an Adversary System* (1975), "when is a lawyer refreshing recollection, and when is he or she prompting perjury?" (p. 59).

In theory, the question is not hard to answer. Professor Richard C. Wydick (1987) has accurately stated the appropriate boundary line:

> The lawyer may probe the witness's memory, explore the basis of the witness's knowledge, point out holes and fallacies in the witness's story, and seek to refresh the witness's recollection by proper means. However, the lawyer must not try to "bend" the testimony or put words in the witness's mouth. New York's Judge Finch put the matter this way in a 1880 disciplinary case: "[The lawyer's] duty is to extract the facts from the witness, not to put them into him; to learn what the witness does know, not to teach him what he ought to know." [*In re Eldridge*, 82 N.Y. 161 (1880)]. (p. 72)

In practice, however, it is very difficult to know when the lawyer's obligations to "zealously" represent his or her client and to "present [the] client's case with persuasive force" (American Bar Association, 1983, comment to Rule 3.3) turns legitimate cajolery into unethical coercion. The expert will need to be sensitive to the fact that the lawyer's desire to get maximum mileage from the expert's opinions may lead the lawyer to want more than the expert feels can professionally be given. Ironically, the same attorney who argues in court that hypnotically refreshed recollection is inadmissible because it is the product of undue suggestion may attempt similar undue suggestion to shape the therapist's testimony.

Pretrial rehearsals are essential to iron out potential differences between lawyer and therapist, if they occur.

WAITING TO TESTIFY

One aspect of appearing as an expert witness that is least acknowledged is the amount of time spend *not* appearing. Many factors contribute to the complex organization and unfolding of a trial. Therefore a witness inevitably will spend a certain amount of time in the courthouse, but not necessarily in the courtroom.

Witnesses often are not allowed to hear the testimony of other witnesses, so they must wait outside the courtroom to be called in to testify. In some cases, the witnesses for both sides are sequestered together, which can be extremely uncomfortable. One of us (Shapiro) was called by the district attorney's office to testify in a criminal trial regarding his hypnotizing of the victim. He found himself sequestered with the defendant's family, whose opinions were expressed mainly by spitting on him.

Scheflin, in another case, was allowed to wait in the courtroom. And wait he did, for four nonconsecutive days. Each day he was summoned to testify, and each day he sat in the courtroom nursing a case of unrequited performance anxiety. When his name was finally called, it almost came as a surprise. Waiting, and its attendant anticipation, are to be expected. Some witnesses review their notes; others work on unrelated tasks; still others bring along a book or newspaper. In any case, witnesses should be prepared to occupy their time fruitfully while waiting to be called.

THE WITNESS IN THE COURTROOM SETTING

The courtroom is a new and foreign environment for most witnesses. The expert may want to make a pretrial visit to this formal, and often bewildering, setting. Some experts like to observe another trial in progress, in order to see how witnesses are called to the stand and how direct examinations and cross-examinations are conducted. Others prefer to visit an empty courtroom and sit in the witness stand to get used to the view. Familiarity with the physical environment makes the expert more at ease on the stand.

Appearance of the Witness

There are some obvious general rules regarding a witness's behavior in the courtroom that are helpful to keep in mind (Morrill, 1979):

1. Do not chew gum.
2. Do not smoke.
3. Do not wear flashy jewelry.
4. Be groomed in accordance with local custom.

    5. Do not slouch; it suggests indifference or disrespect.
    6. Look pleasant. Juries like to see happy faces.
    7. Do not talk with, wave or wink at jurors.
    8. Appear attentive and interested in the course of the trial.
    9. Do not react to another witness's testimony.
  10. Look at the jury when answering questions.
  11. Be courteous in general to all people in court.
  12. Use simple words. (pp. 37–38)

When the expert arrives at the courthouse, potential jurors or the judge may observe his or her entrance. The witness should be on his or her best behavior from the moment of arrival at the halls of justice. It would be unfortunate if the expert's valuable testimony were discounted in the jury room because one jury saw the expert acting in a rude or otherwise inappropriate manner on the courthouse steps before the trial began.

Communicating Effectively with a Jury

A jury is in the unusual position of absorbing and considering evidence almost exclusively by hearing oral testimony. In our modern, visually oriented culture, aural learning has a vastly lower effectiveness. Trial lawyers are told that approximately 85% of what is learned has been acquired through sight—seeing and reading. Only 5–10% of human knowledge is acquired by hearing (Bergman, 1979, p. 45).

To help overcome this learning barrier, lawyers have increasingly resorted to using visual materials to reinforce or augment spoken testimony wherever possible. Charts, diagrams, and blown-up photographs have long been popular courtroom tools. For several decades, lawyers have also been using films to emphasize their legal and emotional points. The most widely known are the "day in the life" films, which graphically depict the daily pattern of an accident victim's tragic existence as a consequence of the accident. The advancing technology of video has created a generation of dazzling courtroom presentations. Today computer simulations are making more frequent appearances before courts and juries. In short, lawyers are aware that a jury is more likely to pay attention to oral testimony if such testimony is interspersed with visual data of some kind.

Unfortunately, in hypnosis cases, visual constructs are quite rare. However, therapists trained in hypnosis bring special talents and abilities to the direct examination process. Because hypnosis focuses on the precise use of the *spoken word*, an hypnosis expert may be especially gifted in his or her ability to reach the jury with words that convey a message convincingly. In preparing for testimony, therapists should pay the same careful attention to word choice and phrasing as they would when utilizing hypnosis for clients.

Demeanor of the Witness

Although the jury *hears* what the witness testifies, without doubt as strong a message is delivered by how the jury *sees* the witness. There is no denying that appearance and demeanor are critical. The bottom line, lawyers firmly believe, is that juries evaluate a witness more on whether or not they *like* that witness than on whether or not they agree with the expert's substantive testimony. A witness's "likability" is based primarily on a pleasant demeanor. A witness who makes easy eye contact with a jury and does not condescend to them will generally make a favorable impression.

Morrill (1979) has catalogued the various "problem personalities" that can emerge on the witness stand. Among the prime evils he has listed are these:[1]

1. *The long-winded witness.* This witness does not know when he or she has said enough. Besides boring the jury, the tendency can create ammunition for cross-examination. A long-winded presentation is likely to include items on which the witness is vulnerable to attack.

2. *The short-winded witness.* This witness can undermine the value of testimony by appearing to have it dragged out of him or her by the attorney. The testimony will seem coaxed and insincere, even if in fact it is neither.

3. *The opinionated witness.* An opinionated witness tends to inflate his or her testimony with a profusion of adjectives, metaphors, and exaggeration. By constantly providing opinions about the testimony, such a witness deprives the jury of its role as evaluators of the evidence. A profusion of opinions also leaves the witness open to attack on cross-examination.

4. *The antagonistic witness.* The antagonistic witness arrives in court prepared to do battle. He or she is on the defensive and takes the experience personally and emotionally. The jurors will not be persuaded by this witness's testimony; they will be too distracted by the hostile manner in which it is presented.

5. *The dull witness.* A dull individual can be a serious danger on the witness stand. A significant message can be lost in a dogged, pedantic speaking style. Often this type of witness will insist on meticulously recounting extraneous technicalities. The forest will be lost for the trees.

6. *The ham witness.* The ham witness bursts onto the stand ready to

---

[1] The following is adapted from *Trial Diplomacy* (pp. 34–36) by A. Morrill, 1979, Chicago: Court Practice Institute. Copyright 1979 by Court Practice Institute, Inc.

enact some favorite movie role. He or she is prepared to give a performance replete with grimaces and overstated delivery. It will receive a negative review from the jury.

7. *The stage fright witness.* Like the short-winded witness, a witness with stage fright freezes as he or she ascends the witness chair. A panic can lead to irrational or incomplete responses. Usually a few moments of reassurance by the lawyer with easy questions will allow this witness to regain his or her composure.

8. *The shifty-eyed witness.* This type can be very ineffective on the witness stand. Jurors who are denied eye contact will have less trust in the content of the witness's testimony. Even worse, the expert who persists in looking at the floor and around the courtroom may convey to the jury a sense of guilt or deception. Often this behavior is a reflection of shyness and discomfort with the circumstances, but it can signal a more negative message to the jury.

9. *The VIP witness.* The VIP witness behaves as if he or she is just too good, too busy, too wise, or too important to squander precious, valuable time in court. Such a witness is apt to be condescending and petty. Jurors resent anyone who patronizes them by word or gesture.

10. *The thinker witness.* The thinker hesitates too long before answering the simplest question. Although the basis for this action can be genuine thoughtfulness, in the courtroom environment such pauses may appear to the jury to signify either uncertainty or conscious deception. The thinker may have difficulty holding the jury's attention.

11. *The disorganized-thinker witness.* This witness takes the roundabout route in answering questions, raises preliminary issues that are not in controversy, and sidetracks both himself or herself and the jury. The core of the testimony becomes lost in the morass of extraneous details or convoluted explanations.

12. *The qualifier witness.* This witness, in the effort to appear clear and precise, can sound confused and unknowledgeable. He or she begins answers with "I think . . ." or "As best I can recall . . ." or "I believe . . .". This phrasing suggests a lack of confidence.

13. *The "everyone's friend" witness.* The witness who cannot bear to disappoint another human being makes a terrible witness. He or she will want to please even the opposing attorney on cross-examination. The overwhelming need to avoid negativity by being agreeable makes it impossible for the witness to speak conclusively about the issues.

14. *The vacillator witness.* This witness insists on altering the versions of the testimony each time he or she speaks. Because the witness switches certain elements of facts and ideas, the jury may discount his or her entire testimony as untrustworthy. If the testimony mirrors that of other witnesses, the vacillations that undermine the witness's own testimony may adversely affect this other testimony as well.

THE STRUCTURE OF THE TESTIMONY

It is the lawyer's job to see that the expert witness tells the jury a truthful story that the jurors will understand and believe. To create a sympathetic atmosphere, a lawyer will conduct the direct examination in a gentle manner. Famed trial lawyer Louis Nizer (1963) describes how "[his] questions [draw the witness] into a description of events, as one leads a child into deeper water by gentle persuasion" (p. 228). The jury will be encouraged to look kindly upon a witness the lawyer treats with respect. The therapist will be encouraged to appear confident, relaxed, and professional.

It is during direct examination that the lawyer must build the solid foundation for the case. The expert will have a great deal of information to convey to the jury. Lawyers will want the sequence in which that information is presented to have maximum persuasive impact. Every lawyer will have a preference for the way in which the direct examination is structured. The unique facts of the case, the availability of witnesses to testify, the applicable legal rules and regulations, and the lawyer's own style and perceptions will shape that preference.

Principles of primacy and recency have had an especially profound effect on the structure and sequence of direct testimony. Research indicates that juries remember most clearly the first and last portions of testimony (Sannito & McGovern, 1985). Lawyers keep this psychological premise in mind when they plan the structure of an expert's direct examination.

Most trial lawyers follow a traditional pattern in the presentation of direct expert testimony. This pattern is designed to maximize the "human" element and minimize the "technical" elements of the expert's opinions.

The Opening: Qualifications of the Expert

The jury's first reaction to the expert must be favorable: "Studies have shown that people are reluctant to change their initial impressions when confronted by unfavorable facts. Hence, first impressions can often be lasting ones" (Mauet, 1980, p. 96).

The opening of direct examination focuses on the expert. The lawyer's goal is to introduce the expert to the jury and have them like and believe him or her. For this reason, lawyers generally prefer a strong, affirmative opening that introduces the expert to the jury as both a *person* and a *professional*. Direct examination usually begins with questions about the expert's education, experience, and practice. Lawyers refer to these opening exchanges as the "love and affection" questions that present the "human" side of the expert (Mauet, 1980, p. 99). The jurors hear about the expert; they become familiar with part of his or her life story and career achievements. If they like the expert, they will believe and stay with him or her later when the testimony turns technical.

Opening the direct examination with questions about the expert's qualifications also allows him or her to get acclimated to the witness stand. There will be no trick questions about past background and achievements. These questions relax the expert while building up his or her prestige in the eyes of the jury.

A witness must be qualified as an expert before the court will permit the witness to testify. To prepare for qualification as expert witnesses, therapists should undertake a careful review of their credentials. They should be able to talk about *where* they learned hypnosis; *when* that training took place; *who* trained them in hypnosis; *what* was learned; and *how* what was learned has been utilized.

The court will be interested in knowing all university courses taken in which hypnosis was taught, as well as all professional training sessions, workshops, and hypnosis institutes attended. In addition, an expert witness should tabulate the number of clients with whom hypnosis has been used, and what proportion of the total practice hypnotherapy represents. Finally, of particular interest to the court and jury will be the question of whether the expert has had any practical experience with the precise issues present in the trial.

A sample, though necessarily abbreviated, direct examination may proceed as follows:

LAWYER: Dr. Wallabee, would you be so kind as to describe for the court your training in hypnosis? Please begin with your educational background.

WITNESS: Yes, I will be pleased to do so. I received a B.A. in psychology from the University of Massachusetts in 1954. I earned a Ph.D. in psychology from Johns Hopkins 6 years later, in 1960. Only one of my courses focused directly on hypnosis, but I did research on hypnotherapy, supervised by two of my professors, as an independent study project.

LAWYER: Thank you, Dr. Wallabee. Would you please describe for us any additional training in hypnosis you received during these academic years?

WITNESS: Gladly. I received training in hypnosis while I was in graduate school. The school had a clinic where doctoral candidates had an opportunity to conduct therapy under the careful supervision of a licensed therapist who was also a member of the faculty. During the 2 years I saw clients in this setting, my hypnotherapy work was observed and reviewed by my supervisors.

LAWYER: Thank you, Doctor. After leaving the academic environment, did you continue to receive instruction from others on hypnosis or hypnotherapy?

WITNESS: Yes, I did. I attended a hypnosis seminar in 1969 at the American Society for Clinical Hypnosis, and in 1972 I attended another seminar at the International Association for Clinical and Experimental Hypnosis. In the years after those seminars, I have made it a point to attend lectures, workshops, or training seminars at least twice a year on average.

LAWYER: Doctor, let us now turn to your practical experience with hypnosis. Would you please describe the extent to which hypnosis has played a role in your clinical research work?

WITNESS: Yes. I did clinical hypnosis research from 1974 to 1976 at the American Hypnosis Institute. The results of that research were published in the *American Journal of Clinical Hypnosis* in 1977.

LAWYER: Have you ever taught hypnosis in a university setting?

WITNESS: Yes, I have. For the last 4 years I have been teaching a course on hypnotherapy in the graduate psychology department of the University of Toledo.

LAWYER: So you have been practicing and studying hypnosis for a good number of years, have you not?

WITNESS: Yes, that is correct.

LAWYER: Doctor, are you licensed to practice hypnotherapy in this state?

WITNESS: Yes. I am licensed as a clinical psychologist.

LAWYER: With how many clients, would you say, have you used hypnotherapy in the years in which you have been in practice?

WITNESS: I would estimate from 225 to 275. Not all of my cases have required hypnosis.

LAWYER: Would you estimate for us approximately how many of those cases have involved retrograde amnesia?

WITNESS: I would say about 60%. I primarily use hypnosis for amnesia work, and I receive referrals mainly on this point.

LAWYER: Thank you, Dr. Wallabee.

Notice how instead of simply asking Dr. Wallabee to tell the court her complete qualifications, the attorney has segmented the witness's answers into manageable descriptive pieces. This prevents the impression that the expert is bragging about her accomplishments. The lawyer has also used words like "kind" and "good" in the questions posed, thus implanting those evocative, suggestive images with the jury. The witness begins most answers with an affirmative comment, once again reinforcing positive feelings.

By the end of the opening portion of the direct examination, a lawyer hopes to have accomplished two goals. First, the court has been favorably disposed to the expert's *credentials* to permit him or her to testify. Second, the judge and jury have been favorably disposed to the expert's *personality* so that they will believe his or her testimony. After the conclusion of the qualification phase, the details of the expert's opinion are explored in the second phase of the direct examination.

The Middle: The Details of Hypnosis

In the middle portion of the direct examination, when the attention of the jurors is likely to wane or wander, the technical details, the academic squabbles in the literature, and the still unanswered scientific questions are discussed. Although jurors will want to maintain their interest during the discussion of these issues, they will have little basis for judging whether the expert is accurate in his or her responses as the details become more and more technical. Juror attention and recall are apt to be lowest when complicated matters are involved and highest when an emotional or human element is at center stage.

The middle portion of the testimony is where all the tedious information can be buried. Intricate details and intellectual theories are what bore jurors most, what they understand least, and what they are most apt to forget. Unfortunately, these very same details may be the source of the expert's greatest pleasure. The expert witness's own fascinated involvement with the tough and much-debated questions in his or her field is natural; it is based on dedication and desire. But the jurors are strangers to the contest being unveiled in the courtroom. They want technical information made simple and direct, with particular emphasis placed on "the bottom line."

As a consequence, the expert faces the most danger in this middle portion of the testimony. The danger is that the expert will commit either of two potential sins: (1) speaking too far above the heads of the jurors; or (2) saying too much, thereby providing material for cross-examination.

During this phase of the testimony, the expert witness will be asked about his or her knowledge of the scientific literature about hypnosis and about the prevailing scientific attitudes on some of the many key questions relevant to the factual aspects of the trial. Particular attention is likely to be focused on memory, susceptibility, inductions, suggestions, and the relationship between trance and telling the truth.

To continue with the sample testimony begun above, Dr. Wallabee may well be asked to define each of the above-mentioned terms; for example, she may have to describe what an induction is and why a particular one was chosen. She may further be asked how it can be determined whether a client is a good hypnotic subject and what the consequences of being one are. The lawyer may inquire as to what assurances she had that the client was in trance. Dr. Wallabee may then be asked to define the trance state and to tell the jury whether someone can fake being in trance. Additional questions may focus on whether subjects can lie in trance, whether experts can tell if clients are lying, and whether hypnotically refreshed memory is apt to be accurate.

Experts are well advised, in preparation for trial, to read the literature well beyond the usual limits of clinical practice. A legally qualified hypnosis expert must be ready to demonstrate familiarity with the current state of the field, as represented in the books and journal articles of one's peers. It is also advisable to review one's own publications.

In addition to knowledge of the therapeutic literature on hypnosis, the therapist should have some background on the legal issues in the jurisdiction in which he or she is testifying. As Chapters Three through Five indicate, the law is always changing and growing; therapists should be familiar with the latest crucial legal rulings.

The Closing: Focus on the Facts

The therapist's direct examination will close with a focusing of attention on the client to revive the jurors' attention and arouse their sympathy. If the hypnotherapist has been successful in telling his or her story, the jury will be "rooting" for the client. The lawyer examining Dr. Wallabee, for example, may begin to wind up her testimony as follows:

LAWYER: Dr. Wallabee, please tell the jury why you used hypnosis in this particular case.

WITNESS: This woman was suffering from amnesia, which is a very painful thing—to know that something happened and not be able to remember it. Hypnosis has great potential to help. I did a very substantial evaluation of this person with regard to her ability to be hypnotized. She was a good subject. In my judgment, hypnosis was valuable in helping her reclaim her memory.

LAWYER: Thank you, Doctor. What type of inductions did you use in assisting her into trance?

WITNESS: I used one induction only. It was a relaxation induction. You're probably familiar with it. I asked her to let her body relax—let the muscles relax and achieve a state of relaxation. Then I did some backward counting, and as the numbers went down she was able to go into deeper and deeper levels of trance.

LAWYER: And you said that in your opinion she was generally, and in this specific instance, a good hypnosis subject?

WITNESS: Yes, I would say she was a good subject.

There are many factual questions to be addressed about the use of hypnosis and the susceptibility of the client. The induction techniques will be carefully scrutinized for undue suggestion. Questions about memory and amnesia, posthypnotic suggestions, confabulation, and a multitude of other issues will be raised. All of them will need to be answered with specific reference to the particular facts of the present case.

The direct examination should close strongly and confidently. The attorney will decide what question or series of questions is apt to make the expert look best. One possibility is suggested in the following section.

THE TRANSITION FROM DIRECT EXAMINATION TO CROSS-EXAMINATION

Witnesses often hear the warning: "Don't change your tone of voice from friendly to defensive when direct examination ends and cross-examination begins." If the jury senses discomfort or resistance in the expert, they may get a feeling that he or she has something to hide.

The manner in which the direct examination concludes can assist a witness in making a smooth transition to cross-examination. Two points are of importance in this concluding exchange. First, the direct examination should end on a strong, positive point; the jury should be left pleased, impressed, and satisfied. At the same time, however, the expert should be guided from the direct examination into anticipation of the forthcoming cross-examination.

Here is the example of Dr. Wallabee:

LAWYER: Dr. Wallabee, you have testified honestly and completely here today, and we thank you. I have just a few remaining questions to ask. Are there many different views about the nature of hypnosis?

WITNESS: Yes.

LAWYER: So not all hypnosis practitioners have the same opinions about the subject?

WITNESS: That is also correct.

LAWYER: Is there a consensus about certain aspects of hypnosis in the therapeutic process?

WITNESS: I believe there is a consensus. The American Medical Association, the American Psychiatric Association, and the American Psychological Association all passed guidelines between 1958 and 1961 describing hypnosis as a standard medical practice or standard psychological practice. Although hypnosis is used by a wide variety of theoreticians and practitioners, most would recognize these guidelines as speaking authoritatively to the subject.

In this exchange, the witness's own lawyer has begun to discuss issues that the opposing attorney will raise on cross-examination. In an agreeable, open format, the expert witness has acknowledged that there is a range of opinion among professionals. Because the admission of other possible viewpoints has first been made on direct examination, the cross-examining attorney may look like a mean-spirited quibbler if he or she bears down on the expert witness.

Furthermore, the witness has established that even with different perspectives, there is a reasonable foundation upon which all professionals base their analyses. Indirectly, Dr. Wallabee has linked her name in the minds of the jurors with the prestige of the leading therapeutic organizations in the country.

HANDLING SPECIAL PROBLEMS

Using a Secret Signal System

No matter how thoroughly a lawyer and witness have gone over pretrial documents and prepared for the upcoming direct examination, miscommunications can arise. The best means of overcoming a witness's confusion while he or she is on the stand is to establish ahead of time a signal system to cue the lawyer. The signal should be a very simple statement, or perhaps a certain prearranged word, to alert the lawyer to stop the process.

The advantage to having a prearranged signal is that the witness loses no credibility with the jury because the jurors are unaware of his or her hesitations. It is a minimally embarrassing method that still provides some assurance to the witness that help can be obtained once he or she has taken the stand.

A different signal can be used by the lawyer to trigger the witness's memory. Given the likelihood that the courtroom environment will be foreign to the expert witness, it is natural that his or her testimony may be missing elements the lawyer finds critical to an effective presentation. If the witness fails to mention some pertinent item, the lawyer will not want to appear as if he or she were putting words into the witness's mouth. For this reason, leading questions are generally not permitted on direct examination.

The lawyer can prompt the expert with a secret sentence, phrase, or word. This should alert the expert that something essential has been omitted. If the expert still does not remember what the lawyer is driving at, he or she can return an "open" answer that allows the lawyer to gracefully attempt a leading question if needed. A sample exchange may occur as follows:

LAWYER: Do you recall anything further, sir? ["Sir" is the secret word here.]

WITNESS: There is nothing I can recall at this moment.

LAWYER: Are any other facts about your client's suggestibility important as you think back?

WITNESS: Yes, I did conclude from my evaluation of my client that he would be an excellent subject for hypnosis.

There is good reason for the lawyer to hint to the expert *before* using a leading question on direct examination. The main body of testimony heard on direct examination should be in the witness's own words, told directly to the jury.

Addressing the Judge

Many witnesses are unsure whether they can or should address the judge directly. Usually it is the lawyer who will approach the judge if the witness is being mistreated in any fashion by the opposing counsel. However, it is within a witness's rights to talk directly to a judge for any of the following reasons (Danner, 1983):

1. If the expert witness is unsure how to answer a question.
2. If the expert witness wants a ruling from the judge about whether he or she *must* answer a question.
3. If the expert witness is unsure about the privileged status of information requested.
4. If the expert witness wants to know whether he or she can be permitted to qualify or expand upon a "yes" or "no" answer.

An additional issue is whether the judge may directly address the expert and question him or her; the answer is "yes." The expert should answer the judge's questions politely. If the questioning is unfair or involved, the attorney may object.

The Use of Notes

Therapists routinely maintain and refer to notes about clients and about the theories and techniques of their trade. There is no law against a therapist's referring to notes while on the witness stand. There is, however, one important consideration: Once notes are used during testimony, they become part of the testimony. Thus, they must be admitted into evidence, and the opposing attorney and the jury are permitted to see them. Furthermore, the contents of and omissions in the notes themselves may provide additional avenues for potential cross-examination.

From a lawyer's point of view, it is unwise to give the opposition access to the private papers of an expert witness. The lawyer wants the other attorney to know only what the law demands he or she know about the expert. From a therapist's point of view, there may be a further problem of confidentiality: If the notes are client-centered, the client may have personal information unnecessarily exposed to a courtroom full of strangers. Nevertheless, the expert is entitled to have his or her memory refreshed by consulting any notes he or she has prepared. These notes should be shown to the attorney as part of pretrial preparation.

With direct examination concluded, it is time for cross-examination to begin.

CHAPTER 9

Cross-Examination

INTRODUCTION

"Well, when I wake up in the morning with a smile on my face," internationally renowned attorney Melvin Belli recently told a television audience, "my wife says, 'You must have been cross-examining someone and winning in your dreams' " (Rosene, 1981). The suspense involved in watching a skilled advocate maneuver with questions to encircle an apprehensive witness has captivated the attention of lawyers and the imagination of laypeople from the very beginning of trial by jury in Greece 2,500 years ago.

In most of their professional lives, therapists view themselves as advocates of their clients. Their expertise is focused on fostering awareness and enhancing the healing process. Lawyers also view their role as one of advocacy, though their advocacy is of a very different kind. While a therapist trains clients to fight their own battles, an attorney is obligated to do the reverse. The lawyer's job is to be the client's champion. Cross-examination is a major tool by which the lawyer most effectively combats views and opinions that threaten the client's interests.

For anyone who has not actually experienced a cross-examination during a trial, his or her conception of what it must be like has probably been formed by sensational news media accounts of current trials, Hollywood movies, and popular television programs such as the classic *Perry Mason*. Cross-examination is the very height of the contemporary courtroom drama—the most potent weapon in the advocate's arsenal of armaments to ferret out a favorable view of truth from unsure, discordant, or unscrupulous witnesses.

Wigmore (1974) calls cross-examination "beyond any doubt the greatest legal engine ever invented for the discovery of truth" (p. 32). For those who have sat in the witness chair and been cross-examined, it can feel more like the torture it was designed to replace. For experts and professionals, it has often, in the graphic words of an old Southern judge, turned the witness box into "a slaughterhouse of reputations" (quoted in Wigmore, 1970, p. 841).

The expert testifying on behalf of a client may experience the cross-examination as painful and frightening. Not only the therapist's professional work, but also his or her personal credentials and competence, may be questioned. Many therapists absolutely refuse to do mental health work that might result in court proceedings. The prospect of an unpleasant day of insult, embarrassment, verbal assault, and other humiliations weighs heavily in their decision.

Hypnotherapists with minimal or no court experience face twin concerns: "What will happen to me, and how do I handle it?" The hypnotherapist has one cardinal means of defense: preparation. The expert who has done his or her homework has little to fear. Knowing what to expect from a cross-examiner, and knowing how to respond professionally, can give the hypnotherapist the confidence essential to make him or her a convincing witness.

THE CROSS-EXAMINATION PROCESS

The Witness's View of Cross-Examination

Cross-examination usually begins with a dialogue very similar to the following:

LAWYER: I have no further questions on direct examination, Your Honor.
JUDGE: *(Turning toward the opposing attorney)* Do you wish to cross-examine?
OPPOSING ATTORNEY: We do, Your Honor. *(Turning to the witness stand)* Now, Dr. Brown . . .

A new and very different aspect of the trial is beginning. Up until this point, the hypnotherapist has been testifying about matters that have been previously discussed with the lawyer who brought him or her into the case. No trick questions have been posed. All inquiries into credentials have been undertaken with the goal of making the therapist look good. The sequence of questions has been carefully designed to permit the therapist to provide a logical and coherent story. The lawyer has endeavored to create a friendly environment supportive of the therapist's testimony. In short, everything so far has been tailored to the expert's comfort.

Cross-examination has several goals, none of which is geared toward protecting the reputation or emotional sensitivity of the expert witness. Goldberg (1982) recommends that the cross-examining attorney view the trial as a dramatic play, with the witness as actor and the attorney as playwright. It is the playwright's job to maneuver and manipulate each character in order to tell the story best. Leading litigator Gerry Spence, who has not lost a jury trial in 15 years, also touts this approach: "A good cross-examination should have a beginning and an end, should have a purpose, should have a direction, should tell a story" (1984, p. 14).

The cross-examining attorney is bound by professional ethics to present, within certain limits, his or her client's story in its most persuasive light. This attorney will view an expert witness whose testimony has done damage to his or her case as an enemy. How the attorney handles the witness will depend upon how skillfully he or she can rewrite the script to shift the witness's character back into the preconceived plot.

To make sure that the witness sticks to the script and does not ad-lib, the cross-examining attorney is authorized—indeed, required—to use "leading questions." These are questions whose purpose is to suggest a definite answer. For example, "Doctor, on the night of August 11 you performed hypnosis on the defendant. *Is that not true?*" This question is asked to receive from the expert a "yes" or "no" and were, nothing else. The attorney does not want the expert to provide any other information or explanation besides what is specifically asked for by the question.

One of the most frustrating aspects of a cross-examination for the therapist is the inability to depart from the opposing attorney's prepared script. After having been given free rein to speak on direct examination, the expert will be tightly controlled on cross-examination. It is uncomfortable for a witness to realize that the person smiling at him or her and asking questions may very well be trying to trap or embarrass the witness. However, as long as the witness keeps calm and remains confident without being arrogant, the jury will identify more with him or her than with the lawyer.

Because the cross-examination is so tightly controlled, the therapist will find it very difficult to clarify or explain his or her answers. For this reason, it is important for the hypnotherapist on the witness stand to make the most clear, careful, and considered responses first, before the attorney has the chance to interrupt, object, or obfuscate.

The Strategy of the Cross-Examiner

The cross-examiner has three basic advantages. The first of these is the carefully constructed question. Essentially, the cross-examiner will design each question so that the answers fit the attorney's preconceived plan for the presentation of his or her case.

The second advantage is the cross-examiner's knowledge of precisely where he or she is going with the questions and intends to end up. Cross-examiners often conceal their game plans by asking questions in what appear to be random sequences. This tactic makes it difficult for witnesses to anticipate potential problems, and it also tends to throw them out of a consistent rhythm. A cross-examiner's plan is to take these pieces and tie them together during closing argument, long after a witness has been denied a chance to fully explain himself or herself.

The third advantage available to the cross-examiner is a thorough knowledge of, and comfort with, the rules and regulations of the courtroom. On his or her "home turf," the attorney will feel at ease in implementing whatever strategic choices the case requires.

The attorney has several basic strategies to devalue damaging direct examination testimony: (1) demolishing or discrediting the expert or the expert's testimony; (2) creating a "yes" set to make it appear that everything the expert says fits the attorney's view of the proceedings; (3) creating a "no" set to make the expert appear negative, uncooperative, and unappealing to the jury; or, finally, (4) eliciting information or data that can later be used during the closing argument. The hypnotherapist who understands the pitfalls in each of these approaches is more likely to avoid falling into one of them.

Demolishing the Expert

Just as therapists at conventions are fond of telling tales of one-sentence or single-session therapy cures, litigators also meet at conventions to swap stories of professional prowess. They are usually most impressed by the recital of a devastating cross-examination that reduced the testimony of an "unbreakable" expert witness to putty. At such conventions, it may sound as if all witnesses are sitting ducks and all attorneys expert shots. But, in reality, the devastating cross-examination is found about as frequently as the miracle therapy cure—more often in the movie house than in the courthouse.

It takes great bravado to undertake the ruination of a reputation. Because the attorney must be entirely successful, or else the jury will strongly sympathize with the hapless witness, so great a risk is rarely undertaken. The demolition of an expert can occur only with the expert's participation. Experts who are completely unprepared, who are dishonest, or who attempt to combat the cross-examiner in legal battle cause their own undoing.

Discrediting the Expert

Discrediting the expert witness is a milder version of demolishing the witness. The attorney's questions may seek to convey to the jury the impression that the witness is biased or prejudiced; stands to personally profit in some way from the testimony; is of bad moral character or reputation; lacks training, qualifications, or experience; or has a bad memory or poor observational skills. The hypnotherapist's best strategy, once again, is thorough preparation. If there are any grounds upon which the expert is vulnerable, answers to embarrassing questions should be thought out in advance with the assistance of the expert's own lawyer. The jury will understand human foibles and will not expect inhuman perfection.

Discrediting the Testimony

In attempting to discredit the testimony, the cross-examiner will pose questions suggesting that the witness was not in a good position to observe or opine; made prior inconsistent statements; told a story that is inconsistent with other evidence or testimony; or told a story that is improbable. The prepared expert will already have considered these possibilities. In all likelihood, some of these difficulties will have been raised during direct examination as a means of defusing the sting of cross-examination. Inconsistency is not a vice, as long as the expert can provide good reasons for a change in viewpoint.

Creating a Positive Set

Suppose that on direct examination, the expert has created a very favorable impression in the minds of the jurors. Rather than bring a frontal assault against this expert, the cross-examining attorney may wish to use this impression positively, to strengthen his or her own case. This may be done in several ways.

First, the attorney may have the witness repeat those parts of his or her direct testimony favorable to the attorney's case. The jury thus gets to hear this beneficial testimony twice.

Second, the attorney may also want to elicit further positive information about which the witness did not testify on direct examination. Using the good will the expert has already established, the attorney will ask a carefully designed sequence of questions forcing the expert to recite material helpful to the cross-examiner's case. It is far better for the jury to hear this positive material from the opposing experts than from the witnesses called by the client, who may be expected to be at least partially partisan.

A third tactic to accomplish this goal borrows from the hypnosis literature itself. In a discussion of Milton Erickson's utilization of the "yes" set, the excellence of this technique as a tool with highly resistant clients is emphasized (Erickson et al., 1976). By asking a series of 20–30 questions, all of which require a "yes" answer, the questioner can make the expert appear favorably predisposed toward him or her. In the hypnosis setting, where treatment is the purpose, this technique is a powerful aid to establish rapport. In the courtroom setting, the "yes" set promotes the impression that everything the witness says is consistent with and sympathetic to the cross-examiner's position.

LAWYER: Dr. Lee, you testified that Mr. Burns was a good hypnotic subject, did you not?

WITNESS: Yes, I did.

LAWYER: You also testified that he went into a deep trance quite easily, isn't that so?

WITNESS: Yes, I did.

LAWYER: You also testified that everyone goes into trances from time to time?

WITNESS: Yes.

LAWYER: Would you say that Mr. Burns is better than most people at doing this?

WITNESS: Yes.

LAWYER: Would you also agree that he had this ability before being hypnotized by you?

WITNESS: Yes.

LAWYER: Would you also agree that his ability is atypical?

WITNESS: Yes.

LAWYER: Isn't it true that people with such atypical ability normally have higher intelligence?

WITNESS: Yes.

LAWYER: Don't such people also tend to have greater imaginations?

WITNESS: Yes.

LAWYER: Do they also tend to have richer fantasy lives?

WITNESS: Yes.

LAWYER: Psychologists often refer to this as the ability to suspend disbelief, don't they?

WITNESS: Yes. It's similar to what happens in a movie. We identify with roles played by characters on the screen.

LAWYER: Would you not agree with other hypnosis experts that people who have greater skills in imagination, fantasy, and intelligence, and are able to go into deeper trances, are also more likely to be unsure of the differences between fantasy and reality?

There is little a hypnotherapist witness can do when this tactic is being used, but there is little the witness would *want* to do, because he or she is still making a favorable impression on the jury. It is up to the retaining lawyer, later in the trial, to make sure that the witness's words are not used out of context. Perhaps the most troubling aspect of this approach is the psychological sense of helplessness as the cross-examiner uses one's own words to one's detriment.

Creating a Negative Set

Clever cross-examination will also employ the opposite approach to great advantage. The attorney may ask the witness two dozen questions, all of which draw a "no" answer. Use of the "no" set can make an impartial witness appear biased, negative, or unfair. Jurors may begin to sympathize with the cross-examiner, who cannot seem to make any headway against this stubborn witness. This strategy is employed when the attorney wants to discredit the witness, but lacks direct information with which to confront him or her on the merits of the testimony.

Use of the "no" set is often accompanied by a tone of voice that becomes increasingly exasperated, and by gestures toward the jury indicating that the witness is particularly obstinate. The obvious intent in eliciting a series of "no" answers is to have the jury believe that the expert is so negative toward the cross-examiner's interest that all of his or her testimony should be considered biased and hence untrustworthy.

One strategy to disrupt the "no" set is to give a confusing positive answer. For example, instead of answering "No," the expert might say, "Yes, I would have to answer that in the negative." Breaking the rhythm of the "no" set also tends to throw the cross-examiner off stride.

Enhancing the Summation

During the summation (the closing argument made after all witnesses have testified), the attorney will tell the client's story to the jury. Material obtained from the cross-examination will be subtly woven into the fabric of the plot long after the expert has left the stand. In order to obtain some of this material, the attorney may have to disguise the purpose of his or her inquiries. The questions put to the hypnotherapist may seem arbitrary, disconnected, or irrelevant.

It may appear tempting to match wits with the attorney. If the attorney has successfully aroused the emotions of the expert, the desire to personalize the adversarial confrontation may seem irresistible. The lawyer who asks disconnected questions would certainly appear to be an especially easy target. However, the expert witness should resist this temptation.

Trying to outguess and outmaneuver the attorney at this point is one way in which a witness's reputation, standing, and testimony may become discredited or demolished. Obviously, the attorney may well have been intending to provoke just such a response. Equally obvious is the fact that the lawyer has been specifically trained to handle these confrontations. After all, the lawyer knows the rules of the legal game.

More importantly, even if the witness handles the confrontation well, the battle may be won, but the war may be lost. Lawyers are continually focused not on what is happening, but on how it will appear to the jury.

Therapists in their own work well know the value of the symbolic meaning of events and the extraordinary role image plays in each person's conception of reality. The expert being cross-examined who does battle with the attorney may turn off the jury's natural emotional sympathy.

The Jury as Audience

Despite the intention and desire of the hypnotherapist on the stand to present a balanced, complete, and truthful account of the facts, the therapist is essentially competing with the cross-examiner in a popularity contest.

The expert begins with an advantage: The natural sympathies of the jury will normally not be with a cross-examining attorney. Each juror will imagine what it must feel like to sit all alone in that tiny witness box facing a highly skilled, professionally trained interrogator. Within the jury, there is often strong support for the underdog, and perhaps more than a little mistrust of lawyers as amoral manipulators.

Despite an infinite and kaleidoscopic potential arrangement of facts, two questions are pre-eminent in the attorney's mind. First, did the jury *like* the witness? Second, did the jury *believe* the witness? The hypnotherapist also can profit from keeping these two questions uppermost in mind. All of the work of a trial is geared to influencing the jury, without seeming to be doing so. Walter (1980) states that the effective cross-examiner must *control* the witness, but must not appear to do so in an obviously unfair manner.

Younger (1977) and Applebaum (1963) train attorneys to cross-examine by stressing certain points. Among these are the following:

1. Be brief and concise.
2. Ask short questions.
3. Use words the jury can understand.
4. Never ask a question to which you do not already know the answer.
5. Never appear to be attacking a witness unless the jury has already lost sympathy with that witness.
6. Do not allow a witness to explain an answer.
7. Make it appear to the jury that if a witness does not answer the question in a favorable way, he or she is not to be trusted.

CROSS-EXAMINING THE HYPNOSIS EXPERT WITNESS

Expert evidence is essential in every trial where the use of hypnosis is at issue. Although most people are fascinated by hypnosis, the actual mechanics of trance and the nature of the hypnotic state are outside their ordinary realm of knowledge. Expert testimony helps guide the jury through the technical aspects of hypnosis, suggestion, confabulation, memory, regression, and simulation.

How should a hypnosis expert prepare for cross-examination? Broadly speaking, there are three "fields of vulnerability" that an opposing lawyer will exploit: the qualifications of the expert, the actual performance of hypnosis, and the infirmities of knowledge about hypnosis.

Qualifications of the Expert

A person's claim to be an expert in a particular field, such as hypnosis, is always subject to careful scrutiny in the eyes of the law. This scrutiny often comes in the form of cross-examination. What are the qualifications of an expert?

Education

Courts usually require experts to have extensive schooling, especially where evidence involving medical or scientific opinion is at issue. As Judge Larry C. Smith of the Florida District Court of Appeal observed in a 1984 hypnosis case, "certainly one of the main criteria by which the qualifications of an expert witness may be determined and his testimony evaluated are the institutions attended and the degrees earned in a special field of expertise" (*Kline v. State*, 1984, p. 1104). Most experts easily meet schooling requirements; as a result, cross-examination in this area is usually nonproductive and unthreatening to the witness. But not always.

Judge Smith's concerns about credentials were stated in the course of a most unusual case involving internationally known hypnosis authority Milton V. Kline. In 1979, at a pretrial hearing, Kline was questioned about his education and training. For some inexplicable reason, he claimed to have earned "a doctoral degree in Clinical Psychology at Penn State University" when in fact he had no such degree at all. This misrepresentation would ordinarily be enough to disqualify any expert witness; the trial judge, however, found Kline still qualified even without the degree. Whether Kline actually testified we do not know, for the opinion is silent on this point. But it was Judge Smith's unpleasant duty to uphold Kline's conviction for perjury. According to the court, "misrepresentations which tend to bolster the credibility of a witness" easily fall within the definition of perjury (p. 1104).

Even in Florida, cases like *Kline* are rarer than whooping cranes. An attorney could never gear an entire cross-examination strategy on the possibility that the expert would lie about his or her schooling. However, there is one line of questioning more or less unique to hypnosis that may be employed to some advantage.

Hypnosis has been studied at American colleges and universities at least since 1890, when William James (1890) wrote accounts of his own experiments at Harvard, as well as descriptions of work being done by Jevons and Cattell. Milton Erickson (1964) reported early experiments with trance in 1923 at the University of Wisconsin when he was a sophomore. However, hypnosis has not been studied in academia very often, nor at very many institutions of higher learning. For much of this century, hypnosis was considered an inappropriate and insufficiently respectable area of scholarly inquiry Furthermore, the nature of the hypnosis that was experimentally studied at such institutions was quite different in kind from the clinical hypnosis used by practitioners in the mental health field. As Hilgard and Loftus (1979) have indicated, the bridge between experimental and clinical hypnosis is not always easily crossed.

There is some possibility that an expert will never have taken a specific course on hypnosis during college or professional academic training. Prior to the trial, the cross-examining attorney can obtain this information by contacting the schools the expert has attended. He or she may attempt to diminish the expert's overall educational credentials by asking a series of pointed questions about the number of hypnosis courses the expert took in college, graduate school, or postgraduate work. When each answer is "none," the prestige of the degrees may be weakened in the minds of the jurors. Such questions can also have the effect of making the hypnotherapist quite uncomfortable on the witness stand, unless he or she is already prepared for them.

The following is an example of this line of questioning:

ATTORNEY: Dr. Brown, at which schools did you receive your degrees?

WITNESS: I received my doctorate at the University of California, Berkeley; my master's degree at UCLA; and my B.A. at Amherst.

ATTORNEY: OK, Doctor, how many courses on hypnosis did you take at Berkeley?

WITNESS: There were no specific courses at Berkeley. I was part of a major research project, and studied clinical hypnosis as part of my internship at the Palo Alto VA.

ATTORNEY: That's fine, Doctor. You had no courses at Berkeley. How many courses in hypnosis did you take at UCLA?

WITNESS: No specific courses. I was also part of . . .

ATTORNEY: So no courses in your master's program either. And you had no courses in hypnosis as an undergraduate, isn't that correct?

WITNESS: That's correct.

ATTORNEY: Then, Doctor, in your 4 years at Amherst, 2 years at UCLA, and 3 years at Berkeley, did you earn even one single credit in hypnosis?
WITNESS: No.

It is embarrassing to appear foolish, which the cross-examining attorney is counting on. An expert who gets flustered may make mistakes. Even worse, visible discomfort will adversely affect the jurors, who want experts to be confident and self-assured. After all, the jurors are being asked to respect the opinion of a stranger. A witness who appears insecure loses credibility.

In a case like the one above, the witness should let the attorney make his or her points here. The witness's demeanor will count more than his or her answer. Furthermore, after the cross-examination is over, the retaining counsel can have the witness explain on re-direct examination that the schools he or she attended followed standard curricula guidelines. In not offering hypnosis courses, they were neither unique nor remiss.

This attack on credentials can only be expected to earn the attorney a few points at best. After all, the expert with undoubtedly have more to offer in the way of expertise than a handful of diplomas. However, if an opposing expert can be rattled without offending the jury, then the cross-examiner has nothing to lose.

Licenses and Certification

Every state requires individuals to have some type of license or certification to practice therapy or medicine. The regulations among the states are likely to differ. Within a state, the right to practice hypnosis may be based upon a different set of credentials for each professional group. In California, for example, licensed physicians and psychologists may practice hypnotherapy without any evidence of prior training. Licensed marital and family therapists (who must have a master's degree) must take and pass a 40-hour course in hypnotherapy to be able to use these techniques (Shapiro, Edmonson, & Wallace, 1986).

It is essential that anyone testifying in court as an expert be knowledgeable about the applicable laws governing the practice of hypnosis. Even licensed and credentialed therapists will be vulnerable if they do not know the legal regulations they are required to obey.

Training

Training is another topic on which the cross-examiner may not gain major victories, but may try to obtain some advantage through gradually whittling away at the expert's qualifications. The approach here is very similar to the challenge to academic credentials discussed earlier.

Most serious training in clinical hypnosis occurs outside the standard academic curricula. There are a small number of graduate programs for the study of hypnosis, but they are mainly restricted to experimental hypnosis rather than clinical training. Since the 1950s, primary responsibility for training in hypnosis has been assumed by privately run seminars or by nonprofit foundations' programs and conferences. In more recent years, these organizations have proliferated to satisfy the increasing interest in hypnotic phenomena.

Regulation of hypnosis training has been slow in coming. Many of the privately run seminars were led by imaginative people with great vision, but without professional degrees. The fact that noncredentialed individuals have been conducting nonregulated programs has lessened confidence in the value of the training received. This may appear especially true if the company or foundation offering the training has long since gone out of business. The opposite attack is also possible when training was received under the auspices of a new organization—one that had not yet had time to prove itself.

As we have seen in the matter of the expert's education, the cross-examiner may take a few opportunities here. Even if an expert was not trained under the best of conditions, the number of years of practice must still be considered. However, years of experience practicing inadequate theories can be similar to a solid house on a flimsy foundation: Neither will stand for long.

Most major hypnosis conferences today have some state-approved certification for the instructional programs they provide. The expert should be aware of this certification and should make a note of it in his or her records when conferences are attended.

Practice

An expert's qualifications are measured in large part by the record of what he or she has accomplished with the education and training received. What has this expert done? In particular, does this expert have actual experience with cases similar in facts to the present case? The cross-examiner can be effective in showing that a hypnotherapist is testifying from the literature and not from personal experience, as in the following example:

ATTORNEY: Now, Dr. Brown, how many patients do you see in your practice in an average week?

WITNESS: Approximately 20–25.

ATTORNEY: And in how many of these cases do you use hypnosis?

WITNESS: At any given time, maybe five.

ATTORNEY: So you use hypnosis with only 20–25% of your patients. Now, are all of these patients seeing you for the same reason?

WITNESS: No.

ATTORNEY: Well, what percentage of the hypnosis patients do you work with for memory enhancement or amnesia?

WITNESS: Maybe 20%.

ATTORNEY: So at any one time you would be treating 20% of five patients for memory loss. That's only one patient.

WITNESS: That's the average over time.

ATTORNEY: You testified earlier that you had been in practice for 10 years. Well, how many of these memory loss patients have you seen in your 10 years of practice?

WITNESS: Perhaps 10–12.

ATTORNEY: And of these 10–12 patients, how many have been for the most part similar to the current case, involving global amnesia after a traumatic criminal assault?

WITNESS: Approximately half.

ATTORNEY: So your expertise over the years consists of possibly five or six patients in 10 years.

A related problem arises when the expert is an experimentalist and not a clinician. Suppose the expert is a heavily degreed professor at a prestigious university. This witness ordinarily will have high believability. The cross-examiner may use structured questions to show that the expert has confined his or her work with hypnosis to experimentation on volunteer college students or interested graduate students. The fact that the expert has never handled hypnosis with victims of traumatic shock may lessen the jury's belief in the expert's competence to speak with authority.

As we have seen in Chapter Seven, many hypnosis authorities believe that the nature of the hypnotic encounter varies, depending upon whether the memory loss is a product of traumatic shock or of normal lack of retention. In some instances, observations from the laboratory may not be as persuasive as observations drawn from real clinical cases.

To make sure that the jury receives this impression, at closing argument the attorney may comment, "There is no doubt that the professor is indeed an expert, but not in this particular branch of hypnosis." The jury will still appreciate the expert's qualifications, but will be more inclined to find him or her mistaken if they believe that his or her real talent lies elsewhere. This reconciles for the jury the dilemma of having to decide that a person labeled as an expert may in fact not be one. The jury is now free to respect the expert but disregard his or her testimony.

Publications

The cross-examiner may make two major uses of an expert's publications. The first is to show that these publications do not address the specific issues in question. If, for example, the question before the court is the reliability of hypnotically refreshed recollection, and the expert's articles focus on whether a hypnotist can manipulate a subject into committing antisocial acts, these writings do not demonstrate an expertise in the precise issues before the court.

The other use cross-examiners make of the publications of experts is to check for inconsistencies, contradictions, or disagreements with other experts. Occasionally, something the expert has written will fly in the face of the testimony given on direct examination.

Such a moment occurred in the trial of Patty Hearst (*The Trial of Patty Hearst*, 1976), during the cross-examination of psychiatrist and hypnotist Dr. Louis J. West. West had been called by the defense to support their argument that Hearst had been brainwashed. The prosecutor found a statement in one of West's earlier publications in which he claimed that brainwashing did not exist. Although the contradiction could have been explained, the witness was not given the opportunity to provide that explanation.

Cross-examiners know that when experts prepare for trial, they often neglect to reread their own writings. It is therefore possible for a cross-examiner to pull out small passages and ask the expert to comment upon them. If the cross-examiner has planned the questions correctly, there is a good chance that the expert may unknowingly condemn his or her own opinions. The transcripts of dozens of trials testify to this incredible fact.

It is natural to think of an expert's publications as those books and articles that have been officially issued to the public. There are, however, two additional types of publications that cross-examiners often study and master: (1) the transcript of the deposition hearing or any other pretrial documents in which the expert's testimony has been recorded, and (2) the transcripts of other cases in which the expert has testified. The expert may be tempted to ignore this material; this is an oft-proven serious error. Therapists should obtain all legal documents in which their testimony plays a part, summarize the contents, store the documents in a safe manner permitting easy retrieval, and study them carefully before any court appearance.

The formidable reputation of many a cross-examiner has been forged upon the poor preparation of experts. Morrill (1979) underscores the significance of the pretrial and deposition hearing transcripts as fuel for a powerful cross-examination:

> The cross-examination conducted under today's rules may even take on the complexion of a game to see who remembers the contents of the deposition better—the trial lawyer or the witness. The trial lawyer has the advantage in that he has played the game before and is, therefore, a bonzer marksman. The witness must remember all of the answers he has given, whereas the questioner is interested only in a limited bailiwick and can

direct his questioning in those areas. Any deviation from the answers given previously in the deposition provides ammunition for the cross-examiner. (p. 56)

Impartiality

There may be reasons why the expert, though otherwise qualified, ought not to be fully believed. Bias, prejudice, financial reward, loyalty, or other forms of partiality may color the expert's judgment.

An expert who has testified many times in many trials, but always for the same side, may be suspect in the eyes of the jury. One who uses every occasion to sell a particular viewpoint may be perceived as self-interested and zealous rather than earnest and convincing. The jury's attention shifts from the truth of the matter to the expert's desire to be believed. This tears the cloak of impartiality, an essential garment for the expert to wear.

In their excellent reference work *Clinical Handbook of Psychiatry and the Law*, Gutheil and Applebaum (1982) point out that an ethical dilemma of the hypnotherapist may provide a basis for the attorney to challenge the impartiality of the expert witness. If the expert was initially hired by a patient for therapy that involved hypnosis, there may be a conflict about whose interests the witness must serve: "In short, is the expert a 'hired gun' who is being employed to express only the opinion that would favor her employer's [patient's] case, or does she owe allegiance to some loftier principle?" (p. 342).

In such a case, the attorney may seek to exploit the fact that the expert may be driven to be an advocate for his or her client's cause rather than an objective, neutral witness. Even worse, the attorney may attempt to whipsaw the witness between the professional duty to provide effective therapy and the courtroom oath to provide the truth. The cross-examiner may, for instance, try to show that the hypnotherapist's testimony is influenced by the therapeutic circumstances:

LAWYER: Dr. Brown, you have worked with Ms. Jones for 10 months, is that correct?

WITNESS: Yes.

LAWYER: Do you like her?

WITNESS: Yes.

LAWYER: Would you like to help heal her?

WITNESS: Yes.

LAWYER: Is it your opinion that if Ms. Jones loses this case, it will cause her mental grief?

WITNESS: I believe it could.

LAWYER: Is Ms. Jones wealthy?

WITNESS: I do not believe she is.

LAWYER: Dr. Brown, do you have an estimate of how much more time in therapy with you Ms. Jones will spend?

WITNESS: I believe another year would be valuable to her.

In this brief exchange, the lawyer has managed to imply that Dr. Brown likes the patient, wants to help her, knows she is not wealthy, and believes that a loss in the case would have an adverse affect on Ms. Jones's mental health (and her pocketbook). Under such conditions, can Dr. Brown's testimony be viewed as strictly neutral?

Dr. Brown might have tried to "fence" with the lawyer by qualifying each answer given. But the lawyer would have asked the judge to instruct Dr. Brown to limit the answers. Dr. Brown's best strategy is to respond truthfully and briefly. If the cross-examiner provides an opening, Dr. Brown might point out that professional obligations to a client do not require a therapist to commit perjury and face a jail term.

An even more effective response is possible if Dr. Brown has anticipated this line of questioning and discussed it with Ms. Jones. In that situation, Dr. Brown could respond as follows:

WITNESS: In our last conversation before trial, I told Ms. Jones that I was bound by the oath to tell the truth, even if the truth might hurt her case or cause her mental pain. She said she understood. We reduced this conversation to writing. I have a copy of it with me if you would like to see it.

An expert's lack of impartiality can even be suggested by innuendo. A surprising advocate of this tactic is Erle Stanley Gardner, the creator of Perry Mason. Before achieving fame as a mystery writer, Gardner was a trial lawyer. In February 1957, he addressed the American Academy of Forensic Sciences; his address was reprinted a year later in the academy's journal. When he was practicing law, Gardner told the audience, he "more or less specialized in cross-examining experts" (1958, p. 374). He then described one of his favorite strategems:

> The cross-examiner, trying to be as unfair as possible, looks witheringly at the witness and says, "Doctor, you expect to be paid for your testimony in this case, don't you?"
> That's the way I did it. (1958, p. 374)

The question was framed so as to suggest that the witness expected to be paid for his or her *testimony*. As mentioned above, the question was deliberately unfair. Most cross-examiners do no want to be fair; they want to discredit the witness. The expert who always beat him, according to Gardner, was the one who looked him in the eye and said, "No, I am being paid for my time, not my testimony" (1958, p. 375).

The Actual Performance of Hypnosis

After the question of qualifications has been explored, the cross-examiner may next choose to consider the expert's testimony about the actual use of hypnosis in the present case. There are two possibilities here: Either the expert performed the hypnosis, or the expert has been called for an independent evaluation of the hypnotic work.

The Hypnosis Practitioner

Once the hypnotist's credentials have been established, inquiry will shift to whether the hypnosis was competently performed in the present situation. In any cross-examination, the attorney will explore the specifics of the hypnotherapy sessions and attempt to convince the jury that it was not done according to minimum standards or was impermissibly suggestive.

Most jurisdictions that permit the introduction of hypnosis evidence require that tapes or certified transcripts of all sessions be provided to the cross-examiner prior to the trial. This transcript will then be scrutinized by other experts in an attempt to find errors or problems with the sessions. As all therapists know, even when a session is expertly completed, it is subject to a vast array of criticism from those who approach hypnotherapy from different theoretical perspectives. The therapist on the stand will be expected to defend every word, intervention, and motive that emerges from the transcript.

In addition to defending the hypnotherapy that was provided, the clinician also may be asked to state an opinion on a great many questions concerning the actual performance of the hypnosis. Some of these questions may include the following:

1. Was the client a good hypnotic subject?
2. Was the subject simulating or faking?
3. How did the hypnotist evaluate veracity?
4. Could the subject have confabulated?
5. Was there undue suggestion during the induction or from the surrounding circumstances?
6. Was the information given while in trance likely to be truthful or accurate?
7. Did the subject go into a trance, and how deep was the trance?
8. By what standards was the depth of the trance evaluated?
9. Why was hypnosis used in this particular case?

The Hypnosis Expert Consultant

Not all therapists who testify in a trial will have performed the actual hypnosis. Indeed, for each practitioner called to testify, there will be at least one other expert prepared to support or criticize the practitioner's handling of the session.

This consultant will have already studied the transcript of the case. All of the questions posed above will also be asked of this expert, with the addition of further crucial questions:

1. Was the practitioner qualified to perform hypnosis?
2. Was the hypnosis competently performed?
3. Should hypnosis have been used in this case?

Whenever an expert consultant seeks to evaluate the performance of another, there are problems involving lack of first-hand observation. The cross-examiner may very well attempt to throw into doubt the expert's ability to make a meaningful assessment.

Suppose, for example, that the hypnotic session was audiotaped only. The expert consultant has testified on direct examination that the hypnosis was free from undue suggestion. The cross-examiner may approach this expert slowly and indirectly. The initial questions would explore the richness of hypnotic induction techniques, ranging from Mesmer's "magnetic passes" to syncopated metronomes, whirling disks, swinging watches, and blinking eyelids. Now the jury has a vivid picture of nonverbal suggestion that would not appear on a sound recording. The expert can do little more than confirm the substantial literature on the centuries-old use of these induction procedures.

The more sophisticated nonverbal induction techniques developed by Milton Erickson and others provide an additional challenge. The cross-examiner will have become fully acquainted with these references, or at least specific components that serve his or her current purposes. He or she will ask whether the expert is familiar with the publications in which these techniques appear.

If the expert answers "yes," the next series of questions will force the expert to describe these techniques on nonverbal suggestion to the jury. If the expert makes any mistakes, the cross-examiner will be certain to point out corrections. If the description is accurate, however, the expert will have conveyed to the jury that nonverbal suggestion is a powerful form of induction.

If the expert answers "no," claiming unfamiliarity with the publications, the cross-examiner will then demonstrate that the expert is unaware of the precise literature directly relevant to the issue of nonverbal suggestion.

When an expert is called upon to evaluate the hypnosis work of another, this evaluation necessarily stems from an incomplete source of information. The expert may be asked to read a transcript, watch a videotape, hear an audiotape, or interview a person after the event has occurred. All of these sources are imperfect. The subtlety and elusiveness of indirect suggestions force the expert to admit the deficiencies of the record upon which his or her opinion has been based. An expert who fails to concede these limitations will be denying the obvious and will lose believability. An expert who concedes thereby admits that his or her opinion contains some measure of speculation, but jurors will accept the limitations of the expert's role.

Infirmities of Knowledge about Hypnosis

In any field of scientific inquiry, observers are likely to maintain distinct perspectives. Hypnosis has managed to fascinate humanity since the beginning of recorded time. It has been studied scientifically since the sensational exploits of the 18th-century pioneer, Anton Mesmer. Two hundred years of experimentation and investigation have produced an enormous wealth of knowledge, but the experts still debate the same major questions that plagued the early European experimenters two centuries ago.

The "battle of experts" is a familiar scene in courtrooms. If an attorney wishes to cast doubt on the use of hypnosis in any given situation, the cross-examination will be designed to show to the jury that fundamental disagreements exist among hypnosis experts as to even the most basic question of all—does hypnosis exist? Indeed, one of the most prolific authors in the field of hypnosis disclaims any such special phenomena as "hypnosis" or "trance" (Barber, 1957, 1969).

One obvious reason for widespread divergent viewpoints addresses the very nature of the mind itself. Intellectual historian Bruno Snell (1953) reminds us that "we cannot speak about the mind without falling back on metaphor" (p. vi). The figurative language used to describe hypnosis and trance does not lend itself comfortably to calibration, quantification, and measurement. This fact can also be exploited by the cross-examiner.

What Hypnosis Is Not

As an authority on what hypnosis is, the expert must also be ready to state what it is not. On cross-examination, the expert may be asked to supply precise descriptions and definitions of any or all of the following concepts:

- Daydreaming
- Sleep
- Visualization
- Meditation
- Guided imagery
- Somnambulism
- Fugue state
- Brainwashing

- Mind control
- Mesmerism
- Programming and deprogramming
- The unconscious mind
- The preconscious mind
- The coconscious mind
- Neurolinguistic programming
- Trance
- Deep trance

The expert witness may *understand* the differences among these concepts very well, but may find it difficult to *articulate* these differences with convincing clarity. Descriptive words may become repetitive, or the expert may sound confused. Steering a clear channel through these related but distinct ideas, without simultaneously losing the jury to boredom or befuddlement, requires truly expert navigation.

For the hypnotherapist, the best answers to many of these general questions are examples and metaphors. The jury will appreciate images over ideas, especially when those ideas are highly abstract and technical. Even where a more technical answer is necessary, the expert is advised to provide a down-to-earth analogy that the jurors can grasp or picture.

Another possibility when faced with a question that calls for a complex or technical answer is to be straightforward and say, "You are asking a very difficult question. Do you prefer a general answer that is short, or a more detailed answer that is more precise?" The cross-examiner is now on the defensive: He or she must either accept the general answer, knowing in advance that its simplicity sacrifices accuracy, or must hear the more detailed answer so as not to appear to be suppressing the truth.

What Hypnosis Is

The discussion above proceeds on the premise that an hypnosis expert should be familiar with what hypnosis *is not*. Equal problems exist for the expert in defining what hypnosis *is*.

Cross-examiners have always been able to profit from the disagreements among experts and the frailties of human knowledge. In Chapter Six, we have presented a variety of definitions and disputes currently prevalent in the fields of clinical and experimental hypnosis. Experts may be unfamiliar with or unprepared to discuss the range and depth of hypnosis theories, especially when confronted with the task of explaining, comparing, and contrasting them in the anxiety-provoking courtroom setting.

An expert who is articulate and conversant with the spectrum of agreements and disagreements within the hypnosis field may be unwittingly demonstrating that there is so much disagreement over fundamental questions that expert opinion about hypnosis is more a matter of perspective than of actual fact. This tactic clearly does not bring the discredit or embarrassment to the expert that unfamiliarity does. From the therapist's point of view, the best strategy is to provide clear, concise, and informed answers. The jurors are not stupid; they know that experts will disagree. The expert who conveys sincerity, admits the incomplete state of human knowledge, and yet holds his or her opinions with confidence will be believed.

Familiarity with the Literature

Professional experts are normally busy people. Even if they were not so busy, there would still be insufficient time to read and reread the vast volume of information that appears monthly on hypnosis, memory, and related topics. Professor James V. McConnell (1968/1970), a psychologist and leading memory researcher, suggested in a speech to lawyers several techniques that take advantage of the difficulty of keeping abreast with the literature.

The "latest research" gambit. McConnell (1968/1970) encouraged lawyers on the eve of trial to check the most recent issues of technical journals, as well as newly published books. The odds favor the expert's falling behind in his or her reading and perhaps being unaware of the newly published information. If this new material has any relevance to the trial, the cross-examiner may linger on the expert's unfamiliarity with the latest findings in the field.

An expert facing a court appearance should become acquainted with the latest issues of the major hypnosis periodicals, and might also contact the leading publishers of hypnosis books to learn of forthcoming texts. Prepublication copies, or discussions with the authors, will give the therapist a distinct edge if the cross-examiner ventures into this avenue of questioning.

The "original source" gambit. Shifting gears into reverse, McConnell (1968/ 1970) encouraged lawyers to exploit the fact that experts have probably not read the original source material of their profession, or at least have not read that material for quite some time. In regard to hypnosis, the cross-examiner can ask the witness whether he or she has read the works of Mesmer, Braid, Bernheim, Charcot, Freud, Janet, William James, Morton Prince, and a host of other hypnosis pioneers. The expert may have read interpretations of these writings, but not the originals. Even if the originals were read, it is not likely that they were read recently. The impact of an expert's unfamiliarity with pioneering thinkers in the field is to diminish the prestige and authority of the rest of the testimony.

The "double whammy" gambit. If the cross-examiner succeeds in getting the expert to admit that he or she has not read the original source material or the latest publications, the attorney may administer the "double whammy" by remarking to the jury, "It is an extraordinary expert who is unfamiliar with both the oldest and the newest work in the field."

The "hindsight history" gambit. Another strategy McConnell (1968/1970) suggested highlights the fact that all scientific disciplines have their fair share of ideas that ultimately prove mistaken. Most of the beliefs held about hypnosis through the ages have in fact been wrong. A wily cross-examiner may have handy a list of theories about hypnosis that have not withstood the test of time. The expert may testify clearly and correctly about these theories, but after a goodly number of them are discussed, the jury may catch the implication that the attorney considers the expert's own opinion another item to be added to the list.

This gambit also works in reverse. Many theories have been proposed in science, only to be met with professional scorn and derision until later proven to be true. Indeed, hypnosis itself was not granted professional respectability until the late 1950s. Suppose that an expert testifies against a hypnotherapist's clinical procedures because they follow a minority viewpoint, while the expert's position is more in line with the mainstream. The cross-examiner may ask questions about different instances in which valid scientific discoveries were rejected by the conservative medical establishment, which later would reverse itself. The jury will catch the implication that the expert is part of a stuffy professional establishment that is reluctant to test new ideas.

The Mystery of Memory

In almost all cases involving forensic hypnosis, expert testimony about the nature of memory is pertinent. A hypnosis expert testifying about the use of hypnosis to refresh recollection may be questioned about memory and the effect of hypnosis on recall.

Research on memory has accelerated in recent years. As with most questions of knowledge, investigation seems more apt to pose new issues than to resolve old ones. Mark Twain's remark about the various endeavors to satisfactorily complete Charles Dickens's unfinished novel *The Mystery of Edwin Drood* applies equally here: "The investigations which a number of researchers have carried out have already thrown a great deal of darkness on the subject, and it is possible, if they continue, that we shall soon know nothing about it at all."

Reiser (1985a), in a paper delivered at the Second International Congress on Ericksonian Approaches to Hypnosis and Psychotherapy, observed, "The fact is that *no one* yet knows how memory really works despite a hundred years of laboratory research. . . . There are dozens of theories and models of memory" (p. 517). In support of this view, Reiser listed an abundance of theories currently held about memory:

1. The two-stage theory
2. Levels-of-processing theory
3. The repression–blockade model
4. The cybernetic communication theory
5. The tape recorder model
6. The two-system theory of episodic and semantic memories
7. Neo-dissociation and parallel-processing theory
8. The holographic model
9. The RNA molecule storage model
10. The two-component theory of long-term and short-term memory
11. Associative-interference theory and trace decay theory
12. The theory of context-bound recall
13. The "uniqueness increases depth of processing" theory
14. The selective-amnesia theory
15. State-dependent learning theory
16. The theory of multiaccess and multichecking modes of retrieval
17. Encoding specificity theory
18. The superiority of cued-recall over uncued-recall theory

Reiser's list, which may now be supplemented by even more recent research (described in Chapter Seven), touches mainly on the workings of memory. To be prepared for the cross-examiner, the expert should also have some familiarity with the literature on amnesias, dissociative states, and confabulation. The jury may reasonably expect an expert on hypnotically refreshed recollection to be acquainted with these related subjects.

Careful preparation by an expert necessarily involves pretrial anticipation. It is expected that any expert will have the general principles and ideological conflicts in the field at ready access, but nobody can reasonably be expected to carry all the minute details around in his or her head. The advantage the cross-examiner possesses here is that while the expert must be conversant with an enormous body of material, the questioner need only be conversant with precisely those portions that will enable him or her to discredit or weaken the testimony.

To help overcome this disadvantage, we advise experts to prepare a set of notes that can be brought into the trial. When the attorney for either side requests very specific information, the therapist can ask permission to answer from these prepared notes. The law permits a witness to use notes to help recall information accurately. Before an expert's notes may be used, the court will have to rule on the procedure. The content of the notes may have to be shared with both sides prior to such a ruling, unless the notes are covered by therapist–client privilege.

Simulation

One of the most serious and hotly contested issues in the field of hypnosis is the determination of whether a subject actually has been in trance or has merely been simulating it. Most of the leading authorities find it difficult to articulate factors that clearly determine trance from trickery (Barber et al., 1974; Kroger, 1963; Orne, 1979).

In the Hillside Strangler case, which baffled police in two states for years, at least three experts were called in to use hypnotic questioning techniques on the suspect, Kenneth Bianchi, with his consent. All three professionals, at least two of whom are international authorities on multiple personality, agreed that the suspect was indeed possessed of at least two distinct personalities. All three were quite prepared to testify to that effect in court.

But before trial, one more opinion was sought. Martin Orne, a leading authority on the issue of simulation, also interrogated the suspect. Through careful questioning and the laying of a hidden trap, Orne was able to show that the witness was not only simulating multiple personalities, but most likely was also simulating being hypnotized at all. Bianchi, who had no formal training in psychology other than some books he had read on his own, had briefly fooled the experts (Barnes, 1984).

Tangential Questions

There are other questions, not directly related to the issues in a trial, that may be asked of a hypnosis expert. The purpose of these questions may include satisfying the curiosity of the jury, increasing their attentiveness, or conducting a "fishing expedition" to find weaknesses to exploit in the expert's knowledge of the field. Hypnosis experts should be prepared to respond to the following lines of inquiry:

1. Can a person be hypnotized against his or her will?
2. Will a hypnotized person do something against his or her personal moral code?
3. Can a person lie in hypnosis?
4. Is the subject under the control of the hypnotist?

These topics are controversial, and a wide range of opinions about them may be found in both the historical and the current literatures. There have been few modern instances where the dark side of hypnosis has been featured in legal proceedings. The brainwashing headlines of the 1950s, the Charles Manson and Patty Hearst cases, and the continuing disputes about the methods used by cults involve more than just hypnosis. Nevertheless, cross-examiners may want an expert to express an opinion about these matters.

It is not necessary for the hypnotherapist to venture an opinion on these questions unless he or she is well versed on these issues. One need not hesitate to decline to answer questions tangentially related to one's expertise. It is better to say "I don't know" than to have the jury discover that an expert knows far less than he or she thinks.

CONCLUSION

This chapter has provided hypnotherapists with an assortment of tactics used in cross-examination, and some techniques to make the experience less inhibiting and more rewarding.

To those professionals not trained in the law and not experienced with lawyers, cross-examination may very well appear unfair and unjust. After all, an effective cross-examiner relies for persuasion primarily on innuendo, inference, and implication. Truth often seems to be a forgotten guest in the courthouse. Many of the techniques of cross-examination may appear underhanded or unnecessarily demeaning.

The cross-examiner's strongest weapon is often the failure of the witness to prepare adequately for the truly partisan nature of advocacy. It is essential, however, that the hypnotherapist not fall into the trap of partisanship. Naturally the therapist may have strong feelings for the client he or she has labored to cure. These feelings must not interfere with the expert's obligation to testify honestly, accurately, and neutrally. In *Psychological Evaluation and Expert Testimony*, David L. Shapiro (1984) recommends that the "therapist should generally not become the patient's advocate in the litigation" (p. 132). This is very good advice.

A therapist will best withstand cross-examination by being properly prepared. This chapter has suggested a means by which one can tailor this preparation to the specific requirements of the legal arena. Because every case is unique in terms of its facts and personalities, the expert witness is encouraged to work closely with the lawyer who seeks his or her testimony.

A therapist's best strategy is to fulfill the oath to tell the truth to the best of his or her ability. It is not the job of the therapist to influence the outcome of a trial other than as a well-prepared, professional, informed expert.

CHAPTER 10

The Psychotherapist's Experience

THE PHONE CALL

DR. BIRD: Hello, Ms. Roberta Green, please.

MS. GREEN: I'm Roberta Green.

DR. BIRD: Hello. I'm Jeffrey Bird, returning your call. How can I help you?

MS. GREEN: My physician suggested I call you for hypnosis. I've been having a lot of physical problems, and she says they may be psychological.

DR. BIRD: Why has she suggested hypnosis?

MS. GREEN: Well, I can't remember some parts of my past, and she thinks it will help relax me.

DR. BIRD: Please tell me a little about what some of the problems are.

MS. GREEN: I think I may have been molested or assaulted last year. I was out on a date, and my boyfriend and I got into a fight and I started to walk home alone. I think some guy offered me a ride or something. Anyhow the next thing I remember is being in the hospital. I was bruised up pretty bad. I just don't remember what happened, but I've been real scared and nervous since then and afraid to go out, and I've got lots of painful infections that Dr. Bernstein, my gynecologist, says may be psychological.

DR. BIRD: Well, it does sound like it is something I may be able to help you with. I can see you Tuesday at 11 A.M. Will that time work for you?

MS. GREEN: OK. Where is your office?

This type of phone call, or some variation of it, is commonplace in the practice of psychotherapy and hypnotherapy.

In a customary return phone call, Dr. Bird typically makes only a few notes during the conversation, and needs no special preparation prior to meeting with a patient. He expects that she will arrive at 11:00 A.M. on

Tuesday and that he will begin his intake procedure at that time. However, this is potentially an unusual case. Because there is a possibility that the patient is suffering from amnesia, and because there is reason to believe that she may be the victim of a crime, any procedure that Dr. Bird employs with Ms. Green will have legal implications. Recognizing this possibility, Dr. Bird must make some immediate arrangements to protect both his potential client and himself.

PROFESSIONAL PREPARATION

Several inconvenient adjustments are mandated when therapy practice interfaces with the legal system. Psychotherapy and the law are widely different traditions. Psychology favors narrative truth, the law historical truth (Spence, 1982). Therapists strive for patients' comfort and symptom relief; the law strives for precision, justice, and punishment. A therapist seeks remedies to a patient's suffering and encourages the client's participation in the cure. An attorney determines what legal remedies are available and appropriate, then helps a client decide whether he or she wishes to pursue those remedies.

Pragmatic Considerations

As soon as he realizes that the new case may involve both hypnosis and legal issues, Dr. Bird must begin to employ atypically comprehensive record-keeping procedures. He will be best advised to recreate, in his own memory, the phone call to Ms. Green in as much detail as possible, and to place it in writing in the patient's file folder. In addition, he must make preparations to record (preferably on videotape) all sessions in which Ms. Green and he meet. Such arrangements should be made prior to the first session.

If forensic cases are not normally part of Dr. Bird's practice, he should also arrange for supervision and/or consult with experienced colleagues.

Emotional Considerations

Most therapists faced with novel situations look forward to them with a combination of excitement and anxiety.

Excitement at Referral

Treatments of psychosomatic disorders can be quite sensational and involve very visible "cures" of the patients. Amnesia cures in which memory is restored during, or as a result of, therapy sessions also have tremendous appeal for therapists who enjoy the dramatic turn of events.

In addition, for most independent practitioners, a referral from a gynecologist for a psychosomatic disorder is an indication of acceptance from a medical community that customarily refrains from embracing hypnotherapists. In short, Dr. Bird's pride may be engaged by the referral.

Anxiety about This Referral

Together with the excitement, there may be some anxiety about the referral. Although psychosomatic cures are sometimes dramatic, the problems are quite resistant to cure. Similarly, hypermnesia is not always easy to achieve. The combination of a patient who is in considerable distress and a delayed amelioration of symptoms is potentially troubling for any healer.

Anxiety about Dealing with Lawyers and Laws

Therapists and attorneys think differently, approach problems with opposite goals, and pursue divergent processes in attaining those goals. Whenever a therapist ventures onto the home court of attorneys, these are reasons for caution.

Anxiety about Using Hypnosis

Unless a therapist specializes in hypnosis, there may be some extra anxiety about using any approach that is not a part of one's everyday practice. In addition, patients and therapists may both have inordinately optimistic expectations about the benefits attainable through hypnosis. Patients often anticipate magical, instantaneous cures, and are subsequently disappointed with the reality of prolonged treatment.

Potential Conflicts between Best Therapy and Legal Rights

Perhaps the most perplexing concern for a hypnotherapist is the possibility of doing everything correctly from a therapeutic perspective and still having the client suffer from a loss of legal rights. Furthermore, it is possible that a hypnotherapist may engage in best therapeutic practice and subsequently find himself or herself the object of a lawsuit for failing to protect the client's legal as opposed to psychological rights.

We have addressed these problems in two ways. First, the general guidelines and procedures in this chapter are provided for therapists concerned about making the best attempts at protecting clients' legal rights without compromising therapeutic integrity. Second, the Appendix provides the current status of legal rulings in state and federal jurisdictions.

Therapists are advised to use the legislative and judicial guidelines prevailing in their own jurisdictions.

Initial Professional Planning

Equipment Readiness

Therapists should have videotape equipment set up and in working condition. It is imperative that a therapist be knowledgeable about such equipment; too frequently, therapists take pride in a lack of knowledge of things mechanical. Blank tapes should be at the ready and in the room. Tests of the equipment should be conducted before the session. If therapists cannot run the equipment themselves, they may need a video operator.

One common problem with professional videotapes involves the audio component. Clip-on lapel microphones or sensitive directional pickups that cut down on ambient noise are extremely useful. Sound-activated recorders are not appropriate, since they only record part of the session. A complete record is necessary.

Scheduling for Hypnosis

Hypnotic hypermnesia sessions do not always fit comfortably into the 50-minute hour. Most experienced hypnotherapists clear at least a 2-hour block when amnesia recovery sessions are to occur. This will probably not happen during the first session, but the therapist should have the necessary time flexibility before taking on such a case.

Many hypnotherapists working with deep trances and regressive hypnosis need "personal time" to recover after a session. The traditional 10-minute break between clients may be insufficient with a client like Roberta Green, Jennifer L. (see Chapter Two), or Andrea H. (see Chapter One).

Reviewing the Relevant Literature

Reading the relevant literature prior to meeting with a client whose treatment is likely to involve hypermnesia can protect the therapist against some easily made errors, such as leading the client, creating situations that promote confabulation, and failing to recognize the importance of historical accuracy to the court.

FIRST DIRECT CONTACT WITH CLIENT: A CHECKLIST

Videotaping and Informed Consent

The therapist should begin with videotaping. The patient should be informed as to the taping and reasons for taping. The therapist should explain carefully the limits of confidentiality for the taped session: Sessions are confidential except as limited by state law, unless they become part of a legal action, in which control may be lost to legal agencies.

The therapist should then get informed consent. If the client eschews the taping, he or she should be clearly informed that the refusal could have an impact on later legal rights; if possible, the therapist should keep the tape of that warning. Should the client insist that the taping be discontinued, the therapist should obtain the client's signature on a document stating that he or she has declined to have the session taped, with full knowledge that this may eliminate later opportunities to testify in court.

Fully informed consent may not be initially possible from a client under great emotional stress. The client should be given the option of later having the tape erased, once he or she fully understands the implications of the tape. If the client agrees to the taping, the therapist should continue taping all contact during this session and future sessions. Waiting room contact that is not on the tape should be kept to a minimum.

Intake/Diagnostic Evaluation

Every hypnotherapist has a standard intake/diagnostic procedure. This normal procedure should be followed.

Not every patient is a candidate for hypnosis, particularly regressive hypnosis. Patients diagnosed with marginal ego strength, borderline personality, potential for psychosis, or hysteria have a higher probability of being harmed by the procedure. The therapist must weigh the potential benefits of memory recapture against detrimental psychological effects. Novice hypnotherapists are not encouraged to take on such cases. Sometimes a memory is best repressed, and aggressive attempts at hypermnesia can be deleterious.

The evaluation should include, but should not be limited to, the therapist's normal indications and counterindications for hypnosis in any case; evaluation of the client's understanding of hypnosis; history of the client's experience with hypnosis; explanation of hypnotic procedures; clear definition as to who is the client, what are the fees, and who pays them; and other usual preparation of the client for what is to follow.

Special History-Taking Considerations

After the normal history taking and diagnostic interview, there are special considerations for memory-refreshing cases, especially if forensic work may be involved. The hypnotherapist must take down the client's complete extant memory of events prior to any hypnosis.

Before attempting any actual hypnosis, *the therapist must again carefully inform the client as to potential loss of legal rights if hypnosis is undertaken.* It is prudent to offer the client alternatives to hypnosis, such as Geiselman et. al.'s (1985) mnemonic recovery technique, free association, and so on.

Evaluation of the Client's Hypnotizability

The therapist should use a standard test to determine the client's current level of hypnotizability. If the client appears to be a good candidate for the procedure, the therapist can then schedule an appointment and prepare to go ahead with the hypnotic memory refreshing.

Establishment of Rapport

Hypnosis should be instituted only when there is sufficient rapport between the therapist and patient. This may take several hours, especially if the hypnosis is conducted by the primary psychotherapist.

AFTER THE INITIAL SESSION

After rapport is established, the hypnotherapist should institute the trance state with the client, using effective cues from any prior inductions the client might have experienced. The client can then return to the scene where the missing memories may have occurred. Once the client can achieve clear memories, the trance can be deepened, prior to utilizing the client's natural imagery, in a primary attempt to recreate in a present sense what he or she experiences.

Professional Responsibilities during the Memory Retrieval Sessions

During the sessions, the therapist should do the following:

1. Observe client reactions carefully.
2. Watch for any evident signs of confabulation, impact of demand characteristics, or pleasing-response bias.
3. Monitor the client's ability to stay with the level of affect displayed.
4. Take care to avoid creating stronger-than-normal expectancies or hope for achievement of memories.
5. Regardless of the client's ability to regain memory, provide the best possible therapeutic treatment with due regard to the legal considerations.
6. Debrief the client carefully.
7. Safely store the tape, notes, and transcripts to ensure confidentiality.

Emotional Responsibilities during the Memory Retrieval Sessions

Few types of cases are as ripe for countertransference problems as hypermnesia cases. The opportunity to be a part of memory recovery and to help a client overcome some trauma is most enticing. Add to that the feeling of being the client's advocate against the perpetrator of a crime and a general sensitivity to the underdog (common among professionals in the helping professions), and one has an almost irresistible package.

Most therapists must regularly assess their own propensity to take care of clients or help them out of their dilemmas in some active ways. If a hypnotherapist becomes at all biased in favor of a client and lets that bias emerge during the emotionally wrenching hypnosis sessions, he or she may invalidate the hypnosis in the eyes of the court.

Partiality can, in subtle ways, create pressure on the client to create a cohesive, coherent story. Such demand characteristics have commonly been shown to enhance confabulation and increase inaccuracy in laboratory experiments. It is especially important to monitor personal reactions to a client's experience, and to be extraordinarily aware of one's own identification with the client as victim.

In interactions with the law, countertransference issues are not only a significant component of therapy to be worked through; evidence of countertransference can also affect admissibility of the hypnosis sessions. If a judge believes that the hypnotherapist's feelings in any way affected the content of the client's refreshed memory, that information, as well as the witness's other testimony, may be barred from the trial.

FOLLOW-UP THERAPY

Although the law may only be interested in the existence and accuracy of the memories elicited, the elimination of amnesia is only the beginning for the hypnotherapist. Few therapists today believe that the recall of events along with an emotional catharsis will be sufficient to cure a client of emotional or psychological difficulties. Once the memories are exposed or remembered, the client is faced with accepting and integrating those memories into his or her psyche and working through the new thoughts and awareness.

Posttraumatic stress disorders are resistant to simple or quick cures. Often amnesia is not completely eliminated. Vestiges of lost memories will frequently emerge as therapy progresses. Psychodynamically oriented therapists maintain that as the client's ego is better integrated and stronger, it can accept more of the repressed material. Thus, more and more is remembered.

Amnesia as an Unexpected Component of Psychotherapy

All of the planning described above presumes that the therapist is aware in advance that the amnesia is present and is directly attempting to refresh memory. It is quite possible that the therapist and patient will accidentally achieve such insight.

One of us (Shapiro) was recently treating a couple with marital difficulties, which were related to their difference of opinion regarding having a child. In the course of the treatment, the husband atypically began reacting to his wife as if she had wronged him in some grievous manner, and became quite defensive and threatening. He was unable to articulate exactly what she had done. During that week he experienced terrible nightmares and "a feeling I was back in the [Marine] Corps."

With the permission of both spouses, Shapiro scheduled a few individual sessions to work with the husband. What emerged in those sessions was a terrible memory of having applied the *coup de grace* to a mortally wounded comrade during the Vietnam War. Once that memory was available to him, he was flooded by a host of other horrible war memories and his feeling of certainty that his first wife had deserted him because of what he had done during the war. Shapiro suggested that this issue be addressed prior to a resumption of marital therapy.

It was only after the husband had worked through these memories, and feelings of terror at any events that related to life-and-death issues, that he was able to rationally consider having a child with his current wife. Marital therapy resumed in 6 months.

Hypnosis as a Subcontract to Psychotherapy

It is, of course, possible that the hypnotherapy is designed solely to elicit the repressed memories, as in the case of Jennifer L. (see Chapter Two). In such circumstances, the psychotherapy will be done by another therapist, who may actually sit in on the hypnosis sessions. It is our contention that this procedure is optimal as it will not interfere as much with the transference between the patient and primary therapist.

Sometimes the hypnotherapist will do the hypermnesia work and then will refer the client to another therapist. It is essential in such referrals that the patient does not experience a feeling of rejection or violation of trust from a therapist who has probed deeper recesses of his or her mind. (A similar but usually less strong reaction can occur if the hypnotherapy involves pain control, motivation, fear of a medical procedure, anesthesia, test anxiety, or any of the host of other problems commonly treated by hypnotherapists.)

If the therapist is aware of these possible difficulties at the beginning, they can be potentially ameliorated by being absolutely clear about the limits of the hypnotherapy contact prior to or during the very first session.

Sometimes a decision to refer can be made only after the specific memories appear. In such situations, the referral must be made with care and with attention to the termination of the hypnotherapy.

WHEN A CASE GOES TO COURT

Pretrial Preparation

Cases involving litigation and courtroom testimony bring special considerations to bear in communicating one's professional opinions. One must be aware of the judicial process, rules of evidence, and the ethos of the adversarial system, especially with regard to testifying under direct examination and cross-examination (see Chapters Eight and Nine).

Determining Who Is the Client

In general, the therapist who is hired solely as an expert witness will be working for an attorney rather than a clinical patient. It is crucial to establish specifically what the attorney is requesting, and the extent to which what is being requested is a possible outcome of consultation and/or testimony. Frequently the therapist must educate the attorney as to the bounds of conscientious and ethical practice in psychotherapy.

When the therapist is contacted by an attorney or investigatory agency and asked to testify on behalf of a client who is currently or has recently been under treatment, the therapist can cooperate with the request only with the expressed (preferably written) permission of that client. If the client agrees or requests the therapist's collaboration, and the therapist consents, there is a substantive alteration in the client–therapist relationship. The attorney becomes the primary client rather than the (former) patient. Should continuing or additional therapeutic work be required, the therapist's role in a court case will seriously affect the transference relationship and other relevant aspects of the therapy. These matters are best worked through carefully with patients prior to any agreement to testify on their behalf.

Financial Arrangements

The financial arrangements for hypnotherapy should be consistent with a therapist's regular hourly charges. Financial charges for participation in the legal proceedings are separate.

It is important to determine who will be billed for the time spent on legal proceedings. This must be prearranged, preferably in a written contract. Normally, the client is the attorney who retains the therapist, or, in criminal trials, the prosecutor's office. The number of hours, the hourly rate, and the services that will be included must all be established. In most cases, time will be spent in reading and reviewing the case and relevant materials, meeting with the attorney, giving depositions, waiting at court, actually testifying, making phone calls, writing reports, and so forth. It is recommended that the therapist charge for all work time, even if the lawyers settle out of court and no testimony is ultimately necessary.

Therapists vary widely in their charges for legal and court work. Some charge their typical hourly rate for "contact hours" only. Others charge their standard hourly rate for all the time they spend working on the case. Still others have different rates and charges for contact and noncontact hours. Finally, some charge flat rates for participation in any legal setting. Since most therapists feel that work in court is particularly trying, they tend to charge higher rates than they would for normal therapy hours.

One point to remember is that cross-examining attorneys commonly inquire about the fees that an expert witness charges. If the fees are atypically high for time in legal proceedings, the cross-examiner may attempt to convince the jury that the expert witness is more interested in personal remuneration than justice in the current trial. Appropriate responses to such tactics are detailed in Chapter Nine.

Meetings with the Attorney Who Has Retained the Therapist

Some of the most important contacts for a therapist will be with the retaining attorney(s). Several matters must be established at these meetings: the therapist's relationship with the patient/client, impressions of the client, belief in the veracity of the hypermnesia, and willingness to testify at a trial; the intent of the attorney making the case; the probable nature of the case; and prior rulings and laws in the jurisdiction.

If the expert agrees to testify, the attorney should make available the legal briefs, literature, and documents that detail the law and background of rulings on similar cases, to help the expert prepare his or her testimony. Case materials will have to be studied, along with relevant reading for the legal and psychological aspects of the case. The therapist should also review guidelines for expert witnesses.

The attorney should go over with the witness the ground that will be covered, and should at least warn the expert of the tactics likely to be used in cross-examination (i.e., the points of law on which the opposing side will try to discredit the witness). The therapist should request that the attorney anticipate any legal difficulties in the case. The therapist would be wise to make every effort to learn about similar cases in law, the likelihood of plea bargaining, and judicial preferences or prejudices toward expert witnesses in general and hypnosis specifically.

One common difficulty is that the testimony may be disallowed entirely.

It is disconcerting to spend hours of preparation time and to expend emotional energy getting "psyched up" to testify, only to be summarily dismissed without explanation by the court.

It will also be determined whether the testimony will enhance or hurt the case. In some cases, the best way to be helpful is to be unavailable for testimony. It is prudent to decline to testify if the questions are beyond the therapist's scope of expertise, if the data do not support any definitive conclusions that could be made on the witness stand, or if the conclusions may weaken the case of the attorney retaining the therapist. It must be remembered that the client is the attorney, not the justice system at large. Of course, the therapist may still be subpoenaed to testify for the opposing side.

Sometimes attorneys will try to convince experts that certain opinions will be unhelpful, and will subtly request that those not be volunteered. On occasion an attorney will try to co-opt a therapist's testimony by telling the therapist what it is that needs to be said to win the case. It is particularly important that the expert not be swayed by such tactics. The therapist's job is to provide the most accurate data and impressions possible, without later contamination. Since memory is so much a recreative rather than a replicative process, it is incumbent upon the therapist to stay as close to the actual data as possible.

Deposition Hearings

A "deposition" is a part of the legal process that occurs during the "discovery" (fact-finding from adversaries) phase. Depositions are increasingly common in legal cases to reduce the load on court dockets, to give the opposition a chance to defend its position, to find evidence, and to evaluate whether a case should proceed to court. The deposition takes place in an informal setting, such as a lawyer's office or even the therapist's own office, and it can have an almost casual atmosphere. *This informality can be deceptive.*

The therapist who will testify must be cautious during depositions. To the therapist, such a gathering of professionals somewhat resembles a case conference in which everyone is working toward the same goal—the best solution for a single client, couple, or family. In such a setting, casual comments or errors will rarely later come back to haunt the participants. The deposition is quite different. Despite the apparent informality and friendly demeanor, the deposition hearing involves sworn testimony that can and will be utilized in court.

Preparation for the Deposition

Prior to the deposition hearing, the expert witness will be asked to produce all records and tapes to both attorneys. Often the opposing attorney will serve the therapist with a *subpoena duces tecum*—a court order requiring the recipient (1) to produce these documents at a given place and time, and (2) to be prepared to answer questions posed by the opposing attorney.

Before the actual deposition hearing, it is wise to meet with the retaining attorney and go over the ground that is likely to be covered, expected questions, likely strategies of cross-examination, anticipated problem areas, and so on. Everything said in a deposition hearing is under oath, is recorded, and has full standing in subsequent court proceedings. The therapist who becomes casual and makes social comments may be grilled over discrepancies in his or her testimony. The lawyers are at the deposition hearing to gain an advantage.

The testimony the expert gives during the deposition will be the most significant source of information used in subsequent cross-examination. An expert witness who makes contradictory statements in the deposition and the court, or even in the deposition itself, may have impeached himself or herself.

The Deposition Process

The deposition will normally include the expert witness, lawyers and their assistants from each side, and a court reporter with stenographic machine or tape recorder. The deposition typically consists of eight stages:

1. Swearing in of the witness.
2. Describing the witness's qualifications.
3. Presenting the expert and obtaining the essential facts and opinions desired by the retaining attorney (this somewhat resembles direct examination).
4. Questioning by the opposing attorney (this is somewhat similar to cross-examination).
5. Re-examining and clarifying certain points by the retaining attorney (this is somewhat similar to re-direct examination).
6. Questioning in areas covered in re-direct examination (this somewhat resembles re-cross-examination).
7. Requesting production of additional records.
8. Certifying the deposition.

The Therapist's Role during a Deposition

As in court, the therapist will first be administered an oath, by the court reporter, to "swear [or affirm] to tell the truth, the whole truth, and nothing but the truth—so help you God." The therapist will then be offered as an expert witness by the side that is employing him or her.

First, the lawyer who has called the witness may ask a series of questions that will establish certain choice aspects of the case and position for the record. The opposing attorney can object to any question on the record. The attorney calling the witness can then request that the witness continue or refrain from answering.

Just as during a court appearance, it is customary for the opposing lawyers to argue points of law "off the record." These discussions pertain primarily to questions of admissibility of evidence or the proper form of questioning. They are not recorded nor retained for the written record of the deposition. These arguments about admissibility or the like may seem to a therapist like lengthy exercises in obfuscation. It is important for witnesses not to let the frustration bother them to the point where they become emotionally expressive or try to help out the situation by jumping into the fray.

Once the initial presentation is complete, the examination by the opposing attorney will begin. The opposing attorney will ask questions that are designed to cast doubt upon or discredit the witness's testimony, either by providing alternate theories to explain events, or by directly casting doubt on the expert witness's perception of events or understanding of crucial matters. Although this "cross-examination" will, in most cases, be fairly short, and is supposed to be limited to facts of the case, it can be most pointed and uncomfortable. (However, many attorneys will save some of their best tactics for the court if that best suits their case.) Here, the attorney who called the witness will object and instruct the witness when he or she should refrain from answering the questions.

Therapists must take care of themselves during this time. Even the supportive attorney is interested primarily in what the witness can do for his or her case, not in what happens to the witness. Therapists need to request appropriate breaks when needed, and to keep fatigue from playing a huge role (hearings can last for several hours and even days). Lengthy, exhausting depositions may serve attorneys in two ways: (1) Fatigued witnesses may let down their guard and make inopportune comments; and (2) attorneys are often paid by the hour—the longer the deposition, the greater the remuneration. This is particularly true in civil cases involving third-party (insurance company) settlements.

The most important rule for the therapist to follow is always to approach the deposition as a competent (usually conservative) professional would. Some other significant rules include these:

- Do not allow lawyers to employ bullying or wearing-down tactics.
- Do not answer questions that go beyond the available data.
- Do not answer any questions until they are specifically asked.
- Never offer additional information that goes beyond the questions asked.
- Do not guess at any answers. If an estimate must be given, it should

be accompanied by a clear statement that the answer is an estimate or probability.

- Do not try to argue with the attorneys and beat them at their own game.
- Ask for clarification if any questions are unclear.
- Always keep in mind what the attorneys are doing at the hearing. At the content level, they are eliciting facts that they will use during the trial. At the process level, they are checking the therapist out as a witness, looking for flaws or chinks in the armor that can be later exploited.

"Loose Lips Sink Ships"

Opposing attorneys will use the occasion of the deposition hearing to gain any additional benefit. Therapists are advised not to lower their guard even while in the bathroom or in the parking lot. It is in such places that lawyers sometimes seek their most useful information. Anything said to an opposing attorney or others, on or off the record, can be made the subject of cross-examination.

In a case familiar to us, the attorney for the defense (apparently coincidentally) accompanied the expert to the parking lot at the termination of the hearing. As they walked, he proposed an alternative theory of the case and concluded with this question: "Just between us, isn't it possible that the client imagined the rape and is stuck with her story now, since she made it up while faking hypnosis?" Any response besides the one given— "Just between us, I gave my testimony at the hearing"—could have been later used at the trial. The expert also reported this "incidental" contact to the retaining attorney from the prosecutor's office.

At the conclusion of the deposition hearing, the attorney who called the hearing may ask the expert witness to stipulate the accuracy of the court reporter's record. This should *never* be done. Inaccuracies are inevitable, even with the best intentions of everyone concerned. Uncorrected, as they must be if the witness agrees *at the hearing* that the record is accurate, they remain as permanent and sworn testimony in a court. Some inaccuracies are relatively harmless (if annoying), such as being referred to as a "political" instead of a "clinical" psychologist. Others, such as the omission of the word "not" in the middle of a sentence, can completely change the meaning of one's testimony. If the record is unchecked, such errors could cause grievous harm in a court of law.

The usual practice is for a draft of the deposition to be sent to the witness for corrections within 6 weeks of the deposition. After these corrections have been made and notarized, the deposition is returned to the retaining attorney. A copy of the corrected deposition should be retained in the expert's files. Because deposition hearings can take place months or even years before a trial, a comprehensive review is essential before trial. A zealous cross-examiner may take a piece of the deposition out of context and cause the witness to appear foolish or confused unless the witness has had the opportunity to study the deposition transcript prior to trial. If the retaining attorney fails to object to the introduction of an unsupported quotation, the witness may ask the cross-examiner for the opportunity to consult the original document.

Pretrial Conferences

If the case is not settled or plea-bargained, and if the prosecutor (in criminal cases) or plaintiff (in civil cases) is hopeful that the case can be won, it will be brought to trial. The case will be scheduled on the court docket, and the expert witness will be called to confirm his or her availability during that approximate time period. It is important to remember that actual court dates can vary by months from the original docket date.

It is essential that the expert witness confirm that the trial will be held as scheduled and reconfirm the date of expected testimony. It is imperative to meet with the retaining attorney prior to the court appearance. A modified rehearsal of anticipated testimony should occur. Blau (1984) indicates that the rehearsal should cover at least the following material:

1. Questions to be used in qualification.
2. The sequence of questions and responses in the direct examination.
3. Hypothetical questions the attorney is likely to pose to the witness following direct examination.
4. The limits of the [expert's] findings.
5. Probable approaches to be used by opposing counsel during cross examination.
6. Something about the demographics and responses of the jury members.
7. The presiding judge's style and special expectancies.
8. Any special limitations the physical environment of the courtroom may pose for presentation of charts or other visual materials. (pp. 217–218)

For cases involving hypnosis and hypermnesia in particular, we would add the following:

9. Points of law that will be argued regarding admissibility.
10. Examination and discussion of notes or materials that the expert plans to take into the courtroom.

At the same time, the therapist must give the attorney a clear estimation of the clinical and scientific weaknesses in his or her testimony. The attorney must know what kinds of questions to ask and what types of rejoinders to anticipate.

THE TRIAL

General Considerations

Demeanor and Availability

Whenever people are called upon to enter an alien arena, it is incumbent upon them to try to fit into that environment as well as possible. Therapists who testify frequently in court learn to think like attorneys, learn to dress like them, learn a certain cultural demeanor appropriate to the court, and learn how to become effective communicators in that venue. The unofficial rules of the court are important for therapists to understand.

Appearance should be neat, appropriate, and conservative for a formal setting. Language should be as precise as possible and devoid of off-hand remarks. Experts should never try to put on a performance for the jury. They are called by the court to help resolve a serious matter, and must conduct themselves in a manner appropriate to such weighty decision making. Indeed, it is always important to keep in mind the implications of the trial's outcome for others.

Experts must be available when the court calls them. Arriving late and appearing hassled are not acceptable and will cause the jury or judge to question the expert's consideration and caring. By contrast, the expert may well have to wait for several hours while the trial goes on, motions are filed, the jury is removed from the court for legal arguments, and other delays occur. It is generally advisable to bring reading materials to occupy time.

Waiting to Be Called to Testify

The court is not run on an easily understood timetable; therefore, witnesses are often summoned to court at the earliest time they will be called to testify. This can create long hours of waiting for a witness.

Hours of waiting once one is prepared and ready can be quite anxiety-producing. Therapists who are in such a position must do what it takes to take care of themselves. In some ways, it is particularly hard to get "psyched up" and then have to wait long hours for the main event. It is easy to lose one's edge.

Witness Exclusion Rules and Their Impact

The witness exclusion rule is common in many jurisdictions. This rule states that witnesses to any aspect of a trial cannot be present while other witnesses are testifying at the trial. Unlike the famous courtroom scenes of Perry Mason and other celebrated fictional trials, the principals are not all present in the courtroom while the clever attorney unearths the buried truth.

As expert witnesses, hypnotherapists will only be allowed in court for their own testimony. They are not officially privy to any other information about the trial. This rule is designed to keep witnesses from being influenced by other witnesses or from developing credible stories that become intertwined in their own memories.

However, while the law is designed to protect the truth, there are often informal procedures that mitigate the procedure and create a far more dangerous potential for confabulation on the part of the witnesses. It is not unusual, for example, for all of the expert witnesses to be called at the same time to testify. Since they are not allowed in the courtroom, they are often relegated to a bench outside the courtroom. There they sit for hours waiting to be called to testify. With nothing else in common, it is hard to believe that they will not discuss the case, since there is often no formal specific injunction against their doing so.

Waiting on the Stand

Frequently, in the course of testimony, witnesses, observers, and the jury are excluded from knowing what is happening. Sometimes the lawyers and judge argue points of procedure in front of the court. Either of the opposing attorneys or the judge may request a conference at the bench. The judge then cups his or her hand over the microphone and converses with the two lawyers, while the witness, jury, defendant, and spectators all await the decision to continue or discontinue some aspect of the trial. It is rare when others are made privy to the content of such conversations, although the witness can often overhear the discussion.

Frequently the public court proceedings are interrupted and the action all takes place *in camera*— that is, in the judge's chambers. Witnesses and jury members are often surprised at the bulk of trial time that is spent out of their view. Many leave a court feeling quite unfulfilled because they do not know what happened or why. In court cases involving hypnosis, or other subjects that involve complicated rulings, this *in camera* time is likely to be considerable.

Rulings made during judge–attorney conferences almost always involve the admissibility of evidence and points of law.

Entering the Courtroom

All courtrooms have similarities and differences. The bench where the judge
sits is on a raised platform. Next to the judge is a witness box, where the
expert will be seated during testimony. The jury is usually seated further
away at a 90-degree angle, on the same side of the judge as the witness
stand. The litigants and attorneys will be seated at tables on either side,
facing the judge and witness box.

The feeling that some witnesses experience on entering the formal and
intimidating atmosphere of the court was summed up by Lewis Carroll in
Alice's Adventures in Wonderland (1865/1960), when the King of Hearts says
to the witness, "Give your evidence . . . and don't be nervous, or I'll have
you executed on the spot" (p. 99). A prior visit to the courtroom can alleviate some of the initial discomfort of a novel setting.

Justice and the Legal System

One of the biggest emotional traps for the hypnotherapist as expert witness is the perception that the legal system obfuscates and ameliorates justice instead of serving it. An expert witness, concerned that the alleged
criminal will be set free, and fearful that the client will be revictimized by
the system, may well be unconsciously swayed to add more surety to observations; to color or slant evidence that is potentially more damning; or
to be more certain than is justified by the data.

This may actually have an impact on the outcome of the trial. A conviction may result that will serve the psyche of the therapist's client, but may
seriously and unfairly affect the life of the defendant. Of course, the opposite is possible. In at least one hypnosis trial, the expert hypnotherapist
was so sure of himself that the jury dismissed his testimony as biased.

Direct Examination

Components of Direct Examination

The direct examination is conducted by the attorney who retained the expert witness. The purpose of direct examination is to present additional
evidence supportive of the retaining attorney's perception of the truth. Because the witness is an expert, special weight is given to his or her testimony. The expert has the unique right within the court of law to give
opinions and estimate probabilities of occurrence.

The direct examination should proceed smoothly and logically. Specific
questions, hypothetical queries, and their sequence will have been practiced and/or discussed in pretrial conferences.

Being Qualified as an Expert

In order to have any special influence in the court, the therapist/witness must be accorded expert status. To the court, a witness who is not an expert cannot give opinions, but may only state observations and facts as he or she knows them. Being an expert allows a witness greater latitude.

In order to be an expert witness, therapists normally need to hold the appropriate licenses to practice hypnotherapy in the jurisdictions in which they work. They need to have completed at least journeyman's-level training in their field. They need to show that they have a reasonable right to treat patients with the disorders being discussed. They must be knowledgeable about their profession.

The expert will be judged as qualified on the basis of credentials, education, training, experience, and professional accomplishments. It is also important that the expert be able to show familiarity with the precise factual issues facing the court. Thus the expert needs to demonstrate competence in psychotherapy and hypnotherapy generally, and hypermnesia in particular. Prior qualification as an expert in these matters is persuasive to a court.

This phase of the direct examination concludes with the following:

ATTORNEY: Your Honor, at this time I would tender the witness as an expert in psychology and as an expert in hypnosis.

JUDGE: *(Addressing the opposing attorney)* Ms. Phelps?

OPPOSING ATTORNEY: No objection, Your Honor.

JUDGE: I find the witness so qualified.

Manner of Presentation

It is most important that, as the expert witness, the therapist educate the judge and jury. While the procedure will have a question-and-answer format, it is important that the witness make a coherent, understandable presentation. Methods and procedures must be explained carefully and intelligently. It is also important to make the presentation interesting and concise.

The first questions will require that the witness provide a definition and description of the scope of hypnosis. The purpose is to let the expert appear informed and knowledgeable and to educate the court.

ATTORNEY: Dr. Bird, could you explain the different uses of hypnosis?

WITNESS: There are four basic uses: three in medical/psychological practice and one in entertainment. The three medical uses are pain control, relief from psychosomatic symptoms, and memory enhancement. The entertainment use is what you might see in a Las Vegas nightclub.

ATTORNEY: How is the last one different from the other three?

WITNESS: The stage hypnotist will choose people from the audience who seem compliant and willing to perform up on the stage. He will then, in a sense, give them permission to act in novel and humorous ways. Thus they might bark like a dog, see the entire audience as naked, etc.

ATTORNEY: OK. Now with respect to the medical use or psychological use of hypnosis, you mentioned three different areas. Let us concentrate on the one relevant to us now. Could you explain how hypnosis is used to relieve a patient of the pain of memory loss?

WITNESS: As a result of some traumatic, sudden, painful event, a victim might suffer a loss of memory for that event. In some cases the event is so shocking, the mind makes no record of it. In others, memory of the event was too painful to acknowledge consciously, and the unconscious component of the mind has protectively kept it from consciousness. Hypnosis allows the unconscious memories to become available to the conscious mind. Is that a sufficient answer to the question, or do you wish more detail?

ATTORNEY: Could you give us an example?

WITNESS: Yes. I worked with a young woman who had no memories of her mother prior to her 13th birthday. She had a total block of all such memories of her mother and herself. This was causing her some pain and confusion as her wedding day approached. Under hypnosis, she was able to recall vividly her mother's wedding to her stepfather just prior to her 13th birthday. She feared that she was losing her mother just as she had her father. Once she recaptured that memory, she also was able to recall much of her preadolescent past.

The jury now has a context in which to consider the use of hypnosis for memory recall. It has learned that there are four uses of hypnosis, only one of which is relevant. Notice also that the expert has refrained from using overly technical terms in this initial phase. Explanations have been kept simple and understandable, yet the expert has indicated readiness to offer much more, if needed.

Another important factor in this piece of testimony is the expert's use of an illustrative story. It is always a good idea to provide real-life dramas as a context for more abstract ideas. The story in this case also indicates that the therapist played a healing role and that hypnosis was a positive force for mental health.

The more general direct questions will be followed by hypothetical questions designed to highlight crucial aspects of the particular case at trial

ATTORNEY: Now that you have described the reasons for doing hypnosis with this client, and the results of that hypnosis, I would like to pose a question to you. Is it possible for a normal person to suddenly develop symptoms of anxiety, nightmares, frightening thoughts, fears of the unknown, and a variety of psychosomatic symptoms without something like the alleged attack occurring?

WITNESS: There may be a lot of causes for such symptoms, but it would be quite rare for them to occur suddenly without something happening to elicit them.

ATTORNEY: Could an assault and rape cause all of these symptoms?

WITNESS: In my opinion, they could.

ATTORNEY: Could a person be assaulted and have no memory of the assault or assailant for many months?

WITNESS: Yes.

ATTORNEY: Would you explain how such a memory loss could happen?

If the expert witness was also the hypnotherapist, the retaining attorney will follow the hypothetical questions with a fact pattern that is designed to connect these questions and answers to the current case, to make a coherent story that will sway the jury.

ATTORNEY: Having done the hypnotherapy with Ms. Green, do you believe that, from her symptoms, she could have been the victim of such an assault?

WITNESS: Yes.

ATTORNEY: Do you have reason to believe that the memory which she regained in therapy is accurate, to the best of her knowledge?

WITNESS: I do.

ATTORNEY: Is there any possibility that she could have made up the story under hypnosis, and that it is not true?

WITNESS: There is no way of absolutely knowing whether anyone has been telling the truth. The question is one of believability, and I believe that her memory is as accurate as if she had regained her memory without hypnosis.

ATTORNEY: Do you have some way of supporting this belief?

WITNESS: A number of things strongly support the view that what she now remembers is essentially what her mind recorded earlier: the sudden relief of her symptoms after the memory was recovered; her intense emotion—sobbing and evident surprise—shown during the sessions; physiological signs such as rapid eye movements and changes in breathing during the trance state; and so on.

ATTORNEY: Could you say that this hypnotically refreshed memory is more accurate than regular memory?

WITNESS: I'd say that her hypnotically refreshed memory is no more or less accurate than that of any victim or eyewitness to a crime.

Notice that the direct examination is designed to anticipate some difficult areas that will be broached on cross-examination. Bringing these up here diffuses their impact and also minimizes the surprise factor.

Other potentially problematic areas that are likely to be addressed include definitions of hypnosis, memory, and psychotherapy; requests for distinctions between memory refreshing and memory induction; the possibility of the hypnotherapist's being influential in helping the patient *create* a credible story versus eliciting an accurate memory; confabulation; demand characteristics; and the difference between alcohol or drug blackouts and trauma-induced memory loss. If the witness was also the hypnotherapist, the direct examination will probably also include a careful review of the therapy, particularly of the hypnosis sessions.

In closing, the retaining attorney will say:

ATTORNEY: Thank you, Doctor. I have no further questions of the witness.

The Calm before the Storm

After the direct examination is complete, the cross-examination begins. If the direct examination has continued for some time, the judge will normally call a recess. This is an opportunity for the witness to relax, take care of physical needs (e.g., a bathroom break, a snack or beverage), take psychological stock of himself or herself, go for a short walk, and the like.

Most of the time, the retaining attorney will join the expert on the break and make suggestions as to where the vulnerabilities may be for cross-examination. The court bailiff is a source of information about bathrooms, food and drink, and the time of reconvening.

Cross-Examination

Wellman (1936) called cross-examination "a mental dual between counsel and witness." It is essential that the witness refrain as much as possible from engaging in the duel on the attorney's terms. Blau (1984) describes the purposes of cross-examination as follows: "to cast some doubt or question on the quality of the witness as an expert, on the thoroughness of the material presented, or on the credibility of the opinion that has been rendered by the expert" (p. 239). Few situations in a professional therapist's life will have prepared him or her for this type of ordeal. Even presentations to colleagues who are committed to punching holes in one's theory or data do not approximate the personal attacks that are possible during cross-examination of a witness. The one shield that a professional has during this joust is preparation.

Although the cross-examiner is supposed to limit questioning of the witness to the topics covered on direct examination, the court will give him or her considerable latitude. Many questions will be designed to create an impression that the expert is not competent, and the actual content of the questions is not fully pertinent. Other questions will try to create an impression that the expert has been biased. Still others will try to elicit contradictions to impeach the witness's testimony.

The most effective responses to such tactics are to respond as professionally, accurately, and carefully as possible. Consulting notes to be sure that one's definitions are accurate is acceptable. It should be remembered, however, that the opposing attorney has the right to request a copy of any such notes prior to their use in court.

One point is most important: It is crucial that the witness understand each question fully before responding. If a question is confusing, it is essential that the witness ask for a clarification. If an answer misrepresents the witness's intent, the witness may ask the judge for permission to clarify the answer.

ATTORNEY: Isn't it true that psychology is an inexact science?

WITNESS: Yes.

ATTORNEY: So what you report here about the accuracy of your belief that the memory is valid is really a guess.

WITNESS: It's a statement of belief based on experience.

ATTORNEY: Your Honor, please instruct the witness to answer the question.

WITNESS: Your Honor, may I ask you for a clarification?

JUDGE: What is it you wish clarified?

WITNESS: In order to answer the attorney's question accurately, I must establish the difference between a guess and a probability.

Dangers during Cross-Examination

One of the things a witness does not want to do is to present himself or herself as uncaring, imprecise, or overemotional. Engaging the attorney in a shouting match, showing high levels of emotion, or becoming otherwise flustered during the testimony will serve the desire of the opposing attorney to get the jury to discount what the expert has to say. It is truly a pyrrhic victory to get the cross-examiner more emotional than the witness. If both have lost control, the witness still loses.

Presentation and Preparation

Therapists can be expected to function as broadly knowledgeable mental health professionals. Therapists who testify in a case should be knowledgeable about all matters pertaining to the case. It may not be possible to limit testimony to the actual hypnosis performed without also being asked to diagnose the patient and to argue why hypnosis was indicated for a person with that diagnosis. It is also important to be aware of the patient's past. It can be quite embarrassing to discover on the stand that a client has been hospitalized for schizophrenia several times previously, with delusions that she was raped.

Therapists who try too hard to narrow the range of their testimony can fall victim to a cross-examiner's portrayal of them as secretive and withholding. Conversely, while it is important to be relevant and informative, extemporaneous speaking from the witness stand should be carefully limited, and no additional information should be offered. It is not always what a psychotherapist says about the relevant issues that is used to discredit him or her; it is extra material that is elicited by a clever attorney playing to the ego needs of the witness.

The jury will generally want the expert to look good. They want the best possible information with which to make their decisions. If the therapist remains helpful and informative and appears well prepared and respectful, the jury will tend to listen closely to his or her opinions. If the jury finds the expert arrogant, secretive, easily swayed, untrustworthy, boring, or overconcerned with minutiae, they will disregard the evidence he or she presents.

The jury will generally identify and sympathize with the therapist on the witness stand unless the therapist does something to destroy that projection. Thus, being natural, cordial, responsive, and careful will contribute a great deal to the jury's belief in the therapist.

A well-prepared cross-examiner will be able to make points on almost any issue. Note, for example, how the use of a standard suggestion for permissive amnesia can be exploited:

ATTORNEY: Dr. Russell, what is a posthypnotic suggestion?

WITNESS: It is a suggestion given during the hypnotic trance state that will be acted upon once the subject is awake, but without conscious thought.

ATTORNEY: What would be an example of one of these?

WITNESS: I might suggest to a patient who has undergone a root canal under hypnosis that if any pain begins to surface, the patient will automatically feel it as pressure instead of pain, just like during the surgery.

ATTORNEY: Could you get subjects to do anything under posthypnotic suggestion?

WITNESS: Not if it violated their personal moral code.

ATTORNEY: Could you give a person a posthypnotic suggestion to remember a trauma even if she had amnesia?

WITNESS: Yes, but it most likely wouldn't work as a posthypnotic suggestion.

ATTORNEY: Did you use a posthypnotic suggestion with your patient in this case, such as instructing her to remember all the allegedly missing details?

WITNESS: I used no posthypnotic suggestions with my patient.

ATTORNEY: Doctor, what is permissive amnesia?

WITNESS: That is a standard suggestion to subjects in a hypnotic trance to remember what is best remembered and to leave behind in the unconscious anything that is best left behind. It is done to add protection and reduce the possibility that unmanageable, painful unconscious material does not intrude into the conscious mind.

ATTORNEY: You used *that* posthypnotic suggestion with Ms. Smith at each of the nine hypnosis sessions you had with her, didn't you?

WITNESS: Yes.

ATTORNEY: Well, Doctor, I wonder what other posthypnotic suggestions you forgot you gave her.

Consulting Notes

In any situation where accuracy is important, it may be helpful to have notes. Prior to consulting such notes, the witness should always ask the judge for permission. It is important to remember that any notes will be made part of the court record and will be offered to the opposing attorney. Many expert witnesses carefully prepare notes and make copies for each attorney in the eventuality that the attorneys ask to see the notes. Therapists should always retain the original documents or tapes, if possible. In no event should a therapist give up his or her only copy of anything. Among the notes, it is important to keep a copy of prior depositions available.

The jury will respect the witness's desire to be precise by consulting notes. They will lose that respect, however, if such notes are disorganized and the desired passages elude the witness.

Emotional Preparation

Three areas of the therapist's emotional life are most likely to be engaged during cross-examination: performance anxiety; protective feelings for the client; and combative, competitive feelings toward the cross-examining attorney.

Performance anxiety. The cross-examiner will exploit every avenue to undercut the expert's credentials, schooling, professionalism, standing in the community, or true understanding of the current situation. As personal doubt creeps in, the attorney will press the point, attempting to portray the witness as unsure or incompetent.

The witness on the stand is faced with an adversary who is looking for weaknesses. This adversary hopes that the witness will either buckle under from sheer nervousness or fatigue, or become combative and lose his or her cool. In short, the therapist's ego will be the target. One psychiatrist of our acquaintance maintains his equilibrium by imagining that he is being questioned by a screaming psychotic patient.

The best antidotes to these feelings of personal insecurity are careful preparation and prior consultation with the retaining attorney, in which the concerns are openly discussed.

Protective feelings toward the patient (victim). The cross-examiner, using a pseudofriendly approach, may well try to show that the witness is biased in the case. If the therapist believes that it is essential that the patient win the case, he or she may well appear biased, and hence not credible.

Therapists who feel this way prior to trial must seek consultation and work through their own feelings of protectiveness well before the trial date. A witness perceived by the jurors as partial to one side of the case may paradoxically cause them to lean in the opposite direction for fairness.

Competition with the cross-examiner. If a person's expertise is as an accountant, it is foolish to challenge Michael Jordan to a slam-dunk contest. The competitor probably will be outmatched unless the contest involves accounting. Similarly, therapists have considerable skill in their own arenas of evaluation or therapy. The therapist who wishes to compete with an attorney would be best advised to do so in the therapy center, not the courtroom. Not only will the lawyer have the advantage of experience, training, and practice, but the rules of a courtroom are different for a witness and an attorney.

For this reason, the cross-examiner will frequently bait the witness to fight, or seduce the witness to try to look good at the expense of the "foolish" attorney. As soon as the witness falls for the bait, the trap is sprung: The witness appears egotistical, argumentative, difficult, and obtrusive, and the attorney who has trapped the witness will appear to be the underdog defender of truth who has to deal with experts who are trying to hurt his or her client. As a rule of thumb, a therapist who feels compelled to fix court procedures, ensure justice against the distortions of the legal system, or compensate for a less skilled retaining attorney has already been hooked into this competitive role.

As a witness, the therapist must accept the attacks, abuse, and seduction, and respond only as a competent professional who is present to help the court with specialized know-how. The jury is much more likely to empathize with a therapist who is less than completely successful in standing up to the cross-examiner's attack than with a bellicose combatant.

AFTER THE TRIAL

Follow-Up with the Patient

Whatever the trial outcome, the patient may need follow-up treatment. When the witness is also the psychotherapist, there are likely to be continuing obligations to the client. It may be appropriate for the person who testified to work subsequently with the patient on some vestiges of the problem. It is possible that the ordeal of a trial or the content of some of the testimony will create or rekindle difficulties for the patient. As a therapist whose initial loyalty was to the patient, but whose allegiance shifted to the retaining attorney when the therapist was hired as an expert witness, there will be remaining ethical and emotional responsibility for the patient.

At the very least, a follow-up evaluation session is in order. Future therapy with the client or referral to other professionals should be carefully considered. The therapist who testifies on behalf of a client must be particularly sensitive to changes in the therapeutic relationship. Regardless of the nature of the testimony or the trial outcome, the transference relationship will be powerfully affected. These changes will have to be addressed as a precursor to continuing therapy.

A debriefing and referral at the patient's request would be appropriate. In an ironic way, the more effective the therapy has been, the more likely it is that the patient has effectively overcome the trauma. However, if the client does not appear to be a victim, the jury may well have less sympathy for him or her. Thus, effective therapy may aid the patient psychologically but diminish his or her legal redress.

Record Keeping

Most trials involving hypnosis will be appealed. Although most appeals are based strictly on points of law and thus will not involve witness testimony, it is possible that further testimony will be requested, especially for retrials.

Legal requirements for record keeping are far more stringent than normal mental health standards. There is a potential need to be conversant with clinical cases that may have concluded therapeutically but not legally. Careful record keeping and confidential storage of records are necessary.

Billing

Lawyers frequently pay for services well after they are billed. For therapists who are accustomed to receiving payment at each session, forensic work may involve setting up an entire accounts-receivable system, with reminders for delinquent accounts. One therapist who does extensive forensic work in testing, competency, and sanity cases estimates that attorneys pay their bills 120 days later than other sources. It is thus important that therapists bill properly and keep track of delinquent payments.

SUMMARY

Much of the material that is discussed in court must be professionally prepared in advance. It is of value to know the questions beforehand and to take all precautions before ever seeing a client for evaluation. In cases of hypermnesia and hypnotically refreshed recall, this is especially crucial.

Therapists who fail to recognize the legal changes that bear on modern psychotherapy practice will probably fail to take the requisite precautions and to follow strict guidelines. Such therapists not only may reduce their clients' legal rights, but may be open to law suits themselves. If a therapist is unwilling to observe the tenets and guidelines put forth in this text, he or she is best advised also to avoid cases of hypermnesia and any other type of hypnotherapy that is likely to interface with the legal system.

A day in court is no picnic. People's lives are often in great jeopardy when they involve the law. Judgments made in court can have lifelong effects on individuals and families. Only the highest level of professionalism and preparation is acceptable under those circumstances.

Part VI

Conclusion

Conclusion

CHAPTER 11

Final Comments

Because the inductions and suggestions common to hypnosis are readily learned and practiced, these techniques are often portrayed as deceptively simple and unrealistically powerful. This depiction, together with the public's ever-increasing interest in miracle cures, has provided the soil for the mushrooming popularity of hypnosis.

Currently, hypnosis is employed by a vast array of professionals and nonprofessionals for healing, self-help, motivation, investigation of the past, forensic work, and entertainment. An increase in both the number and sophistication of professional tracts is matched by the proliferation of "one size fits all" self-help and growth tapes available at most bookstore counters.

The professional psychotherapist who utilizes hypnosis is faced with the dilemma of debunking myths about the "magical cure" quality of hypnosis, and simultaneously employing the powerful placebo and treatment effects that are possible. Effective hypnotherapy involves a comprehensive understanding of the ego state and pathology of the individual patient; a solid perception of operative transference and countertransference phenomena; the choice of methods consistent with the patient's personal style; the timing of inductions to coincide with patient readiness; and the application of many other skills that are consistent with the ethical standards customary in professional psychotherapy.

In hypnotherapy involving refreshed memory or evocation of unconscious material, the skilled therapist must be able to help elicit the material from the client and assist the client's integration of the freshly conscious material into current ego functioning. It is a job that requires a great deal of skill. However, proficiency alone may not be sufficient when nontherapeutic considerations mandated by the legal system are added to the equation.

HYPNOSIS AND THE LAW

Psychotherapy and the law are awkward companions. Therapists' and lawyers' goals and methods are quite different; indeed, they are often in opposition. Nowhere is this incongruity seen so clearly as in the situation of hypnotherapeutic hypermnesia.

For therapists confronted with patients such as Jennifer L., a trauma victim doubly pained because of amnesia (see Chapter Two), the goal is clear. These patients must be helped to regain their lost memories, work through the trauma psychologically, pick up the pieces of their lives, and face the future with hope and meaning. It is tragic that hypnosis performed in such quests for mental health can inadvertently create an additional loss for the victims: It can cost them the right to testify in court against the persons who have harmed them.

In this book, we have presented a series of methods and safeguards that can best protect clients and therapists against that possibility. As we have described, court rulings have followed confusing, and often dramatically differing, directions throughout the last two decades. The application of the law to therapy and the changing nature of legal rulings have created complications for hypnotherapists in terms of preparation and practice.

Preparation

Prior to taking any hypermnesia cases, therapists should do the following:

1. Carefully review the literature on hypnotically refreshed memory.
2. Understand the current status of the law in their own states regarding such memory.
3. Be sufficiently trained in hypnosis and therapy to help evoke repressed memories and help patients work through and integrate such memories once they have been elicited.

Practice

We believe that the most conservative approach is also the wisest for any cases in which recovered memories are likely to produce subsequent legal action (e.g., rape/amnesia cases). Therapists who accept such cases should do the following:

1. Eschew hypnosis per se in favor of alternative mnemonic retrieval procedures, when possible.
2. Obtain written informed consent prior to using any hypnosis. This

consent must include an understanding that any refreshed memory may be inadmissible in subsequent legal proceedings.
3. Use the safeguards described in this text if hypnosis is used.

The Scope of This Book

Because it is our firm belief that the best way to deal with the extension of the legal system into the therapy room is knowledge and careful preparation, this book has been designed to provide practitioners with a guide to the issues, literature, and workings of the legal system. A step-by-step examination of the process when a case goes to trial—from the initial phone call through court proceedings and posttrial record keeping—has been provided, along with recommendations for practice. The literature on forensic hypnosis and hypermnesia has been extensively discussed, and an extensive bibliography, containing a thorough listing of relevant psychological and legal references, has been provided. The current rulings on the admissibility of hypnotically refreshed testimony in each state and federal jurisdiction have also been discussed. (Readers are encouraged to get updates on the situation in their own jurisdictions as time progresses.)

FUTURE CONSIDERATIONS

Status of the Admissibility of Hypnosis

Although it is necessary that therapists practice hypnosis within proper legal guidelines, it is also important to anticipate future legal rulings in this area. Beahrs (1988) argues, on the basis of available research, that per se exclusion laws are shortsighted and unreasonable. He notes that for hypnosis to be excluded in any specific case, four criteria must be met:

1. The exclusion must respect other legal principles.
2. Hypnosis must be shown to be a separable state of consciousness.
3. If there is unreliability in the testimony, it must be shown that the hypnosis is the dominant source thereof.
4. There must be an established absence of spontaneous (informal trance) states.

Beahrs's position may be a harbinger of the next trend in the admissibility of hypnotically refreshed memory. The Colorado Supreme Court (*People v. Romero*, 1987) has recently opined that hypnosis is admissible when reliability is shown by the preponderance of the evidence, and other courts are following this analysis. Such positions not only will encourage further legal debate, but underscore the need for clinicians to proceed with the utmost regard for safeguards. It is precisely when testimony is potentially admissible that the greatest risk of malpractice occurs.

It is a fact of modern life that the law has very much infiltrated the inner sanctum of the therapist's office. The explosive increase in litigation, and issues such as the extended duty to warn, abuse of the therapeutic relationship, and the limits of confidentiality and privilege, have created an environment in which an increasing percentage of the articles in professional journals address legal rather than clinical issues. There is every reason to believe that as the basic questions involving forensic hypnosis approach solution, the law will continue its interest in, and investigation of, hypnosis issues in general.

The Right to Do Hypnosis

One major area of controversy that seems ripe for legal exploration is a renewal of the century-old debate regarding to whom hypnosis belongs. Healers, investigators, purveyors of self-help, mentalists, and entertainers all claim ownership of some aspects of hypnosis.

To date, the use of hypnosis has not generally been restricted by legislators or the courts. It has enjoyed protected status as a form of free speech and communication. Attempts to limit the use of hypnosis (except as a form of medicine or psychotherapy) have been sporadic, ill-planned, and ineffective. Lay hypnotists are prepared with data and numbers to keep it that way.

If professionals wish to effectively restrict the use of hypnosis to skilled licensed practitioners, they must show that they use it successfully and that others use it improperly or dangerously. They must then lobby effectively to limit its use. Anything short of a complete effort in this direction will surely fail. Such an effort will require consensus on a definition of hypnosis; a truce between experimental and clinical disciplines; and reliable, verifiable research on relevant questions involving the application and consequences of hypnosis. Because professionals all zealously protect their own specialized arenas, it is unlikely that anything approaching a cooperative venture will be forthcoming in the near future.

As the ambiguity persists about basic questions that have remained unsolved since the 18th century, legal rulings will surely follow. In the debate over forensic hypnosis, when the law approached mental health professionals expecting clear information in a consistent voice, it heard diversity and stridency instead. When the debate turned acrimonious, the mental health community was further divided; clinicians were left without satisfactory guidelines, and clients were left with their mental health and legal rights in peril. The law was led into confusing and sometimes unjust rulings, occasionally under the influence of individuals taking extreme positions on every side of every question.

A far better solution for all concerned is to recognize that the law will inevitably turn to clinical and experimental experts for guidance on hypnosis issues. It is imperative that the differing factions in the mental health community settle their differences and find common ground. At that time, an approach can be made to the legal system that is harmonious and persuasive. It is our hope that our book will contribute to the attainment of that goal.

State, Federal, and Foreign Law Pertaining to Forensic Hypnosis

LAW OF THE STATES

Alabama

The Alabama Court of Criminal Appeals first directly addressed the issue of hypnotically refreshed recollection in *Prewitt v. State* (1981), a case involving a defense witness who had been hypnotized. The court held that the requirements of *Frye v. United States* (1923) had not been met; the defendant introduced no evidence showing the reliability of hypnotically refreshed recollection or the general acceptance of such evidence by the scientific community. Furthermore, the defendant failed to lay a proper foundation for the receipt of hypnotically refreshed recollection. No evidence was presented concerning the following:

> the nature of the pre-hypnosis interrogations of [the witness], the identity or the qualifications of the hypnotist, the hypnotic technique or procedure used, the nature and extent of hypnotic suggestions, or the nature and extent of any "safeguards" taken to enhance the reliability of the information obtained. (*Prewitt*, 1981, p. 303)

The Court declined to adopt a general rule until a case with an appropriate record was presented. In one paragraph, however, the judges provided a hint that the door might not be completely closed:

> We do, however, acknowledge the efficacy of hypnosis as an investigatory tool. We caution those who so use it to properly document pre-hypnosis evidence to insure its admissibility in appropriate cases, to refute claims that it is somehow "tainted" by hypnosis. (*Prewitt*, 1981, p. 304)

In 1986, the Alabama Court of Criminal Appeals was faced with a claim in the case of *Johnson v. State* that the State's use of hypnosis to "strengthen the victim's recollection of her assailant" (p. 75) was so impermissibly suggestive as to require reversal of the conviction because of the likelihood of misidentification. The court admitted that the hypnosis was suggestive, but held that it was not so *unduly* suggestive as to create a *substantial* likelihood of misidentification. The court found that the victim had an independent basis to identify the defendant; it then went on to state that "we do not mean to say, however, that an identification after hypnosis would necessarily be inadmissible" (p. 75). The court cited none of its prior language concerning the problems with the reliability of hypnosis as a memory refresher.

Prehypnotic recall will most likely be admissible in Alabama, and there is good reason to believe that the court will be lenient with prosecutorial claims for admissibility of hypnotically refreshed recollection.

1. Chamblee v. State, 527 So. 2d 173 (Ala. Crim. App. 1988).
2. Johnson v. State, 500 So. 2d 69 (1986).
3. Adams v. State, 484 So. 2d 1160 (Ala. Crim. App. 1985).
4. Prewitt v. State, 460 So. 2d 296 (Ala. Crim. App. 1984).
5. McKinley v. State, 441 So. 2d 1040 (Ala. Crim. App. 1983).
6. Kuhlman v. Keith, 409 So. 2d 804 (1982).
7. Voudrie v. State, 387 So. 2d 248 (1980).
8. Coon v. State, 380 So. 2d 980 (Ala. Crim. App. 1979), *aff'd, Ex parte* Coon, 380 So. 2d 990 (1980), *vacated,* Coon v. Alabama, 449 U.S. 810, 101 S. Ct. 58, 66 L.Ed.2d 14 (1980).
9. Pollard v. State, 358 So. 2d 778 (1978).
10. Barfield v. State, 54 Ala. App. 15, 304 So. 2d 257 (1975).
11. Louis v. State, 24 Ala. App. 120, 130 So. 904 (1930).
12. *Ex parte* Smith, 183 Ala. 116, 63 So. 70 (1913).
13. Smith v. State, 8 Ala. App. 352, 63 So. 28 (1913).

Alaska

The Alaska Court of Appeals in a lengthy and careful 1983 decision *(State v. Contreras)* permitted the introduction of hypnotically refreshed recollection. This decision was reversed by the Alaska Supreme Court in 1986 in favor of a per se exclusion rule except for well-documented prehypnotic recall.

The Supreme Court stated that the *Frye* standard of reliability had not been met, and that under Alaska Evidence Code Section 403, hypnotically adduced testimony would have to be excluded because it is more prejudicial than probative. The court rejected the safeguards approach because leading experts did not agree on which safeguards were appropriate and because a case-by-case approach was time-consuming, created a risk of nonuniform results, and required judges to become experts in hypnosis.

1. Contreras v. State, 767 P.2d. 1169 (Alaska Ct. App. 1989).
2. Contreras v. State, 718 P.2d 129 (1986).
3. State v. Contreras, 674 P.2d 792 (Alaska Ct. App. 1983).

Arizona

Arizona courts have addressed hypnosis issues quite frequently. The Arizona Supreme Court has adopted a per se exclusion rule subject to two important exceptions:

1. A witness is not disqualified from testifying after having been hypnotized if the hypnosis was conducted to obtain investigative leads and the witness does not testify at trial concerning matters discussed during the hypnosis. In the *State v. Rodriquez* (1984) case, the hypnosis was used only to aid in obtaining a photo composite. All hypnosis sessions were taped. Because there was no potential of creating false memories, according to the court, the witness was not disqualified from testifying.

2. Prehypnotic recollection is admissible. A witness is qualified to testify as to matters remembered before hypnosis was used. A videotape of all prehypnosis, hypnosis, and posthypnosis sessions is preferable. All posthypnotic statements—those induced by hypnosis or those that the hypnosis has altered from prehypnotic recollection—are inadmissible.

Arizona courts have held that these same rules apply to both criminal and civil cases.

1. State v. Poland, 144 Ariz. 388, 698 P.2d 183 (1985).
2. State v. Rodriquez, 145 Ariz. 157, 700 P.2d 855 (Ariz. App. 1984).
3. State v. Tison, 142 Ariz. 454, 690 P.2d 755 (1984).
4. State v. Tison, 142 Ariz. 446, 690 P.2d 747 (1984).
5. State v. Superior Court in and for Pima County, 142 Ariz. 375, 690 P.2d 94 (1984).
6. State v. McMurtrey II, 136 Ariz. 93, 664 P.2d 637 (1983).
7. State v. Young, 135 Ariz. 437, 661 P.2d 1138 (Ariz. App. 1982).
8. State v. Woratzeck, 134 Ariz. 452, 657 P.2d 865 (1982).
9. State v. Gerlaugh, 134 Ariz. 164, 654 P.2d 800 (1982).
10. State v. Thomas, 133 Ariz. 533, 652 P.2d 1380 (1982).
11. State v. Encinas, 132 Ariz. 493, 647 P.2d 624 (1982).
12. State v. Stolp, 133 Ariz. 213, 650 P.2d 1195 (1982).
13. State v. Poland, 132 Ariz. 269, 645 P.2d 784 (1982).
14. Lemieux v. Super. Ct., 132 Ariz. 214, 644 P.2d 1300, 31 A.L.R. 4th 1231 (1982).
15. State *ex rel.* Collins v. Super Ct., 132 Ariz. 180, 644 P.2d 1266 (1982).
16. State v. Grier, 129 Ariz. 279, 630 P.2d 575 (Ariz. App. 1981).
17. State v. Mena, 128 Ariz. 226, 624 P.2d 1274 (1981).

18. State v. Henry, 128 Ariz. 204, 624 P.2d 882 (Ariz. App. 1980).
19. State v. Mena, 128 Ariz. 244, 624 P.2d 1292 (Ariz. App. 1980).
20. State v. LaMountain, 125 Ariz. 547, 611 P.2d 551 (1980).
21. State v. Austin, 124 Ariz. 231, 603 P.2d 502 (1979).
22. State v. Allen, 27 Ariz. App. 577, 557 P.2d 176 (1976).
23. State v. Dante, 25 Ariz. App. 150, 541 P.2d 941 (1975).
24. Wilburn v. Reitman, 54 Ariz. 31, 91 P.2d 865 (1939).

Arkansas

The Arkansas Supreme Court, in *Rock v. State* (1986), applied its per se exclusion rule to defendants. The U.S. Supreme Court reversed this decision in 1987, holding that it violated the defendant's constitutional rights. Arkansas is still free to apply an exclusion rule to victims and witnesses, but not to defendants. Whether it will choose to back away from the per se exclusion of the testimony of victims and witnesses is not yet known.

1. Rock v. State, 288 Ark. 566, 708 S.W.2d 78 (1986), *cert. granted*, Rock v. Arkansas, 107 S. Ct. 430, 93 L.Ed.2d 381 (1986), *vacated and remanded*, Rock v. Arkansas, 107 S. Ct. 2704, 97 L.Ed.2d 37 (1987).
2. Wilson v. State, 282 Ark. 551, 669 S.W.2d 889 (1984).
3. Pitts v. State, 273 Ark. 220, 617 S.W.2d 849 (1981).

California

California has faced hypnosis issues more often in its courts than any other state. In its influential *People v. Shirley* decision in 1982, the California Supreme Court adopted a per se exclusion rule. The court adhered to that ruling 2 years later in *People v. Guerra*. Courts of appeal, however, found many loopholes to avoid disqualifying witnesses who had been hypnotized.

The legislature stepped into the forensic hypnosis debate to provide that a previously hypnotized witness could testify concerning prehypnotic recall if certain carefully articulated safeguards were met.

Chapter Five contains a full discussion of California law, and a complete reprint of California Evidence Code section 795.

1. People v. Johnson, 47 Cal. 3d 1194, 255 Cal. Rptr. 569, 767 P.2d 1047 (1989).
2. People v. Alcala, Crim. No. 25693/SOO4724 (Filed in Supreme Court, June 3, 1988).
3. People v. Johnson, 47 Cal. 3d 576, 253 Cal. Rptr. 710, 764 P.2d 1087 (1988).
4. People v. Caro, 46 Cal. 3d 1035, 251 Cal. Rptr. 757, 761 P.2d 680 (1988).
5. People v. Rich, 45 Cal. 3d 1036, 46 Cal. 3d 584B, 248 Cal. Rptr. 510, 755 P.2d 960 (1988).
6. People v. Milner, 45 Cal. 3d 227, 246 Cal. Rptr. 713, 753 P.2d 669 (1988).

7. Tushinsky v. Arnold, 195 Cal. App. 3d 666, 241 Cal. Rptr. 103 (1987).
8. People v. Burroughs, 188 Cal. App. 3d 1162, 233 Cal. Rptr. 872 (1987).
9. People v. Johnson, 43 Cal. 3d 296, 233 Cal. Rptr. 562, 730 P.2d 131 (1987).
10. People v. Huber, 181 Cal. App. 3d 601, 227 Cal. Rptr. 113 (1986).
11. People v. Thompson, 176 Cal. App. 3d 554, 222 Cal. Rptr. 262 (1986) [depublished].
12. People v. Mackey, 176 Cal. App. 3d 177, 221 Cal. Rptr. 405 (1985).
13. People v. Brown, 40 Cal. 3d 512, 230 Cal. Rptr. 834, 726 P.2d 516 (1985).
14. People v. Zamarripa, 174 Cal. App. 3d 595, 220 Cal. Rptr. 173 (1985) [depublished].
15. Spiritual Psychic Science Church v. City of Azusa, 39 Cal. 3d 501, 217 Cal. Rptr. 225, 703 P.2d 1119 (1985).
16. People v. Guerra, 37 Cal. App. 3d 385, 208 Cal. Rptr. 162, 690 P.2d 635 (1984).
17. People v. Pugh, 156 Cal. App. 3d 544, 203 Cal. Rptr. 43 (1984) [depublished].
18. Spiritual Psychic Science Church v. City of Azusa, 154 Cal. App. 3d 1176, 201 Cal. Rptr. 852 (1984).
19. People v. Glaude, 141 Cal. App. 3d 633, 190 Cal. Rptr. 479 (1983).
20. People v. Parrison, 137 Cal. App. 3d 529, 187 Cal. Rptr. 123 (1982).
21. People v. Adams, 137 Cal. App. 3d 346, 187 Cal. Rptr. 505 (1982).
22. People v. Williams, 132 Cal. App. 3d 920, 183 Cal. Rptr. 498 (1982).
23. Guadalupe v. Super. Ct., 132 Cal. App. 3d 754, 183 Cal. Rptr. 568 (1982) [depublished].
24. People v. Aquino, 131 Cal. App. 3d 966, 182 Cal. Rptr. 656 (1982), *cause retransferred*, 211 Cal. Rptr. 690, 696 P.2d 83 (1985).
25. People v. Shirley, 31 Cal.3d 18, 723 P.2d 1354, 181 Cal. Rptr. 243 (1982), *stay denied*, California v. Shirley, 458 U.S. 1125, 103 S. Ct. 13, 73 L.Ed.2d 1400 (1982), *cert. denied*, California v. Shirley, 459 U.S. 860, 103 S. Ct. 133, 74 L.Ed.2d 114 (1982).
26. People v. Bicknell, 114 Cal. App. 3d 388 (1980) [depublished], *hearing granted*, Crim. 21852, (Feb. 11, 1981), *opinion filed* (Jan. 28, 1986).
27. People v. Diggs, 112 Cal. App. 3d 522, 169 Cal. Rptr. 386 (1980).
28. People v. Lopez, 110 Cal. App. 3d 1010, 168 Cal. Rptr. 378 (1980).
29. People v. Blair, 25 Cal. App. 3d 640, 159 Cal. Rptr. 818, 602 P.2d 738 (1979).
30. People v. Colligan, 91 Cal. App. 3d 846, 154 Cal. Rptr. 389 (1979).
31. People v. Blair, 89 Cal. App. 3d 563, 152 Cal. Rptr. 646 (1979).
32. Shea v. Bd. of Medical Examiners, 81 Cal. App. 3d 564, 146 Cal. Rptr. 653 (1978).
33. People v. Woods, et. al. No. 63187ABNC (Alameda Co., December 15, 1977).
34. People v. Barbosa, No. 2211183 (Super. Ct., Fresno Co., December 13, 1977).
35. People v. Quaglino, No. 109524 (Santa Barbara Super. Ct., 1976), *aff'd*, Crim. 29766 (Cal. Ct. App., 2d Dist., Sept. 30, 1977), *appeal denied*, California v. Quaglino, *cert. denied*, California v. Quaglino, 439 U.S. 875, 99 S. Ct. 212, 58 L.Ed. 2d 189 (1978), *reh. denied* Quaglino v. California, 439 U.S. 997, 99 S. Ct. 599, 58 L.Ed. 2d 670 (1978).
36. People v. Thomas, Crim. No. 3274 (Cal. Ct. App., 4th Dist., Jan. 9, 1969) [unreported].
37. People v. Hiser, 267 Cal. App. 2d 47, 72 Cal. Rptr. 906, 41 A.L.R. 3d 1353 (1968).

38. People v. Modesto, 59 Cal. 2d 722, 31 Cal. Rptr. 225, 382 P.2d 33 (1963).
39. People v. Cantor, 198 Cal. App. 2d Supp. 843, 18 Cal. Rptr. 363 (1961).
40. People v. Busch, 56 Cal. 2d 868, 16 Cal. Rptr. 898, 366 P.2d 314 (1961).
41. People v. Marsh, 170 Cal. App. 2d 284, 338 P.2d 495 (1959).
42. Cornell v. Super Ct., 52 Cal. 2d 99, 338 P.2d 447, 72 A.L.R. 2d 1116 (1959).
43. People v. Ebanks, 117 Cal. 652, 49 P. 1049, 40 L.R.A. 269 (1897).
44. People v. Worthington, 105 Cal. 166, 38 P. 389 (1894).
45. People v. Royal, 53 Cal. 62 (1878).

Statute:

Cal. Evid. Code § 795, "Hypnosis of Witnesses—Admissibility" (West 1984, amended 1987).

Colorado

The Colorado Supreme Court first addressed hypnotically refreshed recollection in the *People v. Romero* case in 1987. The court adopted a "totality of the circumstances" test, whereby the trial judge makes an individualized inquiry in each case as to the reliability of the proposed testimony. The party requesting the admissibility has the burden to show, by a preponderance of the evidence, that the testimony is reliable.

In assessing the "totality of the circumstances," the trial judge should consider the following factors:

the level of training in the clinical uses and forensic applications of hypnosis by the person performing the hypnosis; the hypnotist's independence from law enforcement investigators, prosecution, and defense; the existence of a record of any information given or known by the hypnotist concerning the case prior to the hypnosis session; the existence of a written or recorded account of the facts as the hypnosis subject remembers them *prior* to undergoing hypnosis; the creation of recordings of all contacts between the hypnotist and the subject; the presence of persons other than the hypnotist and the subject during any phase of the hypnosis session, as well as the location of the session; the appropriateness of the induction and memory retrieval techniques used; the appropriateness of using hypnosis for the kind of memory loss involved; and the existence of any evidence to corroborate the hypnotically enhanced testimony" (p. 1017).

1. People v. Romero, 745 P.2d 1003 (1987).
2. People v. McKeehan, 732 P.2d 1238 (Colo. App. 1986).
3. People v. Rivers, 727 P.2d 394 (Colo. App. 1986).
4. People v. Beyette, 711 P.2d 1263 (1986).
5. Garcia v. Scimemi, 712 P.2d 1094 (Colo. App. 1985).
6. People v. Romero, 712 P.2d 1081 (Colo. App. 1985).
7. People v. Angelini, 706 P.2d 2 (Colo. App. 1985).
8. Mondragon v. Poudre School Dist., 696 P.2d 831 (Colo. App. 1984).

9. People v. Rex, 689 P.2d 669 (Colo. App. 1984).
10. People v. Bell, 669 P.2d 1381 (1983).
11. People in the Interest of M.S.H., 656 P.2d 1294 (1983).
12. People v. Quintanar, 659 P.2d 710 (Colo. App. 1982).
13. People v. District Ct., 652 P.2d 582 (1982).
14. People v. Angelini, 649 P.2d 342 (Colo. App. 1982).
15. People v. District Ct., 647 P.2d 1206 (1982).
16. People v. Diaz, 644 P.2d 71 (Colo. App. 1981).
17. Bernie v. State Bd. of Chiropractic Examiners, 36 Colo. App. 229, 538 P.2d 1345 (1975).

Connecticut

In *State v. Pollitt* (1987), the Connecticut Supreme Court permitted the introduction of prehypnotic testimony, but did not address the admissibility of posthypnotic testimony that is inconsistent with facts remembered prior to trance. A case a year later (*State v. Palmer, 1988*) also involved prehypnotic testimony, so the court has yet to rule on the major issue.

1. State v. Palmer, 206 Conn. 40, 536 A.2d 936 (1988).
2. State v. Pollitt, 205 Conn. 61, 530 A.2d 155 (1987).
3. State v. Atwood, 39 Conn. Supp. 273, 479 A.2d 258 (Super. Ct. 1984).
4. State v. Nims, 180 Conn. 589, 430 A.2d 1306 (1980).
5. State v. Darwin, 155 Conn. 124, 230 A.2d 573 (1967).

Delaware

The Delaware Superior Court, in *State v. Davis* (1985), adopted a per se exclusion rule. When the Delaware Supreme Court addressed the issue in *Elliotte v. State* (1986), it noted that "a major difficulty with prehypnotic testimony is the danger that hypnosis may artificially enhance a witness's confidence in his prior recollection, and this in turn could inhibit meaningful cross-examination" (p. 679). Nevertheless, the court permitted the introduction of such testimony, provided a pretrial hearing on the issue demonstrated that the hypnosis was not unduly suggestive and did not "substantially impair" the defendant's ability to cross-examine. The court did not decide whether posthypnotic testimony is admissible, but cited the Superior Court case a year earlier, which suggests that it might follow that exclusion approach.

1. Elliotte v. State, 515 A.2d 677 (1986).
2. State v. Davis, 490 A.2d 601 (Del. Super. Ct. 1985).
3. McKinney v. Reardon, 337 A.2d 514 (Del. Super. Ct. 1975).
4. State v. Lawson, 65 A. 593 (Del. Ct. Gen. Sess. 1907).

District of Columbia

No appellate cases on hypnosis have been found.

Florida

Serial killer Theodore Bundy filled the courts with litigation concerning his murderous rampages. The Florida Supreme Court in *Bundy v. State* (1984), discussed the admissibility of hypnotically refreshed recollection but did not decide the issue. A year later, however, Bundy was back (*Bundy v. State*, 1985); this time, the court adopted a per se exclusion rule. The court did permit, however, the admissibility of prehypnotic recollection.

In *Morgan* (1989), the Florida Supreme Court extended the *Rock* case to mandate the admission of the testimony of a criminal defendant's experts. A psychologist and a psychiatrist were prepared to testify that the defendant was insane at the time he killed his victim. The experts based their opinion in part upon the hypnotically refreshed statements of the defendant while in trance. The court noted that after *Rock*, Florida's per se exclusion rule would have to be amended "to the extent it affects a defendant's testimony or statements made to experts by a defendant in preparation of a defense" (p. 976). A concurring opinion raises the possibility of abolishing the per se exclusion rule entirely.

1. Morgan v. State, 537 So. 2d 973 (1989).
2. Pate v. State, 13 F.L.W. 1797, 529 So. 2d 328 (Fla. App. 2nd Dist. 1988).
3. Dowell v. State, 12 F.L.W. 2463, 516 So. 2d 271 (Fla. App. 2nd Dist. 1987).
4. Duvall v. State, 11 F.L.W. 2568, 500 So. 2d 570 (Fla. App. 2nd Dist. 1986).
5. Spaziano v. State, 11 F.L.W. 230, 489 So. 2d 720 (1986).
6. Bundy v. State, 10 F.L.W. 269, 471 So. 2d 9 (1985), *cert. denied*, Bundy v. Florida, 479 U.S. 894 107 S. Ct. 295, 93 L.Ed.2d 269 (1986).
7. Doyle v. State, 460 So. 2d 353 (1984).
8. Dobbert v. State, 456 So. 2d 424 (1984).
9. Bundy v. State, 455 So. 2d 330 (1984), *stay granted*, Bundy v. Florida, 475 U.S. 1041, 106 S. Ct. 1254, 89 L.Ed.2d 362 (1986), *cert. denied*, Bundy v. Florida, 476 U.S. 1109, 106 S. Ct. 1958, 90 L.Ed.2d 386 (1986).
10. Kline v. State, 444 So. 2d 1102 (Fla. App. 1st Dist. 1984).
11. Crum v. State, 433 So. 2d 1384 (Fla. App. 5th Dist. 1983).
12. Key v. State, 430 So. 2d 909 (Fla. App. 1st Dist. 1983).
13. Wiley v. State, 427 So. 2d 283 (Fla. App. 1st Dist. 1983).
14. Brown v. State, 426 So. 2d 76 (Fla. App. 1st Dist. 1983).
15. Snead v. State, 415 So. 2d 887 (Fla. App. 5th Dist. 1982).
16. McIlwain v. State, 402 So. 2d 1194 (Fla. App. 5th Dist. 1981).
17. Clark v. State, 379 So. 2d 372 (Fla. App. 1st Dist. 1979).
18. State v. Hostzclaw, 351 So. 2d 1033 (Fla. App. 4th Dist. 1976).
19. Shockey v. State, 338 So. 2d 33 (Fla. App. 3rd Dist. 1976), *cert. denied*, 345 So. 2d 247 (1976).

20. Rodriguez v. State, 327 So. 2d 903 (Fla. App. 3rd Dist. 1976), *cert. denied*, 336 So. 2d 1184 (1976).
21. State v. Pitts, 241 So. 2d 399 (Fla. App. 1st Dist. 1970).
22. Peller v. Kisiel, 161 So. 2d 573 (Fla. App. 3rd Dist. 1964).

Georgia

In *Walraven v. State* (1985), the Georgia Supreme Court surveyed the variety of rules adopted by the different states and chose the rule that permitted the witness to testify about matters recollected before trance. Posthypnotic identification, where the witness or victim identifies the defendant only after being hypnotized, is admissible if it can be shown by clear and convincing evidence that the hypnosis did not create or concretize the identification.

1. Walraven v. State, 255 Ga. 276, 336 S.E.2d 798 (1985).
2. Bobo v. State, 254 Ga. 146, 327 S.E.2d 208 (1985).
3. Felker v. State, 252 Ga. 351, 314 S.E.2d 621 (1984).
4. Henley v. State, 169 Ga. App. 682, 314 S.E.2d 697 (1984).
5. Tucker v. State, 249 Ga. 323, 290 S.E.2d 97 (1982).
6. Collier v. State, 244 Ga. 553, 261 S.E.2d 364 (1979), *cert. denied*, Collier v. Georgia, 445 U.S. 946 (1980).
7. Alderman v. State, 241 Ga. 496, 246 S.E.2d 642 (1978).
8. Creamer v. State, 232 Ga. 136, 205 S.E.2d 240 (1974).
9. Emmett v. State, 232 Ga. 110, 205 S.E.2d 231 (1974).

Hawaii

In a brief two-page opinion, the Hawaii Supreme Court ruled in *State v. Moreno* (1985) that only prehypnotic testimony was admissible. The Court noted that it was "unwilling to . . . adopt a bright line rule, which would require either, that the victim of such a crime [rape] forego the use of hypnotherapy for therapeutic purposes until the trial, or, that the State abandon the use of the victim's testimony in attempting to prosecute the crime" (p. 105).

1. State v. Moreno, 709 P.2d 103 (1985).

Idaho

The Idaho Supreme Court in *State v. Iwakiri* (1984) adopted a "totality of the circumstances" test whereby the trial judge, during a pretrial hearing, determines whether the proposed hypnotically refreshed recollection is sufficiently reliable to merit admission. Safeguards, similar to those adopted in the New Jersey *State v. Hurd* (1981) case, assist the trial judge in making this determination. The court made it clear that a failure to follow the safeguards will not necessarily require exclusion of the testimony and that a strict adherence to them will not guarantee admission. The trial judge must examine the "totality of the circumstances" and make an individualized ruling in each case. According to the court,

> [T]he process of hypnosis, which sometimes results in a modification of memory, is not the only subsequent event that could serve to modify memory and render it untrustworthy. . . . An idle conversation with another witness to the same occurrence can, according to some of the experts, lead to a modification of a witness's memory. While the possibility of alteration of memory through the use of hypnosis is much greater than in other subsequent events, the question is only one of degree. (*Iwakiri*, pp. 578–579)

Quick v. Crane, a 1986 civil case, involved almost none of the safeguards being met. The court sent the case back to the trial judge for a hearing on admissibility.

1. Quick v. Crane, 111 Idaho 759, 727 P.2d 1187 (1986).
2. Matter of X, 110 Idaho 44, 714 P.2d 13 (1986).
3. State v. Bainbridge, 108 Idaho 273, 698 P.2d 335 (1985).
4. State v. Joblin, 107 Idaho 351, 689 P.2d 767 (1984).
5. State v. Iwakiri, 106 Idaho 618, 682 P.2d 571 (1984).

Illinois

Illinois appellate courts have consistently followed an open-admissibility rule in holding that the use of hypnosis to refresh recollection goes to the weight to be given to the testimony ("credibility") and not to its admissibility ("competency" of the witness to testify). The first case suggesting this approach was *People v. Harper* (1969).

Ten years later, in *People v. Smrekar* (1979), an appellate court adopted safeguards as a prerequisite to admission. These safeguards, augmented by later decisions, include (1) proof that the hypnotist was competent; (2) proof that the hypnotist was independent of the prosecution and defense; (3) evidence that suggestion was not used in the hypnosis; (4) substantial evidence corroborating any identification; and (5) evidence that the witness had ample opportunity to view the defendant or the scene.

Whether these requirements have been met, however, has provoked some disagreement. In *People v. Gibson* (1983), one appellate court held that a police officer with 30 hours of training was not competent, whereas another appellate court in *People v. Cohoon* (1983) held the opposite by permitting the hypnosis to stand while acknowledging that the police officer, who called himself a "technician," would not qualify as an expert.

The Illinois Supreme Court has had two opportunities to rule on investigative hypnosis. In *People v. Cohoon* (1984) the court declined to do so, and in *People v. Wilson* (1987) the court limited its ruling to a holding that prehypnotic recall is admissible. The more crucial question, whether posthypnotic recollection is admissible, was deliberately ducked.

The consistency of Illinois law was disrupted in a 1987 appellate court ruling in *People v. Zayas*, where the court broke with all other decisions in the state and adopted a per se exclusion rule. The court made specific reference to the evolving legal trend toward exclusion and the growing scientific literature demonstrating the unreliability of hypnotically refreshed recollection. It remains to be seen whether the *Zayas* decision will be viewed as encouragement to other courts to follow its lead or whether the opinion will be rejected as an aberration.

1. People v. Wilson, 161 Ill. App. 3d 995, 113 Ill. Dec. 827, 515 N.E.2d 812 (1987).
2. People v. Zayas, 159 Ill. App. 3d 554, 110 Ill. Dec. 94, 510 N.E.2d 1125 (1987).
3. People v. Wilson, 116 Ill. 2d 29, 506 N.E.2d 571 (1987).
4. People v. Duckett, 133 Ill. App. 3d 639, 88 Ill. Dec. 742, 479 N.E.2d 355 (1985).
5. People v. Cohoon, 104 Ill. 2d 295, 84 Ill. Dec. 443, 472 N.E.2d 403 (1984).
6. People v. Jordan, 120 Ill. App. 3d 836, 76 Ill. Dec. 461, 458 N.E.2d 1115 (1983).
7. People v. Cohoon, 120 Ill. App. 3d 62, 75 Ill. Dec. 556, 457 N.E.2d 998 (1983).
8. People v. Byas, 117 Ill. App. 3d 979, 73 Ill. Dec. 152, 453 N.E.2d 1141 (1983).
9. People v. Gibson, 117 Ill. App. 3d 270, 72 Ill. Dec. 672, 452 N.E.2d 1368 (1983).
10. People v. Renslow, 98 Ill. App. 3d 288, 53 Ill. Dec. 556, 423 N.E.2d 1360 (1981).
11. People v. Kempinski, No. W8OCF 352 (Cir. Ct., 12th Dist., Will County, October 21, 1980) (unreported).
12. People v. Kester, 78 Ill. App. 3d 902, 34 Ill. Dec. 216, 397 N.E.2d 888 (1979).
13. People v. Smrekar, 68 Ill. App. 3d 379, 24 Ill. Dec. 707, 385 N.E.2d 848 (1979).
14. People v. Harper, 111 Ill. App. 2d 204, 250 N.E.2d 5 (1969).

Indiana

From 1980 to 1989, the Indiana Supreme Court discussed investigative hypnosis issues in 21 different cases. The first four times the issues were raised, the court declined to make a general ruling because defense counsel in each case had failed to object properly at trial or had failed to preserve the issue properly on appeal. Eventually, however, the court was able to develop an approach to the admissibility of hypnotically refreshed recollection.

In *Strong v. State* (1982), a composite drawing was developed from information obtained while a witness was in trance. The court held that this drawing was inadmissible: "[E]vidence derived from a witness while he is under hypnosis is inherently unreliable and must be excluded as having no probative value" (p. 970). The court has made it clear, however, that the fact that a witness has been hypnotized will not automatically disqualify that witness from testifying. In *Strong*, the court permitted an in-court identification of the defendant to stand, even though the witness had previously been hypnotized, because there was clear and convincing evidence that the identification had a factual basis independent of the hypnosis session.

One independent factual basis recognized by the Indiana Supreme Court was addressed in *Pearson v. State* (1982), where the court held that a previously hypnotized witness could testify posthypnotically as to what he or she was able to recall before hypnosis. *Pearson* also held that even if posthypnotic testimony is erroneously admitted, reversal is not necessary if the testimony does not present a significant alteration of prehypnotic recollection and if the jury has been presented with sufficient facts to judge the reliability of the witness's prehypnotic recall.

Later Supreme Court opinions have been consistent in following these rules.

1. Daniels v. State, 528 N.E.2d 775 (1988).
2. Pittman v. State, 528 N.E.2d 67 (1988).
3. Taylor v. State, 515 N.E.2d 1095 (1987).
4. Peterson v. State, 514 N.E.2d 265 (1987).
5. Stephens v. State, 506 N.E.2d 12 (1987).
6. Rowley v. State, 483 N.E.2d 1078 (1985).
7. Johnson v. State, 472 N.E.2d 892 (1985).
8. Gentry v. State, 471 N.E.2d 263 (1984).
9. Drake v. State, 467 N.E.2d 686 (1984).
10. King v. State, 460 N.E.2d 947 (1984).
11. Newton v. State, 456 N.E.2d 736 (Ind. App. 2nd Dist. 1983).
12. Peterson v. State, 448 N.E.2d 673 (1983).
13. Clark v. State, 447 N.E.2d 1076 (1983).
14. Morgan v. State, 445 N.E.2d 585 (Ind. App. 2nd Dist. 1983).
15. Stewart v. State, 442 N.E.2d 1026 (1982).
16. Pearson v. State, 441 N.E.2d 468 (1982).
17. Forrester v. State, 440 N.E.2d 475 (1982).
18. Goodwin v. State, 439 N.E.2d 595 (1982).
19. Strong v. State, 435 N.E.2d 969 (1982).
20. Alleyn v. State, 427 N.E.2d 1095 (1981).
21. Riley v. State, 427 N.E.2d 1074 (1981).
22. Pavone v. State, 273 Ind. 162, 402 N.E.2d 976 (1980).
23. Merrifield v. State, 272 Ind. 479, 400 N.E.2d 146 (1980).
24. Parks v. State, 159 Ind. 211, 63 N.E. 862 (1902).

Iowa

Hypnotically refreshed recollection was held to be admissible by the Iowa Supreme Court in *State v. Seager* (1983), but the court noted that the testimony was in complete accord with the witnesses' prehypnotic recollection.

One year later the court, in *State v. Greiman* (1984), upheld the exclusion of a hypnotist's testimony about the defendant's state of mind at the time of the crime, based on the defendant's statements in trance. Later in 1984, in *State v. Groscost*, the Supreme Court again declined to disqualify a witness who had been hypnotized, but noted that her testimony was "substantially in conformance" with her prehypnotic recollection.

No cases since 1984 have addressed the issue still not conclusively decided: Will a witness whose posthypnotic recollection differs from his or her prehypnotic recall be permitted to testify? Iowa is likely to decline to adopt a per se exclusion rule based on the language of its 1983 *Seager* decision.

1. State v.Groscost, 355 N.W.2d 32 (1984).
2. State v. Greiman, 344 N.W.2d 249 (1984).
3. State v. Seager, 341 N.W.2d 420 (1983).
4. State v. Thompson, 326 N.W.2d 335 (1982).
5. Lawson v. State, 280 N.W.2d 400 (1979).
6. State v. Donovan, 128 Iowa 44, 102 N.W. 791 (1905).

Kansas

The Kansas Supreme Court adopted a per se exclusion rule in *State v. Haislip* (1985), but also held that prehypnotic recollection was admissible.

1. Haislip v. Kansas, 1989 W.L. 13126 (Kan. App. 1989).
2. In the Interest of L. C., 758 P.2d 753 (Kan. App. 1988) (Table), (Unpublished Disposition).
3. State v. Haislip, 237 Kan. 461, 701 P.2d 909 (1985), *cert. denied*, Kansas v. Haislip, 474 U.S. 1022, 106 S. Ct. 575, 88 L.Ed.2d 558 (1985).
4. State v. Conley, 6 Kan. App. 2d 280, 627 P.2d 1174 (1981).

Kentucky

There are no definitive cases on point in Kentucky. The only case concerning hypnosis issues involved the interesting issue of police use of hypnosis on a victim who later turned out to be the accused. Unfortunately, the court did not discuss the hypnosis issue and decided the case on other grounds.

1. Pruitt v. Commonwealth, 700 S.W.2d 68 (Ky. 1985).

Louisiana

A civil case (*Watson v. Morrison*, 1976) provided the Louisiana Court of Appeal with an opportunity to rule that a psychiatrist could not testify as to events recalled under hypnosis by a motorist who had no prehypnotic recall of the automobile accident. This testimony was considered to be inadmissible hearsay.

The first criminal case to discuss hypnosis (*State v. Culpepper*, 1982) concluded that hypnotically refreshed recollection is inherently unreliable and therefore inadmissible. The facts of the case clearly demonstrated a failure to meet the safeguards articulated in other states, including the fact that the police officer who conducted the hypnosis was minimally trained and had participated in the investigation of the case.

When the Louisiana Supreme Court addressed the issue in *State v. Wren* (1983), it held that hypnosis did not disqualify a witness whose prehypnosis statements were identical to his or her posthypnotic statements. The Court declined to rule on the issue of "hypnotically-*induced* testimony." Louisiana courts have not yet definitively ruled on this issue, but seem to have a positive attitude toward hypnotically refreshed recollection, provided there is no showing of undue suggestiveness.

In *State v. Porretto* (1985), an unusual twist arose. The victim had given a prehypnotic description of her assailant, but had changed some details under hypnosis. When the defendant asked for any exculpatory evidence, the prosecutors, who did not know of the hypnosis, failed to inform the defendant of the discrepancies. The new details remembered in trance were favorable to the defendant's claim that he had been mistakenly identified as the culprit. The defendant wanted the hypnotically refreshed recollection of the victim admitted to support his claim. He argued that the failure to inform him of the existence of this testimony was reversible error.

The Supreme Court rejected the defendant's position, claiming that the new details were quite minor and that other evidence pointed to his guilt. The court had no difficulty with the victim's posthypnosis out-of-court identification of the defendant. It believed that the hypnosis did not influence her identification.

In *State v. Woodfin* (1989), the Court of Appeal noted that while *Rock* precluded automatic rejection of a defendant's hypnotically refreshed testimony, it did not require automatic admission of it. Such testimony is admissible only if the Orne guidelines adopted in *State v. Hurd* (N.J. 1981) can be satisfied. If the testimony is admitted, the jury should be given a cautionary instruction about the potential dangers of hypnosis as a memory refresher.

1. State v. Woodfin, 1989 W.L. 4345 (La. App., 2nd Cir. 1989).
2. State v. Below, Nos. K88990 & K88977 (La. App., 3rd Cir. 1988), writ denied, 534 So. 2d 445 (1988) [discussed in *State v. Woodfin* (1989)].
3. State v. White, 498 So. 2d 1100 (La. App., 3rd Cir. 1986).
4. State v. Porretto, 468 So. 2d 1142 (1985).
5. State v. Segura, 464 So. 2d 1116 (La. App., 3rd Cir. 1985).

6. State v. Williams, 458 So. 2d 1315 (La. App., 1st Cir. 1984).

7. State v. Rault, 445 So. 2d 1203 (1984).

8. State v. Goutro, 444 So. 2d 615 (1984).

9. Landry v. Garrett, 443 So. 2d 1139 (La. App., 4th Cir. 1983).

10. Landry v. Garrett, 434 So. 2d 1103 and 1105 (1983).

11. State v. Moore, 432 So. 2d 209 (1983), *cert. denied*, Moore v. Louisiana, 464 U.S. 986, 104 S. Ct. 435, 78 L.Ed.2d 367 (1983).

12. Landry v. Garrett, 430 So. 2d 1051 (La. App., 4th Cir. 1983).

13. State v. Wren, 425 So. 2d 756 (1983).

14. State v. Culpepper, 434 So. 2d 76 (La. App., 5th Cir. 1982).

15. Watson v. Morrison, 340 So. 2d 588 (La. App. 4th Cir. 1976).

Maine

The Maine Supreme Judicial Court has decided two cases involving hypnosis issues, but only one paragraph of one opinion *(State v. Commeau)* sheds any light on forensic issues, and the light it sheds is dim indeed. Under the facts of the case there was no undue suggestion, so the court chose not to discuss the admissibility of hypnotically refreshed recollection. There are no definitive rulings on investigative hypnosis and no hints as to what direction the court is likely to take.

1. Johnson v. Gerrish, 518 A.2d 721 (1986).

2. State v. Commeau, 438 A.2d 454 (1981).

Maryland

In *Harding v. State* (1968), the Maryland Court of Special Appeals inaugurated the whole era of the admissibility of hypnotically refreshed recollection by adopting an open admissibility rule.

Fourteen years later, the same court all but closed the door by specifically overruling *Harding* and in its place adopting a per se exclusion rule *(Collins v. State,* 1982). The court did permit, however, the admission of prehypnotic recall.

One year later, in *State v. Collins* (1983), the Maryland Court of Appeals issued a major, extensively researched opinion that reached the same result as the Court of Special Appeals had a year earlier: Hypnotically refreshed recollection fails to meet the *Frye* "general acceptance" standard of reliability, but witnesses will be permitted to testify as to their prehypnotic recall.

1. Herbert v. Whittle, 69 Md. App. 273, 517 A.2d 358 (1986).

2. State v. Calhoun, 306 Md. 692, 511 A.2d 461 (1986).

3. McCoy v. State, 301 Md. 666, 484 A.2d 624 (1984).

4. Calhoun v. State, 297 Md. 563, 468 A.2d 45 (1983).

5. Hughes v. State, 56 Md. App. 12, 466 A.2d 533 (Md. App. 1983).
6. State v. Metscher, 297 Md. 368, 464 A.2d 1052 (1983).
7. State v. McCoy, 297 Md. 5, 464 A.2d 1067 (1983).
8. Grimes v. State, 297 Md. 1, 464 A.2d 1065 (1983).
9. Simkus v. State, 296 Md. 718, 464 A.2d 1055 (1983).
10. State v. Collins, 296 Md. 670, 464 A.2d 1028 (1983).
11. Harker v. State, 55 Md. App. 460, 463 A.2d 288 (1983), *cert. denied*, 297 Md. 312 (1983).
12. Norwood v. State, 55 Md. App. 503, 462 A.2d 93 (1983).
13. Collins v. State, 52 Md. App. 186, 447 A.2d 1272 (1982).
14. Polk v. State, 48 Md. App. 382, 427 A.2d 1042 (1981), *cert. denied*, 290 Md. 719 (1981).
15. State v. Temoney, 45 Md. App. 569, 414 A.2d 240 (1980), *rev'd on other grounds*, 290 Md. 251, 429 A.2d 1018 (1981).
16. Chaney v. State, 42 Md. App. 563, 402 A.2d 86 (1979).
17. Harding v. State, 5 Md. App. 230, 246 A.2d 302 (1968), *cert. denied*, Harding v. Maryland, 395 U.S. 949, 89 S. Ct. 2030, 23 L.Ed.2d 468 (1969).

Massachusetts

The Massachusetts Supreme Judicial Court first ruled in three cases in 1983 (*Commonwealth v. Kater; Commonwealth v. Watson; Commonwealth v. Brouillet*) that hypnotically refreshed recollection is inadmissible. Prehypnotic recollection is admissible, provided certain safeguards have been met. The person seeking to introduce prehypnotic testimony must show that the testimony is uninfluenced by the hypnosis.

1. Commonwealth v. Cifizzari, 397 Mass. 560, 492 N.E.2d 357 (1986).
2. Commonwealth v. McDonald, 21 Mass. App. 368, 487 N.E.2d 224 (1986).
3. Commonwealth v. Burke, 20 Mass. App. 489, 481 N.E.2d 494 (1985).
4. Commonwealth v. Leaster, 395 Mass. 96, 479 N.E.2d 124 (1985).
5. Commonwealth v. Kater, 394 Mass. 531, 476 N.E.2d 593 (1985).
6. Commonwealth v. Dodge, 391 Mass. 636, 462 N.E.2d 1363 (1984).
7. Commonwealth v. Paszlko, 391 Mass. 164, 461 N.E.2d 222 (1984).
8. Commonwealth v. Brouillet, 389 Mass. 605, 451 N.E.2d 128 (1983).
9. Commonwealth v. Watson, 388 Mass. 536, 447 N.E.2d 1182 (1983).
10. Commonwealth v. Kater, 388 Mass. 519, 447 N.E.2d 1190 (1983).
11. Commonwealth v. Stetson, 384 Mass. 545, 427 N.E.2d 926 (1981).
12. Commonwealth v. A Juvenile, 381 Mass. 727, 412 N.E.2d 339 (1980).
13. Commonwealth v. Jewelle, 199 Mass. 558, 85 N.E. 858 (1908).

Michigan

Michigan courts first met hypnosis issues in *People v. Hangsleben* (1978), when the Court of Appeals was asked by the defendant to rule (1) that he could have a psychiatrist testify as to what he had said in trance and (2) that he could have an attorney refer to the hypnosis sessions in opening argument to the jury. The defendant lost both points.

Two years later, in *People v. Tait* (1980), the Court of Appeals was again asked to rule on the use of hypnosis, but this time it was the state seeking admissibility. The prosecuting attorney, an amateur hypnotist, had conducted the hypnosis sessions and did not tell the defense about them. The court held that this constituted prosecutorial misconduct, requiring that the case be reversed and the witness be disqualified from testifying at retrial.

By 1982 the Michigan Supreme Court was prepared to rule that hypnotically refreshed recollection was inadmissible per se. Four months later, the court amended its opinion to specify that it was leaving open the question of the admissibility of prehypnotic recall. In 1984, not surprisingly, the Supreme Court in *People v. Nixon* held such prehypnotic testimony admissible. Safeguards to record and preserve the recollection were deemed advisable.

In December 1987, the Michigan Supreme Court granted an order for an appeal in the *People v. Lee* case on the issue of the admissibility of hypnotically refreshed recollection. It is possible that the court is planning a major examination of this question. No decision has yet been issued.

1. People v. Lee, 429 Mich. 885, 416 N.W.2d 312 (1987).
2. People v. Rosengren, 407 N.W.2d 391 (Mich. App. 1987).
3. People v. Sorscher, 151 Mich. App. 122, 391 N.W.2d 365 (1986).
4. People v. Reese, 149 Mich. App. 53, 385 N.W.2d 722 (1986).
5. People v. Gonzales, 424 Mich. 908, 385 N.W.2d 585 (1986).
6. People v. Perry, 144 Mich. App. 420, 375 N.W.2d 10 (1985).
7. People v. Wallach, 143 Mich. App. 537, 372 N.W.2d 609 (1985).
8. People v. McIntosh, 142 Mich. App. 314, 370 N.W.2d 337 (1985).
9. People v. Centers, 141 Mich. App. 364, 367 N.W.2d 397 (1985).
10. People v. Nixon, 421 Mich. 79, 364 N.W.2d 593 (1984).
11. People v. Simonds, 135 Mich. App. 214, 353 N.W.2d 483 (1984).
12. People v. Wallach, 131 Mich. App. 539, 345 N.W.2d 607 (1984).
13. People v. Perry, 126 Mich. App. 86, 337 N.W.2d 324 (1983).
14. People v. Nixon, 125 Mich. App. 807, 337 N.W.2d 33 (1983).
15. People v. Gonzales, 417 Mich. 1129, 336 N.W.2d 751 (1983).
16. People v. Gonzales, 415 Mich. 615, 329 N.W.2d 743 (1982).
17. People v. Jackson, 114 Mich. App. 649, 319 N.W.2d 613 (1982).
18. People v. Nixon, 114 Mich. App. 233, 318 N.W.2d 655 (1982).
19. People v. Wallach, 110 Mich. App. 37, 312 N.W.2d 387 (1981).
20. People v. Gonzales, 108 Mich. App. 145, 310 N.W.2d 306 (1981).
21. People v. Tait, 99 Mich. App. 19, 297 N.W.2d 853 (1980).
22. People v. Hangsleben, 86 Mich. App. 718, 273 N.W.2d 539 (1978).

Minnesota

In 1980 the Minnesota Supreme Court issued the highly influential *State v. Mack* decision, which was the first major state supreme court opinion to articulate a per se exclusion rule. As of 1984, the last year in which hypnosis issues were addressed by the appellate courts, the exclusion rule remains in force.

1. State v. Ture, 353 N.W.2d 502, 45 A.L.R. 4th 575 (1984).
2. Rodriguez v. State, 345 N.W.2d 781 (Minn. App. 1984).
3. Matter of J.R.D., 342 N.W.2d 162 (Minn. App. 1984).
4. State v. Blanchard, 315 N.W.2d 427 (1982).
5. State v. Koehler, 312 N.W.2d 108 (1981).
6. State v. Mack, 292 N.W.2d 764 (1980).

Mississippi

A 1984 Mississippi Supreme Court ruling *(House v. State)* held that (1) a hypnotist may not testify as to facts related by a victim during hypnosis and (2) the hypnotized victim can testify only if safeguards had been met.

In *Nixon v. State* (1987) the Supreme Court returned to the issue of hypnotically refreshed recollection in a case involving a witness who had undergone "a state of relaxation" to recall a license plate number. She was unable to recall it. At trial, she claimed she was not influenced by the hypnosis. The court noted that in *House* it had approved a safeguards approach, but held that under the facts of the present case the hypnosis did not work, and thus there had been no hypnotically refreshed recollection.

1. Nixon v. State, 1987 W.L. 2104 (1987).
2. House v. State, 445 S. 2d 815 (1984).

Missouri

In 1981, in *State v. Greer*, the Missouri Court of Appeals permitted hypnotically refreshed recollection in any case where the hypnosis was not "impermissibly suggestive."

The Missouri Supreme Court initially declined to rule on the issue in a 1984 criminal case *(State v. Little)*, but did rule in a 1985 civil case *(Alsbach v. Bader)* by adopting a per se exclusion rule. Noting that most of the early cases supporting an open admissibility rule have subsequently been overruled, the Supreme Court rejected the *Greer* approach. The court also rejected the safeguards approach because

> such safeguards do not adequately address how a lay person, such as a trial judge or juror, will recognize when the hypnotized subject has lost

his critical judgment and begun to credit "memories" that were formerly viewed as unreliable. Nor do safeguards provide a means for distinguishing between actual recall and confabulation invented and employed to fill gaps in the story. (p. 827)

The Supreme Court concluded that hypnotically refreshed recollection did not meet the *Frye* test of reliability and accuracy.

1. Howard v. Kysor Indus. Corp., 729 S.W.2d 603 (Mo. Ct. App. 1987).
2. State v. Reasonover, 714 S.W.2d 706 (Mo. Ct. App. 1986).
3. Alsbach v. Bader, 700 S.W.2d 823 (1985).
4. State v. Conley, 698 S.W.2d 542 (Mo. Ct. App. 1985).
5. State v. Barteau, 687 S.W.2d 573 (Mo. Ct. App. 1985).
6. State v. Byrd, 676 S.W.2d 494 (1984).
7. State v. Little, 674 S.W.2d 541 (1984).
8. State v. Williams, 662 S.W.2d 277 (Mo. Ct. App. 1983).
9. State v. Woods, 639 S.W.2d 818 (1982).
10. State v. Greer, 609 S.W.2d 423 (Mo. Ct. App. 1980), *vacated on other grounds,* Missouri v. Greer, 450 U.S. 1027, 101 S. Ct. 1735, 68 L.Ed.2d 222 (1981).
11. State v. Walker, 416 S.W.2d 134 (1967).

Montana

Montana appellate courts have addressed hypnosis issues only twice. In both cases the Montana Supreme Court was faced with unusual fact patterns that did not raise the basic questions of hypnotically refreshed recollection. In *State v. Green* (1984), the defendant was accused of grabbing boys in a park and hypnotizing them. His conviction was upheld. In *In re Raynes* (1984), a police officer with a private hypnosis business was accused of using hypnosis to abuse his clients sexually. His permanent discharge from the police force was upheld. These cases do not afford a basis for an informed prediction about how the Montana courts might rule on investigative hypnosis issues.

1. Matter of Raynes, 698 P.2d 856 (1985).
2. State v. Green, 685 P.2d 370 (1984).

Nebraska

The Nebraska Supreme Court in *State v. Palmer* (1981) adopted a per se exclusion rule, but left open the question of the admissibility of prehypnotic recall. According to the court,

[T]o require the admissibility of hypnotically induced testimony to be determined on a case-by-case basis based on the testimony of expert witnesses produced by the parties . . . is neither sound nor practical. To compare the "recollections" of a witness whose testimony has been hypnotically induced to the "recollections" of an "ordinary" witness, and to determine whether the use of hypnosis was a feasibly reliable means of restoring memory comparable to normal recall in its accuracy, is virtually impossible. (p. 654)

In 1983 the Supreme Court returned to the prehypnotic recall admissibility issue in *State v. Patterson* and held such testimony to be admissible. The court noted that

[T]he question is not whether evidence previously unknown and adduced by reason of hypnosis is admissible but, rather, whether evidence obtained without the benefit of hypnosis and clearly admissible becomes inadmissible simply by reason of the fact that, after relating the facts to a number of witnesses, the facts are once again related to one who purports to be able to hypnotize the witness. (p. 503)

The Supreme Court reaffirmed its position in the 1986 *State v. Palmer* case.

1. State v. Palmer, 224 Neb. 282, 399 N.W.2d 706 (1986).
2. State v. Brown, 214 Neb. 665, 335 N.W.2d 542 (1983).
3. Appeal of Levos, 214 Neb. 507, 335 N.W.2d 262 (1983).
4. State v. Levering, 213 Neb. 686, 331 N.W.2d 505 (1983).
5. State v. Patterson, 213 Neb. 686, 331 N.W.2d 500 (1983).
6. *In re* Estate of McCartney, 213 Neb. 550, 330 N.W.2d 723 (1983).
7. State v. Palmer, 210 Neb. 206, 313 N.W.2d 648 (1981).
8. Dill v. Hamilton, 137 Neb. 723, 291 N.W. 62 (1940).

Nevada

No appellate cases on hypnosis have been found.

New Hampshire

No appellate cases on hypnosis have been found.

New Jersey

In 1980 and 1981, the New Jersey Superior Court and then the Supreme Court decided the *State v. Hurd* case by adopting an approach of admissibility if safeguards were met. A full discussion of *Hurd* may be found in Chapter Four. New Jersey appellate courts have not addressed hypnosis issues since 1981.

1. State v. Hurd, 86 N.J. 525, 432 A.2d 86 (1981).
2. State v. Hurd, 173 N.J. Super. Ct. 333, 414 A.2d 291 (1980).
3. State v. Levitt, 36 N.J. 266, 176 A.2d 465 (1961).

New Mexico

The New Mexico Court of Appeal in the 1981 *State v. Beachum* case, adopted the safeguards approach pioneered by the New Jersey *Hurd* case. The Court stated that the crucial issue was whether hypnosis was reasonably reliable not in eliciting truth, but rather in refreshing a witness's memory. The rule accepted by the court

> is that testimony of pre-hypnotic recollections is admissible in the sound discretion of the trial court, but post-hypnotic recollections, revived by the hypnosis procedure, are only admissible in a trial where a proper foundation has also first established the expertise of the hypnotist and that the techniques employed were correctly performed, free from bias or improper suggestibility. (p. 252)

Two years later, the New Mexico Supreme Court acknowledged the *Beachum* holding without officially endorsing it. The court stated that the *Beachum* rule did not apply because the trance produced no change in testimony.

In *State v. Clark* (1986), the Court of Appeal had another opportunity to discuss hypnosis in a case involving a hypnotist who was a private investigator and polygrapher. The hypnosis was performed on a 6-year-old girl who resisted the procedure. The hypnotist had never used hypnosis on a child and had never performed hypnosis in a forensic setting. During the session, as investigators working on the case watched, the hypnotist told the child that she should "let herself go" and help the police "catch the guy" who had molested her. She was also told that she would remember "more and more."

The Court of Appeal held that the hypnosis was inept and ineffective, but did not affect the child's testimony. The court concluded,

> [W]e express deep concern about law enforcement's use of nonprofessional hypnotists and condemn the failure to adhere to basic safeguards, whether or not required for evidentiary purposes. Our concern is not only for possible evidentiary taint, but also for the physical and mental well-being of the hypnotized subject. (p. 690)

1. State v. Clark, 104 N.M. 434, 722 P.2d 685 (Ct. App. 1986).
2. State v. Hutchinson, 99 N.M. 616, 661 P.2d 1315 (1983).
3. State v. Beachum, 97 N.M. 682, 643 P.2d 246 (Ct. App. 1981), *writ quashed*, 98 N.M. 51, 644 P.2d 1040 (1982).
4. State v. Turner, 81 N.M. 571, 469 P.2d 720 (Ct. App. 1970).

5. State v. Turner, 81 N.M. 450, 468 P.2d 421 (Ct. App. 1970), *cert. denied*, 81 N.M. 506, 469 P.2d 151 (1970).

New York

New York courts have been deciding hypnosis issues for more than 80 years. Only California has a longer history and a greater number of appellate decisions. Despite this longevity, it was not until the 1983 *People v. Hughes* case that the Court of Appeals, New York's highest judicial tribunal, first addressed and finally resolved some questions about investigative hypnosis. The court identified three problems with hypnotically refreshed recollection: (1) The witness may become susceptible to intentional or unintentional suggestion; (2) the witness may confabulate or intentionally fabricate incidents to fill in memory gaps or to please the hypnotist; and (3) the witness's memories may "harden" or "concretize," or the witness may experience an "artificially enhanced confidence" in them, all of which may substantially impair the ability to cross-examine the witness.

Based on these problems, the court stated in *Hughes* that the scope of the witness's prehypnotic recollection establishes the boundaries of admissible testimony. According to the court, pretrial proceedings should explore the extent of the prehypnotic memories and whether the hypnosis "was so impermissibly suggestive as to require exclusion of in-court testimony with respect to such prehypnotic recollection" (p. 267). The prosecution must establish by clear and convincing evidence that the prehypnotic recall is reliable and that there has been no substantial impairment of the defendant's right of cross-examination.

One year later, the defendant in *People v. Tunstall* (1984) asked the Court of Appeals to prevent the introduction of the victim's prehypnotic recall, which was identical to her posthypnotic recollection, because the hypnosis added extra confidence to her testimony. The hypnotist had suggested explicit details and had told the victim that when the trance ended she would remember everything. The court was clearly troubled by the hypnotist's conduct and sent the case back for a hearing on the "boosted confidence" point. At that hearing, the judge was instructed to

> take into consideration the amount of confidence the witness had in her initial recollections prior to being hypnotized, the extent of her belief in the ability of hypnosis to yield the truth, the degree to which she was hypnotized, the length of the session, the type and nature of questioning employed, the effectiveness of the hypnosis in yielding additional details, and any other factors which the court may deem important based upon the specific facts and circumstances of the case. (p. 34)

This hearing ultimately concluded that the defendant's ability to cross-examine was not substantially impaired (*People v. Tunstall*, 1986; *People v. Chamberlin*, 1988).

1. People v. Hughes, 72 N.Y. 2d 1035, 534 N.Y.S.2d 931, 531 N.E. 2d 652 (1988).
2. People v. Chamberlin, 140 A.D.2d 364, 527 N.Y.S.2d 851 (1988).
3. People v. Hughes, 134 A.D.2d 939, 521 N.Y.S.2d 945 (1987).
4. People v. York, 133 A.D.2d 130, 518 N.Y.S.2d 665 (1987).
5. People v. York, 126 A.D.2d 767, 511 N.Y.S.2d 345 (1987).
6. People v. Rhoades, 126 A.D.2d 774, 510 N.Y.S.2d 718 (1987).
7. People v. Tunstall, 133 Misc. 2d 640, 509 N.Y.S.2d 701 (1986).
8. People v. Hults, 122 A.D.2d 857, 505 N.Y.S.2d 723 (1986).
9. People v. Eybergen, 130 Misc. 2d 1, 494 N.Y.S.2d 803 (1985).
10. People v. Smith, 63 N.Y.2d 41, 468 N.E.2d 879, 479 N.Y.S.2d 706 (1984), *cert. denied*, New York v. Smith, 469 U.S. 1227, 105 S. Ct. 1226, 84 L.Ed.2d 364 (1985), *reh. denied*, New York v. Smith, 471 U.S. 1049, 105 S.Ct. 2042, 85 L.Ed.2d 340 (1985).
11. People v. Tunstall, 63 N.Y.2d 1, 468 N.E.2d 30, 479 N.Y.S.2d 192 (1984).
12. People v. Barnes, 123 Misc. 2d 142, 472 N.Y.S.2d 1017 (1984).
13. People v. Douglas, 23 Misc. 2d 75, 472 N.Y.S.2d 815 (1984).
14. People v. Tunstall, 97 A.D.2d 253, 468 N.Y.S.2d 32 (1983).
15. People v. Perrino, 96 A.D.2d 952, 466 N.Y.S.2d 408 (1983).
16. People v. Hughes, 59 N.Y.2d 523, 453 N.E.2d 484, 466 N.Y.S.2d 255 (1983).
17. People v. McAfee, 95 A.D.2d 898, 463 N.Y.S.2d 916 (1983).
18. People v. Porter, 93 A.D.2d 943, 463 N.Y.S.2d 65 (1983).
19. People v. Boudin, 118 Misc. 2d 230, 460 N.Y.S.2d 879 (1983).
20. People v. Smith, 117 Misc. 2d 737, 459 N.Y.S.2d 528 (1983).
21. People v. Hughes, 88 A.D.2d 17, 452 N.Y.S.2d 929 (1982).
22. People v. Smith, 114 Misc. 2d 258, 451 N.Y.S.2d 549 (1982).
23. People v. Fisher, 53 N.Y.2d 907, 423 N.E.2d 53, 440 N.Y.S.2d 630 (1981).
24. People v. Lucas, 107 Misc. 2d 231, 435 N.Y.S.2d 461 (1980).
25. People v. McDowell, 103 Misc. 2d 831, 427 N.Y.S.2d 181 (1980).
26. People v. Lewis, 103 Misc. 2d 881, 427 N.Y.S.2d 177 (1980).
27. People v. Fisher, 73 A.D.2d 886, 424 N.Y.S.2d 197 (1980).
28. People v. Hughes, 99 Misc. 2d 863, 417 N.Y.S.2d 643 (1979), *aff'd.*, 59 N.Y.2d 523, 466 N.Y.S.2d 255, 453 N.E.2d 484 (1983).
29. Bakal v. N.Y. Tel. Co., 97 Misc. 2d 540, 411 N.Y.S.2d 859 (1978).
30. Hird v. Gen. Motors Corp., 61 A.D.2d 832, 402 N.Y.S.2d 429 (1978).
31. People by Lefkowitz v. Therapeutic Hypnosis, 83 Misc. 2d 1068, 374 N.Y.S.2d 576 (1975).
32. People v. Baldi, 80 Misc. 2d 118, 362 N.Y.S.2d 927 (1974).
33. People v. Leyra, 302 N.Y. App. 353, 98 N.E.2d 553 (1951).
34. Austin v. Barker, 110 A.D. 510, 96 N.Y.S. 814 (1906).
35. Austin v. Barker, 90 A.D. 351, 85 N.Y.S. 465 (1904).

North Carolina

In *State v. McQueen* (1978), the North Carolina Supreme Court held that hypnotically refreshed recollection is admissible. The court followed the "open-admissibility" approach then prevalent.

By 1984 the trend had dramatically shifted away from an approach based on "credibility, not admissibility," and toward a per se exclusion rule. In *State v. Peoples* (1984), the Supreme Court overruled its earlier decision and embraced the exclusion of hypnotically refreshed recollection. An exception was made, however, for prehypnotic memory; this was held to be admissible, provided that some record of this recollection was available and provided that the safeguards adopted in the New Jersey *Hurd* case were followed.

A 1985 Supreme Court opinion *(State v. Payne)* followed this approach, but declined to reverse the defendant's conviction in a case where the witness's testimony should have been excluded. The court reasoned that because other evidence clearly demonstrated the defendant's guilt, and the erroneously admitted testimony did not add information not already presented in the testimony of other witnesses, the failure to exclude the hypnotically refreshed recollection was harmless error.

 1. Morris v. Bruney, 78 N.C. App. 668 338 S.E.2d 561, 57 A.L.R. 4th 393 (1986).
 2. State v. Payne, 312 N.C. 647, 325 S.E.2d 205 (1985).
 3. State v. Flack, 312 N.C. 448, 322 S.E.2d 758 (1984).
 4. State v. Bullard, 312 N.C. 129, 322 S.E.2d 370 (1984).
 5. State v. Peoples, 311 N.C. 515, 319 S.E.2d 177 (1984).
 6. State v. Jean, 310 N.C. 157, 311 S.E.2d 266 (1984).
 7. State v. Hunt, 309 N.C. 824, 310 S.E.2d 354 (1983).
 8. State v. Hunt, 64 N.C. App. 81, 306 S.E.2d 846 (1983).
 9. State v. Waters, 308 N.C. 348, 302 S.E.2d 188 (1983).
10. State v. Peoples, 60 N.C. App. 479, 299 S.E.2d 311 (1983), *rev'd on other grounds,* 311 N.C. 515, 319 S.E.2d 177 (1984).
11. State v. Flack, 305 N.C. 588, 292 S.E.2d 8 (1982).
12. State v. McQueen, 295 N.C. 96, 244 S.E.2d 414 (1978).
13. State v. Exum, 138 N.C. 599, 50 S.E. 283 (1905).

North Dakota

A very thorough review of the major issues and viewpoints in the forensic hypnosis debate was conducted by the North Dakota Supreme Court in *State v. Brown* (1983). The court decided to adopt the distinctly minority viewpoint permitting hypnotically refreshed recollection to be admitted even in the absence of guidelines. The court justified its holding by noting that in the circumstances of the case before it, many of the safeguards adopted by other jurisdictions were in fact followed.

North Dakota is one of only a handful of states declining to adopt even minimal safeguards. It is possible, however, that the Supreme Court would decline to admit hypnotically refreshed recollection if the facts of a case demonstrated that indeed few, if any, safeguards had been met.

1. State v. Brown, 337 N.W.2d 138 (1983).
2. State v. Pusch, 77 N.D. 860, 46 N.W.2d 508 (1950).

Ohio

A 1984 Ohio Court of Appeals ruling *(State v. Weston)* held hypnotically refreshed recollection to be admissible if the *Hurd* safeguards are met. A more elaborate set of rules was adopted by the Ohio Supreme Court in *Johnston* (1988).

First, the judges allowed a witness to testify about matters recalled *prior* to hypnosis even though the only record of his memory before hypnosis was some "non-verbatim, handwritten notes by the interviewing officer" (p. 903) which were not signed or initialed by the witness at the time. The Supreme Court did signal a warning, however, that insufficient documentation of the prehypnosis memory of a witness may result in exclusion of the testimony.

Second, *post*hypnotic testimony is admissible on a case by case basis. The trial should conduct a pretrial hearing to determine if the posthypnotic testimony is sufficiently reliable under the totality of the circumstances to merit admission. Trial judges were instructed that the Orne guidelines "should be considered prerequisites to admissibility" (p. 906).

1. State v. Wells, 1989 W.L. 3962 (Ohio App. 1989).
2. State v. Johnston, 39 Ohio St. 3d 48, 529 N.E.2d 898 (1988).
3. State v. Cohen, 1988 W.L. 41545 (April 29, 1988).
4. State v. Maurer, 1988 W.L. 38529 (April 25, 1988).
5. State v. Maurer, 15 Ohio St. 3d 239, 15 Ohio B. Rep. 379, 473 N.E.2d 768 (1984).
6. State v. Weston, 16 Ohio App. 3d 279, 475 N.E.2d 805, 16 Ohio B. Rep. 309 (1984).
7. State v. Papp, 64 Ohio App. 2d 203, 412 N.E.2d 401, 18 Ohio Op. 3d 157 (1978), *cert. denied,* 444 U.S. 886 (1979).
8. State v. Smith, 49 Ohio App. 2d 388, 361 N.E.2d 267, 3 Ohio Op. 3d 454 (1976).
9. State *ex rel.* Sheppard v. Koblentz, 174 Ohio St. 120, 187 N.E.2d 40, 21 Ohio Op. 2d 384 (1962), *cert. denied,* Ohio *ex rel.* Sheppard v. Koblentz, 373 U.S. 911 (1963).
10. Cantrell v. Maxwell, 174 Ohio 51, 186 N.E.2d 621, 21 Ohio Op. 2d 297 (1962).
11. State v. Nebb, No. 39,540, Ohio C.P. Franklin County (May 20, 1962).

Oklahoma

The Oklahoma Court of Criminal Appeals in the *Robinson v. State* (1984) case adopted a per se exclusion rule. The court also held that a witness may not make an in-court identification of the defendant following hypnosis if no identification was made prior to hypnosis. The court did not hold that a witness who has been hypnotized is totally disqualified, however. Testimony from such a witness would be limited to those facts that demonstrably could be shown to have been recalled prior to hypnosis.

In 1985, the Court of Criminal Appeals reaffirmed these rules in *Harmon v. State*.

1. Stafford v. State, 731 P.2d 1372 (Okla. Crim. App. 1987).
2. Stafford v. State, 726 P.2d 894 (1986).
3. Standridge v. State, 701 P.2d 761 (Okla. Crim. App. 1985).
4. Harmon v. State, 700 P.2d 212 (Okla. Crim. App. 1985).
5. Bowen v. State, 715 P.2d 1093 (Okla. Crim. App. 1984).
6. McDoulett v. State, 685 P.2d 978 (Okla. Crim. App. 1984).
7. Robison v. State, 677 P.2d 1980 (Okla. Crim. App. 1984), *cert. denied*, Robison v. Oklahoma, 467 U.S. 1246, 104 S. Ct. 3524, 82 L.Ed.2d 831 (1984).
8. Ferguson v. State, 675 P.2d 1023 (Okla. Crim. App. 1984).
9. Stafford v. State, 669 P.2d 285 (Okla. Crim. App. 1983).
10. Johnson v. State, 665 P.2d 815 (Okla. Crim. App. 1983).
11. Daugherty v. State, 640 P.2d 558 (Okla. Crim. App. 1982).
12. Jones v. State, 542 P.2d 1316 (Okla. Crim. App. 1975).
13. Henderson v. State, 94 Okla. Crim. 45, 230 P.2d 495, 23 A.L.R. 2d 1292 (1951).

Oregon

In *State v. Jorgensen* (1971), the Oregon Court of Appeals opted for an open-admissibility rule, which at that time was the evolving trend. The court reaffirmed this position a year later in *State v. Brom* (1972).

In 1977, the state legislature stepped in to enact this position by permitting hypnotically refreshed recollection to be introduced, provided that (1) the entire proceeding is videotaped or recorded and (2) state or local law enforcement agents seeking to perform the hypnosis obtain the informed consent of the intended subject. In order to obtain this consent, the subject must be told that he or she has the right to refuse and that a request will be honored to have a licensed doctor or psychologist perform the hypnosis free of charge. The subject must also be told that there is a risk of psychological side effects resulting from the hypnosis and that the process may reveal information of which the subject is unaware, or of which the subject is aware and wishes to keep private.

1. State v. King, 84 Or. App. 165, 733 P.2d 742 (1987).
2. Luther v. State, 83 Or. App. 336, 732 P.2d 24 (1987).
3. State v. Cochran, 72 Or. App. 499, 696 P.2d 1114 (1985).
4. State v. Johnson, 66 Or. App. 326, 673 P.2d 1380 (1984).
5. Stage v. Luther, 296 Or. 1, 672 P.2d 691 (1983).
6. *In re* Jordan, 295 Or. 142, 665 P.2d 341 (1983).

7. State v. Luther, 63 Or. App. 86, 663 P.2d 1261 (1983).
8. State v. Brom, 8 Or. App. 598, 494 P.2d 434 (1972).
9. State v. Jorgensen, 8 Or. App. 1, 492 P.2d 312 (1971).
10. State v. Harris, 241 Or. 224, 405 P.2d 492 (1965).

Statutes:

1. Criminal Trials/Procedures §§ 136.675, 136.685, and 136.695, "Hypnotized Witnesses" (Or. Rev. Stat. 1977, amended 1983).
2. Crimes and Punishments § 167.870. "Definition and Classification of the Crime of Exhibiting a Person in a Trance" (Or. Rev. Stat. 1973).

Pennsylvania

The Pennsylvania Supreme Court in *Commonwealth v. Nazarovitch* (1981) came close to adopting a per se exclusion rule, but declined to do so only because it wanted to see more evidence concerning the reliability of hypnotically refreshed recollection. Until such evidence were to be presented, the court held hypnotically refreshed testimony to be inadmissible.

By 1984, however, the court was in a more moderate mood and held in *Commonwealth v. Smoyer* that prehypnotic recall is admissible, provided certain guidelines have been met. These guidelines include a qualified hypnotist who is independent of the parties and issues involved in the case.

Pennsylvania Superior Court decisions since 1984 have admitted prehypnotic statements if these guidelines have been met.

1. Commonwealth v. DiNicola, 502 A.2d 606 (Pa. Super. Ct. 1985).
2. Commonwealth v. DiNicola, 502 A.2d 604 (Pa. Super. Ct. 1985).
3. Commonwealth v. Mehmeti, 347 Pa. Super. 278, 500 A.2d 832 (1985).
4. Commonwealth v. Romanelli, 336 Pa. Super. 261, 485 A.2d 795 (1984).
5. Commonwealth v. Smoyer, 505 Pa. 83, 476 A.2d 1304 (1984).
6. Commonwealth v. McCabe, 303 Pa. Sup. 245, 449 A.2d 670 (1982).
7. Commonwealth v. Taylor, 294 Pa. Sup. 171, 439 A.2d 805 (1982).
8. Commonwealth v. Nazarovitch, 496 Pa. 97, 436 A.2d 170 (1981).
9. Commonwealth v. Langley, 468 Pa. 392, 363 A.2d 1126 (1976).
10. State Bd. of Medical Examiners v. Grumbles, 22 Pa. C. 74, 347 A.2d 782 (1975).

Rhode Island

No appellate cases on hypnosis have been found.

South Carolina

South Carolina appellate courts have addressed hypnosis only once, in a 1974 Supreme Court ruling involving a defendant's request to have a hypnotherapist testify about information revealed by the defendant in trance. The court held such testimony to be inadmissible.

1. State v. Pierce, 263 S.C. 23, 207 S.E.2d 414 (1974).

South Dakota

The South Dakota Supreme Court has addressed hypnosis issues three times. The *State v. Galati* (1985) ruling was not relevant to investigative hypnosis questions; however, in *State v. Adams* (1988), the court held that hypnotically refreshed recollection is admissible, provided that certain safeguards have been met. These safeguards were deemed to be flexible in the sense that compliance with them will not guarantee admissibility and noncompliance will not necessitate exclusion. The trial judge must evaluate all pertinent facts and then rule on admissibility. In the *Adams* case itself, the trial judge found compliance, yet limited testimony to prehypnotic recollection. The Supreme Court's opinion in *Adams* erroneously states in a footnote that the per se exclusion rule is "probably unacceptable" under the 1987 *Rock* decision by the U.S. Supreme Court.

The *Boykin* (1988) case reaffirms *Adams* favoring the admissibility of post-hypnotic testimony when certain procedural safeguards have been met. The witness is limited, however, to testimony corroborated by prehypnotic statements.

1. State v. Boykin, 432 N.W.2d 60 (1988).
2. State v. Adams, 418 N.W.2d 618 (1988).
3. State v. Galati, 365 N.W.2d 575 (1985).

Tennessee

The Tennessee Court of Criminal Appeals, in *State v. Glebock* (1981), accepted a minimal-safeguards approach first adopted by the U.S. Court of Appeals for the Ninth Circuit in *United States v. Adams* (1978). A transcript or tape of the hypnosis session must be furnished to the defendant. The party seeking to introduce hypnotically refreshed recollection must present expert testimony from the hypnotist explaining why hypnosis was used, how the hypnosis was conducted, and how hypnosis affects memory.

The Tennessee Supreme Court, in *State v. Hartman* (1985), did not address the hypnosis issue because the trial judge had limited testimony to prehypnotic statements.

1. State v. Hartman, 703 S.W.2d 106 (1985).
2. State v. Glebock, 616 S.W.2d 897 (1981).

Texas

The first case in Texas that raised issues involving investigative hypnosis was decided by the Court of Criminal Appeals (*Burnett v. State*, 1982). The court held that tape recordings of hypnosis sessions with the defendant were protected under the attorney–client privilege.

One year later, the Texas Court of Appeals permitted the admission into evidence of posthypnotic testimony identifying the defendant as the culprit. The court followed constitutional due process principles and did not treat hypnosis any differently from any other identification issue. The test for the trial judge was held to be that the testimony is admissible if the "totality of the circumstances" surrounding the hypnosis is not so impermissibly suggestive as to give rise to a substantial likelihood of unreliability or a misidentification. Where the identification has an independent origin, the fact of hypnosis should not disqualify the witness from testifying.

Texas courts applied this test for several years until the direct question of the admissibility of posthypnotic recollection was addressed in *Zani v. State* (1988). In that case the Court of Criminal Appeals, on the basis of an erroneous interpretation of the 1987 U.S. Supreme Court ruling in *Rock* (see Chapter Five), felt compelled to hold that such testimony is admissible if the trial judge finds, by clear and convincing evidence, that the hypnosis neither rendered the witness's memory untrustworthy nor substantially impaired the ability of the opponent to fairly test the witness's memory by cross-examination. The *Zani* approach has been followed in the four cases decided after it.

In the 1989 version of *Zani*, the Texas Court of Appeals noted that the proponent of hypnotically refreshed testimony must show, by clear and convincing evidence, that this testimony is trustworthy when measured against the four dangers inherent in hypnosis: hypersuggestibility, loss of critical judgment, confabulation, and memory cementing. The "totality of the circumstances" test should be used to make this determination. *Zani* (1989) lists 10 factors that should be evaluated in deciding whether to admit the testimony.

Legislation in Texas, effective January 1, 1988, requires that a peace officer who uses any "hypnotic interview technique" first complete a specified training course and pass an examination testing the officer's knowledge of investigative hypnosis. The 1988 *Zani* case made no mention of this legislation and it has not been mentioned in any of the later cases as well. It seems likely that the approach taken by the courts and by the legislature will increase the volume of investigative hypnosis practiced in Texas.

1. Zani v. State, 1989 W.L. 17229 (Tex. Ct. App.–Texarkana, 1989).
2. Robinson v. State, 1988 W.L. 109823 (Tex. Ct. App.—Houston 1988).

3. Horst v. State, 758 S.W.2d 311 (Tex. Ct. App.—Amarillo 1988).
4. Tumlinson v. State, 757 S.W.2d 440 (Tex. Ct. App.—Dallas 1988).
5. Zani v. State, 758 S.W.2d 233 (Tex. Crim. App. 1988).
6. Gaudette v. State, 713 S.W.2d 206 (Tex. Ct. App.—Tyler 1986).
7. Vester v. State, 713 S.W.2d 920 (Tex. Crim. App. 1986).
8. Walters v. State, 680 S.W.2d 60 (Tex. Ct. App.—Amarillo 1984).
9. Zani v. State, 679 S.W.2d 144 (Tex. Ct. App.—Texarkana 1984).
10. Vester v. State, 684 S.W.2d 715 (Tex. Ct. App.—Amarillo 1983).
11. Burnett v. State, 642 S.W.2d 765 (Tex. Crim. App. 1982).
12. Mirowitz v. State, 449 S.W.2d 475 (Tex. Crim. App. 1969).
13. Johnston v. State, 418 S.W.2d 522 (Tex. Crim. App. 1967).
14. Masters v. State, 170 Tex. Crim. 471, 341 S.W.2d 938, 85 A.L.R. 2d 1123 (1960).
15. Tyrone v. State, 77 Tex. Crim. 493, 180 S.W. 125 (1915).

Statute:

Texas Gov't. Code Ann. § 415.031(7) (d) and (e) (Vernon 1987).

Utah

The only case raising hypnosis issues in Utah involved a civil tort claim. After trial, the plaintiff was hypnotized and claimed that what he remembered constituted "newly discovered evidence." The Utah Supreme Court rejected this claim, but expressed no opinion on the question of the admissibility of hypnotically refreshed recollection.

1. Mulherin v. Ingersoll-Rand, 628 P.2d 1301 (1981).

Vermont

No appellate cases on hypnosis have been found.

Virginia

In *Greenfield v. Commonwealth* (1974), the Virginia Supreme Court held that hypnotically based evidence—either testimony in court while in trance or a psychiatrist's account of what a defendant said in trance—was inadmissible.

In *Hopkins v. Commonwealth* (1985), the Supreme Court addressed the separate issue of the admissibility of the hypnotically refreshed recollection of a witness. The hypnosis sessions had not been recorded, and standard tests to determine depth of trance had not been administered. The trial judge, however, found that the hypnosis did not alter the witness's story and permitted the witness to testify. The Supreme Court upheld this ruling. The prehypnotic recollections of a witness are admissible, according to the court, despite its conclusion that "the one certainty that emerges from the mass of expert opinion, well documented in the cases, is that manipulation of the mind through hypnosis may lead to uncertain and unreliable results" (p. 271). The court declined to rule on the direct question of whether hypnotically induced testimony, or testimony altered by hypnosis from prior recollection, is admissible.

1. Hopkins v. Commonwealth, 337 S.E.2d 264 (1985).
2. Greenfield v. Commonwealth, 214 Va. 710, 204 S.E.2d 414, 92 A.L.R. 3d 432 (1974).
3. Denis v. Commonwealth, 144 Va. 559, 131 S.E. 131 (1926).

Washington

The Washington Supreme Court has consistently barred hypnotically refreshed recollection. Prehypnotic testimony, however, is admissible if it can be proven that the hypnosis had no effect on these memories. An audiotape, videotape, or transcript will usually be necessary as a record of the prehypnotic recollection. Any identification of a defendant made by a witness after having been hypnotized is also inadmissible, even if a detailed description of the defendant was given by the witness prior to hypnosis. The court has correctly noted that the 1987 U.S. Supreme Court decision in *Rock* applies only to defendants.

1. State v. Coe, 109 Wash. 2d 832, 750 P.2d 208 (1988).
2. State v. Yapp, 45 Wash. App. 601, 726 P.2d 1003 (1986).
3. State v. Coe, 101 Wash. 2d 772, 684 P.2d 668 (1984).
4. State v. Laureano, 101 Wash. 2d 745, 682 P.2d 889 (1984).
5. State v. Martin, 101 Wash. 2d 713, 684 P.2d 651 (1984).
6. State v. Martin, 33 Wash. App. 486, 656 P.2d 526 (1983).
7. State v. Long, 32 Wash. App. 732, 649 P.2d 845 (1982).
8. State v. Thompson, 58 Wash. 2d 598, 364 P.2d 527 (1961).

Statute:

> Crimes and Punishments § 9.94A.440, "Evidentiary Sufficiency: . . . Investigation Techniques" (West Wash. Rev. Code Ann. 1983, amended 1986).

West Virginia

No appellate cases on hypnosis have been found.

Wisconsin

A Wisconsin Supreme Court ruling in *State v. Armstrong* (1983) permits hypnotically refreshed recollection, provided that certain safeguards are met. The trial judge must review the hypnotic session to determine whether the hypnosis has tainted the memory:

There are no experts who can testify as to what specific effects hypnosis has had on the witness' memory; just as there are no experts who can testify that a normal waking memory of an event is in fact a completely accurate representation of what accurately occurred. The most a trial judge can do is review the hypnotic session to ensure that no impermissible suggestiveness has occurred. (p. 393)

1. State v. Wyss, 124 Wis. 2d 681, 370 N.W.2d 745 (1985).
2. State v. Armstrong, 110 Wis. 2d 555, 329 N.W.2d 386 (1983), *cert. denied,* Wisconsin v. Armstrong, 461 U.S. 946, 103 S. Ct. 2125, 77 L.Ed.2d 1304 (1983).
3. State v. White, 26 Crim. L. Rep. (BNA) 2168 (Wis. 1979).

Wyoming

The Wyoming Supreme Court, in *Chapman v. State* (1982), was one of the few courts to adopt an open-admissibility policy without the requirement of even minimal safeguards. A previously hypnotized witness is competent to testify, but the credibility of the witness is open to challenge at trial.

This permissive ruling has been reaffirmed four times. In the first four cases, however, the court has been almost evenly divided in a 3–2 split in each case. The dissenting opinions have pointed out that most of the original cases from other states adopting open admissibility, which were relied on by the majority, have been overruled by those states. In *Prime* (1989), Wyoming's open admissibility rule was challenged only by a lone dissenter.

1. Prime v. State, 767 P.2d 149, 1989 W.L. 374 (1989).
2. Haselhuhn v. State, 727 P.2d 280 (1986), *cert. denied,* Haselhuhn v. Wyoming, 479 U.S. 1098, 107 S. Ct. 1321, 94 L.Ed.2d 174 (1987).
3. Pote v. State, 695 P.2d 617 (1985).
4. Gee v. State, 662 P.2d 103 (1983).
5. Chapman v. State, 638 P.2d 1280 (1982).

FEDERAL CASES

Supreme Court

1. Rock v. Arkansas, 107 S. Ct. 2704, 97 L.Ed.2d 37 (1987).
2. Bundy v. Florida, 107 S. Ct. 295, 93 L.Ed.2d 269 (1986).
3. Darwin v. Connecticut, 391 U.S. 346, 88 S. Ct. 1488, 20 L.Ed.2d 630 (1968).
4. Leyra v. Denno, 347 U.S. 556, 74 S. Ct. 716, 98 L.Ed. 948 (1954).

Courts of Appeal

1. Perry v. Howes, 852 F.2d 568 (6th Cir. 1988) (Table) (Unpublished).
2. Bundy v. Dugger, 850 F.2d 1402 (11th Cir. 1988).

3. United States v. Bercier, 848 F.2d 917 (8th Cir. 1988).
4. Little v. Armontrout, 835 F.2d 1240 (8th Cir. 1987).
5. Porretto v. Stalder, 834 F.2d 461 (5th Cir. 1987).
6. Robison v. Maynard, 829 F.2d 1501 (10th Cir. 1987).
7. Rault v. Butler, 826 F.2d 299 (5th Cir. 1987), *stay and cert. denied,* 108 S.Ct. 14, 97 L.Ed.2d 803 (1987).
8. Chaussard v. Fulcomer, 816 F.2d 925 (3rd Cir. 1987).
9. McQueen v. Garrison, 814 F.2d 941 (4th Cir. 1987).
10. Bundy v. Wainwright, 808 F.2d 1410 (11th Cir. 1987).
11. Country v. Foster, 806 F.2d 182 (8th Cir. 1986).
12. United States v. Kimberlin, 805 F.2d 210 (7th Cir. 1986), *cert. denied,* Kimberlin v. United States, 107 S. Ct. 3270, 97 L.Ed.2d 768 (1987).
13. Beck v. Norris, 801 F.2d 242 (6th Cir. 1986).
14. Harker v. Maryland, 800 F.2d 437 (4th Cir. 1986).
15. United States v. Mest, 789 F.2d 1069 (4th Cir. 1986).
16. Wicker v. McCotter, 783 F.2d 487 (5th Cir. 1986).
17. United States v. Keplinger, 776 F.2d 678 (7th Cir. 1985).
18. Rault v. Louisiana, 772 F.2d 117 (5th Cir. 1985).
19. Spryzczynatyk v. General Motors Corp., 771 F.2d 1112 (8th Cir. 1985), *cert. denied,* 475 U.S. 1046, 106 S. Ct. 1263, 89 L.Ed.2d 572 (1986).
20. United States v. Harvey, 756 F.2d 636 (8th Cir. 1985).
21. United States v. Harrelson, 754 F.2d 1153 (5th Cir. 1985).
22. Clay v. Vose, 771 F.2d 1 (1st Cir. 1985).
23. United States v. McCollum, 732 F.2d 1419 (9th Cir. 1984), *cert. denied,* 469 U.S. 920, 105 S. Ct. 301, 83 L.Ed.2d 236 (1984).
24. United States v. Valdez, 722 F.2d 1196 (5th Cir. 1984).
25. Rhodes v. Chicago Ins., 719 F.2d 116 (5th Cir. 1983).
26. United States v. Brooks, 219 App. D.C., 677 F.2d 907 (D.C. Cir. 1982).
27. Belluso v. Turner Communications Corp., 633 F.2d 393 (5th Cir. 1980).
28. United States v. Awkard, 597 F.2d 667, 50 A.L.R. Fed. 594 (9th Cir. 1979), *cert. denied,* Awkard v. United States, 444 U.S. 885, 100 S. Ct. 179, 62 L.Ed.2d 116 (1979).
29. United States v. Adams, 581 F.2d 193 (9th Cir. 1978), *cert. denied,* 439 U.S. 1006 (1978).
30. Kline v. Ford Motor Co., 523 F.2d 1067 (9th Cir. 1975).
31. Wyller v. Fairchild Hiller, 503 F.2d 506 (9th Cir. 1974).
32. Connolly v. Farmer, 484 F.2d 456 (5th Cir. 1973).
33. Rucker v. Wabash R.R. Co., 418 F.2d 146 (7th Cir. 1969).
34. United States v. Miller, 411 F.2d 825 (2d Cir. 1969).
35. Silver v. Dickson, 403 F.2d 642 (9th Cir. 1968), *cert. denied,* 394 U.S. 990, 89 S. Ct. 1477, 22 L.Ed.2d 765 (1969).
36. Ghadiali v. United States, 17 F.2d 236 (9th Cir. 1927).

District Courts

1. The Petrie Method, Inc. v. Petrie, 1988 W.L. 135375 (E.D.N.Y. 1988).
2. The Petrie Method, Inc. v. Petrie, 1988 W.L. 135377 (E.D.N.Y. 1988).

3. Karas v. Beyer, 690 F. Supp. 1388 (D.N.J. 1988).
4. Byrd v. Armontrout, 686 F. Supp. 743 (E.D. Mo. 1988).
5. McDougall v. Rice, 685 F. Supp. 532 (W.D.N.C. 1988).
6. Mokone v. Kelly, 680 F. Supp. 679 (S.D.N.Y. 1988).
7. Rault v. Blackburn, 187 W.L. 15654 (E.D. La. 1987).
8. Bundy v. Wainwright, 651 F. Supp. 38 (S.D. Fla. 1986).
9. McQueen v. Garrison, 619 F. Supp. 116 (E.D.N.C. 1985).
10. McQueen v. Garrison, 617 F. Supp. 633 (E.D.N.C. 1985).
11. Conley v. Whitener, 617 F. Supp. 86 (E.D. Mo. 1985).
12. Clay v. Vose, 599 F. Supp. 1505 (D. Mass. 1984).
13. Dobbert v. Wainwright, 593 F. Supp. 1418 (M.D. Fla. 1984).
14. McQueen v. Garrison, No. 82-675-HC, slip op. (E.D.N.C. Dec. 3, 1984).
15. United States v. Charles, 561 F. Supp. 694 (S.D. Tex. 1983).
16. United States v. Waksal, 539 F. Supp. 834 (S.D. Fla. 1982).
17. United States v. Kimberlin, 527 F. Supp. 1010 (S.D. Ind. 1981).
18. United States v. Phillips, 515 F. Supp. 758 (E.D. Ky. 1981).
19. Alderman v. Austin, 498 F. Supp. 1134 (S.D. Ga. 1980).
20. United States v. Narcisio, 446 F. Supp. 252 (E.D. Mich. 1977).
21. Greenfield v. Robinson, 413 F. Supp. 1113 (W.D. Va. 1976).
22. Emmett v. Ricketts, 397 F. Supp. 1025 (N.D. Ga. 1975).
23. Shaw v. Garrison, 391 F. Supp. 1353 (E.D. La. 1975).
24. South v. Slayton, 336 F. Supp. 879 (W.D. Va. 1972).
25. Shaw v. Garrison, 328 F. Supp. 390 (E.D. La. 1971).
26. United States v. Miller, 296 F. Supp. 422 (N.D. W.Va. 1968).
27. *Ex parte* Britten, 293 Fed. 61 (W.D. Wash. 1923).

Military Cases

1. United States v. Pacunayen, 1987 C.M.R. Lexis 667 (A.F.C.M.R. 1987).
2. United States v. Stark, 24 M.J. 381 (C.M.A. 1987).
3. United States v. Eshalomi, 23 M.J. 12 (C.M.A. 1986).
4. United States v. Robinson, 21 M.J. 937 (A.F.C.M.R. 1986).
5. United States v. Stark, 19 M.J. 519 (A.C.M.R. 1984).
6. United States v. Harrington, 18 M.J. 797 (A.C.M.R. 1984).

FOREIGN CASES

Canada

1. The Queen v. Clark, Q.B. Alberta, No. 8303 2017 C1 (1984).
2. Regina v. Zubot, (1981) Q.B. Alberta, unreported (1981). Discussed in Brown, R.J. (1985). Hypnosis in Canadian criminal law. *American Journal of Clinical Hypnosis, 27,*153–158.
3. Horvath v. The Queen, 44 C.C.C. 2d 385, 2 S.C.R. 376, 93 D.L.R. 3d 1 (1979).
4. Regina v. K., 47 C.C.C. 2d 436, 10 C.R. 3d 235 (Man. Prov. Ct. 1979).
5. Regina v. Pitt, 68 D.L.R. 2d 513 (1967).
6. Rex v. Booher, 4 D.L.R. 795 (1928).

England

1. Regina v. Blackpool Borough Council *ex parte* Casson, (Crown Office List), No. CO/891/84, (7 September 1984). (Transcript: Marten Walsh Cherer).

New Zealand

1. Regina v. McFelin, 2 N.Z.L.R. 750 (Court of Appeal, Wellington, 6 August 1985).
2. Maxwell v. North Canterbury Hospital Board, 2 N.Z.L.R. 118 (Supreme Court, Christchurch, 29 April 1977).

References and Bibliography

Allen, G. S. (1934). Hypnotism and its legal import. *Canadian Bar Review, 12,* 14–22, 81–92.

Alman, B. M., & Carney, R. E. (1980). Consequences of direct and indirect suggestions on success of post-hypnotic behavior. *American Journal of Clinical Hypnosis, 23,* 112–118.

American Bar Association. (1983). *Model rules of professional conduct.* Chicago: Author.

American Psychological Association. *Division on Law and Psychology Newsletter.* 1985–present.

American Society of Clinical Hypnosis (ASCH). (1983, November). *Code of ethics.* Des Plaines, IL.: Author.

Applebaum, J. A. (1963). *Cross-examination.* London: Colner.

Applebaum, P. S. (1984). Hypnosis in the courtroom. *Hospital and Community Psychiatry, 35,* 657–658.

Araoz, D. (1981). *The new hypnosis.* Paper presented at annual convention of the American Psychological Association, Los Angeles.

Arnold, M. B. (1946). On the mechanism of suggestion and hypnosis. *Journal of Abnormal and Social Psychology, 41,* 107–128.

Arons, H. (1967). *Hypnosis in criminal investigation.* Springfield, IL: Charles C Thomas.

Arons, H. (1977). *Hypnosis in criminal investigation* (2nd ed.). South Orange, NJ: Power.

Arons, H., & Bubeck, M. F. H. (1971). *Handbook of professional hypnosis.* South Orange, NJ: Power.

As, A. (1962). The recovery of forgotten language knowledge through hypnotic age regression: A case report. *American Journal of Clinical Hypnosis, 5,* 19–21.

Ashford, B., & Hammer, A. G. (1978). The role of expectancies in the occurrence of posthypnotic amnesia. *International Journal of Clinical and Experimental Hypnosis, 26,* 281–291.

Atkinson, R. C., & Shiffrin, R. M. (1968). Human memory: A proposed system and its control processes. In K. W. Spence & J. T. Spence (Eds.), *The psychology of learning and motivation: Advances in research and theory* (Vol. 2). New York: Academic Press.

Atkinson, R. C., & Shiffrin, R. M. (1971). The control of short term memory. *Scientific American, 225,* 82–90.

Augustynek, A. (1977). Recalling in state of awareness and under hypnosis. *Przeglad Psychologiczny, 20,* 693–705.

Augustynek, A. (1978). Remembering under hypnosis. *Studia Psychologica, 20,* 256–266.

Augustynek, A. (1979). Hypnotic hypermnesia. *Prace Psychologiczno Pedagoglczne, 29,* 25–34.

Ault, R. L. (1979). FBI guidelines for use of hypnosis. *International Journal of Clinical and Experimental Hypnosis, 27,* 449–451.

Ault, R. L. (1980, January). Hypnosis: The FBI's team approach. *FBI Law Enforcement Bulletin,* pp. 1–2.

Bailey, F. L. *The defense never rests.* New York: New American Library.

Baker, E. L. (1982). *Developmental aspects of the hypnotherapeutic relationship: Theoretical, clinical and empirical observations.* Paper presented at the 34th Annual Meeting of the Society for Clinical and Experimental Hypnosis, Indianapolis.

Baker, E. L. (1987). The state of the art of clinical hypnosis. *International Journal of Clinical and Experimental Hypnosis, 35,* 203–214.

Baker, R. A., Haynes, B., & Patrick, B. S. (1983). Hypnosis, memory and incidental memory. *American Journal of Clinical Hypnosis, 25,* 253–262.

Bandler, R., & Grinder, J. (1975a). *Patterns of the hypnotic techniques of Milton H. Erickson, M.D.* Cupertino, CA: Meta.

Bandler, R., & Grinder, J. (1975b). *The structure of magic.* Palo Alto, CA: Science and Behavior Books.

Barber, J. (1980). Hypnosis and the unhypnotizable. *American Journal of Clinical Hypnosis, 23,* 4–9.

Barber, T. X. (1957). Hypnosis as perceptual–cognitive restructuring: III. From somnambulism to autohypnosis. *Journal of Psychology, 44,* 299–304.

Barber, T. X. (1962). Toward a theory of hypnosis: Posthypnotic behavior. *Archives of General Psychiatry, 7,* 321–342.

Barber, T. X. (1969). *Hypnosis: A scientific approach.* New York: Van Nostrand Reinhold.

Barber, T. X., & Calverley, D. S. (1964). Effects of E's tone of voice on "hypnotic-like" suggestibility. *Psychological Reports, 15,* 139–144.

Barber, T. X., & Calverley, D. S. (1966). Effects on recall of hypnotic induction, motivational suggestions and suggested regression: A methodological and experimental analysis. *Journal of Abnormal Psychology, 71,* 169–180.

Barber, T. X., & Glass, L. B. (1962). Significant factors in hypnotic behavior. *Journal of Abnormal and Social Psychology, 64,* 222–228.

Barber, T. X., Spanos, N. P., & Chaves, J. F. (1974). *Hypnotism, imagination and human potentialities.* New York: Pergamon Press.

Barnes, M. (Producer and Director). (1982). *Hypnosis on trial* [Television program]. London: British Broadcasting Corporation.

Barnes, M. (Producer and Director). (1984). *The mind of a murderer* [Television program; a segment of *Frontline*]. Boston: WGBH Educational Foundation.

Bartlett, F. C. (1932). *Remembering.* Cambridge, England: Cambridge University Press.

Bateman, W. (1980). The use of hypnosis in the interrogation of witnesses. *Australian Journal of Clinical Hypnotherapy, 1,* 87–90.

Baudouin, C. (1920). *Suggestion and autosuggestion* (E. Paul & C. Paul, Trans.) London: George Allen & Unwin.

Beahrs, J. O. (1986). *Hypnosis cannot be excluded from the courtroom.* Paper presented at the 29th Annual Scientific Meeting of the American Society of Clinical Hypnosis, Las Vegas.

Beahrs, J. O. (1988). Hypnosis can not be fully nor reliably excluded from the courtroom. *American Journal of Clinical Hypnosis, 31,* 18–27.

Bekerian, D. A., & Bowers, J. M. (1983). Eyewitness testimony: Were we misled? *Journal of Experimental Psychology: Learning, Memory, and Cognition, 9,* 139–145.

Bell, C. (1889). Hypnotism. *Medico-Legal Journal, 7,* 363–371.

Belli, M. (1982). The expert witness. *Trial, 17*(7), 35–37.

Belmore, S. M. (1981). Imagery and semantic elaboration in hypermnesia for words. *Journal of Experimental Psychology: Human Learning and Memory, 7,* 191–203.

Bergman, P. (1979). *Trial advocacy.* St. Paul, MN: West.

Bergson, H. (1911). *Matter and memory* (M. Paul & W. Palmer, Trans.). New York: Macmillan. (Original work published 1896.)

Bernheim, H. (1890). *Suggestive therapeutics* (2nd ed., C. A. Herter, Trans.). London: Young Pentland.

Bernheim, H. (1973). *Hypnosis and suggestion in psychotherapy.* New York: Jason Aronson. (Original work published 1886.)

Bernheim, H. (1980). *New studies in hypnotism* (R. S. Sandor, Trans.). New York: International Universities Press. (Original work published 1891)

Bernstein, M. (1956). *The search for Bridey Murphy.* Garden City, NY: Country Life Press.

Binet, A., & Fere, C. (1988). *Animal magnetism.* New York: D. Appleton.

Blau, T. H. (1984). *The psychologist as expert witness.* New York: Wiley.

Block, E. B. (1976). *Hypnosis: A new tool in crime detection.* New York: David McKay.

Bower, G. H. (1981). Mood and memory. *American Psychologist, 36,* 129–148.

Bowers, K. S. (1966). Hypnotic behavior: The differentiation of trance and demand characteristic variables. *Journal of Abnormal Psychology, 71,* 42–51.

Bowers, K. S. (1977). Hypnosis: An informational approach. *Annals of the New York Academy of Sciences, 296,* 222–237.

Bowers, K. S., & Hilgard, E. R. (1988). Some complexities in understanding memory. In H. M. Pettinati (Ed.), *Hypnosis and memory.* New York: Guilford Press.

Bowers, P. G., & Bowers, K. S. (1979). Hypnosis and creativity: A theoretical and empirical rapproachment. In E. Fromm & R. E. Shor (Eds.), *Hypnosis: Developments in research and new perspectives* (2nd ed.). Chicago: Aldine.

Braid, J. (1843). *Neurypnology; or the rationale of nervous sleep considered in relation with animal magnetism.* London: J. Churchill.

Braid, J. (1960). *Braid on hypnotism: The beginnings of modern hypnosis* (A. E. Waite, ed.). New York: Julian Press.

Bramwell, J. M. (1903). *Hypnotism, its history, practice and theory.* Philadelphia: J. B. Lippincott.

Braun, B. G. (1986). Introduction: The uses of hypnosis in psychiatry. *Psychiatric Annals, 16,* 81–86.

Brenman, M. (1942). Experiments in the hypnotic production of anti-social and self-injurious behavior. *Psychiatry, 5,* 49–61.

Breuer, J., & Freud, S. (1955). Studies on hysteria. In J. Strachey (Ed. & Trans.) *The standard edition of the complete psychological works of Sigmund Freud* (Vol. 2). London: Hogarth Press. (Original work published 1895)

Brigham, J. C., Maass, A., Snyder, L. D., & Spaulding, K. (1982). Accuracy of eyewitness identifications in a field setting. *Journal of Personality and Social Psychology, 42,* 673–681.

British Medical Journal. (1955, April 23). Supplementary annual report of council, 1954–5. Supplement, 190–193.

Broadbent, D. E. (1958). *Perception and communication.* New York: Pergamon Press.

Brodie-Innes, J. W. (1891). Legal aspects of hypnotism. *Juridical Review, 3,* 51–62.

Brosnahan v. Brown, 32 Cal. 3d 236, 186 Cal. Rptr. 30 (1982).

Brown, D. P., & Fromm, E. (1986). *Hypnotherapy and hypnoanalysis.* Hillsdale, NJ: Erlbaum.

Brown, J. (1958). Some tests of the decay theory of immediate memory. *Quarterly Journal of Experimental Psychology, 10,* 12–21.

Brown, R. J. (1985). Hypnosis in Canadian criminal law. *American Journal of Clinical Hypnosis, 27,* 153–158.

Bryan, W. J., Jr. (1962). *Legal aspects of hypnosis.* Springfield, IL: Charles C Thomas.

Bryan, W. J., Jr. (1971). *The chosen ones.* New York: Vaɪ.tage Press.

Buckhout, R., Eugenio, P., Kramer, T. K., Licitra, T., & Oliver, L. (1982). *Hypnosis eyewitness memory: The effects of unintentional bias.* Unpublished manuscript.

Buckhout, R., Eugenio, P., Licitra, T., Oliver, L., & Kramer, T. K. (1981). Memory, hypnosis and evidence: Research on eyewitnesses. *Social Action and the Law, 7,* 67–72.

Burgess, A. W. (1983). Rape trauma syndrome. *Behavioral Sciences and the Law, 1,* 97–113.

Burrows, G. D., Dennerstein, L., & Frenader, G. (1982). A note on hypnosis and the law. *Australian Journal of Clinical and Experimental Hypnosis, 11,* 83–88.

Canadian Medical Association Journal. (1958). Miscellany: Hypnotism and medicine. *78,* 367–368.

Carrizosa, P. (1982, March 29). Deputy AG doubts court review of hypnosis ruling. *Los Angeles Daily Journal,* p. 1.

Carroll, L. [C. L. Dodgson]. (1960). *Alice's adventures in Wonderland.* New York: Washington Square Press. (Original work published 1865.)

Cautela, J. R. (1975). The use of covert conditioning in hypnotherapy. *International Journal of Clinical and Experimental Hypnosis, 23,* 15–27.

Cheek, D. B., & LeCron, L. M. (1968). *Clinical hypnotherapy.* New York: Grune & Stratton.

Chertok, L. (1981). *Sense and nonsense in psychotherapy: The challenge of hypnosis.* New York: Pergamon Press.

Chertok, L. (1982). The unconscious and hypnosis. *International Journal of Clinical and Experimental Hypnosis, 30,* 95–107.

Chertok, L. (1984). Hypnosis and suggestion in a century of psychotherapy: An epistomological assessment. *Journal of the American Academy of Psychoanalysis, 12,* 211–232.

Clarapede, E. (1951). Recognition and me-ness. In D. Rapaport (Ed. and Trans.), *Organization and pathology of thought.* New York: Columbia University Press. (Original work published 1911)

Clark, B. D., Hungerford, L. E., & Reilley, R. R. (1984). Doctoral dissertations on hypnosis 1923–1980. *Psychological Reports, 54*, 203–209.

Clifford, B. R., & Hollin, C. R. (1981). Effects of the type of incident and the number of perpetrators on eyewitness memory. *Journal of Applied Psychology, 66*, 364–370.

Clifford, B. R., & Hollin, C. R. (1983). The effects of discussion on recall accuracy and agreement. *Journal of Applied Social Psychology, 13*, 234–244.

Coe, W. C. (1966). Hypnosis as role enactment: The role demand variable. *American Journal of Clinical Hypnosis, 8*, 189–191.

Coe, W. C. (1977). The problem of relevance vs. ethics in researching hypnosis and antisocial conduct. *Annals of the New York Academy of Sciences, 296*, 90–104.

Coe, W. C. (1978). The credibility of posthypnotic amnesia: A contextualist's view. *International Journal of Clinical and Experimental Hypnosis, 26*, 218–245.

Coe, W. C., Baugher, J. R., Krimm, W. R., & Smith, J. (1976). A further examination of selective recall following hypnosis. *International Journal of Clinical and Experimental Hypnosis, 24*, 13–21.

Coe, W. C., Kobayashi, K., & Howard, M. L. (1972). An approach toward isolating factors that influence antisocial conduct in hypnosis. *International Journal of Clinical and Experimental Hypnosis, 20*, 118–131.

Coe, W. C., & Sarbin, T. R. (1977). Hypnosis from the standpoint of a contextualist. *Annals of the New York Academy of Sciences, 296*, 2–13.

Coe, W. C., & Steen, P. (1981). Examining the relationship between believing one will respond to hypnotic suggestions and hypnotic responsiveness. *American Journal of Clinical Hypnosis, 24*, 225–243.

Cohn, A., & Udolf, R. (1979). *The criminal justice system and its psychology.* New York: Van Nostrand Reinhold.

Conn, J. H. (1972). Is hypnosis really dangerous? *International Journal of Clinical and Experimental Hypnosis, 20*, 61–79.

Cooke, G. (Ed.). (1980). *The role of the forensic psychologist.* Springfield, IL: Charles C Thomas.

Coons, P. M. (1988). Misuse of forensic hypnosis: A hypnotically elicited false confession with the apparent creation of a multiple personality. *International Journal of Clinical and Experimental Hypnosis, 36*, 1–11.

Cooper, L. M., & London, P. (1973). Reactivation of memory by hypnosis and suggestion. *International Journal of Clinical and Experimental Hypnosis, 21*, 312–323.

Council, J. R., Kirsch, I., Vickery, A. R., & Carlson, D. (1983). "Trance" versus "skill" hypnotic inductions: The effects of credibility, expectancy and experimenter modeling. *Journal of Consulting and Clinical Psychology, 51*, 432–440.

Council on Mental Health, American Medical Association (AMA). (1958). Medical use of hypnosis. *Journal of the American Medical Association, 168*, 186–189.

Council on Mental Health, American Medical Association (AMA). (1962). Training in medical hypnosis. *Journal of the American Medical Association, 180*, 693–698.

Council on Scientific Affairs, American Medical Association (AMA). (1985). Scientific status of refreshing recollection by the use of hypnosis. *Journal of the American Medical Association, 253*, 1918–1923.

Coue, E. (1922). *Self mastery through conscious autosuggestion* (A. S. Van Orden, Trans.). New York: Malkan.

Craik, F. I. M., & Jacoby, L. L. (1979). Elaboration and distinctiveness in episodic memory. In L.-G. Nilsson (Ed.), *Perspectives on memory research*. Hillsdale, NJ: Erlbaum.

Craik, F. I. M., & Lockhart, R. S. (1972). Levels of processing: A framework for memory research. *Journal of Verbal Learning and Verbal Behavior, 11*, 671–684.

Craik, F. I. M., & Tulving, E. (1975). Depth of processing and the retention of words in episodic memory. *Journal of Experimental Psychology: General, 104*, 268–294.

Craik, F. I. M., & Watkins, M. J. (1973). The role of rehearsal in short term memory. *Journal of Verbal Learning and Verbal Behavior, 12*, 599–607.

Crasilneck, H. B., & Hall, J. A. 1959). Physiological changes associated with hypnosis: A review of the literature since 1948. *International Journal of Clinical and Experimental Hypnosis, 7*, 9–50.

Crasilneck, H. B., & Hall, J. A. (1975). *Clinical hypnosis: Principles and applications*. New York: Grune & Stratton.

Crawford, H. J., & Allen, S. N. (1983). Enhanced visual memory during hypnosis as mediated by hypnotic responsiveness and cognitive strategies. *Journal of Experimental Psychology: General, 112*, 662–685.

Criminal Law Magazine. (1891). Hypnotism. *13*, 421–424.

Crosswell, G. L., & Smith, E. W. L. (1974). Evaluation of a hypnotist by subjects in hypnotic, hypnotic simulator and control conditions. *American Journal of Clinical Hypnosis, 17*, 102–107.

Crouse, E., & Kurtz, R. (1984). Enhancing hypnotic susceptibility: The efficacy of four training procedures. *American Journal of Clinical Hypnosis, 27*, 122–136.

Danner, D. (1983). *Expert witness checklists*. Rochester, NY: Lawyers Co-operative.

Das, J. P. (1961). Learning and recall under hypnosis and in the wake state: A comparison. *Archives of General Psychiatry, 4*, 517–521.

Davis, S., Dawson, J. G., & Seay, B. (1978). Prediction of hypnotic susceptibility from imaginative involvement. *American Journal of Clinical Hypnosis, 20*, 194–198.

DeBetz, B., & Sunnen, G. (1985). *A primer of clinical hypnosis*. Littleton, MA: PSG.

Deffenbacher, K. A. (1980). Eyewitness accuracy and confidence. *Law and Human Behavior, 4*, 243–260.

DeLeon, P. H., & Donahue, J. (1983). Overview: The growing impact of organized psychology in the judicial arena. *Psychotherapy in Private Practice, 1*, 109–121.

DePiano, F. A., & Salzberg, H. C. (1981). Hypnosis as an aid to recall of meaningful information presented under three types of arousal. *International Journal of Clinical and Experimental Hypnosis, 29*, 383–400.

Demster, C. R., & Balson, P. M. (1982). *Hypnotherapy of the victim experience*. Paper presented at the 9th International Congress of hypnosis and Psychosomatic Medicine, Glasgow, Scotland.

de Puysegur, M. (1837). *An essay of instruction on animal magnetism* (J. King, Trans.). New York: J. C. Kelley.

Derrick, C. D. (1959). Interrogation by hypnosis. *The Police Chief, 26*, 26–29.

Deyoub, P. L. (1984). Hypnotic stimulation of antisocial behavior: A case report. *International Journal of Clinical and Experimental Hypnosis, 32*, 301–306.

Dhanens, T., & Lundy, R. M. (1975). Hypnotic and waking suggestions and recall. *International Journal of Clinical and Experimental Hypnosis, 23*, 68–79.

Diamond, B. L. (1980). Inherent problems in the use of pretrial hypnosis on a prospective witness. *California Law Review, 68,* 313–349.

Diamond, M. J. (1972). The use of observationally presented information to modify hypnotic susceptibility. *Journal of Abnormal Psychology, 79,* 174–180.

Diamond, M. J. (1974). Modification of hypnotizability: A review. Psychological Bulletin, 81, 180–198.

Diamond, M. J. (1977). Hypnotizability is modifiable: An alternative approach. *International Journal of Clinical and Experimental Hypnosis, 25,* 147–166.

Diamond, M. J. (1984). Other voices. In G. J. Pratt, D. P. Wood, & B. M. Alman (Eds.), *A clinical hypnosis primer.* La Jolla, CA: Psychology and Consulting Associates Press.

Diamond, M. J. (1987). The interactional basis of the hypnotic experience. *International Journal of Clinical and Experimental Hypnosis, 35,* 95–115.

Diamond, M. J. (1988). Accessing archaic involvement: Toward unraveling the mystery of Erickson's hypnosis. *International Journal of Clinical and Experimental Hypnosis, 36,* 141–156.

Diggett, C., & Mulligan, W. C. (1982). *Hypnocop.* Garden City, NY: Doubleday.

Dinges, D. F. (1987). Hypnotic hypermnesia: By what criterion? In B. L. Diamond (Chair), *Fifty years after Hull: Assessing the issues and data in hypnotic hypermnesia.* Symposium conducted at the 38th Annual Meeting of the Society for Clinical and Experimental Hypnosis, Los Angeles.

Dolby, R. M., & Sheehan, P. W. (1977). Cognitive processing and expectancy in hypnosis. *Journal of Abnormal Psychology, 86,* 334–345.

Dorcus, R. M. (1960). Recall under hypnosis of amnestic events. *International Journal of Clinical and Experimental Hypnosis, 8,* 57–60.

Dorn, N. K. (1981, March 29). Finally: Light on *Light. San Francisco Examiner and Chronicle,* p. 42.

Doucé, R. G. (1979). Hypnosis: A scientific aid in crime detection. *The Police Chief, 46,* 60.

Dubreuil, D. L., Spanos, N. P., & Bertrand, L. D. (1982–1983). Does hypnotic amnesia dissipate with time? *Imagination, Cognition and Personality, 2,* 103–113.

Duncan, B., & Perry, C. (1977). Uncancelled hypnotic suggestions: Initial studies. *American Journal of Clinical Hypnosis, 19,* 166–176.

Dynes, J. B. (1947). Objective method for distinguishing sleep from hypnotic trance. *Archives of Neurology and Psychiatry, 57,* 84.

Dywan, J. (1987). What is the criterion shift in applied memory research? In B. L. Diamond (Chair), *Fifty years after Hall: Assessing the issues and data in hypnotic hypermnesia.* Symposium conducted at the 38th Annual Meeting of the Society for Clinical and Experimental Hypnosis, Los Angeles.

Dywan, J., & Bowers, K. S. (1983). The use of hypnosis to enhance recall. *Science, 222,* 184–185.

Ebbinghaus, H. (1885). *On memory.* (H. A. Ruger & C. E. Bussenius, Trans.). New York: Teachers College.

Ebert, B. W. (1988). Hypnosis and rape victims. *American Journal of Clinical Hypnosis, 31,* 50–56.

Edmonston, W. E., Jr. (1981). *Hypnosis and relaxation: Modern verification of an old equation.* New York: Wiley.

Edmonston, W. E., Jr. (ed.). (1977). *Conceptual and investigative approaches to hypnosis and hypnotic phenomena.* New York: New York Academy of Sciences.

Edmonston, W. E., Jr. (1986). *The induction of hypnosis.* New York: Wiley.

Ellenberger, H. F. (1965). Charcot and the Salpêtrière school. *American Journal of Psychotherapy, 19,* 253–267.

Elliotson, J. (1843). Cases of cures by mesmerism. *The Zoist, 1,* 161–208.

Erdelyi, M. H. (1982). A note on the level of recall, level of processing, and imagery hypotheses of hypermnesia. *Journal of Verbal Learning and Verbal Behavior, 21,* 656–661.

Erdelyi, M. H. (1984). The recovery of unconscious (inaccessible) memories: Laboratory studies of hypermnesia. In G. Bower (Ed.), *The psychology of learning and motivation* (Vol. 18). New York: Academic Press.

Erdelyi, M. H., & Becker, J. (1974). Hypermnesia for pictures: Incremental memory for pictures but not words in multiple recall trials. *Cognitive Psychology, 6,* 159–171.

Erdelyi, M. H., & Stein, J. B. Recognition hypermnesia: The growth of recognition memory (d') over time with repeated testing. *Cognition, 9,* 23–33.

Erickson, M. H. (1939). An experimental investigation of the possible antisocial use of hypnosis. *Psychiatry, 2,* 391–414.

Erickson, M. H. (1964). Initial experiments investigating the nature of hypnosis. *American Journal of Clinical Hypnosis, 7,* 152–162.

Erickson, M. H. (1967). Further experimental investigations of hypnosis: Hypnotic and nonhypnotic realities. *American Journal of Clinical Hypnosis, 10,* 87–135.

Erickson, M. H. (1977). Hypnotic approaches to therapy. *American Journal of Clinical Hypnosis, 20,* 8–19.

Erickson, M. H. (1980). *The collected papers of Milton H. Erickson* (4 vols., E. L. Rossi, Ed.). New York: Irvington.

Erickson, M. H., & Erickson, E. M. (1941). Concerning the nature and character of post hypnotic behavior. *Journal of General Psychology, 24,* 299–309.

Erickson, M. H., Hershman, S., & Secter, I. L. (1961). *The practical application of medical and dental hypnosis.* New York: Julian Press.

Erickson, M. H., Rossi, E. L., & Rossi, S. I. (1976). *Hypnotic realities: The induction of clinical hypnosis and forms of indirect suggestion.* New York: Irvington.

Estabrooks, G. H. (1951). The possible anti-social use of hypnotism. *Personality: Symposia on Topical Issues, 1,* 294–299.

Estabrooks, G. H. (Ed.). (1962). *Hypnosis: Current problems.* New York: Harper & Row.

Eugenio, P., Buckout, R., Kostes, S., & Ellison, K. W. (1982). Hypermnesia in the eyewitness to a crime. *Bulletin of the Psychonomic Society, 19,* 83–86.

Evans, F. J. (1979). Contextual forgetting: Posthypnotic source amnesia. *Journal of Abnormal Psychology, 88,* 241–256.

Evans, F. J., & Kihlstrom, J. F. (1973). Posthypnotic amnesia as disrupted retrieval. *Journal of Abnormal Psychology, 82,* 317–323.

Evans, F. J., Kihlstrom, J. F., & Orne, E. C. (1973). Quantifying subjective reports during posthypnotic amnesia. *Proceedings of the 81st Annual Convention of the American Psychological Association, 8,* 1077–1078.

Faria, L'Abbe de. (1819). *Du sommeil lucide ou étude de la nature de l'homme.* Paris: D. G. Delgado.

Fellows, B. J., & Creamer, M. (1978). An investigation of the role of hypnosis, hypnotic susceptibility and hypnotic induction in the production of age regression. *British Journal of Medical Hypnosis, 7*(2), 21–24.

Ferrera, S. J., & Wade, N. L. (1982). Hypnotic testimony: To be or not to be. *Medical Hypnoanalysis, 3,* 112–117.

Fischer, R. (1977). On flashback and hypnotic recall. *International Journal of Clinical and Experimental Hypnosis, 25,* 217–235.

Fisher, S. (1954). The role of expectancy in the performance of posthypnotic behavior. *Journal of Abnormal and Social Psychology, 49,* 503–507.

Fisher, S. (1955). An investigation of alleged conditioning phenomena under hypnosis. *Journal of Clinical and Experimental Hypnosis, 3,* 71.

Fitch, W. L., Petrella, R. C., & Wallace, J. (1987). Legal ethics and the use of mental health experts in criminal cases. *Behavioral Sciences and the Law, 5,* 105–117.

Fourie, D. P. (1980). Relationship aspects of hypnotic susceptibility. *Perceptual and Motor Skills, 51,* 1032–1034.

Frank, J. D. (1974). *Persuasion and healing.* New York: Schocken.

Frankel, F. H. (1974). Trance capacity and the genesis of phobic behavior. *Archives of General Psychiatry, 31,* 261–263.

Frankel, F. H. (1976). *Hypnosis: Trance as a coping mechanism.* New York: Plenum.

Frankel, F. H., & Zamansky, H. S. (Eds.). (1978). *Hypnosis at its bicentennial: Selected papers.* New York: Plenum.

Franklin, B., et al. (1970). Report of Benjamin Franklin and the other commissioners, charged by the King of France, with the examination of animal magnetism, as now practiced in Paris. In M. M. Tinterow (Ed.), *Foundations of hypnosis: From Mesmer to Freud.* Springfield, IL: Charles C Thomas. (Original work published 1785)

Frauman, D. C., Lynn, S. J., Hardaway, R. A., & Molteni, A. L. (1984). Effect of subliminal symbiotic activation on hypnotic rapport and susceptibility. *Journal of Abnormal Psychology, 93,* 481–483.

Freedman, M. H. (1975). *Lawyers' ethics in an adversary system.* Indianapolis: Bobbs-Merrill.

Freud, S. (1949). Repression. In *Collected papers* (A. A. Brill, Trans.). London: Hogarth Press. (Original work published 1915)

Fromm, E. (1972). Activity and passivity of the ego in hypnosis. *International Journal of Clinical and Experimental Hypnosis, 20,* 238–251.

Fromm, E. (1977). An ego psychological theory of altered states of consciousness. *International Journal of Clinical and Experimental Hypnosis, 25,* 372–387.

Fromm, E. (1987). Significant developments in clinical hypnosis during the past 25 years. *International Journal of Clinical and Experimental Hypnosis, 35,* 215–230.

Fromm, E., & Shor, R. E. (Eds.). (1979). *Hypnosis: Developments in research and new perspectives* (2nd ed.). Chicago: Aldine.

Frye v. United States, 54 App. D.C. 46, 293 F. 1013 (D.C. Cir. 1923).

Furst, A. (1973). *Post-hypnotic instructions.* Hollywood, CA: Wilshire.

Gard, B., & Kurtz, R. M. (1979). Hypnotic age regression and cognitive perceptual tasks. *American Journal of Clinical Hypnosis, 21,* 270–277.

Gardner, C. G., & Olness, K. (1981). *Hypnosis and hypnotherapy with children.* New York: Grune & Stratton.

Gardner, D. S. (1933). The perception and memory of witnesses. *Cornell Law Quarterly, 18,* 390.

Gardner, E. S. (1958). Confessions of a cross-examiner. *Journal of Forensic Sciences, 3,* 374–376.

Garver, R. B., Fuselier, G. D., & Booth, T. B. (1981). The hypnotic treatment of amnesia in an Air Force basic trainee. *American Journal of Clinical Hypnosis, 24,* 3–6.

Gaunitz, S. C. B., Nystrom-Bonnier, E., & Skalin, M. (1980). Posthypnotic suggestions and behavior change: Highly hypnotizables compared with simulators. *Scandinavian Journal of Psychology, 21,* 269–273.

Geiselman, R. E., Bjork, R. A., & Fishman, D. L. (1983). Disrupted retrieval in directed forgetting: A link with posthypnotic amnesia. *Journal of Experimental Psychology: General, 112,* 58–72.

Geiselman, R. E., Fisher, R. P., Cohen, G., Holland, H. L., & Surtes, L. (1986). Eyewitness responses to leading and misleading questions under the cognitive interview. *Journal of Police Science and Administration, 14,* 31–39.

Geiselman, R. E., Fisher, R. P., MacKinnon, D. P., & Holland, H. L. (1985). Eyewitness memory enhancement in the police interview. *Journal of Applied Psychology, 27,* 358–418.

Geiselman, R. E., Fisher, R. P., MacKinnon, D. P., & Holland, H. L. (1987). Eyewitness memory enhancement in the police interview: Cognitive retrieval mnemonics versus hypnosis. In K. S. Bowers (Chair), *Hypnosis and memory: Recent findings.* Symposium conducted at the 38th Annual Meeting of the Society for Clinical and Experimental Hypnosis, Los Angeles.

Geiselman, R. E., MacKinnon, D. P., Fishman, D. L., Jaenicke, C., Larner, B. R., & Swartz, S. (1983). Mechanisms of hypnotic and nonhypnotic forgetting. *Journal of Experimental Psychology: Learning, Memory, and Cognition, 9,* 626–635.

Gerber, S. R. (1959, January 25). Hypnotism—new weapon against crime? *This Week Magazine,* pp. 7–8.

Gerber, S. R., & Schroeder, O., Jr. (Eds.). (1962). *Criminal investigation and interrogation.* Cincinnati: W. H. Anderson.

Giannelli, P. C. (1980). The admissibility of novel scientific evidence: *Frye v. United States,* a half-century later. *Columbia Law Review, 80,* 1197–1250.

Gibson, H. B. (1982). The use of hypnosis in police investigations. *Bulletin of the British Psychological Society, 35,* 138–142.

Gill, M. M., & Brenman, M. M. (1959). *Hypnosis and related states: Psychoanalytic studies in regression.* New York: International Universities Press.

Goldberg, S. H. (1982). *The first trial: Where do I sit? What do I say?* St. Paul, MN: West.

Goldenson, R. M. (1984). *Longman dictionary of psychology and psychiatry.* New York: Longman.

Goldstein, L. (1982). Some recent advances in research on hypnosis: Introductory remarks. *Research Communications in Psychology, Psychiatry and Behavior, 7,* 145–147.

Goldstein, M. S., & Sipprelle, C. N. (1970). Hypnotically induced amnesia versus ablation of memory. *International Journal of Clinical and Experimental Hypnosis, 18,* 211–216.

Goodman, J., & Loftus, E. F. (1984, April). Social science looks at witness examination. *Trial, 20,* 52–57.

Goodman, M. (1985). *Psychotherapy and the legal system.* Paper presented at the annual meeting of the American Psychological Association, Los Angeles.

Graham, C., & Leibowitz, H. W. (1972). The effect of suggestion on visual acuity. *International Journal of Clinical and Experimental Hypnosis, 20,* 169–186.

Graham, M. H. (1978). The confrontation clause, the hearsay rule, and the forgetful witness. *Texas Law Review, 56,* 151–205.

Gravitz, M. A. (1981). Bibliographic sources of nineteenth century hypnosis literature. *American Journal of Clinical Hypnosis, 23,* 217–219.

Gravitz, M. A. (1983). An early case of investigative hypnosis: A brief communication. *International Journal of Clinical and Experimental Hypnosis, 31,* 224–226.

Gravitz, M. A. (1985a). A case of forensic hypnosis. In E. T. Dowd & J. M. Healy (Eds.), *Case studies in hypnotherapy.* New York: Guilford Press.

Gravitz, M. A. (1985b). Resistance in investigative hypnosis: Determinants and management. *American Journal of Clinical Hypnosis, 28,* 16–19.

Gregg, V. H. (1982). Posthypnotic amnesia for recently learned material: A comment on the paper by J. F. Kihlstrom (1980). *Bulletin of the British Society of Experimental and Clinical Hypnosis, 1982 (5),* 27–30.

Gross, M. (1980). Hypnosis as a diagnostic tool. *American Journal of Clinical Hypnosis, 23,* 47–52.

Gruber, L. N. (1983). Hypnotherapeutic techniques in patients with affective instability. *American Journal of Clinical Hypnosis, 25,* 263–266.

Gruenewald, D. (1982). Some thoughts on the distinction between the hypnotic situation and the hypnotic condition. *American Journal of Clinical Hypnosis, 25,* 46–51.

Gruenewald, D. (1984). On the nature of multiple personality: Comparisons with hypnosis. *International Journal of Clinical and Experimental Hypnosis, 32,* 170–190.

Gur, R. C., & Reyher, J. (1976). Enhancement of creativity via free-imagery and hypnosis. *American Journal of Clinical Hypnosis, 18,* 258–262.

Gutheil, T. G., & Applebaum, P. S. (1982). *Clinical handbook of psychiatry and the law.* New York: McGraw-Hill.

Haley, J. (1963). *Strategies of psychotherapy.* New York: Grune & Stratton.

Haley, S. (1974). When the patient reports atrocities. *Archives of General Psychiatry, 30,* 191–196.

Halleck, S. (1981). *Law in the practice of psychiatry.* New York: Plenum.

Ham, M. L. (1981). Hypnotic amnesia: A phenomenological and quantitative analysis. *Dissertation Abstracts International, 42,* 2600B.

Ham, M. W., & Spanos, N. P. (1974). Suggested auditory and visual hallucinations in task-motivated and hypnotic subjects. *American Journal of Clinical Hypnosis, 17,* 94–101.

Hammer, E. F. (1954). Posthypnotic suggestion and test performance. *Journal of Clinical and Experimental Hypnosis, 2,* 178–185.

Hammerschlag, H. E. (1957). *Hypnotism and crime.* Hollywood, CA: Wilshire.

Hanley, F. W. (1969). Hypnosis in the courtroom. *Canadian Psychiatric Association Journal, 14,* 351–354.

Hariman, J. (1982). The bearing of the "concentration" theory of hypnosis on the

Freudian conception of the unconscious. *Australian Journal of Clinical Hypnosis,* 5, 82–86.

Hart, M. M. (1981). Memory for details of an aggressive interpersonal interchange as a function of hypnotic induction. *Dissertation Abstracts International, 41,* 4292B.

Hartland, J. (1965). The value of "ego-strengthening" procedure prior to direct symptom removal under hypnosis. *American Journal of Clinical Hypnosis, 8,* 89–93.

Hartmann, H., Kris, E., & Lowenstein, R. M. (1946). Comments on the formation of psychic structure. *Psychoanalytic Study of the Child, 2,* 11–38.

Haward, L., & Ashworth, A. (1980). Some problems of evidence obtained by hypnosis. *Criminal Law Review,* 469–485.

Hegland, K. F. (1978). *Trial and practice skills.* St. Paul, MN: West.

Helwig, C. V. (1978). A comparison of the effectiveness of hypnotic-motivational, task-motivational and relaxation instructions in eliciting the recall of anxiety-inducing material. *Dissertation Abstracts International, 38,* 6013A.

Herman, L. (1964). The use of hypno-induced statements in criminal cases. *Ohio State Law Journal, 25,* 1–59.

Heron, W. T. (1952). Hypnosis as a factor in the production and detection of crime. *British Journal of Medical Hypnotism, 3,* 15–29.

Hibbard, W. S., & Worring, R. W. (1981). *Forensic hypnosis: The practical application of hypnosis in criminal investigation.* Springfield, IL: Charles C Thomas.

Hibler, N. S. (1984a). Forensic hypnosis: To hypnotize or not to hypnotize, that is the question. *American Journal of Clinical Hypnosis, 27,* 52–57.

Hibler, N. S. (1984b). Investigative aspects of forensic hypnosis. In W. C. Wester II & A. H. Smith (Eds.), *Comprehensive clinical hypnosis.* Philadelphia: J. B. Lippincott.

Hibler, N. S. (1986). *The role of suggestion in police interviews.* Paper presented at the 29th Annual Scientific Meeting of the American Society of Clinical Hypnosis, Las Vegas.

Hiland, D. N., & Dzieszkowski, P. A. (1984). Hypnosis in the investigation of aviation accidents. *Aviation, Space and Environmental Medicine, 55,* 1136–1142.

Hilgard, E. R. (1965). *Hypnotic susceptibility.* New York: Harcourt, Brace & World.

Hilgard, E. R. (1968). *The experience of hypnosis.* New York: Harcourt, Brace & World.

Hilgard, E. R. (1973). The domain of hypnosis: With some comments on alternative paradigms. *American Psychologist, 23,* 972–982.

Hilgard, E. R. (1975). Hypnosis. *Annual Review of Psychology, 26,* 19–44.

Hilgard, E. R. (1977). *Divided consciousness: Multiple controls in human thought and action.* New York: Wiley.

Hilgard, E. R. (1982). Hypnotic susceptibility and implications for measurement. *International Journal of Clinical and Experimental Hypnosis, 30,* 394–403.

Hilgard, E. R. (1984). The hidden observer and multiple personality. *International Journal of Clinical and Experimental Hypnosis, 32,* 248–253.

Hilgard, E. R. (1987). Research advances in hypnosis: Issues and methods. *International Journal of Clinical and Experimental Hypnosis, 35,* 248–264.

Hilgard, E. R., & Hommel, L. S. (1961). Selective amnesia for events within hypnosis in relation to repression. *Journal of Personality, 29,* 205–216.

Hilgard, E. R., & Loftus, E. F. (1979). Effective interrogation of the eye-witness. *International Journal of Clinical and Experimental Hypnosis, 27,* 342–357.

Hilgard, E. R., & Tart, C. T. (1966). Responsiveness to suggestions following waking and imagination instructions and following induction of hypnosis. *Journal of Abnormal Psychology, 71,* 196–208.

Hilgard, J. R. (1974). Imaginative involvement: Some characteristics of the highly hypnotizable and the non hypnotizable. *International Journal of Clinical and Experimental Hypnosis, 22,* 138–156.

Hilgard, J. R. (1979). *Personality and hypnosis: A study of imaginative involvement.* Chicago: University of Chicago Press.

Hodge, J. R. (1959). The management of dissociative reactions with hypnosis. *International Journal of Clinical and Experimental Hypnosis, 15,* 20–24.

Hofling, C. K., Heyl, B., & Wright, D. (1971). The ratio of total recoverable memories to conscious memories in normal subjects. *Comparative Psychiatry, 12,* 371–379.

Hosford, S. C. (1980, November 24). Petition for Hearing by the [California] Supreme Court, 4 Crim. 12044.

Howard, M. L. (1979). The effects of changes in the contextual demands on the report of posthypnotic amnesia. *Dissertation Abstracts International, 40,* 755A.

Howard, M. L., & Coe, W. C. (1980). The effects of context and subjects' perceived control in breaching posthypnotic amnesia. *Journal of Personality, 48,* 342–359.

Hull, C. L. (1933). *Hypnosis and suggestibility: An experimental approach.* New York: Appleton-Century-Crofts.

Hull, C. L. (1962). Psychology of the scientist: IV. Passages from the "idea books" of Clark L. Hull. *Perceptual and Motor Skills, 15,* 807–882.

Huse, B. (1930). Does hypnotic trance favor the recall of faint memories? *Journal of Experimental Psychology, 13,* 519–529.

Huston, J. (Director). (1948). *Let there be light* [Film]. Washington, DC: U.S. Army.

Hypnosis Quarterly. (1954–1984). (H. Arons, Ed.). Irvington, NJ: Power Publications. [Superseded by *Hypnosis Reports.* (R. Harte, Ed.). New York: Harte Center for Hypnosis.]

In re Eldridge, 82 N.Y. 161 (1880).

Jacobson, E. (1938). *Progressive relaxation.* Chicago: University of Chicago Press.

Jacoby, L. L., & Witherspoon, D. (1982). Remembering without awareness. *Canadian Journal of Psychology, 36,* 300–324.

Jaensch, E. R. (1923). *Eidetic imagery and typological methods of investigation.* New York: Harcourt, Brace.

James, W. (1890). *Principles of psychology.* New York: Henry Holt.

Janet, P. (1889). *L'automatisme psychologique.* Paris: F. Alcan.

Janet, P. (1925). *Psychological healing: A historical and clinical study.* E. Paul & C. Paul, Trans. New York: Macmillan. (Original work published 1919.)

Jeans, J. W. (1975). *Trial advocacy.* St. Paul, MN: West.

Jenkins, J. A. (1983, December 11). Experts' day in court. *New York Times Magazine,* pp. 98–106.

Jewett v. United States, 15 F.2d 955 (9th Cir. 1926).

Karlin, R. A. (1983). Forensic hypnosis—two case reports: A brief communication. *International Journal of Clinical and Experimental Hypnosis, 31,* 227–234.

Katona, G. (1940). *Organizing and memorizing.* New York: Columbia University Press.

Keeton, R. (1973). *Trial tactics and methods* (2nd ed.). Boston: Little, Brown.

Kellogg, E. R. (1929). Duration of the effects of posthypnotic suggestion. *Journal of Experimental Psychology, 12,* 502.

Kemperer, E. (1965). Past ego states emerging in hypnoanalysis. *International Journal of Clinical and Experimental Hypnosis, 13,* 132–143.

Kerr, N. L., & Bray, R. M. (Eds.). (1982). *The psychology of the courtroom.* New York: Academic Press.

Kihlstrom, J. F. (1977). Models of posthypnotic amnesia. *Annals of the New York Academy of Sciences, 296,* 284–301.

Kihlstrom, J. F. (1978). Context and cognition in posthypnotic amnesia. *International Journal of Clinical and Experimental Hypnosis, 26,* 246–267.

Kihlstrom, J. F. (1979). Hypnosis and psychopathology: Retrospect and prospect. *Journal of Abnormal Psychology, 88,* 459–473.

Kihlstrom, J. F. (1980). Posthypnotic amnesia for recently learned material: Interactions with "episodic" and "semantic" memory. *Cognitive Psychology, 12,* 227–251.

Kihlstrom, J. F. (1982). Hypnosis and the dissociation of memory, with special reference to posthypnotic amnesia. *Research Communications in Psychology, Psychiatry and Behavior, 7,* 181–197.

Kihlstrom, J. F. (1985). Hypnosis. *Annual Review of Psychology, 36,* 385–418.

Kihlstrom, J. F. (1987). *Hypnosis and the cognitive unconscious.* Invited address at the 38th Annual Meeting of the Society for Clinical and Experimental Hypnosis, Los Angeles.

Kihlstrom, J. F., Easton, R. D., & Shor, R. E. (1983). Spontaneous recovery of memory during posthypnotic amnesia. *International Journal of Clinical and Experimental Hypnosis, 31,* 243–248.

Kihlstrom, J. F., & Evans, F. J. (1976). Recovery of memory after posthypnotic amnesia. *Journal of Abnormal Psychology, 85,* 564–569.

Kihlstrom, J. F., & Evans, F. J. (1977). Residual effect of suggestions for posthypnotic amnesia: A re-examination. *Journal of Abnormal Psychology, 86,* 327–333.

Kihlstrom, J. F., & Evans, F. J. (1978). Generic recall during posthypnotic amnesia. *Bulletin of the Psychonomic Society, 12,* 57–60.

Kihlstrom, J. F., Evans, F. J., Orne, E. C., & Orne, M. T. (1980). Attempting to breach posthypnotic amnesia. *Journal of Abnormal Psychology, 89,* 603–616.

Kihlstrom, J. F., & Shor, R. E. (1978). Recall and recognition during posthypnotic amnesia. *International Journal of Clinical and Experimental Hypnosis, 26,* 330–349.

Kihlstrom, J. F., & Twersky, M. (1978). Relationship of posthypnotic amnesia to waking memory performance. *International Journal of Clinical and Experimental Hypnosis, 26,* 292–306.

Kihlstrom, J. F., & Wilson, L. (1984). Temporal organization of recall during posthypnotic amnesia. *Journal of Abnormal Psychology, 93,* 200–208.

Kinney, J., & Sachs, L. B. (1974). Increasing hypnotic susceptibility. *Journal of Abnormal Psychology, 83,* 145–150.

Klatzky, R. L., & Erdelyi, M. (1985). The response criterion problem in tests of hypnosis and memory. *International Journal of Clinical and Experimental Hypnosis, 33,* 246–257.

Kline, M. V. (1966). Hypnotic amnesia in psychotherapy. *International Journal of Clinical and Experimental Hypnosis, 14,* 112–120.

Kline, M. V. (1972). The production of antisocial behavior through hypnosis: New clinical data. _International Journal of Clinical and Experimental Hypnosis, 20_, 80–94.

Kline, M. V. (1976). Dangerous aspects of the practice of hypnosis and the need for legislative regulation. _Clinical Psychologist, 29_, 3–6.

Kline, M. V. (1979). Defending the mentally ill: The insanity defense and the role of forensic hypnosis. _International Journal of Clinical and Experimental Hypnosis, 27_, 375–401.

Kluft, R. P. (1982). Varieties of hypnotic interventions in the treatment of multiple personality. _American Journal of Clinical Hypnosis, 24_, 230–240.

Koffka, K. (1935). _Principles of Gestalt psychology._ New York: Harcourt, Brace.

Konecni, V. J., & Ebbesen, E. B. (1986). Courtroom testimony by psychologists on eyewitness identification issues. _Law and Human Behavior, 10_, 117–126.

Kraft, W. A., Rudolfa, E. R., & Reilley, R. R. (1985). Current trends in hypnosis and hypnotherapy: An interpersonal assessment. _American Journal of Clinical Hypnosis, 28_, 20–26.

Kroger, W. S. (1963). _Clinical and experimental hypnosis in medicine, dentistry and psychology._ Philadelphia: J. B. Lippincott.

Kroger, W. S. (1977). _Clinical and experimental hypnosis in medicine_ (2nd ed.). Philadelphia: J. B. Lippincott.

Kroger, W. S., & Doucé, R. G. (1979). Hypnosis in criminal investigation. _International Journal of Clinical and Experimental Hypnosis, 27_, 358–374.

Kroger, W. S., & Doucé, R. G. (1980). Forensic uses of hypnosis. _American Journal of Clinical Hypnosis, 23_, 86–93.

Kroger, W. S., & Fezler, W. D. (1976). _Hypnosis and behavior modification: Imagery conditioning._ Philadelphia: J. B. Lippincott.

Kubie, L. S., & Margolin, S. (1944). The process of hypnotism and the nature of the hypnotic state. _American Journal of Psychiatry, 100_, 611–622.

Labelle, L., Lamarche, M. C., & Laurence, J.-R. (in press). Potential jurors' opinions on the effects of hypnosis on eyewitness identification. _International Journal of Clinical and Experimental Hypnosis._

Laurence, J.-R., Nadon, R., Labelle, L., Button, J., & Perry, C. (1987). _Hypnosis, imagination and memory: When fantasy becomes reality._ Paper presented at the 38th Annual Meeting of the Society for Clinical and Experimental Hypnosis, Los Angeles.

Laurence, J.-R., Nadon, R., Nogrady, H., & Perry, C. (1986). Duality, dissociation, and memory creation in highly hypnotizable subjects. _International Journal of Clinical and Experimental Hypnosis, 34_, 295–310.

Laurence, J.-R., & Perry, C. (1981). The "hidden observer" phenomenon in hypnosis: Some additional findings. _Journal of Abnormal Psychology, 90_, 334–344.

Laurence, J.-R., & Perry, C. (1983a). Forensic hypnosis in the late nineteenth century. _International Journal of Clinical and Experimental Hypnosis, 31_, 266–283.

Laurence, J.-R., & Perry, C. (1983b). Hypnotically created memory among highly hypnotizable subjects. _Science, 222_, 523–524.

Laurence, J.-R., & Perry, C. (1987). Hypnosis, imagination and memory: When fantasy becomes reality. In B. L. Diamond, Chair, _Fifty years after Hull: Assessing the issues and data in hypnotic hypermnesia._ Symposium conducted at the 38th Annual Meeting of the Society for Clinical and Experimental Hypnosis, Los Angeles.

Laurence, J.-R., & Perry, C. (1988). *Hypnosis, will, and memory: A psycho-legal history.* New York: Guilford Press.

Law Times. (1893, October 14). Hypnotism and the law. p. 500.

Lazar, B. S., & Dempster, C. R. (1981). Failures in hypnosis and hypnotherapy. *American Journal of Clinical Hypnosis, 24,* 48–54.

LeCron, L. M. (Ed.). (1952). *Experimental hypnosis.* New York: Macmillan.

LeCron, L. M. (1953). A method of measuring the depth of hypnosis. *International Journal of Clinical and Experimental Hypnosis, 1,* 4–7.

LeCron, L. M., & Bordeaux, J. (1947). *Hypnotism today.* New York: Grune & Stratton.

Leippe, M. R., Wells, G. L., & Ostrom, T. M. (1978). Crime seriousness as a determinant of eyewitness accuracy. *Journal of Applied Psychology, 63,* 345–351.

Levendula, D. (1972). The possible role of hypnosis in criminal investigation. In S. R. Gerber & O. Schroeder, Jr. (Eds.), *Criminal investigation and interrogation.* Cincinnati: W. H. Anderson.

Levitt, E. E., Aronoff, G., Morgan, C. D., Overley, T. M., & Parrish, M. J. (1975). Testing the coercive power of hypnosis: Objectionable acts. *International Journal of Clinical and Experimental Hypnosis, 23,* 59–67.

Levitt, E. E., & Baker, E. L. (1983). The hypnotic relationship—another look at coercion, compliance and resistance: A brief communication. *International Journal of Clinical and Experimental Hypnosis, 31,* 125–131.

Levitt, E. E., & Harshman, S. (1963). The clinical practice of hypnosis in the U.S.: A preliminary survey. *International Journal of Clinical and Experimental Hypnosis, 11,* 55–65.

Levitt, E. E., Overley, T. M., & Rubinstein, D. (1975). The objectionable act as a mechanism for testing the coercive power of the hypnotic state. *American Journal of Clinical Hypnosis, 17,* 263–266.

Levy, S. S. (1955). Hypnosis and legal immutability. *Journal of Criminal Law, Criminology and Police Science, 46,* 333–346.

Lewin, K. (1936). *Principles of topological psychology.* New York: McGraw-Hill.

Liebeault, A. A. (1889). *Induced sleep and related states.* Paris: Doin.

Loftus, E. F. (1975). Leading questions and the eyewitness report. *Cognitive Psychology, 7,* 560–572.

Loftus, E. F. (1979a). *Eyewitness testimony.* Cambridge, MA: Harvard University Press.

Loftus, E. F. (1979b). *The manipulative uses of language* (*Psychology Today* Cassette, No. 20234). New York: Ziff Davis.

Loftus, E. F., Miller, D. G., & Burns, H. J. (1978). Semantic integration of verbal information into a visual memory. *Journal of Experimental Psychology: Human Learning and Memory, 4,* 19–31.

Loftus, E. F., & Zanni, G. (1975). Eyewitness testimony: The influence of the wording of a question. *Bulletin of the Psychonomic Society, 5,* 86–88.

Lundy, R. M. (1987). How can we account for reports of hypnotic hypermnesia? In B. L. Diamond (Chair), *Fifty years after Hull: Assessing the issues and data in hypnotic hypermnesia.* Symposium conducted at the 38th Annual Meeting of the Society for Clinical and Experimental Hypnosis, Los Angeles.

Lynn, S. J., Kaltenbach, P., & Weekes, J. R. (1987). Hypnosis, Contextual reinstatement and eyewitness recall: The effects of interpretation of events, the recall task and witness sex. In K. S. Bowers (Chair), *Hypnosis and Memory: Recent findings.* Symposium conducted at the 38th Annual Meeting of the Society for Clinical and Experimental Hypnosis, Los Angeles.

MacHovec, F. J. (1979). The cult of Asklipios. *American Journal of Clinical Hypnosis, 22,* 85–90.

MacHovec, F. J. (1981). Hypnosis to facilitate recall in psychogenic amnesia and fugue states: Treatment variables. *American Journal of Clinical Hypnosis, 24,* 7–13.

MacHovec, F. J. (1985). Treatment variables and the use of hypnosis in the brief therapy of post-traumatic stress disorders. *International Journal of Clinical and Experimental Hypnosis, 33,* 6–14.

MacHovec, F. J. (1988). Hypnosis complications, risk factors and prevention. *American Journal of Clinical Hypnosis, 31,* 40–49.

Madigan, S. (1976). Recovery and reminiscence in free recall. *Memory and Cognition, 4,* 233–236.

Madigan, S., & Lawrence, V. (1980). Factors affecting item recovery and hypermnesia in free recall. *American Journal of Psychology, 93,* 489–504.

Malpass, R. S., & Devine, P. G. (1980a). Guided memory in eyewitness identification. *Journal of Applied Psychology, 66,* 343–350.

Malpass, R. S., & Devine, P. G. (1980b). Realism and eyewitness identification research. *Law and Human Behavior, 66,* 347–357.

Marcuse, F. L. (1953). Antisocial behavior and hypnosis. *International Journal of Clinical and Experimental Hypnosis, 1,* 18–20.

Marcuse, F. L. (1959). *Hypnosis: Fact and fiction.* Baltimore: Penguin Books.

Marcuse, F. L. (1976). *Hypnosis: Fact and Fiction* (2nd ed.). Baltimore: Penguin Books.

Marshall, J. (1969, February). The evidence—do we see and hear what it is? Or do our senses lie? *Psychology Today,* pp. 48–52.

Mauet, T. A. (1980). *Fundamentals of trial techniques.* Boston: Little, Brown.

McCabe, M. P., Collins, J. K., & Burns, A. M. (1978). Hypnosis as an altered state of consciousness: I. A review of traditional theories. *Australian Journal of Clinical and Experimental Hypnosis, 6,* 39–54.

McCabe, M. P., Collins, J. K., & Burns, A. M. (1979). Hypnosis as an altered state of consciousness: II. A review of contemporary theories. *Australian Journal of Clinical and Experimental Hypnosis, 7,* 7–25.

McCann, T., & Sheehan, P. W. (1987). Confidence effects in experimental pseudo memory. In K. S. Bowers (Chair), *Hypnosis and memory: Recent findings.* Symposium conducted at the 38th Annual Meeting of the Society for Clinical and Experimental Hypnosis, Los Angeles.

McCloskey, M., & Egeth, H. E. (1983). Eyewitness identification: What can a psychologist tell a jury? *American Psychologist, 38,* 550–563.

McConkey, K. M. (1986). Opinions about hypnosis and self-hypnosis before and after hypnotic testing. *International Journal of Clinical and Experimental Hypnosis, 34,* 311–319.

McConkey, K. M., & Jupp, J. J. (1985). Opinions about the forensic use of hypnosis. *Australian Psychologist, 20,* 283–291.

McConkey, K. M., Sheehan, P. W., & Cross, D. G. (1980). Post-hypnotic amnesia: Seeing is not remembering. *British Journal of Social and Clinical Psychology, 19,* 99–107.

McConnell, J. V. (1970). Doctors are people too. In *Effective utilization of psychiatric evidence*. New York: Practicing Law Institute. (Original work published 1968)

McCranie, E. J., Crasilneck, H. B., & Teter, H. R. (1955). The electroencephalogram in hypnotic age regression. *Psychiatric Quarterly, 29*, 85–88.

McDonald, R. D., & Smith, J. R. (1975). Trance logic in tranceable and simulating subjects. *International Journal of Clinical and Experimental Hypnosis, 23*, 80–89.

McEwan, N. H., & Yuille, J. C. (1982). *The effect of hypnosis as an interview technique on eyewitness memory*. Paper presented at the annual meeting of the Canadian Psychological Association, Montreal.

McGeoch, J. A. (1935). The conditions of reminiscence. *American Journal of Psychology, 47*, 65–89.

Meares, A. (1960). *A system of medical hypnosis*. New York: Julian Press.

Milgram, S. (1969). *Obedience to authority*. New York: Harper & Row.

Miller, G. A., Galanter, E., & Pribram, K. H. (1960). *Plans and the structure of behavior*. New York: Holt, Rinehart & Winston.

Miller, J. (1983). "Spontaneous" age regression: A clinical report. *American Journal of Clinical Hypnosis, 26*, 53–55.

Millwee, S. C. (1979). The hypnosis unit in today's law enforcement. *The Police Chief, 46*, 65–70.

Miner, J. P. (1984). Cognitive functioning in hypnosis: The effect of hypnotic susceptibility and capacity for trance. *Dissertation Abstracts International, 45*, 680B.

Minor, D. (Producer). (1981). *Forensic hypnosis* [Television program; a segment of *Walter Cronkite's universe*]. New York: Columbia Broadcasting System.

Miranda v. Arizona, 384 U.S. 436, 16 L.Ed.2d 694, 86 S. Ct. 1602 (1966).

Mitchell, M. B. (1932). Retroactive inhibition and hypnosis. *Journal of General Psychology, 7*, 343–359.

Moll, A. (1958). *The study of hypnosis*. New York: Julian Press. (Original work published 1889)

Monahan, J., & Loftus, E. F. (1982). The psychology of law. *Annual Review of Psychology, 33*, 441–475.

Moore, E. H. (1949). Elements of error in testimony. *Oregon Law Review, 28*, 293–304.

Morrill, A. E. (1979). *Trial diplomacy*. Chicago: Court Practice Institute.

Morgan, T. R. (1983, January). The power of the trance. *Esquire*, pp. 74–81.

Morse, S. (1978). Law and mental health professionals: The limits of expertise. *Professional Psychology, 9*, 389–399.

Mott, T., Jr. (1982). The role of hypnosis in psychotherapy. *American Journal of Clinical Hypnosis, 24*, 241–248.

Munsterberg, H. (1908). *On the witness stand*. New York: Doubleday.

Mutter, C. B. (1980). Critique of videotape presentation on forensic hypnotic regression: *The case of Dora. American Journal of Clinical Hypnosis, 23*, 99–101.

Mutter, C. B. (1984). The use of hypnosis with defendants. *American Journal of Clinical Hypnosis, 27*, 42–51.

Nace, E. P., & Orne, M. T. (1970). Fate of an uncompleted posthypnotic suggestion. *Journal of Abnormal Psychology, 75*, 278–285.

Nash, M. R., Johnson, L. S., & Tipton, R. D. (1979). Hypnotic age regression and the occurrence of transitional object relationships. *Journal of Abnormal Psychology, 88*, 547–555.

Nash, M. R., Lynn, S. J., Stanley, S. M., Frauman, D., & Rhue, J. (1985). Hypnotic age regression and the importance of assessing interpersonally relevant affect. *International Journal of Clinical and Experimental Hypnosis, 33,* 224–235.

Nebraska Law Review. (1952). Hypnotism, suggestibility and the law. *31,* 575–596.

Newsweek. (1974, August 5). Hypnosis for witnesses. p. 57.

Newsweek. (1981, October 19). The trials of hypnosis. p. 96.

New York Times. (1979, August 19). Cautious use of investigative hypnosis is growing. p. 49.

Nides, M. A. (1987). The use of hypnotic age regression to recover a forgotten language. In K. S. Bowers (Chair), *Hypnosis and memory: Recent findings.* Symposium conducted at the 38th Annual Meeting of the Society for Clinical and Experimental Hypnosis, Los Angeles.

Nilsson, L.-G. (Ed.). (1979). *Perspectives on memory research.* Hillsdale, NJ: Erlbaum.

Nizer, L. (1963). *My life in court.* New York: Pyramid Books.

Nogrady, H., McConkey, K. M., Laurence, J.-R., & Perry, C. (1983). Dissociation, duality, and demand characteristics in hypnosis. *Journal of Abnormal Psychology, 92,* 223–235.

Nogrady, H., McConkey, K. M., & Perry, C. (1985). Enhancing visual memory: Trying hypnosis, trying imagination, trying again. *Journal of Abnormal Psychology, 94,* 195–204.

Norman, D. A. (1968). *Memory and attention* (2nd ed.). New York: Wiley.

Nygard, J. W. (1939). Cerebral circulation prevailing during sleep and hypnosis. *Journal of Experimental Psychology, 24,* 1–20.

O'Brien, R. M. (1979). Hypnosis and task-motivation instructions for "post-experimental" posthypnotic instructions. *Perceptual and Motor Skills, 45,* 1274.

O'Brien, R. M., & Rabuck, S. J. (1976). Experimentally produced self-repugnant behavior as a function of hypnosis and waking suggestion. *American Journal of Clinical Hypnosis, 19,* 182–184.

O'Connell, D. N., Shor, R. E., & Orne, M. T. (1970). Hypnotic age regression: An empirical and methodological analysis. *Journal of Abnormal Psychology Monographs, 76*(3, Part 2).

Olness, K. (1984). Other voices. In G. J. Pratt, D. P. Wood, & B. M. Alman (Eds.), *A clinical hypnosis primer.* La Jolla, CA: Psychology and Consulting Associates Press.

Orne, M. T. (1951). The mechanisms of hypnotic age regression: An experimental study. *Journal of Abnormal and Social Psychology, 46,* 213–225.

Orne, M. T. (1959). The nature of hypnosis: Artifact and essence. *Journal of Abnormal and Social Psychology, 58,* 277–299.

Orne, M.T. (1962). Antisocial behavior and hypnosis: Problems of cont ol and validation in empirical studies. In G. H. Estabrooks (Ed.), *Hypnosis: Current problems.* New York: Harper & Row.

Orne, M. T. (1964). A note on the occurrence of hypnosis without conscious intent. *International Journal of Clinical and Experimental Hypnosis, 12,* 75–77.

Orne, M. T. (1965). Undesirable effects of hypnosis: The determinants and management. *International Journal of Clinical and Experimental Hypnosis, 13,* 226–237.

Orne, M. T. (1966). On the mechanisms of posthypnotic amnesia. *International Journal of Clinical and Experimental Hypnosis, 14,* 121–134.

Orne, M. T. (1967). What must a satisfactory theory of hypnosis explain? *International Journal of Psychiatry, 3*, 206–211.

Orne, M. T. (1971). The simulation of hypnosis: Why, how and what it means. *International Journal of Clinical and Experimental Hypnosis, 19*, 183–210.

Orne, M. T. (1972). Can a hypnotized subject be compelled to carry out otherwise unacceptable behavior? *International Journal of Clinical and Experimental Hypnosis, 20*, 101–117.

Orne, M. T. (1977). The construct of hypnosis: Implications of the definition for research and practice. *Annals of the New York Academy of Sciences, 296*, 14–33.

Orne, M. T. (1979). The use and misuse of hypnosis in court. *International Journal of Clinical and Experimental Hypnosis, 27*, 311–341.

Orne, M. T. (1983, December 12). Hypnosis: Useful in medicine, dangerous in court. *U.S. News and World Report*, pp. 67–68.

Orne, M. T. (1985). *Forensic hypnosis.* Paper presented at the annual meeting of the American Psychological Association, Los Angeles.

Orne, M. T. (1988). *Forensic hypnosis.* Paper presented at the annual meeting of the Association of American Law Schools, Evidence section, Miami.

Orne, M. T., Dinges, D. F., & Orne, E. C. (1984, December). The forensic use of hypnosis. *National Institute of Justice*, 1–6.

Orne, M. T., & McConkey, K. M. (1981). Toward convergent inquiry into self-hypnosis. *International Journal of Clinical and Experimental Hypnosis, 29*, 313–323.

Orne, M. T., Soskis, D. A., Dinges, D. F., & Orne, E. C. (1984). Hypnotically induced testimony. In G. L. Wells & E. F. Loftus (Eds.), *Eyewitness testimony: Psychological perspectives.* Cambridge, England: Cambridge University Press.

Orne, M. T., Whitehouse, W. G., Dinges, D. F., & Orne, E. C. (1988). Reconstructing memory through hypnosis: Forensic and clinical implications. In H. M. Pettinati (Ed.), *Hypnosis and memory.* New York: Guilford Press.

Ornstein, B. (Producer). (1981). *Camera in the court* [Television program]. San Francisco: KQED-TV.

Oteri, J. *The Joe Oteri Show* [Television program]. Boston: February 25, 1979.

Packard, V. (1958). *The hidden persuaders.* New York: Pocket Books.

Parrish, M. J. (1974). Moral predisposition and hypnotic influence of "immoral" behavior: An exploratory study. *American Journal of Clinical Hypnosis, 17*, 115–124.

Pascal, G. R. (1949). The effect of relaxation upon recall. *American Journal of Psychology, 62*, 32–47.

Pattie, F. A. (1943). Some American contributions to the science of hypnosis. *American Scholar, 12*, 444–454.

Pavlov, I. P. (1928). *Lectures of conditioned reflexes: Twenty-five years of objective study of the higher nervous system activity (behavior) of animals* (W. H. Gault, Trans.). New York: Liveright.

Payne, D. G. (1987). Hypermnesia and reminiscence in recall: A historical and empirical review. *Psychological Bulletin, 101*, 5–28.

Penzien, S., Kvinge, D., Lynn, S. J., Bellezza, F., & Abel, M. (1987). The effects of hypnosis, contextual reinstatement and hypnosis plus contextual reinstatement on delayed witness recall. In K. S. Bowers (Chair), *Hypnosis and memory: Recent findings.* Symposium conducted at the 38th Annual Meeting of the Society for Clinical and Experimental Hypnosis, Los Angeles.

Perry, C. (1977a). Is hypnotizability modifiable? *International Journal of Clinical and Experimental Hypnosis, 25,* 367–374.

Perry, C. (1977b). Uncanceled hypnotic suggestions: The effects of hypnotic depth and hypnotic skill on their posthypnotic persistence. *Journal of Abnormal Psychology, 86,* 570–574.

Perry, C. (1979). Hypnotic coercion and compliance to it: A review of evidence presented in a legal case. *International Journal of Clinical and Experimental Hypnosis, 27,* 187–218.

Perry, C., & Laurence, J.-R. (1983). The enhancement of memory by hypnosis in the legal system. *Canadian Psychology, 24,* 155–167.

Perry, C., Laurence, J.-R. D'Eon, J. D., & Tallant, B. (1988). Hypnotic age regression techniques in the elicitation of memories: Applied uses and abuses. In H. M. Pettinati (Ed.), *Hypnosis and memory.* New York: Guilford Press.

Peterson, L. R., & Peterson, M. J. (1959). Short term retention of individual verbal items. *Journal of Experimental Psychology, 38,* 193–198.

Pettinati, H. M. (1979). Selectivity in memory during posthypnotic amnesia. *Dissertation Abstracts International, 40,* 898B–899B.

Pettinati, H. M. (Ed.). (1988). *Hypnosis and memory.* New York: Guilford Press.

Pettinati, H. M., & Evans, F. J. (1978). Posthypnotic amnesia: Evaluation of selective recall of successful experiences. *International Journal of Clinical and Experimental Hypnosis, 26,* 317–329.

Piaget, J. (1953). *The origin of intelligence in the child.* London: Routledge & Kegan Paul.

Poythress, N. C. (1982). Concerning reform in expert testimony. *Law and Human Behavior, 6,* 39–43.

Putnam, W. H. (1979). Hypnosis and distortions in eyewitness memory. *International Journal of Clinical and Experimental Hypnosis, 27,* 437–448.

Rafky, D. M., & Bernstein, J. (1984). Forensic hypnosis and witness recall. *Journal of Police Science and Administration, 12,* 277–286.

Raginsky, B. B. (1969). Hypnotic recall of an aircrash cause. *International Journal of Clinical and Experimental Hypnosis, 17,* 1–19.

Rainer, D. D. (1984). Eyewitness testimony: Does hypnosis enhance accuracy, distortion, and confidence? *Dissertation Abstracts International, 45,* 340B.

Rapaport, D. (1942). *Emotions and memory.* Baltimore: Williams & Wilkins.

Rapaport, D. (Ed.). (1951). *Organization and pathology of thought.* New York: Columbia University Press.

Ray, J. A. (1962). Editorial from America: The adolescent infant. *British Journal of Medical Hypnotism, 13,* 15–16.

Register, P. A., & Kihlstrom, J. F. (1986). Finding the hypnosis virtuoso. *International Journal of Clinical and Experimental Hypnosis, 34,* 84–97.

Register, P. A., & Kihlstrom, J. F. (1987). Hypnotic effects on hypermnesia. *International Journal of Clinical and Experimental Hypnosis, 35,* 155–170.

Reiff, R., & Scheerer, M. (1959). *Memory and hypnotic age regression: Developmental aspects of cognitive function explored through hypnosis.* New York: International Universities Press.

Reiser, M. (1974). Hypnosis as an aid in homicide investigation. *American Journal of Clinical Hypnosis, 17,* 84–87.

Reiser, M. (1976). Hypnosis as a tool in criminal investigation. *The Police Chief, 43,* 39–40.

Reiser, M. (1978). Hypnosis and its uses in law enforcement. *Police Journal* (Great Britain), *51,* 24–33.

Reiser, M. (1980). *Handbook of investigative hypnosis.* Los Angeles: Law Enforcement Hypnosis Institute.

Reiser, M. (1984a, August). Investigative hypnosis: A controversial technique. *Police Chief,* 65–68.

Reiser, M. (1984b). Police use of investigative hypnosis: Scientism, ethics and power games. *American Journal of Forensic Psychology, 2,* 115–143.

Reiser, M. (1985a). Investigative hypnosis: Scientism, memory tricks and power plays. In J. K. Zeig (Ed.), *Ericksonian psychotherapy: Vol. 1. Structures.* New York: Brunner/Mazel.

Reiser, M. (1985b). Some current issues in investigative hypnosis. *International Journal of Investigative Hypnosis, 33,* 41–56.

Reiser, M. (1986, April). Reader's forum. *Division on Psychological Hypnosis Newsletter* (American Psychological Association), pp. 5–6.

Reiser, M., & Neilson, M. (1980). Investigative hypnosis: A developing specialty. *American Journal of Clinical and Experimental Hypnosis, 23,* 75–84.

Reiter, P. J. (1958). *Antisocial or criminal acts and hypnosis: A case study.* Springfield, IL: Charles C Thomas.

Relinger, H. (1984). Hypnotic hypermnesia: A critical review. *American Journal of Clinical Hypnosis, 26,* 212–225.

Relinger, H., & Stern, T. (1983). Guidelines for forensic hypnosis. *Journal of Psychiatry and the Law, 11,* 69–74.

Reyher, J., & Pottinger, J. (1976). The significance of the interpersonal relationship in the induction of hypnosis. *American Journal of Clinical Hypnosis, 19,* 103–107.

Reyher, J., & Smyth, L. (1971). Suggestibility during the execution of a posthypnotic suggestion. *Journal of Abnormal Psychology, 78,* 258–265.

Ritterman, M. (1983). *Using hypnosis in family therapy.* San Francisco: Jossey-Bass.

Rivers, S. M. (1981). Suggested amnesia in the context of directed forgetting. *Dissertation Abstracts International, 41,* 3875B–3876B.

Roberts, A. C. (1982). The abuse of hypnosis in the legal system. *American Journal of Forensic Psychiatry, 3,* 67–86.

Rodolfa, E. R., Kraft, W. A., & Reilley, R. R. (1985). Current trends in hypnosis and hypnotherapy: An interdisciplinary assessment. *American Journal of Clinical Hypnosis, 28,* 20–26.

Roediger, H. L., III, & Payne, D. G. (1982). Hypermnesia: The role of repeated testing. *Journal of Experimental Psychology: Learning, Memory, and Cognition, 8,* 66–72.

Rosen, H. (1960). Hypnosis—applications and misapplications. *Journal of the American Medical Association, 172,* 683–687.

Rosene, J. S. (Producer) (1981). *Miller's Court* [Television program] Boston.

Rosenhan, D., & London, P. (1963). Hypnosis in the unhypnotizable: A study in rote learning. *Journal of Experimental Psychology, 65,* 30–34.

Rosenthal, B. G. (1944). Hypnosis recall of material learned under anxiety and non-anxiety producing conditions. *Journal of Experimental Psychology, 34,* 369–389.

Rosenthal, R. (1966). *Experimenter effects in behavioral research.* New York: Appleton-Century-Crofts.

Rowland, L. W. (1939). Will hypnotized persons try to harm themselves or others? *Journal of Abnormal and Social Psychology, 34,* 114–117.

St. Jean, R., & Coe, W. C. (1981). Recall and recognition memory during posthypnotic amnesia: A failure to confirm the disrupted-search hypothesis and the memory disorganization hypothesis. *Journal of Abnormal Psychology, 90,* 81–86.

Salter, A. (1941). Three techniques of autohypnosis. *Journal of General Psychology, 24,* 423–438.

Salzberg, H. C. (1960). The effects of hypnotic, posthypnotic and waking suggestions on performance using tasks varied in complexity. *International Journal of Clinical and Experimental Hypnosis, 8,* 251–258.

Salzberg, H. C. (1977). The hypnotic interview in crime detection. *American Journal of Clinical Hypnosis, 19,* 255–258.

Sanders, G. S., & Simmons, W. L. (1983). Use of hypnosis to enhance eyewitness accuracy: Does it work? *Journal of Applied Psychology, 68,* 70–77.

Sanders, G. S., & Warnick, D. (1981). Some conditions maximizing eyewitness accuracy: A learning/memory model. *Journal of Criminal Justice, 9,* 136–142.

Sannito, T., & McGovern, P. J. (1985). *Courtroom psychology for trial lawyers.* New York: Wiley (Law Publications).

Sarbin, T. R. (1972). Imaging as muted role taking: A historical–linguistic analysis. In P. W. Sheehan (Ed.), *The function and nature of imagery.* New York: Academic Press.

Sarbin, T. R. (1984). Nonvolition in hypnosis: A semiotic analysis. *Psychological Record, 34,* 537–549.

Sarbin, T. R., & Coe, W. C. (1972). *Hypnosis: A social-psychological analysis of influence communication.* New York: Holt, Rinehart & Winston.

Sarbin, T. R., & Lim, D. T. (1963). Some evidence in support of the role taking hypothesis in hypnosis. *International Journal of Clinical and Experimental Hypnosis, 11,* 98–103.

Schachtel, E. G. (1949). On memory and childhood amnesia. In P. Mullahy (Ed.), *A study of interpersonal relations.* New York: Hermitage.

Schafer, D. W. (1984, May). Forensic hypnosis after Shirley: An interim situation. *Division 30 (Hypnosis) Newsletter.*

Schafer, D., & Rubio, R. (1978). Hypnosis to aid the recall of witnesses. *International Journal of Clinical and Experimental Hypnosis, 26,* 81–91.

Schein, E. H. (1961). *Coercive persuasion.* New York: Norton.

Schilder, P. (1927). *The nature of hypnosis* (I. Corwin, Trans.) New York: International Universities Press.

Scholder, M. H. (1982). The argument against the use of hypnosis to improve or enhance the memory of courtroom witnesses. *Law and Psychology Review, 7,* 71–86.

Schwartz, W. (1980). Hypnosis and episodic memory. *International Journal of Clinical and Experimental Hypnosis, 26,* 307–316.

Scott, E. M. (1977). Hypnosis in the courtroom. *American Journal of Clinical Hypnosis, 19,* 163–165.

Sears, A. B. (1954). A comparison of hypnotic and waking recall. *Journal of Clinical and Experimental Hypnosis, 2,* 296–304.

Serrill, M. S. (1984, September 17). Breaking the spell of hypnosis. *Time*, p. 62.

Shapiro, D. L. (1984). *Psychological evaluation and expert testimony.* New York: Van Nostrand Reinhold.

Shapiro, J. L. (1979). *The use of hypnosis in graduate training of counselors.* Unpublished manuscript.

Shapiro, J. L. (1981). Psychotherapy and hypnotherapy with rape victims and rapists [Videotape]. San Rafael: California Graduate School of Family Psychology.

Shapiro, J. L., & Diamond, M. J. (1972). Increases of hypnotizability as a function of encounter group training: Some confirming evidence. *Journal of Abnormal Psychology, 79*, 112–115.

Shapiro, J. L., Edmonston, B. A., & Wallace, E. (1986). *Handbook of ethical and legal guidelines for MFCC's and psychologists.* Santa Clara, CA: Santa Clara University Division of Counseling Psychology and Education.

Shapiro, J. L., & Scheflin, A. W. (1986). *Trance on trial: The legal implications of Ericksonian hypnotherapy* [Audiotape]. Garden Grove, CA: Infomedix.

Shapiro, S. R., & Erdelyi, M. H. (1974). Hypermnesia for pictures but not for words. *Journal of Experimental Psychology, 103*, 1218–1219.

Shaul, R. D. (1978). Eyewitness testimony and hypnotic hypermnesia. *Dissertation Abstracts International, 39*, 2521B.

Sheehan, P. W. (1973). Analysis of the heterogeneity of "faking" and "simulating" performance in the hypnotic setting. *International Journal of Clinical and Experimental Hypnosis, 21*, 213–225.

Sheehan, P. W. (1980). Factors influencing rapport in hypnosis. *Journal of Abnormal Psychology, 89*, 263–281.

Sheehan, P. W., Grigg, L., & McCann, T. (1984). Memory distortion following exposure to false information in hypnosis. *Journal of Abnormal Psychology, 93*, 259–265.

Sheehan, P. W., & Orne, M. T. (1968). Some comments on the nature of posthypnotic behavior. *Journal of Nervous and Mental Disease, 146*, 209–220.

Sheehan, P. W., & Perry, C. W. (1976). *Methodologies of hypnosis: A critical appraisal of contemporary paradigms of hypnosis.* Hillsdale, NJ: Erlbaum.

Sheehan, P. W., & Tilden, J. (1983). Effects of suggestibility and hypnosis on accurate and distorted retrieval from memory. *Journal of Experimental Psychology: Learning, Memory, and Cognition, 9*, 283–293.

Sheehan, P. W., & Tilden, J. (1984). Real and simulated occurrences of memory distortion in hypnosis. *Journal of Abnormal Psychology, 93*, 47–57.

Sheehan, P. W., & Tilden, J. (1986). The consistency of occurrences of memory distortion following hypnotic induction. *International Journal of Clinical and Experimental Hypnosis, 34*, 122–137.

Shields, I. W., & Knox, V. J. (1986). Level of processing as a determinant of hypnotic hypermnesia. *Journal of Abnormal Psychology, 95*, 358–364.

Shiffrin, R. M. (1976). Capacity limitation in information processing, attention and memory. In W. K. Estes (Ed.), *Handbook of learning and cognitive processes* (Vol. 4). Hillsdale, NJ: Erlbaum.

Shor, R. E. (1959). Hypnosis and the concept of the generalized reality orientation. *American Journal of Psychotherapy, 13*, 582–602.

Shor, R. E. (1962). Three dimensions of hypnotic depth. *International Journal of Clinical and Experimental Hypnosis, 10*, 23–28.

Shor, R. E., & Orne, E. C. (1962). *Harvard Group Scale of Hypnotic Susceptibility.* Palo Alto, CA: Consulting Psychologists Press.

Shor, R. E., Pistole, D. D., Easton, R. D., & Kihlstrom, J. F. (1984). Relation of predicted to actual hypnotic responsiveness, with special reference to posthypnotic amnesia. *International Journal of Clinical and Experimental Hypnosis, 32,* 376–387.

Sidis, B. (1898). *The psychology of suggestion.* New York: D. Appleton.

Simon, M. J., & Salzberg, H. C. (1985). The effect of manipulated expectancies on posthypnotic amnesia. *International Journal of Clinical and Experimental Hypnosis, 33,* 40–51.

Sloane, M. C. (1981). A comparison of hypnosis vs. waking state and visual vs. non visual recall instructions for witness/victim memory retrieval in actual major crimes. *Dissertation Abstracts International, 42,* 2551B.

Slovensko, R. (1973). *Psychiatry and law.* Boston: Little, Brown.

Smith, M. C. (1983). Hypnotic memory enhancement of witnesses: Does it work? *Psychological Bulletin, 94,* 387–407.

Smith, W. H. (1987). Antecedents of post-traumatic disorder: Wasn't being raped enough? In B. W. Newton, (chair), *Perspectives on hypnosis and its application.* Symposium conducted at the 38th Annual Meeting of the Society for Clinical and Experimental Hypnosis, Los Angeles.

Snell, B. (1953). *The discovery of the mind: The Greek origins of European thought.* New York: Harper.

Society for Clinical and Experimental Hypnosis. (1979). Resolution (10/78). *International Journal of Clinical and Experimental Hypnosis, 27,* 452–453.

Soper, P. H., & L'Abate, L. (1977). Paradox as a therapeutic technique: A review. *International Journal of Family Counseling, 5,* 10–21.

Spanos, N. P. (1986). Hypnotic behavior: A social-psychological interpretation of amnesia, analgesia and "trance logic." *Behavioral and Brain Sciences, 9,* 449–502.

Spanos, N. P., & Barber, T. X. (1974). Toward a convergence in hypnosis research. *American Psychologist, 29,* 500–511.

Spanos, N. P., & Bodorik, H. L. (1977). Suggested amnesia and disorganized recall in hypnotic and task motivated subjects. *Journal of Abnormal Psychology, 86,* 295–305.

Spanos, N. P., & McLean, J. (1985–1986a). Hypnotically created false reports do not demonstrate pseudomemories. *British Journal of Experimental and Clinical Hypnosis, 3,* 167–171.

Spanos, N. P., & McLean, J. (1985–1986b). Hypnotically created pseudo-memories: Memory distortions or reporting biases? *British Journal of Experimental and Clinical Hypnosis, 3,* 155–159.

Spanos, N. P., & Radtke, H. L. (1982). Hypnotic amnesia as strategic enactment: A cognitive, social-psychological perspective. *Research Communications in Psychology, Psychiatry and Behavior, 43,* 565–573.

Spanos, N. P., Radtke-Bodorik, H. L., & Shabinsky, M. A. (1980). Amnesia, subjective organization and learning of a list of unrelated words in hypnotic and task-motivated subjects. *International Journal of Clinical and Experimental Hypnosis, 28,* 126–139.

Spanos, N. P., Tkachyk, M. E., Bertrand, L. D., & Weekes, J. R. (1984). The dissipation hypothesis of hypnotic amnesia: More disconfirming evidence. *Psychological Reports, 55,* 191–196.

Spence, D. P. (1982). *Narrative truth and historical truth: Meaning and interpretation in psychoanalysis.* New York: Norton.

Spence, G. (1984). Questioning the adverse witness. *Litigation, 10,* 13–18, 64.

Spiegel, D. (1981). Vietnam grief work using hypnosis. *American Journal of Clinical Hypnosis, 24,* 33–40.

Spiegel, D. (1987). The *Shirley* decision: The cure is worse than the disease. In R. W. Rieber (Ed.), *Advances in forensic psychology and psychiatry* (Vol. 2). Norwood, NJ: Ablex.

Spiegel, D., & Spiegel, H. (1987). Forensic uses of hypnosis. In I. B. Weiner & A. K. Hess (Eds.), *Handbook of forensic psychology.* New York: Wiley.

Spiegel, H. (1980). Hypnosis and evidence: Help or hindrance? *Annals of the New York Academy of Sciences, 347,* 73–85.

Spiegel, H., & Spiegel, D. (1978). *Trance and treatment: Clinical uses of hypnosis.* New York: International Universities Press.

Stager, G. L., & Lundy, R. M. (1985). Hypnosis and the learning and recall of visually presented material. *International Journal of Clinical and Experimental Hypnosis, 33,* 27–39.

Stalnaker, J. M., & Riddle, E. E. (1932). The effect of hypnosis on long delayed memory. *Journal of General Psychology, 6,* 429–440.

Stark, E. (1984, February). Hypnosis on trial. *Psychology Today,* pp. 34–36.

Stern, W. (1939). *General psychology from a personalistic standpoint.* New York: Macmillan.

Stratton, J. G. (1977). The use of hypnosis in law enforcement criminal investigations. *Journal of Police Science and Administration, 5,* 399–406.

Strentz, T. (1980). The Stockholm syndrome: Law enforcement policy and ego defenses of the hostage. *Annals of the New York Academy of Sciences, 347,* 137–150.

Stromberg, B. V. (1975). The use of subjective questioning in hypnotic psychotherapy. *Journal of Clinical Psychology, 31,* 110–115.

Stump, A. (1975, October 4–10). "That's him—the guy who hit me!" *TV Guide,* pp. 32–35.

Sturm, C. E. (1982). *Eyewitness memory: Effects of guided memory and hypnotic hypermnesia techniques and hypnotic susceptibility.* Unpublished doctoral dissertation, University of Montana.

Suggs, D. L. (1979). The use of psychological research by the judiciary. *Law and Human Behavior, 3,* 135–148.

Swiercinsky, D., & Coe, W. C. (1970). Hypnosis, hypnotic responsiveness and learning meaningful material. *International Journal of Clinical and Experimental Hypnosis, 18,* 217–222.

Swiercinsky, D., & Coe, W. C. (1971). Hypnosis, hypnotic responsiveness and learning meaningful material. *International Journal of Clinical and Experimental Hypnosis, 19,* 146–153.

Symonds, M. (1980). Victim responses to terror. *Annals of the New York Academy of Sciences, 347,* 129–136.

Tarasoff v. Regents of the University of California, 17 Cal. 3d 425, 551 P.2d 334, 131 Cal. Rptr. 14 (1976).

Task Force on the Victims of Crime and Violence. (1983, May). *Interim report*. Washington, DC: American Psychological Association.

Teitelbaum, M. (1963). Admissibility of the hypnotically adduced evidence and the Arthur Nebb case. *St. Louis Law Journal, 8,* 205–214.

Tellegen, A. (1978–1979). On measures and conceptions of hypnosis. *American Journal of Clinical Hypnosis, 21,* 219–237.

Terr, L. (1983). Chowchilla revisited: The effects of psychic trauma four years after a school bus kidnapping. *American Journal of Psychiatry, 140,* 1543–1550.

Teten, H. D. (1979). *A discussion of the precepts surrounding the use of hypnosis as an investigative aid by the FBI.* Paper presented at the 87th Annual Meeting of the American Psychological Association, New York.

Thorne, D. E. (1969). Amnesia and hypnosis. *International Journal of Clinical and Experimental Hypnosis, 17,* 225–241.

Time. (1953, March 30). The uses of hypnosis. p. 34.

Time. (1968, April 12). Trials: Hypnotic film. p. 57.

Time. (1968, May 24). Evidence: Hypnosis and the truth. p. 59.

Time. (1976, September 13). The Svengali squad. p. 56.

Timm, H. W. (1981). The effect of forensic hypnosis techniques on eyewitness recall and recognition. *Journal of Police Science and Administration, 9,* 188–194.

Timm, H. W. (1983). The factors theoretically affecting the impact of forensic hypnosis techniques on eyewitness recall. *Journal of Police Science and Administration, 11,* 442–450.

Tinterow, M. M. (1970). *Foundations of hypnosis: From Mesmer to Freud.* Springfield, IL: Charles C Thomas.

The trial of Patty Hearst. (1976). San Francisco: Great Fidelity Press.

True, R. M. (1949). Experimental control in hypnotic age regression states. *Science, 110,* 583–584.

Tuite, P. A., Braun, B. G., & Frischolz, E. J. (1986). Hypnosis and eyewitness testimony. *Psychiatric Annals, 16,* 91–95.

Tulving, E. (1967). The effects of presentation and recall of material in free recall learning. *Journal of Verbal Learning and Verbal Behavior, 6,* 175–184.

Tulving, E. (1985). Memory and consciousness. *Canadian Psychology, 26,* 1–12.

Turco, R. N., & Scott, E. M. (1982). Hypnosis: Complications—an illustrative clinical example. *International Journal of Offender Therapy and Comparative Criminology, 26,* 133–137.

Udolf, R. (1981). *Handbook of hypnosis for professionals.* New York: Van Nostrand Reinhold.

Udolf, R. (1983). *Forensic hypnosis.* Lexington, MA: Lexington Books.

Udolf, R. (1987). *Handbook of hypnosis for professionals* (2nd ed.). New York: Van Nostrand Reinhold.

U.S. News and World Report. (1978, October 2). Hypnotic detectives. p. 75.

Valdiserri, E. V., & Byrne, J. P. (1982). Hypnosis as emergency treatment for a teenage rape victim. *Hospital and Community Psychiatry, 33,* 767–769.

Venn, J. (1988). Misuse of hypnosis in sexual contexts: Two case reports. *International Journal of Clinical and Experimental Hypnosis, 36,* 12–18.

Wadden, T. A., & Anderton, C. H. (1982). The clinical use of hypnosis. *Psychological Bulletin, 91,* 215–243.

Wagstaff, G. F. (1977a). An experimental study of compliance and post-hypnotic amnesia. *British Journal of Social and Clinical Psychology, 16,* 225–228.

Wagstaff, G. F. (1977b). Post hypnotic amnesia as disrupted retrieval: A role playing paradigm. *Quarterly Journal of Experimental Psychology, 29,* 499–504.

Wagstaff, G. F. (1981). *Hypnosis, compliance and belief.* New York: St. Martin's Press.

Wagstaff, G. F. (1982). Hypnosis and recognition of a face. *Perceptual and Motor Skills, 55,* 816–818.

Wagstaff, G. F. (1984). The enhancement of witness memory by "hypnosis": A review and methodological critique of the literature. *British Journal of Experimental and Clinical Hypnosis, 2,* 3–12.

Wagstaff, G. F. (1986). Paradigms of hypnosis: A real or false dichotomy. *Behavioral and Brain Sciences, 9,* 486–487.

Wagstaff, G. F., & Ovenden, M. (1979). Hypnotic time distortion and free recall learning—an attempted replication. *Psychological Research, 40,* 291–298.

Wagstaff, G. F., & Sykes, C. T. (1984). Hypnosis and the recall of emotionally-toned material. *IRCS Medical Science: Psychology and Psychiatry, 12,* 137–138.

Wain, H. J., & Amen, D. G. (1986). Emergency room use of hypnosis. *General Hospital Psychiatry, 8,* 19–22.

Waldfogel, S. (1948). The frequency and affective character of childhood memories. *Psychological Monographs, 62,* 39–48.

Wall, P. D., & Lieberman, L. R. (1976). Effects of task motivation and hypnotic induction on hypermnesia. *American Journal of Clinical Hypnosis, 18,* 250–253.

Wallace, B. (1978). Restoration of eidetic imagery via hypnotic age regression. *Journal of Abnormal Psychology, 85,* 335–337.

Walter, M. J. (1980). Controlling the witness on cross-examination. *Litigation, 7,* 36–37, 53–55.

Warner, K. E. (1979). The use of hypnosis in the defense of criminal cases. *International Journal of Clinical and Experimental Hypnosis, 27,* 417–436.

Watkins, J. G. (1947). Antisocial compulsions induced under hypnotic trance. *Journal of Abnormal Psychology, 44,* 256–259.

Watkins, J. G. (1963). Psychodynamics of hypnotic induction and termination. In J. M. Schneck (Ed.), *Hypnosis in modern medicine* (3rd ed). Springfield, IL: Charles C Thomas.

Watkins, J. G. (1972). Antisocial behavior under hypnosis: Possible or impossible? *International Journal of Clinical and Experimental Hypnosis, 20,* 95–100.

Watkins, J. G. (1984). The Bianchi (L. A. Hillside Strangler) case: Sociopath or multiple personality? *International Journal of Clinical and Experimental Hypnosis, 32,* 67–101.

Watkins, M. J., Ho, E., & Tulving, E. (1976). Context effects in recognition memory for faces. *Journal of Verbal Learning and Verbal Behavior, 15,* 505–517.

Weiner, I. R. (1985). Preparing forensic reports and testimony. *Clinical Psychologist, 38,* 78–80.

Weitzenhoffer, A. M. (1949). The production of antisocial acts under hypnosis. *Journal of Abnormal Psychology, 44,* 420–422.

Weitzenhoffer, A. M. (1953). *Hypnotism: An objective study in suggestibility.* New York: Wiley.

Weitzenhoffer, A. M. (1957). *General techniques of hypnotism*. New York: Grune & Stratton.

Weitzenhoffer, A. M. (1963). Special book review: Bryan's *Legal aspects of hypnosis*. *American Journal of Clinical Hypnosis, 5*, 214–222.

Weitzenhoffer, A. M. (1972). Open-ended distance hypnotherapy. *American Journal of Clinical Hypnosis, 14*, 236–248.

Weitzenhoffer, A. M., & Hilgard, E. R. (1959). *Stanford Hypnotic Susceptibility Scales, Forms A & B*. Palo Alto, CA: Consulting Psychologists Press.

Weitzenhoffer, A. M., & Hilgard, E. R. (1962). *Stanford Hypnotic Susceptibility Scales, Form C*. Palo Alto, CA: Consulting Psychologists Press.

Wellman, F. L. (1936). *The art of cross-examination* (4th ed.). New York: Macmillan.

Wellman, F. L. (1962). *The art of cross-examination* (5th ed.). New York: Collier.

Wells, G. L., Ferguson, T. J., & Lindsay, R. C. L. (1981). The tractability of eyewitness confidence and its implications for triers of fact. *Journal of Applied Psychology, 66*, 688–696.

Wells, G. L., Lindsay, R. C. L., & Ferguson, T. J. (1979). Accuracy, confidence and juror perceptions in eyewitness identification. *Journal of Applied Psychology, 64*, 440–448.

Wells, G. L., & Loftus E. F. (Eds.). (1984). *Eyewitness testimony: Psychological perspectives*. Cambridge, England: Cambridge University Press.

Wells, W. R. (1940). The extent and duration of posthypnotic amnesia. *Journal of Psychology, 2*, 137.

Wells, W. R. (1941). Experiments in the hypnotic production of crime. *Journal of Psychology, 11*, 63–102.

West, L. J. (1960). Psychophysiology of hypnosis. *Journal of the American Medical Association, 172*, 672–675.

West, L. J., & Deckert, G. H. (1965). Dangers of hypnosis. *Journal of the American Medical Association, 192*, 9–12.

Wester, W. C. (1986). *Judicial approaches to the question of admissibility of hypnotically refreshed testimony: A history and analysis*. Paper presented at the 29th Annual Scientific Meeting of the American Society of Clinical Hypnosis, Las Vegas.

Wester, W. C., & Smith, H. (Eds.). (1984). *Clinical hypnosis: A multidisciplinary approach*. Philadelphia: J. B. Lippincott.

White, R. W. (1941). A preface to the theory of hypnotism. *Journal of Abnormal and Social Psychology, 36*, 477–505.

White, R. W., Fox, G. F., & Harris, W. W. (1940). Hypnotic hypermnesia for recently learned material. *Journal of Abnormal and Social Psychology, 35*, 88–103.

Whitehouse, W. G., Dinges, D. F., Orne, E. C., & Orne, M. T. (1987). Hypnotic hypermnesia assessed by forced interrogatory recall. In K. S. Bowers (Chair), *Hypnosis and memory: Recent findings*. Symposium conducted at the 38th Annual Meeting of the Society for Clinical and Experimental Hypnosis, Los Angeles.

Wigmore, J. H. (1909). Professor Munsterberg and the psychology of testimony. *Illinois Law Review, 3*, 399–445.

Wigmore, J. H. (1970). *Evidence* (rev. ed., J. H. Chadbourn, Ed., Vol. 3A). Boston: Little, Brown.

Wigmore, J. H. (1974). *Evidence* (rev. ed., J. H. Chadbourn, Ed., Vol. 5). Boston: Little, Brown.

Wiley, S. K., Critelli, J. W., & Nash, M. R. (1987). Hypnosis and recognition memory: Peripheral versus central detail. In K. S. Bowers (Chair), *Hypnosis and memory: Recent findings*. Symposium conducted at the 38th Annual Meeting of the Society for Clinical and Experimental Hypnosis, Los Angeles.

Wilkes, J. (1986). A study in hypnosis: Conversation with Ernest R. Hilgard. *Psychology Today, 20*, 23–27.

Williamsen, J. A., Johnson, H. J., & Erickson, C. W. (1965). Some characteristics of posthypnotic amnesia. *Journal of Abnormal Psychology, 70*, 123–131.

Wilson, L., Greene, E., & Loftus, E. F. (1986). Beliefs about forensic hypnosis. *International Journal of Clinical and Experimental Hypnosis, 34*, 110–121.

Wolpe, J. (1961). The systematic desensitization treatment of neurosis. *Journal of Nervous and Mental Disease, 132*, 189–203.

Worthington, T. S. (1979). The use in court of hypnotically enhanced testimony. *International Journal of Clinical and Experimental Hypnosis, 27*, 402–416.

Wydick, R. C. (1987). *Professional responsibility*. San Francisco: Harcourt Brace Jovanovich.

Yarmey, A. D. (1979). *The psychology of eyewitness testimony*. New York: Free Press.

Young, J., & Cooper, L. M. (1972). Hypnotic recall amnesia as a function of manipulated expectancy. *Proceedings of the 80th Annual Convention of the American Psychological Association, 7*, 857–858.

Young, P. C. (1925). An experimental study of mental and physical functions of the normal and hypnotic states. *American Journal of Psychology, 36*, 214–232.

Young, P. C. (1940). Hypnotic regression—fact or artifact? *Journal of Abnormal and Social Psychology, 35*, 273–278.

Young, P. C. (1952). Antisocial uses of hypnosis. In L. M. LeCron (ed.), *Experimental hypnosis*. New York: Macmillan.

Younger, I. (1976). *The art of cross-examination* (Section of Litigation Monograph Series, No. 1). Chicago: American Bar Association.

Younger, I. (1977). A letter in which Cicero lays down the ten commandments of cross-examination. *Litigation, 3*, 18–21.

Yuille, J. C., & McEwan, H. (1985). Use of hypnosis as an aid to eyewitness memory. *Journal of Applied Psychology, 70*, 389–400.

Zeig, J. K. (Ed.). (1982). *Ericksonian approaches to hypnosis and psychotherapy*. New York: Brunner/Mazel.

Zeig, J. K. (1985). *Ericksonian psychotherapy*. New York: Brunner/Mazel.

Zelig, M., & Beidleman, W. B. (1981). The investigative use of hypnosis: A word of caution. *International Journal of Clinical and Experimental Hypnosis, 29*, 401–412.

Ziskin, J., & Coleman, L. (1981). Two professionals urge ban on psychiatric testimony. *The California State Psychologist, 15*(5), 1–13.

Zonana, H. V. (1979). Hypnosis, sodium pentathol and confessions. *Bulletin of the American Academy of Psychiatry and the Law, 7*, 18–28.

Index